COULTER LIBRARY ONONDAGA COMM.
E840.8.S53 A38 1983
Shannon, Elizabeth. Up in the park

3 0418 00085276 2

D0853035

E
840.8
.S53
A38
1983

Shannon, Elizabeth

Up in the park

DATE DUE

| AUG 17 1983 | | |
| OCT 1 | | |

0165   01 899226   01 0   (IC=0)
SHANNON, ELIZABETH
UP IN THE PARK
(4) 1983 . E 840.8 .S53 A38 1983

The Sidney B. Coulter Library
Onondaga Community College
Rte. 173, Onondaga Hill
Syracuse, New York 13215

Up in the Park

The Sidney B. Coulter Library
Onondaga Community College
Rte. 173, Onondaga Hill
Syracuse, New York 13215

UP IN
THE PARK

*The Diary of the Wife of
the American Ambassador to Ireland
1977–1981*

Elizabeth Shannon, 1937-

Atheneum   New York   1983

The following photographs are reprinted with permission. Page 20: Department of State, Audio Visual Services; pages 25, 31, 56, 82, 326, and 346: Lensmen Press Photo Agency, Dublin; page 132 from *The American Ambassador's Residence—Dublin,* No. 28 in the Irish Heritage Series, Eason & Son Ltd., Dublin; page 289: Pat Cashman, *Irish Press;* page 329: Robert Allen Photography, Dublin.

LIBRARY OF CONGRESS CATALOGING IN PUBLICATION DATA

Shannon, Elizabeth, ———
Up in the park.

Includes index.
1. Shannon, Elizabeth, ———.   2. Shannon,
William Vincent.   3. Ireland—Social life and
customs—20th century.   4. Ambassadors' wives—
United States—Biography.   5. Ambassadors—
United States—Biography.   I. Title.
E840.8.S53A38   1983   941.50324'092'4   82-73037
ISBN 0-689-11364-1

Copyright © 1983 by Elizabeth Shannon
All rights reserved
Published simultaneously in Canada by McClelland and Stewart Ltd.
Composed by American-Stratford Graphic Services, Inc., Brattleboro, Vermont
Manufactured by Fairfield Graphics, Fairfield, Pennsylvania
Designed by Mary Cregan
First Edition

This book is dedicated with love
to my parents
CHARLES BOWMAN MCNELLY
CECILIA BROWER MCNELLY
one born Irish
the other an enthusiastic convert

Acknowledgments

One day when we were lunching at Deerfield with our American friends Bill and Joan Roth, I regaled them with some quixotic incident that had happened to me on my daily diplomatic rounds. Bill Roth said: "You must write a book about it all." I assured him that I was keeping a diary and being faithful to it.

"Then you must publish your diary," he said. And a short time afterward he had put me in touch with Atheneum Publishers, which, happily, agreed with him. I am deeply grateful to the Roths for their push in the right direction.

Friends in Ireland and in America read the manuscript. They not only cheered me enormously by laughing out loud in my hearing but also offered ideas and helpful suggestions. Novelist John Broderick used to come up from Athlone to visit us at Deerfield, and before he could take off his coat I had him seated on the sofa saying: "Here are pages 107 to 309, John. Take your time. Here's a pencil." And he, poor fellow, thought he was just coming to dinner.

Mab Moltke read it all and made valuable corrections and gave me editorial advice. Anne Woodward and Elizabeth Donahue were both enthusiastic and helpful readers.

Like every author, I had a list of twenty-five possible titles, each worse than the next. One evening I mentioned to Seamus Heaney that I planned to call my book *A Rare Auld Time*. He made a wry face and suggested: "Why not call it *Up in the Park*?" I knew instantly that was just right.

Eventually it appeared on the desk of my editor at Atheneum, Judith Kern, and she edited it with skill and sensitivity.

My sons Liam and Christopher were patient, encouraging, and always remembered to ask: "How's it coming?" And David gave me great encouragement by measuring the height of the manuscript each week as it grew and grew and kept me up to date on its size.

I have special thanks for the wonderful staff at Deerfield. While I wrote, they managed the house, did the shopping, cooking, laundry and gardening, ran the errands, answered the phone and brought me a thousand cups of tea. It was just like having a wife.

But my deepest debt of gratitude goes to my husband, Bill, who took us all to Ireland in the first place.

1977

MAY 4: *Washington, D.C.*

I was sitting in the kitchen this evening when the telephone rang. It was our "melted phone" that had been put too near the stove one day, so that the yellow plastic cover softened into an intricate pattern of ridges and peaks. We try to keep it hidden from telephone repairmen.

The long distance operator asked for Bill, and when I said he wasn't home I heard the voice of President Mortimer Appley of Clark University on the line saying: "I'll talk to Mrs. Shannon." He was speaking from Worcester, Massachusetts, Bill's hometown.

"Liz? I'm calling to say congratulations. Congressman Early just called and told me the news. I think it's wonderful."

Was it true then?

I stood up, holding the receiver in my hand, which had begun to shake, and walked over to the kitchen table to sit nearer my boys.

"I think you've heard more than I've heard," I replied evasively. And my caller realized that he had broken the news to me.

"Oh, dear," he said. "I guess I've spilled the beans. I assumed you knew."

I couldn't talk further. I thanked him and hung up. I would have to hear it from Bill to believe it. I dialed him at his office in the *New York Times* Bureau, and he picked up immediately.

"Is it true?" I asked, without preliminaries.

"Yes," he said. "Darn. I wanted to come home and tell you in person and see your face." News in our land of communication travels too fast for face-to-face encounters.

"Are you happy?" I asked him.

I could hear him smiling.

The boys had stopped eating and were staring at me. They had known for the past few weeks that their father was on the short list of five candidates for the ambassadorship, but they had been warned not to mention it. We knew that President Carter was making a trip out of the country this week, and rumor had gone round that he would announce some ambassadors before he left.

Now three pairs of unblinking brown eyes stared at me, and waited for me to say it: yes or no. I began to grin at their curious, tense expressions, and then they knew, too.

Liam responded first and with customary enthusiasm. "Wow!" he kept saying, over and over. "Wow!"

Christopher held back comments, weighing and judging as always. David, who didn't quite understand the meaning of it all, knew something very exciting was in the air, and he hugged and kissed me.

I picked up the melted phone again and called my parents in Texas. They had been in on the secret for weeks.

"Well, I always knew he'd get it," my mother began matter-of-factly, then burst into tears.

Christopher asked if they could run out and "tell everyone" now, but I told him to wait a little longer, and I began dialing again, this time to friends and neighbors.

"Come over after dinner," I told one after another of them, trying to sound natural and offhand. "Nixon is doing an interview with David Frost tonight. Let's have a drink and talk about it." A pretty flimsy excuse, but everyone I reached agreed to come.

"Finish your dinner," I said automatically to the boys, as if they could or as if I cared. "I'm going to run down to Higger's and buy champagne."

While my old friend behind the counter put the bottles into a box, he said: "What are you grinning for?"

I didn't even know I was.

"Big celebration tonight?"

"Yes," I said, and started to tell him, but suddenly I felt shy about saying it. It just seemed too strange.

By 9:30, all our friends had gathered in the living room and were spilling out on the screened-in porch. I was pouring them drinks and beer, hiding the champagne for the Announcement. I was also hiding Bill.

I stood up in the middle of the room and said: "You may wonder why you were invited here tonight. It isn't really to discuss the Nixon-Frost interview. It's to meet a new neighbor." Some of them began to grin and others looked puzzled.

Then Bill stepped into the room and I said: "Meet the new American ambassador to Ireland!"

Their enthusiasm burst over us in a rush of affection and excitement. After all the hugs and kisses and squeals and "I *knew* its," we settled down to champagne and explanations of our not-too-well-kept secret.

4

Most of them had heard rumors, but being good friends and well-seasoned Washingtonians, they were kind enough and discreet enough not to say anything to us.

I sat on the floor, and the warm sweet air of a Washington May evening drifted into the room from the open porch. With azaleas, rhododendron and dogwood blazing away, Washington in May is a city filled with color and scent. "Downright gaudy," one of my more aesthetic friends said once. As I sat there, surrounded by familiar faces, the joy of the evening dimmed with the thought of leaving them and our home on Gramercy Street. But this was an evening of emotions, and they rarely come unmixed.

Everyone had gone by midnight. Elated, weary, apprehensive and excited, Bill and I picked up empty bottles, stacked glasses, and then he climbed into bed. I came in here, to my little office off our bedroom. It was originally David's nursery; when he was two, I turned him out and took over the room as my office. The blue-flowered wallpaper and the white fluffy rug stayed. The crib gave way to a desk and files. It's my place now, and I feel at home being alone here. Other rooms in the house seem empty and incomplete without other people in them, but when I come in here and shut the door I fill the room.

Now, with the curtains pulled back and the windows open, the spring air ruffles papers on my desk. I decided, while we were downstairs at the party, that I would keep a journal of everything that happens to us on this grand adventure. So, dear journal, this is the beginning, and I promise to be faithful for as long as we're together.

MAY 5

I was up very early this morning, a miracle induced by spring and euphoria. Bill was still sleeping when I climbed out of bed, and I whispered: "Good morning, Mr. Ambassador," but he didn't even stir.

I went outside to pick up the *Times* and the *Post* from the dew-damp ivy along the front walk. To my astonishment, there was no banner headline in either paper saying: SHANNONS EN ROUTE TO IRELAND! Don't they know this is the biggest news story in the world? But news has its own routes, and by 8 AM the melted phone was ringing steadily. We squeezed in breakfast between calls. I had to leave the house by 8:30 to get downtown to the Stevens Elementary School, where I was helping to put on an arts festival.

Later

It's so hot, the children are wilted and the grown-ups exhausted. The temperature hit 90 degrees, and the black asphalt playground shimmered in the heat. But the festival is over, and by all accounts, it was a glorious success.

Sandy Fitzpatrick and Susan Deerin, two friends who had masterminded the festival, and I gathered up our boxes and briefcases and purses and headed for home, stopping en route at a downtown restaurant for a cold beer. It was dark and cool in the bar, and the beer was gloriously icy. I sat with my skirt lifted up from under me, like Spanish girls do, to feel the coolness of the leather banquette on the backs of my legs. "Ireland won't be hot like this, will it?" Sandy asked, and I lifted my right hand and swore: "I vow on this spot, here and now, never to complain about the rain in Ireland." We asked the waiter to turn down the Muzak and ordered another beer.

MAY 9

I read off my list at the breakfast table this morning: "Pediatrician. Dentist. Movers. Storage. Insurance. Trunks (buy more). Car (take? leave?). Dog (take? leave?). Quarantine (ask about). Schools in Dublin. Clothes (?). Cancel Liam's camp. Change Christopher's camp dates. Barbecue spit (ask Brian). House (Rent. Call Louise)."

I phoned Louise Sullivan, my neighbor and friend in the real estate business, and asked her to put our house on the market. "No groups," I cautioned, remembering the "legal secretaries" who moved into a house across the street a few years ago. They turned out to be less than legal and their working day appeared to begin about 7 PM.

I've promised to give a fund-raising dinner for the children's school with my neighbors, the Staceys. Nevzer Stacey had an inspiration from her Turkish childhood to roast a whole lamb on a spit. We got the lamb with no difficulty and it's in my freezer now, sitting upright and staring reproachfully at me through frozen eyes every time I open the door. But we are having trouble finding an electric spit big enough to hold a whole lamb.

Bill is in New York. I've got to finish a paper I've contracted to write about sex discrimination on television. The lights burn late in my office tonight. Little Nell, our Welsh terrier, sat at my feet and kept me company while I worked. I scratched her tight, wiry curls and wondered if the quarantine facilities in Dublin were good. All animals coming into Ireland have to go into quarantine for six months. That's a long time in a dog's life, Little Nell. I haven't even *mentioned* it to the children.

MAY 10

I've shown the house twice already. Once to an unfriendly diplomat's wife, who said sourly: "I don't think I could ever be happy in your kitchen."

I didn't think she could be happy anywhere. "Don't rent it to her," I whispered to Louise as they went out the door.

"She doesn't want it," Louise whispered back.

We found the spit. It's electric and very fancy. Bill Rice, the food editor of the *Washington Post,* is coming over early tomorrow to help us thread the lamb onto the spit, head and all. Thank goodness I'll be rid of those glassy eyes in my freezer. They stunned one of the prospective tenants when she opened the door today.

I phoned the Irish Desk officer at the State Department today and introduced myself. I think he was startled by my call. He's supposed to call me, but I wanted to find out when the Seminars for Spouses begin. I'm ready to get this show on the road.

MAY 18

Bill and I went to Senator Javits' birthday party this evening at the Watergate apartments. Zbigniew Brzezinski was there and came over to Bill to congratulate him on his appointment. Eric Sevareid was there, too, but I didn't ask him about the rumor that he may become ambassador to Norway. We left early; Sandy Fitz has arranged a birthday party/farewell outing for me tomorrow. It's a mystery. I'm supposed to "be ready" at 11 A.M.

MAY 19

Sandy, Marie Hawke, Ann Brower and I went to Middleburg, Virginia, today for my surprise party. I can't think of a nicer outing. The Virginia countryside was awash with dogwood blossoms as we drove out of Washington. We had lunch and then nosed around the small, chic, pretty town, shopping and looking. I had a sudden inspiration and said to the girls: "*One* last practical joke before I become dignified." I whispered my plans, and we all put on our serious, young-matron look and rolled into a chi-chi riding outfitters'. (Middleburg is horsey.)

"Good afternoon," I said to a very thin, young clerk. "As you may know, Miss Elizabeth Taylor has recently married John Warner and has moved to Middleburg. I am her secretary."

"Good afternoon," said the unsmiling clerk.

"Miss Taylor is going to take up riding again, now that she is here in horse country. You, perhaps, are too young to remember *National Velvet.* Anyway, she will want to try on riding outfits. Size eighteen."

The clerk's eyebrows shot up but she remained unsmiling. "I'm afraid our jodhpurs only go up to size sixteen. But I'm sure Miss Taylor could have some specially made." She gave me the name of an outfitter, and I said: "Miss Taylor will be in touch."

(Miss Taylor, wherever you are, will you forgive us?)

7

MAY 20

I drove to the Hay Adams Hotel this morning to meet Mrs. Walter Curley, whose husband Bill is replacing in Ireland. I couldn't find a parking place for ages and drove around and around, getting later and later and becoming more and more frenzied by the moment, thinking: I shouldn't keep an ambassador's wife waiting. Then I remembered, *I'm* an ambassador's wife, too, and I burst out laughing. This role is going to take some getting used to.

Mrs. Curley turned out to be fun and charming and didn't mind being kept waiting, and we talked for two hours about the residence in Dublin, and the staff, the gardens, her friends in Ireland and all the things she loved about living there. She told me that they have a home in the west of Ireland and will go back frequently.

I wondered all the time she was talking to me what she was thinking: Was she sad to be leaving? Relieved? Does she feel angry or hostile toward me for moving into her house? I think *I* will, when the time comes. Or is she simply resigned to the inevitable? It must be hard to leave. I feel proprietary about the residence already, and I haven't even seen it!

There was a Seminar for Spouses on "Protocol" today at the State Department. Most of it seemed rather mysterious to me, with overtones of a middle-brow mid-Victorian novel.

"If you leave your calling card personally at someone's home, turn down the right- [or was it left?] hand corner. If you have your driver deliver it, turn down the left- [right?] hand corner." I don't even have any calling cards. I turned to the section on "Calling Cards" in the thick blue book I was given today at the seminar. "Ambassadors," it said, "are required to provide their own stationery, cards, informals, invitations, notes, etc. etc."

What I want to know is: What do I *do?* What can make my side of the job more interesting, productive, helpful, original and fun? There are many more seminars coming up, and I hope I'll find the answers I'm looking for.

MAY 21

The boys and I went to the Chevy Chase library this afternoon and took out all the children's books on Ireland we could find. Coming home in the car, Christopher said: "These are the same books you got out for us last year, when we went to Ireland on our holiday."

Well, I said, read them again.

We went to a party tonight. Mark Shields and I share a birthday, and

Anne, his wife, gave us a great evening. I didn't ask Mark how old he was, and he didn't ask me. We're that sort of age.

MAY 23

I crossed the Potomac this morning against the flow of rush-hour traffic pouring into Washington to visit the State Department's Interior Decorating Division. It's a fascinating operation. Mrs. Susan McQueen, the chief decorator, and a very small staff, working out of a few overcrowded rooms, are in charge of the interior decor of all the chanceries, residences, consulates and embassy-owned houses all over the world. New chanceries and residences are constantly being built (and sometimes burned down) or refurnished. With the excessive wear and tear of embassy entertaining, and with constant personnel changes, there are vast decorating projects going on everywhere, all the time, all over the world.

"Some new ambassadorial families are status quo people," Mrs. McQueen told me. "They can move in and nest, and are perfectly happy to leave everything just as it is. Others are changers and movers, or decorators at heart, and they welcome the challenge of a worn-out decor."

I sat in the midst of ringing telephones, surrounded by mountains of fabric samples, catalogs, architectural drawings, photographs of interiors, and I saw rooms around the world being put together with amazing speed and deftness. Fabrics and furniture to complement a hot and humid climate were being matched in one room. "This is going to take a lot of sun," Susan muttered, as she pulled out a brilliant orange denim fabric. Warm tones and heavy-textured upholstery fabrics were laid out for a bedroom in a frigid zone. "They're going to want the room to look warm in a snowstorm," was Susan's decision about the apricot-colored tweed.

Period reproductions were ticked off in catalogs for an eighteenth-century home. Chrome and glass tables were being ordered for a new, contemporary residence.

Besides planning the decor for a new building or the restoration of an old one, picking a fabric to recover a sofa or replacing a worn coffee table, the women on Susan's staff play a juggling act. While I was there, one of them came in to say that a large Persian carpet in Prague was no longer needed. "Send it to London," said Mrs. McQ. without a pause. "It'll fit there and it's just what they're looking for."

I found it all amazing and exciting. Susan McQueen is a dynamo, full of energy and good ideas, tempered with patient humor, despite being inundated with new ambassadors' wives, all wanting her undivided attention for their top-priority requirements.

I had a short lesson in diplomacy as I watched her dealing with a New

Wife, who came in with a friend. The two of them were going to do over the *entire* residence, from *top* to *bottom,* without ever having seen it, and they were just *full* of good ideas and they knew *exactly* what they wanted; the friend was a professional decorator, so she had come along to take charge, and if Mrs. McQueen would *just* be kind enough to show them photographs of the residence and turn them loose in the fabric room, etc. etc. etc. Mrs. McQueen had both of them, within a very short time, sitting glumly in chairs poring over complicated architectural drawings of the house (*so* much more demanding than color photographs), and had convinced them both how difficult it is to do a top-to-bottom job without having seen the house. Their enthusiasm was distinctly dampened.

I hadn't seen our new home in Dublin, either. Bill had been to a reception there in 1972, when John Moore was ambassador, and the boys and I plagued him with questions about what it looked like. All he could come up with was: "It's big and white."

"Like the White House?" Christopher asked.

"Smaller."

"Sort of like Monticello painted white?" Liam tried.

"Bigger."

Obviously we'd have to wait to see for ourselves. Mrs. McQueen showed me color photographs, and I was enchanted. It looks beautiful. It's a large, white Georgian house with a "diplomatic entrance" portico added on. It's set in a magnificent garden of green lawns, stone walls and rose beds, with a lovely old sycamore tree shading the entrance. It's in the middle of the Phoenix Park, "the largest urban park in Europe," the caption says, "filled with free-ranging deer." I just can't *wait* to see it.

The photographs of the interior of the house are out of date, and Mrs. McQueen has never visited it herself, so it's hard for me to tell much about the decor. Except for picking out some fabrics for the boys' rooms, I'm going to wait until I'm there and have lived in the house for a while before I make any changes.

There is only one thing that puzzles me about the house. It doesn't have a name. It is simply called "the residence," which sounds awfully portentous and heavy. Perhaps while I'm there, I can name it.

MAY 24

The days are flying by and so crammed with the minutiae of moving that we don't even have time to sit down and talk with each other. Bill is busier than I am, trying to wind down his work at the *New York Times,* fill out the innumerable forms sent to him every day by the State Department: health forms, insurance forms, security forms, net worth forms. It's endless. He's undergoing a security investigation and then he has to have a Senate Foreign Relations Committee hearing on his nomination. The vote on his appointment will go to the floor of the Senate, with committee approval, and *then* he will be sworn in.

We both had to go to the Department for physical examinations this morning, for the first of two long sessions in the medical division. Judging from the thorough poking, prodding and testing done on us, and the amount of blood we left behind in small vials, the United States must have a remarkably healthy foreign service. I'm glad we are going to Ireland. Some of the possible innoculations listed for more exotic places would send me looking for a new line of work.

MAY 31

I took all three boys to see Beale Ong, their pediatrician, for their own physical exams, and to tell him good-by. He has tended their broken arms (3), broken leg (1), broken nose (1), stitches (lost count), chicken pox and colds since Liam was a baby, and we shall all miss his patient support and wise counseling. He has never made me feel that any call was too unimportant or too silly for him to advise on, even when Christopher put his tongue on the door of the freezing compartment and it stuck there.

He had read a recent editorial in the Washington *Star*, praising Bill's work as a journalist and his appointment as ambassador, and he told the boys that they should be proud of their father because praise from one's colleagues was to be valued above all other.

When we return from Ireland, Liam will be too old for a pediatrician, so as we left, they said good-by as doctor and patient. Our first farewell.

JUNE 1

The long series of good-bys began this evening at a party given by Kate Alfriend and Dode Jackson, at Dode's lovely old gray clapboard house in Georgetown. One of the guests drove down from New York for the party and en route picked up a boy who was hitchhiking. He turned out to be a young Irishman visiting the States, and the two of them decided it would be a shame for him to miss a party given for the new ambassador to Ireland, so he joined in, too. I think the Irish have a special instinct that guides them to parties. And guards them on the way home!

JUNE 5

Our neighborhood gave us a rousing, rollicking beer and hot dogs send-off today on the grounds of Alice Deal Junior High School. They filled the trees with balloons, draped the branches with green crepe-paper streamers, and put up an Irish flag on a makeshift pole. All the children, more than fifty of them, posed for a group picture, and then all the adults lined up for the same thing. We're promised a big blowup of both pictures to hang on our wall in Dublin.

The "committee" had arranged for a school of Irish dancers to come and perform. The little girls were charming in their blue and white costumes, and although it wasn't easy to dance in the grass (or in 92 degree heat), they gave us a superb performance. Someone suggested that the grown-ups in the audience join in, and the girls tried to teach us the steps. Within minutes, most of the adults were in danger of mass heat exhaustion and heart failure. We all gave up.

The blazing sun finally disappeared over Deal Hill and we sat in the grass and talked about the things we always talked about: politics (local and national), the D.C. school system, cars that break down, vacation plans, the children—and, today, Ireland. We told everyone to come and visit us, and I hope they do, because what will I do without them?

June 9

Another gala affair to send us on our way, this time at a party given for us in New York by Ambassador and Mrs. Eamon Kennedy, the Irish ambassador to the United Nations. Mrs. Kennedy, an American, is famous for her cuisine, and it was a most elegant and sumptuous dinner.

Governor Hugh Carey was there, and the talk all evening was about Ireland and the elections that are about to be held there. I tried to follow the fortunes of Fianna Fáil, Fine Gael, and Labour, the three Irish political parties, but it's all new territory to me. I've got so much to learn, and such a short time to do it in.

The ambassador made a stylish after-dinner toast to Bill. What a marvelous talent to have, and how well it sounded in his soft Irish tones. Bill will have to start polishing up his after-dinner speeches, but he's good at that anyway, and, I must say, his response this evening was more than passable. He's Irish, too.

June 10

And another farewell party, given by the American Irish Foundation at the F Street Club. Bill has been on the board of the AIF for years, and they were all proud to have one of "theirs" named ambassador. They gave us a beautiful silver tray, engraved with our names, as a parting gift. It will travel to Ireland with us and be in use at the residence.

We are still impatiently awaiting word from the Irish government on the *"agrément."* Every host country of a newly appointed ambassador has to agree on the choice of envoy. Usually it is only a formality, but the government may, with good reason, deny the *agrément* to a prospective ambassador. Until the *agrément* is signed, the Senate Foreign Relations Committee can't hold its hearings on Bill's appointment, and thus each step along our route to Dublin is held up.

There was some rumor that the *agrément* was going to be put on the back burner in Dublin until after their elections, when the newly elected government would vote on it. I hope that rumor proves to be unfounded.

JUNE 14

And it was. Jack Rendahl, the deputy chief of mission at the embassy in Dublin, phoned today to tell us the *agrément* has been signed. One more item checked off our long list.

JUNE 16

The representative from the storage company arrived this morning to look us over. Nearly everything in our house will go into storage. Ambassadors' families have to provide their own personal linen and towels; otherwise, our residence is completely furnished. We'll take clothes, books, records, knickknacks, pictures, toys and bikes. I still haven't made a decision about Little Nell.

We're going to have a huge garage sale and get rid of ten years' worth of junk. If I could persuade Himself to clean out that *mound* of yellowing magazines, newspapers, clippings (and probably dead mice) in his study, all my throwing-away instincts would be satisfied. But I'm sure when the movers come, it will probably all be neatly stacked into cartons for storage, labeled "newspapers, clippings, and dead mice."

With such a peripatetic population, Washington has dozens of garage sales each spring. We had a young Irish poet visiting us last year, and one day, when we were driving him around on a sight-seeing tour of northwest Washington, he suddenly asked: "Why are so many people here selling their garages?"

JUNE 21

Bill's nomination went to the Senate yesterday and this morning we set out for Capitol Hill to attend the hearings. It was sunny, windy and unusually cool for June. Our good friend Libby Donahue came by the house early to drive the boys and me downtown. Bill had to go on ahead to the State Department for briefings. Senator Edward Kennedy is going to introduce Bill at the hearings.

The boys were dressed up and slicked down, and they looked marvelous. They are so excited and proud of their dad today. David has been "briefed" about the hearings, too, and warned to sit still, to listen, to observe, to be quiet, to be good, and to go to the bathroom *before* we go into the Senate Hearing Room.

The room began filling up very quickly after we arrived, and soon it was crowded. Bill wasn't there yet, but his name was fourth on the list of ambassadorial appointees to be heard that day, so he had plenty of time. So we thought.

Suddenly there was a flurry at the door. Senator Kennedy came in with an aide, and spoke to the chairman, John Sparkman of Alabama. Senator Sparkman then rapped his gavel on the table and in his soft, southern tones, he brought the hearings to order, announcing that since Senator Kennedy had another hearing to attend, he would speak first, and he was introducing the ambassador-designate to Ireland.

At this point, Senator Kennedy turned around in his seat and mouthed to me: "Where's Bill?" I could only shrug my shoulders, as I looked frantically at the doorway, still jammed with people coming in. God help us all, was my chronically late husband going to miss his own Senate hearing? Had that ever happened before? Would he be disqualified? Would we leave Washington in disgrace? Would it be an item in "Ear"?

The boys were shuffling nervously in their seats and Libby looked as if she were going to burst out either laughing or crying. "Where could he be?" I whispered to her. She shrugged.

The room quieted down as Senator Sparkman banged the gavel again, and Senator Kennedy stood up and began speaking:

"Mr. Chairman, I am delighted, as I am sure all of us in the Senate are, that President Carter has nominated William V. Shannon of Massachusetts, the distinguished editorial writer of the *New York Times,* to be the next ambassador of the United States to the Republic of Ireland."

He glanced down at the empty chair beside him and as he continued: "I am pleased to accompany him here this morning . . ." a faint titter went around the room; then exactly at that moment, as if he had been waiting for his cue, the door opened and Bill burst in, accompanied by another aide from the senator's office. He smiled at us as he went up to take his seat. The boys sighed audibly, and the senator continued without a break, making a very warm and generous statement about Bill's qualifications, background and potential as an outstanding ambassador.

I breathed again and sat back to enjoy and savor this high point in Bill's career and our lives.

After Senator Kennedy finished his statement, a few members of the committee asked Bill questions about Ireland. Most of them were long-time acquaintances, and many had read his books, columns and editorials over the years. They had very complimentary things to say about him. There was some banter and some jokes, and then it was all over. It had taken exactly twenty-two minutes.

Of course, the instant we were all out in the corridor we pounced on Bill to ask: "Where *were* you??" And naturally, it had all been a silly misunderstanding. The person bringing him to the hearings from the State Department thought they were meeting Senator Kennedy in his office, instead of at the Hearing Room. Bill went one place and Kennedy another, and there were miles of corridors between the two.

Later in the day, Bill received a call saying that the vote for his confirmation was going to be brought to the floor of the Senate that very evening, so he dashed back to the Hill in time to hear the vote being taken. He had to miss Liam's father-son banquet at the Army-Navy Club, and he was upset by that, but Liam assured him that he didn't mind. "It'll be a lot of football stories and jokes, Dad," he said, "not your scene." I drove Liam downtown to the banquet, and as he got out of the car, I said: "Are you sure you don't want me to come in drag? I could lower my voice an octave and tell all my dirty jokes." Liam was laughing as he walked alone through the "Men Only" entrance of that oh-so-male bastion.

JUNE 25

I'm beginning to worry about the style and content of this journal. It seems to me that it is too filled with personal anecdote and family trivia to be of interest, and it doesn't include anything of serious import. I decided to reread some of my favorite diaries to try to see what it was exactly that I enjoyed about them, so this evening I pulled Harold Nicolson's second volume of *Diaries and Letters* out of the bookcase and opened the book at random to page 147. To my amused astonishment, I read: "I am rather fussed about this diary. It is not intimate enough to give a personal picture . . . the day-to-day impressions of a greengrocer in Streatham would really be more interesting. I must try henceforward to be more intimate and more illuminating."

He persevered and so shall I.

JUNE 29

Don and Paula Jeffries, the couple who introduced Bill to me, and Libby Donahue gave us a beautiful, gala farewell party in the Jeffries' garden in Georgetown. Jack Molloy, the Irish ambassador to the United States, was there, and he and I did a Washington version of an Irish jig (or perhaps it was an Irish version of a Washington jig). A group of young Irish singers and guitarists kept our feet tapping all night. So many of our friends were there to wish us bon voyage, and before the evening was out we had invited all of them to come to Ireland and see us, and I expect most of them will.

We've been receiving press cuttings from the Irish papers announcing Bill's appointment and, of course, stressing our Irish roots. The *Irish Times,* which I had enjoyed reading so much of when I was in Ireland last summer, got major facts wrong about Bill's career: He is not a "vice-president" of the *New York Times,* nor is he chief of the Washington Bureau, and he did not win a Pulitzer Prize for *The Heir Apparent.* A glance into Who's Who would have set them straight.

The *Sunday Press* of May 15 had a long article by a "special correspondent" (I'm always suspicious about the motives behind an unsigned article. Why hide?) making the most astounding speculation that Bill's appointment as ambassador "could be seen in some quarters as a 'reward' to Father Sean McManus and the Irish National Caucus for their support for Carter in the presidential election last year." The "special correspondent" went on to pick up some sentences from a speech Bill had made to the Eire Society in Boston in 1975 to try and show that he was sympathetic to the IRA.

Bill has never had anything to do with the Irish National Caucus, abhors violence for any cause, and supports fully the anti-IRA line taken by Governor Carey, Senator Kennedy, and Speaker Tip O'Neill. He wrote an answer to the "special correspondent" which the *Sunday Press* printed on May 22. It began: "I am astonished that any correspondent stationed in the United States and supposedly familiar with American opinion could contrive such an inaccurate and misleading account of President Carter's views and my own."

That was his first experience of being on the other side of the news, being written about instead of doing the writing.

"Very educational," he said.

Anyway, it was all a tempest in a teapot. I think the Irish are very fond of teapots.

July 1

The company that is packing us for Ireland sent their packers this morning. They were young women in jeans and white T-shirts with their company name emblazoned across their bosoms. Each one had a very large wad of gum in her mouth, which she worked on diligently all day. They were fast and efficient. I had to leave them at noon to go to lunch with a neighbor and foreign service wife, Peggy Barry. The Barrys had been posted to Russia, and Mrs. Jacob Beam, the wife of an ex-ambassador to Russia, was another luncheon guest.

We had a long talk about the role of ambassadors' wives, and I found it more helpful than the seminars have been so far. Some of their tips:

Don't play favorites among embassy wives (or husbands, either!); don't demand that the staff dance attendance on your own functions when it is inconvenient for them; stay out of embassy business and run your home; make your reputation by example rather than pronouncements; be discreet with the press.

They told me that the role of a foreign service wife has changed drastically in this decade. In 1972, on the initiative of the Foreign Service Wives' Association, the State Department decided that wives were no longer to be judged and evaluated along with their husbands as to whether they were "good hostesses" or "did their share of the entertaining," as they had been judged in the past. Their husbands are State Department personnel, they are not, and therefore they are free to run their personal lives as they wish with no detriment to their husbands' careers. Along with these new directives, they are not to be at the beck and call of a tiresome ambassador's wife who doesn't have the energy or the confidence to do her own job herself.

Our luncheon was interrupted sporadically by telephone calls from my mother, who was at home overseeing the packers, with questions about what was to stay and what was to go. "They're packing *everything*," she said desperately at one stage. "They've put in the garbage."

Elaine Greenstone, a friend and neighbor, has been coming over every afternoon to give me a quick survey of Irish literature. She received her master's degree in it, and I, although an English major, am quite ignorant about Ireland's literature, except for the contemporary writers whom I read and love. One of the thousand things that I'm looking forward to in Dublin is the chance to meet all those names that have meant so much to me: Mary Lavin, Benedict Kiely, Terence de Vere White, Dervla Murphy, Seamus Heaney, John Broderick. It's a long list for such a small country.

Alas, Elaine knows too much and I know too little and here it is July 1, and we haven't gotten beyond the *Cattle Raid of Cooley!* I told Elaine today: "Give me names and outlines and I'll do the reading when I get to Ireland." She gave us a farewell party tonight and her film-buff cousin, Howard Kolodny, showed *The Quiet Man*. It was marvelous to sit back and roam the wild beauty of Connemara with John Wayne and forget about movers and packers and Seminars for Spouses. I can't believe in less than a month we'll be walking those same green hills. Sometimes I get so busy with the logistics of our move that I quite literally forget where we're going.

JULY 7

A good seminar today. The morning session was on the emotional adjustments the family must make during and just after the move abroad. It will be easier for us than for some families, who will have a foreign language to learn and a different culture to assimilate. I think we will slide smoothly into Irish life, but the breaking of old ties and the making of new friends will be an adjustment for all of us. We were warned not to be misled by the initial euphoria of arriving; the fun and excitement of new experiences and the warm welcome we receive will soon wear off when we all get down to the day-to-day business of work and school.

"It's very common," our seminar leader said, "for families to experience a common period of depression, sadness, and anxiety about a month after they have settled into their new home. That's when you need the support of each other, and when parents need to give the most support and understanding to the children. Some of you may not experience this phase at all, but you'll be the lucky ones."

She warned about other common pitfalls: the frustration of a wife's having to give up an interesting and lucrative job to follow her husband halfway around the world to a country where no job possibilities exist for her; the dangers of alcoholism, which members of the foreign service, with the constant demands of entertaining, are more than normally vulnerable to; the health hazards of difficult climates.

The afternoon session, which included both ambassadors and spouses, was equally enlightening. One hour was given over to a psychiatrist who offered us guidelines on how to react if we were kidnapped or held hostage. "Think about the small details of everyday life," he suggested. "Plan a new garden. Redecorate your house. Keep your mind busy thinking about pleasant, positive, unemotional things. Get as much exercise as you can."

I'm glad once again that it's Ireland we're going to. I don't think Americans are likely victims of IRA terrorism. People ask me all the time if I am afraid of living in Ireland because of the political unrest in the North. Many of them have a misconception both geographical and historical about the violence in Ireland and the division between Northern Ireland and the Republic of Ireland; about the six counties in Ulster that are still part of Great Britain, and the twenty-six counties that are the Republic.

In the summer of 1976, the British ambassador to Ireland, Christopher Ewart-Biggs, was blown up and killed by IRA terrorists when a bomb exploded under his car in Dublin. But I don't think the American ambassador is a political target there. Anyway, I always answer, when asked, that I am not afraid of being shot, blown up, knee-capped or kidnapped and, except when asked, I never even think of it.

Another sad and final farewell today. Little Nell has gone to her new home. I groomed her before she left, and for once she looked like a Welsh terrier is supposed to look instead of like a small ball of brown and black fur. Her new owner came for her this afternoon, and only his enthusiasm about having her kept me from changing my mind at the very last minute. He pulled his car away from the curb with Little Nell looking at me out the back window. She's going to a farm in Maryland, among dog lovers, and I can think of her chasing rabbits in the woods instead of sitting lonely and cooped up in a six-foot concrete run in quarantine for six months.

I had told the boys that we would have to leave Little Nell behind. They understood. Tonight at dinner, I told them she had actually gone. And then we all cried.

July 9

A farewell trip to my hairdresser of many years, with a new, short cut, a perm, and good-bys to everyone in the shop. "Keep it short," was Sylvan's last but firm piece of advice. Only afterwards did I wonder if he was referring to my hair or my stay in Ireland.

And then a trip downtown with Bill to Copenhaver's to order all our stationery. They are used to ambassadorial needs there, and it was a quick and decisive transaction:

200 "Ambassador" calling cards
200 "Mrs." calling cards
100 "Ambassador and Mrs." calling cards
200 Engraved invitations with the gold ambassadorial seal
200 "Ambassador and Mrs." fold-over informal notes
200 "Mrs." fold-over formal notes
200 "Ambassador" gold seal stationery
10 Pads "Office of the Ambassador"

Total cost: $364.20

July 11

Bill was sworn in today at the State Department. He asked our longtime friend Judge Frank Coffin to come down from Portland, Maine, to preside. My cousin Martin Coyne loaned us a family Bible for the ceremony.

All of Bill's family from Worcester arrived for the event. Along with several dozen friends and State Department officials, we assembled at 4 PM in the beautiful, ornate Jefferson Room on the eighth floor of the Department. I wore a brand new green, white and red silk dress, with a red straw hat. The ceremony was short, simple and, for us, very moving. I stood between Bill and Frank Coffin and held the Bible. The boys stood with us, and Bill, with one hand on the Bible, repeated his oath of office. When it was over, everyone lined up and shook hands with us, congratulating Bill. One of the warmest handshakes and broadest grins came from Bill's great friend Congressman Joseph Early, from Worcester. Two hometown Irishers who made good.

Bill's swearing-in at the State Department

I had organized a small champagne reception for the guests immediately after the ceremony, and David Patrick Shannon decided that the significance of the occasion called for champagne instead of ginger ale. Alas, the waiter thought so, too, and before anyone realized what had happened, we had a tipsy five-year-old on hand.

After the reception, we all went back to the Staceys', where we grilled hamburgers in the garden and had cold salads. Brian had made strawberry daiquiris as a surprise for everyone. They were delicious and one of our guests, a lady who scarcely has a glass of sherry from one year to the next, had three and said it was the best strawberry sherbet she had ever tasted.

We sat in the garden till well past midnight. I've seldom seen Bill in such high spirits, enjoying himself so much, so happy.

July 12

The movers and packers from the storage company have been here for the past two days, and they are finished now. Our front yard looked ghostly this afternoon, with chairs, tables, beds and lamps, each one wrapped in heavy brown storage paper, lined up in rows to be loaded on the truck. The house echoes, and has the eerie, lonely feeling of a house newly emptied. I gave my last plant to one of the movers. It was a gigantic rubber tree, so big none of my friends wanted it, but I have nursed it to gargantuan size for seven years, carefully watching each new leaf unroll, and I couldn't let it die. The mover promised to take good care of it.

My cleaning lady, Lola, phoned this morning to tell of a ghastly accident involving her sister in California; Lola was on her way to the airport to go to her. Another helper, Ada, promised to come out tomorrow and help me sweep, scrub and polish the house for the new tenants.

The boys carried our suitcases across the street to the Staceys', where we shall stay until we leave the day after tomorrow.

July 13

I was sitting in the Staceys' kitchen this morning, telling Nevzer how wonderful it was to have everything finished and behind me so I could enjoy my last day in Washington. I suddenly put down my teacup and stared at her in horror:

"Bill's morning suit! It's still at the tailor's."

Bill had a morning suit made by a Georgetown tailor, and it was supposed to be finished and picked up last week. All of us had forgotten about it. He would have to wear it, shortly after our arrival in Dublin, to present his credentials to President Patrick Hillery.

"I'm glad I remembered," I said, dialing the tailor's number. "Bill would have been devastated to have forgotten it. It's almost an ambassador's uniform."

There was no answer. "Let's drive over," Nevzer suggested. "They'll be open by the time we get there."

But when I walked up to the door of the small shop, I saw the notice and my heart sank. "Closed for summer holidays. Back August 1."

I couldn't believe it. I walked around to the back of the shop, peering in all the windows. And I saw it there, looking smart and elegant in a row of light-colored summer suits.

Nevzer and I drove home disheartened. "He can rent one in Dublin," she suggested.

"I know, but the rented ones never fit well. He so much wanted to wear it when he presents his credentials. Darn."

When we reached home, I had an inspiration and phoned my real estate friend, Louise. "Could you find out who owns the building?" I begged. "They might have a key to the shop, or know where the tailor is."

Louise was back on the phone in an hour. She had traced the landlord, and he did know where the tailor had gone: Rehoboth Beach, Delaware. She even had his phone number there. I had him on the line in minutes. I was prepared to beg, cajole, threaten or bribe. But he said instantly: "I can get back to Washington in three hours. The suit is ready. I'll meet you at the shop."

And so, on a sweltering hot summer's day, in mid-holiday, he drove back to town, opened the shop, and fitted the suit. It was splendid. Bill stood patiently in the hot, stuffy shop, sweat pouring off his face as the tailor pulled and tugged and circled, admiring his craftsmanship. He finally reached his verdict: Perfect. A tailor like that is not only an artist, but an advertisement for humanity.

When we got back to Gramercy Street, the phone was ringing. Ada had dropped a knife on her foot while carving a chicken and had to go to the hospital to have it stitched. I headed back across the street to my empty house, bucket, broom and mop in hand, and spent what was left of my last, leisurely day in Washington cleaning. It was 97 degrees. It can rain in Ireland until I mildew.

We had our final Washington dinner with the Englishes, our next-door neighbors. Despite the heat, Penny had prepared a splendid farewell dinner. "Even better," I told her, "than the casserole you made for us the night we moved in, seven years ago." I walked back to the Staceys' tonight barefoot, and the sidewalk and street were still warm from the day's heat.

JULY 14

Just as I was zipping up David's bag this morning, we received a call from the State Department. There was a blackout in New York last night and Kennedy Airport was closed. We were told we probably wouldn't be able to leave after all. What an anticlimax.

Bill went this morning to call on President Carter. We all pounced on him when he returned an hour later. "What did he say?"

"He said, 'Be an ambassador to all of Ireland. Get out of Dublin and meet the people in the country.'"

"Is that *all* he said?" I asked. Bill, always teasing my insatiable curiosity, said gravely: "The rest was confidential."

He was saved from grave injury for that remark by the telephone ringing again.

"The airport is open," the Department reported. "You should plan to leave after all."

Sandy Fitz brought her Volvo to the Staceys' front door, and we loaded up bags and boys and waved good-by to the little crowd standing in the street as our car turned up 39th Street. We passed the box of Kleenex all around.

Our TWA flight left on time. I spent an hour writing thank-you notes and then put on my earphones to listen to music and await dinner. I promptly fell asleep. The next thing I knew, we were on the ground at Shannon Airport. So much for my first-class, champagne flight!

JULY 15

There is an hour's wait at Shannon for passengers going on to Dublin. I went into the ladies' room and reconstituted myself. It's amazing how much a change of clothes and new makeup will convince you that you aren't jet-weary. I put on slacks, a plaid shirt and a white wool blazer. Women in Ireland seldom wear slacks, but I often do, and I decided that I would arrive as myself.

We took off from Shannon on time and began the final lap of our long journey. It's just a twenty-five minute flight from Shannon Airport, in the west of Ireland, to Dublin, on the east coast. The soft, rounded green hills and stone fences of the Irish midlands, rich farm and grazing country, rolled by under me. I turned from the window to look at my gang of four. Bill looked fresh and excited, although as always he hadn't slept a wink on the plane. Poor David was still woozy after being awakened from a sound sleep, and was grumpy and apprehensive. Liam was excited, eager and smiling, and Christopher looked thoughtfully out the window, not reacting until he could appraise the situation. I knew that the minute we stepped off the plane in Dublin we would cease to be the people we left behind last night. We would be playing a role as long as we stayed in Ireland, and that role would define us.

I took out my small purse-sized diary and wrote: "My Eight Commandments" (to be changed later according to circumstances):

1. I will play my role with energy and try to leave my mark. I will *not* leave Ireland known merely as "the American ambassador's wife."

2. The children will have to come before official duties, no matter how important those seem.

3. I will not allow the children to be treated differently from their friends, and they will not ride around town in a limousine (Liam's dream).

4. I will write in my journal every day. (Well, every other day.)

5. I will try to be at Bill's side when he needs me, and definitely *not* be at his side when he doesn't.

6. I will not be lazy about trying to learn all I can about Ireland, by reading, traveling, meeting people and listening.

7. I will not complain about the weather.

8. I will have fun.

The plane landed with the tiniest of bumps and sped smoothly down the runway. In seconds, we were saying good-by to the crew and waiting for the heavy doors to slide open. I stepped out first, with the boys close behind, and Bill bringing up the rear. There was a platoon of men standing outside the door of the plane. The first hand I shook belonged to Jack Rendahl, the voice behind so many helpful telephone calls. Suddenly, seemingly out of nowhere, the cameras appeared. Bulbs began popping, TV lights turned on, journalists were walking alongside us, asking questions. David tucked his head behind my back and wouldn't look at anyone. I remembered, too late, that I hadn't explained about the cameras to him before he deplaned so that he would be prepared. I also remembered, too late, that I had not brought a "sick bag" off the plane for him. He has an unorthodox habit of throwing up when he gets *off* a plane. I smiled at the flashing cameras and whispered to Bill: "Did you bring a bag for David?"

"No." He smiled back. David looked beige, which is his pre-throwing-up color. We all just smiled.

We were taken into the small VIP waiting room, which was hot and stuffy, and filled with cigarette smoke. I began to feel beige myself. It's an embassy custom for the American staff and their spouses to come to the airport to greet the new ambassador. They were all there this morning, and we shook hands with each of them. It gave the effect of an immediate rapport and warmth surrounding our welcome. Bill was whisked off into another room for a television interview. Poor fellow, no sleep and no breakfast and a TV appearance.

Finally, we went outside to two waiting cars. No limousines, thank goodness. The ambassador's car was a small black Holden; I had never seen one before. We started to pile in, when the boys and I were gently disengaged from Bill and led over to another waiting car. Several men from the embassy staff got in with Bill; he gave me a wistful smile as I walked away. He had wanted to "see my face" when we pulled up in front of our new home, and, once again, we weren't to share a special moment.

The ride from the airport to our house in the Phoenix Park was not memorable, and it was a gray, damp, chilly day, raining lightly; a "heavy" day, the Irish would say. (Mind you, I'm not complaining, only stating the facts.) Our driver, Joe Lewis, chatted about the neighborhoods we were driving through: Drumcondra, Phibsboro, Cabra, the Navan Road, and finally, the Cabra Gate, into the Park.

"That's the home of your nearest neighbor, the papal nuncio," Joe added, as we glimpsed a large white house through the trees on our right. I knew from reading about the Park that we had only two neighbors, the papal nuncio and the president of Ireland. "No dashing out to borrow a cup of sugar," one of my neighbors in Washington had warned.

We crossed the Main Park Road and turned into a short drive which led to two white stucco gate houses framing the large black wrought-iron gate of our new home. The flags, one Irish, one American, were flying above the gate for our welcome. Two polished hardwood plaques on the white stucco pillars read, in gold lettering: "Home of the American Ambassador," and, in Irish, "Áras an Ambasadoir Amurcain."

Slowing down to drive through the opened gates, we saw a dozen children of all sizes lining the driveway, waving little American and Irish flags and smiling at us. David immediately perked up when he saw them and waved back.

Our arrival at the Residence

"They're children of the staff," Joe explained. "They all live here, and they've been waiting to give you a proper welcome."

We drove up the broad avenue toward the house; a white iron fence lined the meadows on either side of the drive, keeping in the herd of black and white Friesian cattle that munched the thick green grass and looked up lazily as we drove past. A dozen huge chestnut trees along the drive shaded them.

The big white house stood at the end of the drive, facing a circle of green lawn hedged by miniature boxwood. A bust of Abraham Lincoln stood opposite the front door against a high garden wall, looking gravely down on all who passed his way. We pulled up to the porticoed green front door, and as we all got out, we were greeted by Dennis Buckley, the chief butler and general manager of the house, and his wife, Maeve, the embassy social secretary.

My first impression as we went into the house was of flowers everywhere: multicolored sweet peas trailing over table tops; Japanese iris, roses, daisies, snapdragons, petunias and dahlias—blues and yellows, pinks, reds, rainbows of color and scent. Bouquets on every table. I've never seen so many flowers.

The rest of the household staff came in to meet us: Maureen Sharkey, who did all the lovely flower arrangements; Anne O'Brien, the cook;

Kitty Horgan, in charge of the family quarters. They are all a blur of friendly, smiling faces and blue eyes at the moment. We needed to retreat into the baths and beds to get our second wind. Bill and I went upstairs to our beautiful, large, light bedroom at the end of the hall. Its three floor-to-ceiling windows look out over our lawn and the Park beyond. The boys were down the hall in two adjoining rooms. I had a cup of tea and fell into bed.

We came downstairs just in time for our first meal here. Anne's roast lamb and tiny potatoes were marvelous. I will happily, eagerly, enthusiastically give up my culinary efforts to her for the next few years. We sat at a small round table at one end of the large dining room, in the bay of three huge windows with the same view as our bedroom. The table must have been in that place for a long time; its dark mahogany finish has been bleached and mellowed to pale gold by years of sunshine.

During dinner the sun broke through dark rifts of clouds and sent flames shooting through the western sky. Shafts of light fell across the smooth green lawn that stretches from the house to the edge of the Park. It was my first experience of the magic of Irish light.

Cows and deer grazed silently in the Park, staring up at the house as we stared back at them. There is a peace and stillness here as the sun still rides high in a long Irish summer evening. Even the cattle seem to have fallen into a reverie of their own.

After dinner we walked slowly through each of the large rooms. The house is graceful and handsome. Now we have to make it home.

JULY 17

We awoke to a dull, gray sky, but I feel rested and excited and keen to get going. Maureen has unpacked all my bags and put everything away, which is a marvelous luxury, except that I can't find anything.

After a huge breakfast—eggs, thick Irish bacon, sausage, brown soda bread and scones, tea (they can't believe that we Americans are tea drinkers)—we went to mass at our neighborhood church in Chapelizod, just outside the Park gate. The pastor, Father McCarthy, welcomed us to the parish in his sermon, and that embarrassed the boys mightily. They hung their heads and smirked and nudged each other. The parishioners eyed us shyly as we filed out, but the Irish have far too much dignity to intrude on one's privacy. No one came up to say hello.

After an enormous Sunday lunch (this can't go on; in fact, tomorrow I will tell Anne that we are a two-meal family on Sundays), we took a ride around Dublin with Gerry Noctor, Bill's driver. Downtown Dublin looked awful in the gray Sunday mist. There are great gaping holes in blocks of buildings that make one think of postwar bombed-out Munich or Vienna. Destruction and demolition seem rampant. Where are the pretty Dublin squares I saw last summer in the sunshine? Surely all this destruction couldn't have happened in a year?

Then we passed a most appalling encampment of broken-down caravans parked in an empty lot right in the city center. Litter was strewn with total abandon; cans, rags, old mattresses, car seats, rusty tins, papers, garbage, and a gaggle of dirty, laughing children playing in the midst of it all.

"Tinkers," Gerry told us. Tinkers to me conjure up gaily painted wagons with dark-haired, pretty boys and girls frolicking about on a grassy verge. This looked like a West Virginia hillbilly scene moved to a New Delhi slum, with a few rusty car parts thrown in for good measure.

Our spirits lifted as we headed out through Ballsbridge toward Dun Laoghaire* ("God's country," Gerry explained, being a Dun Laoghaire man himself). The Vico Road, high over Killiney Bay, with the Wicklow mountains rising in the distance, was remote and mysterious in the mist.

This evening, Jack Rendahl had us all over to his house for dinner. We talked about Dublin, and Ireland, and the embassy and the people here we would want to get to know. Jack is an accurate and observant reporter and good company, and Bill is grateful to have such a cool and professional diplomat to guide him through his first weeks here.

We came home early. Tomorrow Bill has to "go to work."

"What are you going to do when you sit down at your desk tomorrow?" I asked him, as we were getting ready for bed. He thought for a moment, and smiled. "Ask me that tomorrow. What are you going to do?"

"I'm going to walk through the house from top to bottom with Dennis. I'm going to ask a lot of questions and make a list and try to look as if I know what I'm doing."

July 18

I did wander all over the house today with Dennis. It's big and beautiful, but my first impression of it is that it's bland and colorless, despite the lovely flowers everywhere. The walls and carpets are pale gray, elegant and cool, but I like warm houses, filled with color. It was built in 1776, but no one, either here or at the State Department, seems to know much about its history. I want to do some research on it, to know why it was built here in the Park, and who has lived in it.

The downstairs has two small entry halls, which open out into a lovely oval foyer, two stories high, with a graceful Adams-style skylight in the ceiling. Dennis told me that some past ambassador's teenaged son was

*Pronounced "Dun Leary."

climbing on the roof and crashed through that skylight, falling two stories to the hall floor. He lost an eye in the accident. I made a mental note to the boys; warning number two thousand and three: Don't climb on the roof and fall through the skylight.

An American flag and an ambassadorial flag flank a large marble table in the foyer where we put our picture of President Carter. It's our "official" reception room. On either side of the marble table, two doors lead into the two drawing rooms. The house is well designed for entertaining. Four large rooms along the back open into each other. The ballroom is on one end, the two drawing rooms in between, and the large, handsome dining room at the far end. All the rooms have floor to ceiling windows looking out over the lawns of the residence and the Park beyond.

The furniture is mostly eighteenth-century American reproduction, or traditional American "all-purpose." Some of it looks good, some is in need of repair, and some of it should find its way to the nearest garage sale. The draperies in the ballroom and the drawing rooms are lovely. The dining room drapes are so old they are beginning to shred.

Workrooms and storage rooms line the back passage and one of them will make a good crafts/playroom. The end of the house has a sunny, large, old-fashioned workable kitchen. Pantries, a store room, a staff lounge and the laundry make up the rest of the wing.

All the staff live here. I've gone to visit their quarters; Dennis and Maeve are above the kitchen in a lovely apartment they share with their two small boys; the single women are in rooms over a wing to themselves; Gerry, with his wife and children, live in a spacious apartment over the garage.

My first priority will be redecorating the staff bedrooms. They need more storage space, new dressers, paint and curtains. Do I present a list to the general services officer at the embassy, requesting the changes? Do they like ambassadors' wives who initiate new projects? Will they tell me what sort of a budget I have for the house? I didn't learn any of that in my Seminars for Spouses.

Bill came home at six thirty, just as I was coming back from a walk around the gardens.

"What kind of a day did you have?" I asked him, as he unloaded an enormous stack of reading material onto the desk.

"So busy meeting everyone that I didn't have time to 'do' anything. Tomorrow, perhaps, I'll begin. What did you do?"

"Plan," I answered. "Lots of plans."

"Save tomorrow afternoon," he said. "There will be a reception at the chancery with all the staff to welcome us."

I wonder if they are curious to see me. I'm *very* curious to meet them and see what they are like. The short reception at the airport just became a haze of faces unattached to names.

David woke a little while ago, crying for us, something he hasn't done in years. I stumbled in the darkness of the unfamiliar hall, twisted my ankle, cursed, and finally found a light switch. I held him, sobbing and shaking and pleading: "Don't leave me." I finally carried him to our room, his long legs drooping nearly to the floor, and put him into bed with us, usually a "no-no" in our house. It took him a long time to go back to sleep, and between his sobs, it all came out: "I miss Mark and Bart. I miss Little Nell and our house, and Gramercy Street. I miss my room and my Big Wheel." Poor little fellow. I do, too. And just to keep him company, I let a few tears mingle with his on the pillow. Don't tell me we're having our sinking spell already! That's not supposed to come for another month, and we've only been here over the weekend.

JULY 19

I had my first good look at the chancery today, before we joined the staff in the rotunda for the party. It's a sand-colored, round building, the only round American chancery in the world. The building is very controversial in Dublin, but I think it's handsome and interesting. The architects took their inspiration from the Irish round towers of the sixth and seventh centuries, and its oddly shaped rectangular windows are based on Celtic designs. Michael Scott, one of Ireland's leading architects, and an American, John M. Johansen (who also designed a stunning new library building at Bill's alma mater, Clark University, in Worcester), were the codesigners of the building.

Inside, there is a large rotunda, with the offices circling it on five floors, two below ground, three above, in keeping with the local zoning laws regulating the height of buildings in the neighborhood.

The staff was already gathered in the rotunda when we came in. Bill made a short, humorous speech, saying that President Carter had sent them two ambassadors for the price of one, and then introduced me. They clapped, and we circulated, trying to meet and chat with everyone. Was I shy or were they? Somehow, I felt a holding back, a certain aloofness, or perhaps a wariness, particularly on the part of the American staff. Is there a barrier between them and us that can't be crossed? Do they resent a political appointee coming into their camp? For some reason, I found the Irish staff, though shyer and quieter, easier to talk with, and warmer in their reception. Obviously, we all need a lot of getting to know each other. I remembered some of the chilling stories of ambassadors' wives that my foreign service friends in Washington had told me; perhaps some of the Dublin staff had fallen under the baleful eye or wicked tongue of a diplomatic villainess in days gone by. Anyway, although I had been looking forward to this reception, I was relieved when it was over.

Tomorrow is a momentous day for Bill, the last step in the long passage from private citizen to ambassador. He will go to "Áras an Uachtaráin," the President's House, to present his credentials to President Patrick Hillery. Until he actually hands over those credentials, Bill's predecessor here, Walter Curley, is still officially the United States ambassador to Ireland.

We had so much been looking forward to witnessing this ceremony, and then I was told just today that wives and children are excluded. Damn! I was *so* mad when I heard that. The boys and I had been dying to see Himself review the troops, which is part of the ceremony. Liam said this morning: "Dad, I bet you go up to every soldier in the line and say, 'Did you brush your teeth this morning?' the way you review the troops at home." I'm determined that I will figure out a way to get us in there to see it.

JULY 20

Bill dressed in his morning suit. He wore the gray top hat his *New York Times* colleagues had given him as a farewell present, and he carried his new gray suede gloves. He looked like he was born to be an ambassador. We watched him dress, like royalty preparing for a levee, giving him encouraging advice like, "Don't hand the president your top hat and put your credentials on the chair," and "Don't trip over the rug going in." And David, just to even up the score, said: "Go to the bathroom *before* you leave the embassy, Daddy," then roared with laughter at his clever joke. When Bill was dressed, I stuck a carnation in his buttonhole.

The tradition here is for ambassadors to leave their chancery, escorted by an army motorcycle corps, and ride to Áras an Uachtaráin in the Phoenix Park. Since we live in the Park, it was a quick return trip from our residence to the chancery and back to the Park.

The boys and I stood outside the chancery in Ballsbridge, with a small crowd that had gathered to watch. The motorcycle corps, twenty strong, arrived in a flourish of revving motors, gleaming bikes and flashy white gloves. They looked very smart, and even Christopher was impressed. Then a big black Daimler from the Department of Foreign Affairs purred to a stop in front of the chancery and the chief of protocol and his assistant got out.

Bill came down the chancery steps with Jack Rendahl and Colonel John Berres, his military attaché, close behind. The chief of the motorcycle corps came up to him and saluted smartly, then turned on his heel and returned to his motorcycle. Bill got into the Daimler, the motorcycles roared, and off they sped toward the Park. Happily, the sun was shining.

By prearrangement, the boys and I dashed into our waiting car and

"Himself" reviewing the troops

followed the procession through town. We were stopped at the presidential gates as the official party sped through, and, at this point, I put My Plan into action. I will leave my methods to your imagination, dear journal, because I don't want to implicate anyone else in my less-than-diplomatic gate-crashing (and who knows? I might want to use the system again). Suffice it to say that the boys and I watched the entire proceedings, at least that part of it which was held outside, discreetly stationed behind a large clump of rhododendron bushes, close enough to take good pictures, hidden enough to please the Protocol Office. Unorthodox, but effective. And just for the record, I did not bribe, beg or cajole anyone, but I wasn't a Girl Scout for nothing.

After it was over, we came back to the residence, where we had invited all the American embassy staff and their spouses to have lunch with us and celebrate the occasion.

When the party was over and the house was quiet this afternoon, a couple named Matthews from Nebraska arrived at our gates and asked if they could come in and see the house. Ordinarily we have to turn away the hordes of American tourists who arrive in the Park eager to see the residence, but the Matthewses were different. His father had been ambassador to Ireland in 1951–52 and had died while in office here. The present Mr. Matthews hadn't been back to Ireland since, and was taking his wife on a sentimental journey. I was delighted to show them all through the house. I discovered that I love being a guide, although it is obvious that in the future I will have to enlarge my recitation with a few more facts. Today I'm afraid I glossed over facts with fancy.

Bill came back in time to meet them, and they promised that when they get home they would look in their attic to see if they still have the black top hat from Mr. Matthews' father's ambassadorial days. "He had a big head, too," Mr. Matthews said, looking at Bill's dome. "I'm sure it would fit you. We don't have much use for it in Nebraska, except for school plays."

I wonder if my sons will return here in thirty years' time and have nostalgic memories of this house? And happy memories? I hope they will always receive a warm welcome. I think anyone who has ever lived here is a part of this house and leaves something of himself behind.

JULY 21

Ginnie Kennealy of the *Irish Press* came out to the house today to do an interview with Bill. She wanted him to talk about his views on Northern Ireland, but he didn't want to commit himself, nor did he want to stray into controversial subjects. But he said later that he was too sympathetic to the press point of view and remembered all the interviews he had done when he was a young reporter, trying to pry information out of wary officials.

The first signature appeared in our brand-new guest book today: "Alistair Cooke." He's here in Dublin to give a speech at the Royal Dublin Society. He and Bill knew each other covering national political conventions years ago, but it was the first time I had met him. He is just as charming in real life as he is on radio and television, and seems to know everyone in this world and quite a few in the next.

JULY 22

We paid our first "call" together today. It's a tradition for new ambassadors to pay formal calls on their colleagues, and wives do the same thing with each other. After a few weeks go by, each of them repays the call. It seems time consuming, but in fact it is a simple, straightforward way of meeting one's colleagues and establishing the beginnings of a personal rapport.

The Austrian ambassador here is a single woman, so we paid our call on her together. She is a short, plump little Viennese lady with a tart tongue and a great love for Ireland. "This is the last Victorian society," she said, as she poured us each a glass of sherry in her office. She's right, of course. There is a great respect for authority here, inculcated partly by the Catholic Church, which one doesn't find anymore in the rest of Europe or America. There is also a greater emphasis on family life here than one finds at home. I doubt that Ireland has more happy or unhappy marriages than any other country, but divorce is not legal here and so the institutions of marriage and family are still supported and bolstered by society and the law. Whatever people may do in private, they keep up the facade of public morality, which is the essence of Victorian mores.

I had my first group of embassy wives out to the house for tea this afternoon. Remembering the warnings in Washington to be friendly, open, and not to slight any of the wives, even inadvertently, I'm having them all out for the afternoon in small groups, to try to chat and get to know each one. A friend in Washington told me that she and her husband had been posted for a year and a half in a large European embassy when, one day, the ambassador's wife approached her at a reception, put out her hand, and said: "Hello, I'm ——. Do you live here?" Since that occasion had happened twenty years before, my friend's memory of it was not only galling but lasting.

JULY 25

The papal nuncio in Dublin lives just across the Main Park Road from us in a lovely old eighteenth-century house surrounded by enormous trees and a walled garden filled with vegetables. (The day we arrived in Dublin, the nuns who care for the nuncio sent us an overflowing basket filled with a dozen varieties of vegetables from the garden, just to say "Welcome.")

We went to a reception at the nuncio's this evening to say good-by to the departing French ambassador and his wife. I haven't even said hello to them, but departure ceremonies are de rigueur for ambassadors and their wives.

We assembled in the spacious drawing room and were served drinks and hors d'oeuvres (they were *delicious,* definitely not your wilted-cracker variety. The silver trays were filled with tiny puff pastries, miniature pizzas, smoked salmon on brown bread). The farewells in Dublin are always held at the nuncio's because he is dean of the corps. In most countries, the ambassador who has served in the post the longest is dean, but in Catholic countries, it is usually the nuncio. Bishop Alibrandi, the nuncio, would be dean here under either system because he has served longer than any other ambassador.

After thirty minutes of chitchat, we were hushed up and the nuncio and the French ambassador and his wife stood in front of the room while the nuncio read out a little speech of farewell. The ambassador replied, and was then presented with a silver tray engraved with all the ambassadors' names. Champagne was passed around by the nuncio's white-gloved butler, and we toasted the departing ambassador and wished him and his wife bon voyage.

When our turn comes to stand up front and say good-by, I don't want another silver tray to polish. I wonder if one can substitute a nice piece of eighteenth-century furniture instead? Would they be scandalized? I need a sideboard more than I need a silver tray.

This was my first glimpse of the diplomatic corps. There are twenty-three countries represented. For such a formal, traditional reception, it was a warm and friendly occasion. I think I'm going to enjoy the diplomatic life.

JULY 26

I interviewed three candidates for a job as live-in baby-sitter for David. None seemed just right. I'm looking for a university student who will be in school when David is but who will be here to look after him in the late afternoons and evenings.

In the middle of the interviews, I had a most peculiar and rather disturbing phone call. The caller told Maeve, who had answered the phone, that she was phoning in response to the ad in the newspaper for the baby-sitter's job, but when I came on the line she said:

"I want to welcome you to Ireland, but you should know that, although the Irish people will always pretend to like you and to admire America, they don't. It's just a sham. There is a lot of anti-Americanism here and you should be prepared for that." Then she hung up, before I could say a word.

Well, if I came to Ireland expecting everyone to love me, I might as well have stayed at home. Still, it was an odd call and it echoed in my mind all day.

We gave our first big reception here this evening, for an international convention of trade unionists who are meeting in Dublin. Since the planning had been done in advance of our arrival, we were almost like guests ourselves, except for shaking 350 hands.

I was enjoying myself in my first receiving line, meeting everyone and chatting away, and didn't realize at all that disaster had struck in the kitchen. The catering firm had not arrived with the food; Dennis was dashing from the bar in the ballroom, where he was serving drinks, to the pantry to make yet another frantic phone call to the firm, asking what was going on and when were they coming? But Bill and I just went on blithely shaking hands, oblivious to the crisis. By the time we were finished receiving, everyone was enjoying himself and the food finally arrived. I don't think it had even been missed. When it did come, we pressed it on our guests with persistent enthusiasm. I think people come to an embassy reception to see what it's like, to meet the ambassador, to see the house and to have a drink, and not really to eat. Anyway, if a hostess is worried about the arrangements and shows it, the guests will know it and won't enjoy themselves. The best way to give them a good time is to have one yourself. I am glad that for my first reception I was spared the Crisis of the Caterer. I hope it isn't an omen of things to come!

July 27

Two more names appeared in our guest book tonight. Kevin Mallen, an old friend from California, came out to the Park for dinner with Terence de Vere White, the literary editor of the *Irish Times*. We have read several of Terence's books and much of his literary criticism, and were eager to meet him.

It was one of those evenings that sparkle and glitter from the beginning. Terence lived up to an Irishman's reputation for talk; wit, erudition and eloquence flowed from him as naturally as rain from an Irish sky. He must have inspired the rest of us (he is a good listener as well) because we all shone. No subject was left to languish; books and plays, art and architecture, Ireland in general and Dublin in particular, people we should get to know and people we should avoid. Terence is a sensitive, discerning and somewhat incorrigible "Who's Who in Dublin," and I would relish having him as my cicerone to lead me through the maze of Dublin society, where everyone seems to be everyone's cousin or in-law, where family feuds of long ago still simmer on the back burner, and where a stranger must tread carefully to avoid ancient wounds, real or imagined.

July 28

Can we have been here only two weeks? I feel like I am awakened in the mornings by a demanding tempest that swirls me through the day and slings me back down at night, breathless, exhausted and spent. We did not have a quiet, peaceful period to "settle in" as we had hoped. I am always being asked by people I meet if I have "settled in," and I resolutely say yes, hoping that by affirming it, it will be accomplished. I'm so grateful for the competent, caring staff we have at the residence. The house and all its activities purr along; tempting, delicious food appears on the table; the house is shining and spotless; the laundry is done, the linens cared for, the grates and brasses polished, the fires cleared and rebuilt, the floors polished, the walks swept. The house is filled with flowers, and the gardens are majestic. The telephone is answered, the invitations lists made, the table seating arranged, the receiving lines kept straight. What wonderful luck. So many of the other ambassadors' wives complain about their lack of staff and their inability to find anyone to work for them. I couldn't begin to manage without the help and support I'm given here. I seem to be dashing in and out of the house all day and all night, running in through the back door to greet guests coming in through the front, dashing out the front door to pay a call or go to a reception, checking up on the boys or changing clothes. I didn't know that life was going to be so busy, but surely after I find a school for the boys, finish paying my calls, find a baby-sitter for David and (the blessed panacea of all mothers) when school starts! my life will be less hectic.

We visited St. Michael's College today (secondary schools in Ireland are often called colleges). It's an elementary/high school for boys, run by the Holy Ghost Fathers. Although a long way from Phoenix Park, it's near the chancery, so Bill could drive the boys in with him in the mornings. And they take children as young as David, which many of the schools do not. The classrooms are very small, and the classes large, thirty to thirty-five boys to a class. But there are beautiful, spacious playing fields in back.

We liked Father Flood, the headmaster, and St. Michael's has a reputation in town of being a "happy" school, so if they are willing to take David and Christopher, we shall enroll them. Liam is holding out for a coed school.

The curriculum at St. Michael's sounds more demanding than that of the boys' public school in Washington, but one can't really tell until classes begin what the quality of work will be. Our boys will be exempt from studying Irish because they are foreign students, but Irish children must take Irish, taught as a second language, from the first grade through the end of high school. It's amazing how few of the people we have met speak Irish, considering the emphasis on it in the schools. We decided that David will take it because he is just beginning "prep," the kindergarten class at St. Michael's, and all of his classmates will also be beginners.

JULY 29

Our own car hasn't arrived yet, nor has our shipment of clothes and personal effects, so we feel rather like we are still camping out here. Gerry has to drive me everywhere, and although he is a marvelous guide to Dublin, I hate being dependent on him. I'm trying to memorize streets (which isn't easy since street signs are placed in a rather whimsical fashion here), so that I'll know my way when I take the wheel.

The boys are running out of steam, too, with no bikes, balls, tennis racquets and, worst of all, no friends. They are going to start riding lessons next week. I'm more enthusiastic about the lessons than they are, however.

I visited a Christian Brothers School today with Liam, but we weren't seriously interested in it. It's too far away, and it isn't coed. I said to the very friendly brother who showed us around: "The Christian Brothers in America have a reputation for having a heavy hand with a cane."

He laughed merrily and said: "Oh, we're not nearly as bad as we used to be." Rather a chilling reassurance, I thought.

I've interviewed about fifteen boys and girls for the baby-sitting job, and today I hit the jackpot. A freckle-faced girl arrived on her bicycle, in jeans and with curly hair blowing wild in the wind. Her bike fell over as she tried to park it at the front door, and she spilled her tea in her lap and laughed, then told me some hilarious Irish stories, and I hired her on the spot. Her name is Siobhán O'Tierney and she has four brothers and seems to me a girl who could handle anything that David—or Christopher or Liam—put in her way. She's a first-year student at University College in Dublin, and she said she would ride her bike into school each day.

"It's about eight miles each way," I warned her.

"That's not far," she replied cheerfully.

August 2

Horse Show Week. We went to a preshow party a few days ago at the home of Lilian Fay, whose husband was a very popular ambassador to the United States in the 1960s. I'm sure I met half of Dublin in her drawing room, but faces and names are still a fuzzy blur to me. Everyone I met was friendly and welcoming; I don't think I've ever gazed into so many smiling blue eyes in one room.

We were in Dublin for the Horse Show last year, and I remember sitting with friends at the Royal Dublin Society grounds, looking over at the diplomatic boxes, with the Stars and Stripes draped over one of them, wondering who was in it and thinking how much fun it must be to be the host and hostess there.

The Dublin Horse Show is a colorful mosaic of past and present, elegant remnants of Anglo-Irish mingling with country squireens, young farmers and city folk in the tie that binds the Irish together surer than families and funerals; a love of good horseflesh.

Besides being an impressive and exciting competition of international show jumping, it is also a week of balls and receptions, band concerts and craft displays, horse shoeing contests and donkey shows, strolls around the RDS gardens under a summer sun (perhaps!) to meet friends for tea and cakes; blue ribbons for pony and hunter classes, flowered hats and derbies, lost children, and hopeless bottlenecks that bring traffic in Ballsbridge to a standstill. Top hats and tailcoats are brought out of mothballs and worn proudly by the RDS stewards, those stalwarts who keep everyone and everything in order. Ireland's top show jumpers enjoy the adulation of pop-star status for a week, and the talk is horses, horses, horses.

The show jumping events take place each afternoon in the big ring of the RDS grounds. The flag-draped diplomatic boxes along one end are

The Dublin Horse Show

festooned with geraniums and ivy and the ring itself is banked with yellow marigolds. The jumps, freshly painted, stand like formidable barriers along the thick, clipped grass. The scene is brilliant with color, glamour and impending drama. The atmosphere is a curious combination of unhurried languor and electrically charged anticipation.

At 3 PM sharp each afternoon, a crisp, authoritative voice announces over a loudspeaker the arrival in the ring of the first rider and horse. There is a different competition each day, but it is always a jumping event, judged either by time or faults, or both. A rider having a clear round in one event competes with another clear round for better time. At the end of each event, a jump-off may be required to narrow the field down to a winner. Six countries participate, with competitors vying for the individual as well as team points. I was disappointed that the United States had not sent a team. Someone told me they don't come anymore because it is too expensive to fly the horses over. Someone else said they worry about security problems because of the troubles in the North.

The jumps look frighteningly high and wide to me, ranging from four and a half feet to seven feet high, with a four-foot spread. It is an intensely competitive, skilled show, and only the top European riders participate. Eddie Macken is Ireland's darling of the show jumping circuit this year, his blue eyes and handsome smile backed up by formidable skill. Since the United States isn't represented, I'm ready to cheer Eddie and the Irish team to victory.

We invited six guests to share the box with us today. At four thirty, a waiter brought us high tea, trays laden with sandwiches, fruit cake and pastries. By 6 PM the show was over, I was hoarse from cheering, and Ireland's riders had won the day's events. Without our even noticing it, the sun had gone down over the grandstand and the late afternoon air had become chilled.

"Grand show today, miss," the elderly white-coated attendant who takes tickets for the boxes said, and I agreed.

AUGUST 3

I pay calls in the mornings and slip off to the Horse Show in the afternoons. There is always a reception at one of the embassies following the show. This evening we went out to the beautiful Italian embassy in Lucan to meet the Italian riding team. They have been coming to the show in Dublin for years and are very well-known and popular here. One of the women riders shook my hand with a grip of iron; she's obviously been reining in horses for a long time. The men were much smaller than they seem out in the field on those big horses, but in their army uniforms and riding boots, they looked handsome and romantic to me. Alas, they don't speak English, and my Italian begins and ends with *"Arrivederci."*

AUGUST 5

It's our wedding anniversary. Is it sixteen years or seventeen since we rode around Central Park in a buggy on our wedding night? I never know. I can't even remember the years the boys were born, and I have to think back to where we were living at the time to arrive at the right dates.

Today I called on Mrs. Haydon, the wife of the British ambassador. They live in a house called Glencairn, built by, of all people, "Boss" Croker, the notorious head of Tammany Hall in the 1890s, when he retired to Ireland. Ambassador Haydon replaced Christopher Ewart-Biggs last year after Ewart-Biggs was assassinated by the IRA. Although the Haydons are heavily guarded and their house and grounds seemed filled with security men, it must be a terrible strain to live here and try to go about your day-to-day business knowing that you are an obvious target for the masked gunmen who pose as Ireland's liberators.

Mrs. Haydon is a pretty, vivacious strawberry blonde who lived for many years in New York while her husband was posted there. We were very soon engrossed in talk of dogs, flowers, children and gardens, topics safe for ambassadors' wives to begin their friendship when paying calls. Outside the French windows, security guards walked up and down by the flower beds, carrying submachine guns.

AUGUST 6

Today is the big day at the Horse Show when six country teams compete for the "Nations' Cup," the Aga Khan Challenge Trophy. Our invitation said: "Please assemble in the President's box at 2:45 PM." I thought that meant the president of Ireland, but it turned out to be the president of the Royal Dublin Society. Dress for ambassadors was spelled out on the invitation: "Morning coat and top hat." The women were left to use their own imaginations. I wore a white silk suit I had bought in Washington specially for the occasion, with a navy blue straw hat. I wore woolen underwear, and even then, I was happy for the blanket the stewards thoughtfully provided.

The president of Ireland and Mrs. Hillery, the taoiseach (the Irish word for "prime minister") and Mrs. Jack Lynch, and various government officials joined us in the box. It was a cool, gray and misty day, but the show was spectacular. Ireland won the cup in a wildly exciting jump-off overtime, narrowly beating the German team. I found myself on my feet, pounding on the back of an ambassador sitting in front of me, shouting myself hoarse for Ireland. (I rather conspicuously made up for a lack of enthusiasm otherwise displayed in my box.) When the day was won for Ireland, the ambassadorial back I had pounded upon turned round to give me a frosty smile and ask if I was happy that Ireland had won. He turned out to be the German ambassador. "Oh well," I said gamely, "someone has to win. *Jawohl?*"

AUGUST 7

I'm weary of making calls. I've run out of small talk and I'm overflowing with coffee and cakes. My stop today was with an extravagant hypochondriac, who took me on a tour of her liver, her pancreas and her upper intestinal tract. I was spared her bowels, thanks be to God, but we left her bladder reluctantly as time was running out, and we still had to cover her allergies. At least I wasn't forced to contribute to the conversation.

AUGUST 9

I made my grand tour of the gardens today with Michael O'Donohoe, the head gardener here for many years. His interest in every blade of grass, every blossom on the property, is all-consuming, and I share his interest, but with a certain aloofness that I reserve for gardens that aren't really mine. At home, I'm the weed puller, the earth turner, and I watch my garden grow with the possessive, critical eye of its creator. I show off my delphiniums, my clematis, my tomatoes like a proud parent. And although I like the new image of myself here, basket in hand, daintily clipping an endless supply of snapdragons, gladioli, roses and petunias to arrange for the house, I know I won't invest emotion in a garden I haven't planned and planted.

Most of the sixty-nine acres here are in woodland and meadow, circumscribed by a path that goes right around the outer edge of the property. The outside edge of the path drops sharply down about four feet, forming a sort of half-moat, called a ha-ha. It's a sixteenth-century French landscaping innovation designed to keep out deer and livestock without diminishing the view with a fence. Why a "ha-ha"? No one seems to know.

The path is lined with stately ancient beech, oak, elm and lime trees, even a few aspen, rare in Ireland. They bend and groan and creak in the wind in a slightly sinister manner, as if they have stories to tell but don't speak the language. Bill jogs along this path under the trees and does two laps a day, one and a quarter miles in each lap. I watch him flash by each morning from my bedroom window. Well, pass by.

There are two walled gardens; one, called the Pretty Garden, is just for looking at, walking through and admiring. The other is our working garden, filled with vegetables, fruit trees, berry bushes and cutting flowers. And then there is a rather mysterious, unkempt, overgrown hill where David disappears to play for hours each day with the other residence children. When I ask him where he's been, he simply says: "On the Fairy Hill."

I finally queried Michael about it today: "Why is it so wild and unkempt?" I asked.

"It's the Fairy Hill," says he, explaining all.

AUGUST 10

We went to dinner with friends in the country tonight, a soft, mild evening that drew us into the garden for cocktails. During dinner, a neighbor rushed in, greatly excited, to say he had just bought a horse and invited us all to come out to look at it. We filed out, admired it, discussed it, patted it, walked around it, and then we all trooped back in to dinner again.

People keep asking me: What is different between Ireland and America? That's different.

We enrolled Liam today in King's Hospital, a coed, Church of Ireland boarding/day school. It's known locally as the Blue Coat School and was founded in the seventeenth century as a hospice or boarding school for the sons of British Army officers.

I liked the way the headmaster, Dr. Gerald Magahy, talked about teenagers, schools, education, manners and life. I'd like him to be in charge of Liam's education.

During the interview, I asked Dr. Magahy how he handled pot smoking or other drug abuse in the school.

"We don't have much of it," he said, "and when we do, it's grounds for expulsion. We only had to expel one student last year, who was caught smoking pot on the school grounds, and she was an American."

When I told a friend this evening that Liam would be going to King's Hospital, she laughed. "With two of your boys at St. Michael's and one at King's Hos, I can just hear the wags now: 'Sure it must be a mixed marriage!' " I think I'd forgotten about definitions being made in "Catholic" and "Protestant" terms, but I remember now being a little girl at Holy Cross Elementary School and laughing, even then, at a copy of *The Catholic Miss* that had an article entitled: "Do You Want to Grow Up and Be a Catholic Typist?"

August 15

Lunched today at the National Gallery of Art with Terence de Vere White and the director of the Gallery, James White. After lunch, we toured the Gallery. It isn't large, but it has a wide range of good pictures and includes a small American Room. When George Bernard Shaw died, he left a trust to the National Gallery from the proceeds of *Pygmalion*. The royalties dribbled in, until Henry Higgins and Eliza Doolittle landed on Broadway in *My Fair Lady* and then traveled to Hollywood for the movie. GBS could have danced all night, and certainly the trustees of the National Gallery did, as that modest little trust grew into a legacy that enabled them to enlarge substantially. Now a bronze statue of Shaw stands by the Museum's front entrance, a handsome tribute to its patron.

The boys took their second riding lesson today and showed less enthusiasm than with their first. Why am *I* not taking the lessons? I'm the one who loves horses. Why do we parents waste so many lessons on our children when it's really ourselves who would enjoy them? I once made Liam sign up for trumpet lessons at school. "Why?" he asked dourly.

"Why? Because I've always wanted to know how to play the trumpet, that's why."

We gave a big "do" at the residence today, a luncheon for the American Irish Foundation Literary Award presentation. Aidan Higgins, the novelist, received the $7,000 prize, which the Foundation gives each year to an Irish writer, poet, or playwright. He arrived tieless, shy and quiet, probably wishing he were home writing books instead of making a speech in our ballroom.

We sat at round tables of six, and I cornered Seamus Heaney, a poet and past recipient of the Award, to sit at my table. His merry brown eyes twinkled and he kept us laughing through lunch with stories of the trials and tribulations of being a poet. "My *unautographed* books will be collectors' items one day," he said wryly, but he was being modest since his talent is already recognized both here and in the United States.

The ballroom looked beautiful, sparkling with sunlight, banked with pots of flowers and ivy, and with tiny bouquets of sweet peas in baskets on each round table. I put a carnation in everyone's napkin to pin on during the luncheon, which gave us all the festive air of a wedding party. To add to the gaiety, a group of young American harpists studying in Ireland for the summer played for us after lunch. They were good, and they ended the party on a sweet and pleasantly elegiac note.

If anyone comes up to me again and asks me if I "like Ireland," I'm going to throw myself on the ground and plead for mercy.

Yes, yes, *Yes*. I like Ireland!!

AUGUST 25: *Donegal*

We've come to Letterkenny, in the middle of County Donegal, to open the 1977 International Folk Festival. It's our first official "opening," and we arrived here just before lunch in the midst of great excitement. The bank manager's son was kidnapped last night and is being held for ransom by the IRA. All cars coming into town are being stopped and searched by the army and the gardai.* Our own boys, languishing in the backseat of the car and nearly extinguished with boredom after a three-hour drive from Sligo Town, were immediately restored to full vigor at the sight of a fully armed search party.

Our appointed host for the day was Derek Hill, the distinguished portrait painter, who lives in the country just outside Letterkenny. He met us in the hotel lobby and took us to his house for lunch. A big, rotund, handsome, rosy-cheeked man with a youthful, unlined face and friendly

* The Irish word for police is gardai. An individual policeman is a garda. The official name for the Irish police force is Garda Síochána.

brown eyes, wearing a rumpled linen suit, his warm personality made me feel immediately at home and we chatted easily as we drove to his house in a steady, hammering downpour. He had a few local friends in for lunch, and then showed us around his marvelous house, crammed with his "things": his own portraits and paintings on wood of Tory Island, where he camps and paints each summer; shells and skins, pottery, tapestry, needlepoint, vases, china, glass. A wonderful bachelor's nest, happily undisturbed by fussy housekeeping.

The lashing rain had stopped by midafternoon. Before we returned to Letterkenny, we lined up on Derek's back steps for a snapshot, while the sodden roof dripped on our heads.

We were back in town in time to lead the parade from its starting point through town to the bandstand in the square, where Bill officially opened the festival. It's the first time I've led a parade since I was a baton twirler in high school. When the drums began to roll and the band started up, I could feel myself starting to prance like an old circus horse.

"I didn't know we were going to lead a parade," I whispered to Christopher. "I could have brought my boots and my baton and done my figure-eight routine."

"Thank God," Christopher sighed, as the whistle blew and we marched sedately into Letterkenny. The rain had left behind a clear, clean, sunny afternoon. The wet stones of the narrow street glistened, and the cheerful crowd shouted a welcome as we passed by. On the bandstand, Bill made a little speech in which he hinted that, given encouragement, I might be persuaded to participate in the jig and reel contest later that evening. I'll get even with him later. Then he pronounced the festival officially open.

We marched from the town square to the Technical College, where Bill reviewed the troops lined up in front. Then we went inside for a lavish, reviving tea, served up by the Irish Countrywomen's Association. It seemed to me that *all* the men sat down to tea, while *all* the women hurried around, serving us, urging us to eat, taking away plates, refilling cups. Why were there no women at the table? Why were there no men serving tea? I didn't dare ask.

The festival was extraordinarily varied and interesting. A lack of professionalism was more than made up for by enthusiasm, good humor and community spirit. There was Irish dancing, pipe music, folk songs, drama, choral singing. There were harpists and storytellers. There were Dutch and Danish folk musicians, a magnificent high school band from Manchester, England. There were Maltese dancers (how did they ever *hear* about Letterkenny?), Basque folk groups and Irish accordion bands. I did *not* participate in the jig and reel contest. "Thank God," sighed you-know-who.

44

We've come to spend the next three days at Glenveagh Castle, perched on the edge of an icy, gray lough in the middle of the Donegal bogs. It's a nineteenth-century Gothic castle that belongs to Henry McIlhenny, an American whose ancestors came from a neighboring village, emigrated to the United States and made good. It has all the charm and beauty of an Irish castle, and all the comforts and warmth of an American home. Roaring peat fires blaze in every room, keeping the temperature deliciously high.

Our trunks still have not arrived from America, so Bill was without evening clothes and I without much of anything. As a very sweet, shy young servant was helping me unpack, we both realized that I had put only one evening sandal into my bag. "Oh," I quipped, "that's because I have only one foot." Before I could even laugh, she dashed from the room in horror and embarrassment. I *must* stop making dumb jokes like that.

We passed the day in easy comfort, walking through the magnificent gardens that Mr. McIlhenny has developed, eating superb meals, talking, playing bridge, and going into Letterkenny in the evening for the festival. Liam and Christopher went fishing in the lough. David, angry that he was too small to be taken along, went "fishing" by himself on the bank and came back later to report that he had caught a "smoked salmon."

The search for the kidnappers is still going on. Apparently some IRA fugitives have stolen a gardai car and are reported to be in the vicinity of the castle. Two Special Branch men have arrived here to stay until we leave. The boys are insisting that I write a mystery story about it. It's tempting.

There's really no need to write mystery stories with David around. He provides us with enough real-life drama. Today, one of the guests in our house party invited him to come for a walk, but told him to tell his parents where he was going. Being five years old, he made a thirty-second, fruitless search for us and joined his friend, saying that he *had* told us, and off they went.

When I began to be aware that he wasn't around, I made a sweep of the house and gardens. Then I intensified the search with Bill and the two older boys. No sign of him. I asked Gerry, our driver, and some of the other staff to join us, and finally, one by one, the other guests realized a search party was on and joined in.

It was getting dark very quickly. The castle is surrounded by lakes and thousands of acres of marshy bogs, where a small boy could wander for days without being found. I had to keep a tight rein on myself not to give way to the hysteria I felt growing by the second.

One of the staff said that several house guests had gone on a hike up one of the mountains and perhaps they had taken David with them. We drove our car in the direction they had gone as far as the road lasted, then Bill got out and went on foot to meet them as they returned. I watched through binoculars, but when he got to the group he signaled to me that David wasn't with them.

It was a nightmarish repeat of the time he followed the Good Humor truck on Gramercy Street when he was three, became lost, and wasn't found until four hours later, when a friendly policeman brought him home in a squad car. That time, frightened though we were, we clung to the hope that he could be in no real danger in his own neighborhood. This was different. There was no possible way a small child could survive the dangers of that unknown, treacherous bogland. I shifted wildly between rage at David for wandering off, and sick fear that I would never see him again. And I kept remembering the kidnappers who were still on the loose in this neighborhood.

We kept up a steady honking of the horn as we turned up and down the small lanes and "boreens," getting out of the car at intervals, shouting, scanning the beautiful, empty, gorse-filled fields with binoculars. The staff were searching the territory closer to the house: the gardens, the swimming pool, the changing house, the "steps that lead to nowhere." Finally, when we realized that there was less than an hour of daylight left, Bill said, "We must call the gardai and get a helicopter. We can never hope to find him any other way."

I spun the car around in the gravel lane, somehow getting emotional relief in the reckless spinning of wheels and skidding on the narrow path, and then I saw one of the other cars, far in front of us on the road, flashing its lights on and off, on and off. Obviously a signal. I spun the wheels even deeper into the soft, wet gravel as I frantically tried to hurry toward those blinking lights. When we got closer, we could see Patrick, the butler, standing by the open door of the car, waving and smiling. All was well.

When we reached the castle courtyard, a very scared-looking and chastened David was standing with the staff and the young man who had taken him walking. He, too, looked most chagrined. Not knowing the ways of five-year-olds, he had taken David's word that he had told us where he was going. They went further than planned. David grew tired, his legs weren't strong enough to walk fast in bogland, so he had to be carried part way home.

We gave David a stern, incoherent talking to, but we couldn't stop hugging him long enough to spank him.

We left Glenveagh reluctantly after our three-day weekend. It had been a romantic interlude in our lives. Even David's adventure, harrowing though it was, will make another family saga one day. We said good-by to our driver, Gerry, who headed back to Dublin, and took off in our own car for a week's holiday driving from Donegal down to the west coast of Ireland. It's our first time in Donegal, and it's competing with my serious love affair with the Dingle Peninsula and Connemara. Like the coast of Maine, its shore is lined with tiny, pointed fingers that stretch out to sea, only here they point westward toward America. We could spend weeks wandering in and out of the tiny promontories, circling bright estuaries lined with wide, white beaches. The sand is swept clean, and the water is gleaming, blue, icy. Although it is only late August, the tourists have gone home, and we seem to have all of Donegal to ourselves as we picnic on fine powdered sand, warmed by a late summer's sun. Those clouds that come racing each other over the Atlantic and deposit eighty inches of rain each year on Donegal have luckily decided to frolic elsewhere during our holiday. We are traveling under the bluest of skies.

The scenic route takes us through the Derryveagh Mountains out to Burtonport, down through Dungloe and finally to Glencolumbkille, a small village on the outermost tip of the Donegal coast. We had heard of Father James McDyer and the economic miracle he had wrought at Glencolumbkille, how he had taken a dying community and turned it into a thriving, busy town with a healthy tourist trade and successful small crafts industry, and we wanted to see it.

That most enervating and persistent of Irish diseases, immigration, had been slowly undermining Glencolumbkille, robbing it of its young. There were no jobs for them, and so they left. Father McDyer arrived with determination and a plan. He cajoled banks to invest, he nagged young men and women to stay on, to open up small businesses; he persuaded the Irish Tourist Board to build one of their successful thatched "rent-a-cottage" schemes there. He blew on dying embers and kindled sparks.

The drive to Glencolumbkille from Ardara was lonely, remote, and to my eye, beautiful. Another might fear its emptiness or wonder at the isolation. The village was a welcome sight when we came to it, handsome and clean, sitting on the top of Donegal Bay, looking out over the Atlantic.

We had dinner with Father McDyer in a very comfortable hotel overlooking the town, and as he talked, I could sense the vitality, the enthusiasm, and the dedication that made his particular dream come true.

Misery! Montezuma's Revenge, Donegal-style, has struck. I feel like I was hit in the stomach by a two-ton lorry. Between loud moans and dashes to the bathroom, I asked Bill to go down to the lobby and see if he could find a doctor. "If you can't," I gasped, "ask for the undertaker."

Skeptical but dutiful, he disappeared downstairs. An hour later, a sweet, kindly doctor was sitting on my bed, giving me a shot and some pills. To my astonishment, I survived, and was well again by teatime.

AUGUST 30: *Connemara*

Heading south, hugging west, down through Sligo and Mayo, our old haunt of last summer, where we wended our way around Clew Bay in a horse-drawn caravan. Did we actually do that last summer with our four-year-old, the Great Wanderer? Every year, as my children get a year older, I marvel that I coped with the previous age. Have I really had three two-year-olds? Did I really read *Charlie and the Chocolate Factory* through, twice, three times? And now that I have one teenager, will I live through three of them?

The west. Like a lover who thrills to hear her loved one's name, I love to listen to the names of the west: Ballyshannon, Belmullet, Mulrany, Newport, Westport, Louisburgh, Leenane, Clifden, Ballyconneely, Recess (*Recess?*), Oughterard, Galway, Lough Mask, Lough Corrib, Cong, Pontoon.

We had an end-of-summer picnic on a chilled and empty beach near Costelloe, where we had gone in search of Padraic Pearse's holiday home. David soaked his pants playing in the water, and rather than go back to the hotel for a change, I stopped in the general store to buy him a new pair. It was filled with children dashing in to buy afternoon sweets. For the first time in all my travels in Ireland I heard everyone speaking Irish. It isn't common. In fact, it's quite rare to hear Irish being spoken, but we're in the "Gaeltacht" here, a designated Irish-speaking area where even the road signs (to our confusion) are only in Irish.

We picked up an elderly couple by the side of the road, in the desolate bogland that stretches from Costelloe to Oughterard. Their car had broken down as they were going into town for a day's shopping. Realizing that we were Americans, they began to tell us about the new American ambassador who had recently arrived in Ireland, how he had family connections in Clare and his wife was from Newry. The boys went into their nudge-nudge routine in the backseat, so I thought it would be rude not to introduce ourselves. They were predictably delighted and said sure if the car hadn't broken down they would never have met us, so wasn't it all for the best?

Back at the Hotel Corrib, our favorite small hotel in Oughterard, a middle-aged American in plaid pants, green jacket, maroon shirt and polka-dot tie was conversing in the lounge with two women friends. It was hard not to overhear their conversation.

"Americans are so loud," Liam whispered to me.

"No, they aren't," I replied. "It only seems that way because the Irish speak in tones just one decibel over a whisper, making everything they say seem conspiratorial. Anyone would seem loud in comparison. And anyway, don't be such a snob about American tourists."

Just then, our fellow countryman got up and wandered over to the fireplace, where Michael Maguire, the young owner of the hotel, was lighting a fire.

"Want some good advice on how to start a fire, laddy?" he boomed.

I looked at Liam. "You win this round," I said.

September 3: *Dublin*

I've been so busy the last month and my life so crowded with new experiences and new acquaintances, that I hadn't realized how much I've missed a good visit with an old friend. But the minute Marie Hawke arrived on our doorstep today, with her pal Barbara Pelosi in tow, I began laughing and chattering like I haven't done since we arrived here. It was as if we were back on my side porch on Gramercy Street, reliving all the long, hot summer days we've passed together. I've known Marie for so long that our talk needs no explanations. It's a wonderful and relaxing respite from the polite, careful conversation of new-made friends.

We gave a dinner party for the two women tonight, and one of the guests was Sean O'Casey's widow, Eileen. It was the first time Bill and I had met her, and we found her delectable, full of wry stories about herself, her life with Sean, her madcap adventures in New York, her career as an actress. As Barbara said after the party: "That was *not* my preconceived idea of a typical Irish widow!"

September 5

David and Christopher started school today. We'd made a trip to Arnott's Department Store, school list in hand, to outfit them. Gray slacks that feel like flexible cast-iron, gray cotton shirts that won't show dirt for a week, V-necked sweaters, blue blazers, striped ties, gray socks, black shoes. No deviation, and no more fights about what to wear to school.

David is in prep, which is the first year of school for five-year-olds. They all look so tiny; David seems to tower over his classmates. Lots of trembling lips and teary eyes, but the teacher was fully in control, pleasant, smiling, unruffled. We chatted briefly. She's widowed, with young sons of her own to bring up. David seemed happy and calm and somewhat bemused by the emotional scenes of separation going on around him. He's an old pro at this, having started "prenursery" when he was two, and graduated on up through nursery, prekindergarten, half-day kindergarten. When I told him he was going to be in "prep" at St. Michael's, he asked plaintively: "When am I ever going to be in a *real* grade?"

Christopher disappeared down a long hallway jammed with blazer-clad, laughing, shoving boys. He walked alone, and very fast, looking straight ahead. Oh, the misery of a new boy at school.

I was back at noon to pick them up after their half day, and I couldn't believe the chaos as I pulled into the drive. Boys of all sizes shooting out of the three entrances like cannon balls, cars pulling into the drive, fanning out into the small parking space in front of the school, blocking each other, honking for children's attention, and all the time, little blue-coated figures darting everywhere. My boring old PTA "Parking and Pick-Up Committee" self was horrified. I saw a priest cheerfully and ineffectually waving cars backward and forward, adding to the confusion. "It's always like this on the first day," he explained.

I could work out a system for him.

Irish children are so handsome and appealing. Their parents turn out to be as good-looking or as plain as anyone else, so I don't know what happens en route (except the loss of several teeth), but as children, the Irish are all winners.

One tiny little boy was crying desperately, looking up and down the drive. His mother was late, on his first day at school. Will he ever forgive her? Certainly he'll never forget. All the children were carrying large leather briefcases, half as big as they are. They looked like miniature lawyers, running home from court.

Finally, my two came out. I scrutinized their faces for signs, but as usual, they were noncommittal. "It was okay." Both insisted on going into town immediately to buy leather briefcases, obviously an integral part of school life here. Christopher had carefully written down the name of the store and the street where we can get them. On the way into town, David offered one morsel of information about his new class: "A kid in my room threw up."

SEPTEMBER 9

Bill made his first major speech here yesterday at the US Chamber of Commerce (his relieved staff at the embassy were surprised and euphoric that their ambassador writes his own speeches), in which he attacked certain pro-IRA groups, both in Ireland and in the US, who tried to "hitchhike" on President Carter's recent statement on Northern Ireland. The president said last week that the United States was prepared to give financial aid to the North when the troubles there were brought under control.

In his speech, Bill said that there was no "Carter Peace Plan," nor did the American government see the possibility of any made-in-America so-lution. But various organizations, some of them IRA fronts in America, have tried to take credit for the president's statement.

The *Irish Times* in its editorial today said that Bill's speech "far from settling speculation about the president's speech will send the whole caravan rolling more crazily along." They added: "Is there something a bit bald and unfeeling in this insistence that not a dollar will be put into Ireland until the fighting stops?"

I thought the editorial in the *Irish Independent* offered a more positive response: "Peace in the North cannot, of course, be bought. Therefore, the American promise to do everything possible to help the North eco-nomically after a peaceful formula has been found is not a bribe but rather an incentive to those men and women who want peace to keep on trying for it. When the guns are put aside, then the economic develop-ment of the North can be fruitfully tackled—and we all know that the North really needs help to overcome its huge problem of unemploy-ment."

SEPTEMBER 16

All of our belongings arrived from America today. Everyone was put to work tearing open large wooden crates, unpacking smaller cardboard containers, exclaiming with joy over repossessed belongings—David's Big Wheel, Liam's bicycle, my Cuisinart. But joy quickly turned to hor-ror when we began opening the boxes that contained our clothes. I be-came suspicious when the outer, waterproof wrappings on the boxes were pulled off and revealed soggy, sodden inner boxes. As they, in turn, were opened, our worst fears were realized: somehow the original boxes, and their contents, had become soaked, probably left standing in the open on a dock somewhere, and when their condition was discovered, they had been—too late—wrapped in waterproof paper. The wet and sodden clothes then had eight weeks in which to mildew, rot, or simply dissolve.

Tough, sturdy clothes like jeans and T-shirts can be washed and re-stored to their original condition. Other items were sent off to the clean-ers and may become usable again. But many things are lost forever, in-cluding my beautiful suede coat, which grew enough mold on it to culture pounds of penicillin, and several of Bill's best suits. Even after airing, and the cleanings, the unpleasant aroma of mildew is going to ac-company us wherever we go.

SEPTEMBER 19

We've been inviting all the government ministers and their wives to lunch at the residence, to get to know them in an informal and intimate setting. (One minister, who has turned down several invitations, asked that he not be invited again, he is "too busy.")

Our guests today were George and Mary Colley; he is the finance minister and also the "tanaiste," or deputy prime minister. They are both warm and easy guests to entertain. Mary, mother of seven, is going back to university to get her degree, putting this mother of three to shame. Slim and pretty, with sparkling brown eyes and a sharp wit, she charmed us immediately, and we felt we had made a friend on the spot. Minister Colley, tall and broad-shouldered, with a soft, melodious speaking voice, is apparently in ill favor at the moment with various Irish women's groups for criticizing what he called "well-heeled middle-class women" who go out to work and take away jobs from men who have families to support. I didn't ask Mary what *she* intends to do after she gets her degree, but after visiting with her this afternoon, I'm sure she'll make that decision herself. Her soft-spoken, feminine style obviously does not preclude a mind of her own.

SEPTEMBER 21

I think I bombed tonight. I made my first speech, to the Wives of Engineers Club, a loosely knit group with disparate interests, whose only common bond is their husbands' profession. They said: "Oh, just talk about *anything!*" But I took it all too seriously and prepared a long, boring speech about the status of women in America, concentrating on working women, job status and equal pay. I droned on and on. It was too long and I almost put myself to sleep, quoting percentiles, dates and figures. I could tell long before I had finished that neither I nor the speech sparkled.

I discovered later, having tea with the women, that very few of them work outside their home, so they wouldn't be very interested in the status of working women. (They were very curious, though, about the home ownership laws in America and the tax status of wives.) The evening had been their night off, a night to come out and meet the new ambassador's wife, have tea and a good gossip with friends, and I should have given them a light and witty account of what it's like being ambassadorial. The trouble is, I hardly know myself!

SEPTEMBER 29: *Birr, County Offaly*

The third Earl of Rosse lived in Birr Castle, County Offaly, in the nineteenth century. A man of uncommon scientific and intellectual curiosity, he built a giant, fifty-eight-foot telescope on his castle grounds in 1845. For over seventy years, it was the largest telescope in the world.

We went to Birr today to have lunch with the present Earl and Countess of Rosse (she's Lord Snowdon's mother), and to participate in a ceremony to open a museum beside the remains of the telescope. Although only the huge tubular base is left at Birr—the reflector is in the Science Museum in London—the museum will house the eye pieces, lenses, and photographs and drawings connected with it.

The luncheon party before the ceremony gave us a chance to become acquainted with the Rosses and the other guests. Lord Rosse, exuding friendliness and charm, made us feel immediately at home, and took great pleasure in showing us some of the fantastic treasures in the castle, which is one of Ireland's finest homes.

The ceremony was held in the gardens on a platform built for the occasion. It was a windy, chilly day and I, as usual, began my teeth-chattering routine, until Lady Rosse kindly loaned me a long woolen cape to wrap myself in during the speeches. She herself looked elegant in ropes of pearls, a heavy knit dress and matching purple turban. We chatted later about her old friend Ethel Garrett, whose husband had been the American ambassador to Ireland in 1950.

"When Ethel arrived in Ireland, we were all so tacky," she said, though I find it hard to believe. "Ethel was slim and stylish and beautiful. She hunted and danced and her clothes were always elegant. She made us feel like dowdy old matrons. She lit a fire under us, and we all began to dress better and be more stylish under her good example."

Thirty years later, Ethel is still setting that good example.

A Night Best Forgotten, or You Can't Win Them All

Now I know why some diplomats ask for early retirement. A night like tonight would make life as a plucker in a turkey factory seem fun. My first mistake was missing lunch, having had a wildly overscheduled afternoon. My second mistake was to arrive at the dinner party on time. My third mistake, having shivered through evenings in unheated houses, leaving behind a reputation at best for "nerves," at worst for suffering from a rare form of palsy, was to put on woolen underwear and a long, black knit dress.

We walked into a very small room, suitable for an intimate party of ten but gaily crammed with thirty. We were met by a blast of heat reminiscent of stepping off a plane in El Paso in August. "We know how you Americans like warm houses," our thoughtful host announced as he beamed at us, sweat pouring off his face in little rivulets. "Now come and warm yourselves by the fire."

Bill's head was already glistening and I wondered if my woolen underwear would fit into my evening bag. Cocktails were being gulped down eagerly by perspiring guests, more to ward off dehydration than for conviviality, I think. More guests streamed in. Cigarette smoke circled the room and our conscientious host kept replenishing the fire, grinning conspiratorially at me every time he did it. I caught his eye and fanned my face with my napkin, thinking he would take the hint, but no, he just waved his own napkin back at me merrily, and winked.

More cocktails were passed. I was about ready to pass out. A large, friendly woman, with a dark stain widening under each armpit, came up to me and said: "Do you like Ireland? I bet you get asked that all the time."

"No," I said. "You're the first person who ever asked me that."

"Go 'way," she said, pleased with herself, and I did, as soon as I could.

I peeked at my watch. Ten o'clock. Where was the food? Did I mistake the invitation? A man cornered me with my back to the fire, talking to me about energy. Mine was waning. I wondered if he would think it odd if I slipped an ice cube from my drink down my bosom. I fished it out of my glass and he boomed: "Ha ha! You're the American who doesn't like ice in her drink either," and took it out of my hand to toss into the fire. I saw Bill through a haze of smoke; a thin, dark-haired lady was gesticulating in his face and he looked glum. My partner had left solar heat and had moved into windmills and his fourth gin and tonic. I could only stare at him dumbly, hearing nothing, looking longingly over his shoulder toward the closed dining room doors.

At last! Our hostess announced dinner. There was a lavish buffet spread out on the dining room table and I raced toward it, easily outdistancing a small, elderly man who looked undernourished in the best of times.

"Ladies first!" I cried, nearly knocking him over, as I grabbed a plate and heaped food onto it. Salads, meat, fish, rolls, everything. Anything. Lashings and lashings of it, until my plate disappeared under the load. I haven't been so hungry since I went with Liam on a Cub Scout picnic when I was eight months pregnant and, after waiting two hours while the scoutmaster tried vainly to light the bonfire, was reduced to eating raw hot dogs.

I went back into the drawing room, sat down, and shoveled it all into my mouth. Gobble, gobble. Someone brought me a glass of wine, and I just pointed to the nearest table, my mouth too full to speak. And dessert! They brought in dessert. Goody, I said to myself. I had three.

When we finished coffee it was twenty minutes to one. Honest to God. I was exhausted from too much food too late, from the heat and the company. I could only sit dumbly, occasionally burping softly, while I waited for the party to end so I could go home and go to bed.

OCTOBER 3

We left for London tonight on the boat train across the Irish Sea. It's a beautiful and romantic sight to sail out of Dublin Bay after dark, and to see the half-circle of lights, from Dun Laoghaire right around to the lighthouse at Howth Head, twinkling, then disappearing slowly into the night and the sea.

I'm excited and happy to be going back to London for the first time since we lived there for a year in 1969–70.

OCTOBER 5: *London*

We had dinner tonight with Ambassador and Mrs. Brewster at the American embassy residence, Winfield House, in Regent's Park, the home that used to belong to Barbara Hutton and which she gave to the United States government. The embassy sent a car to pick us up and I'm afraid the driver, with his chilly "yes" and "no" and "I'm afraid I wouldn't know," wouldn't have lasted long in Dublin.

Winfield House has been beautifully decorated to the last detail by former Ambassador and Mrs. Walter Annenberg. It is large and impressive, but I like our house in Dublin better. Less grand but more livable. And, lovely as Regent's Park is, it can't hold a candle to the Phoenix Park.

Airey Neave, the shadow minister for Northern Ireland, was one of the dinner guests,* and another was the man who had been in the car with Ambassador Ewart-Biggs when his car was blown up in Dublin last year. He was badly injured in the explosion but recovered. So the talk was once again of Northern Ireland, approaching the problem largely in military and security terms: how to contain, control and finally stamp out IRA terrorism. I sat quietly and listened. I agreed with what they said. But terrorism is only part of the problem.

OCTOBER 6

I went shopping today and bought myself a pair of Ferragamo boots. I had to take out a second mortgage on the house to pay for them, but of course I'll wear them for years. Decades. All the stories one hears these days about extravagant, wildly rich Arabs converging on London may be true. I saw the most extraordinary woman in Harrods today, dressed in long, brown robes and with what looked to me like a wooden face mask leaving only a slit for her eyes. She was heavily veiled and followed by a cortege of seven small, dark men, each in a business suit and each carrying a large basket. Herself was billowing through the aisles from counter to counter. She dropped scores of shirts, ties, scarves, sweaters and socks into the baskets without stopping to look at color, price or size. Bizarre. I wonder if she hires out for Christmas shopping.

*In May 1979, Airey Neave was leaving the basement parking garage of the House of Commons when the car he was driving blew up, killing him instantly. The Irish National Liberation Army claimed "credit" for the assassination.

The old folks entertain me at tea

October 13: *Dublin*

I had the second of my old folks' teas here today. The "Golden
Oldies," the guard at the front gate calls them. I enjoy visiting with old
folks, listening to their endless stories of the "auld days," and I'm beginning to sound not too unlike them myself.

The group today was lively, full of songs and stories, and no one
needed to tell them to eat up when the tea and cakes came around. I took
them for a walk in the gardens after tea, and since there was only one
man in the group, he took my arm and walked with me.

"How old do you think I am?" he asked.

"Seventy-three," I lied.

"Wrong," says he. "I'm ninety-one, and I walk three miles every day.
How do you think I look?"

"Great." He did. Rosy cheeks and clear blue eyes.

Later, when he had dropped behind me, one of the ladies came up to
me and whispered conspiratorially: "Did *he* [tossing her head in the old
man's direction] tell you he was ninety-one?" I said that he did.

"Ha!" she cackled triumphantly. "I knew he would try that line on
you. He's only eighty-seven, *and,* if he said he walks three miles a day,
don't believe that, either. He can't walk no more than one, maybe

one and a half on a good day. He's always puttin' on airs."

I was just seeing the old folks into their bus in the courtyard when Dervla Murphy arrived on her bicycle from her home in Lismore, County Waterford. We hugged like long-lost friends, which in a way we are, although we've never met before today. We've corresponded ever since she won the American Irish Foundation Literary Award in 1975. I heard of her then for the first time from. Bill and went to the Library of Congress to get out her book *In Ethiopia with a Mule*. I *didn't* think, I have to confess, that I was going to find it riveting, but I read on until four o'clock in the morning and have been her devoted fan ever since.

She's one of the world's most intrepid travelers. On foot or with her bike, she's traveled across India, Afghanistan, Tibet, Ethiopia, Nepal; wherever the mountains are the highest, the gorges the deepest, the terrain most hazardous and beautiful, you'll find Dervla, notebook in her pocket, pencil behind her ear, and a pack on her back. I am astonished all over again, with each book, at her bravery, her curiosity, her stamina. She is one of the unique women of our day. Here she came, on the same old, dilapidated bike that took her from Ireland to India more than a decade ago.

We sat down in the library over a beer (*she* makes her own beer at home; I could only offer her bottled) and began to talk. She is as vivid as her prose; friendly, strong, attractive, with keen brown eyes, roses in her cheeks and a firm handshake that isn't meant for the fragile-boned.

She's writing a book about Northern Ireland, traveling all over Ulster on her bike, talking to people on all sides, listening, recording. Given the paranoid suspicions in Northern Ireland, I shouldn't think that would be a very safe undertaking, but Dervla would only scoff at my caution.

We talked on and on about the North, about the intransigence of the Unionist leaders, the viciousness of the Reverend Ian Paisley's attacks on Catholics (I had just finished reading Patrick Marrinan's book on Paisley and was still reeling under the flood of moral depravity that flows from his "sermons"); on the horrors of IRA murders; on the gulf between the two societies, the distrust, the suspicion that is fed and nourished by self-serving zealots. I asked Dervla the standard questions: Is it economic? Is it religious? Are the two so intertwined that they can't be separated? Is it better now? Will it ever end? Those same old questions that one goes on about endlessly, and for which no one has an answer.

The afternoon stretched into early evening. We were having a dinner party for our houseguest, Ben Welles, a former colleague of Bill's from the *New York Times*. Would she stay for dinner?

"In my jeans and boots?" she asked.

"They don't worry me if they don't worry you," I replied, and so she stayed and it was a good evening. She pedaled off into the dark and the rain at midnight while the other guests got into their cars and drove home.

OCTOBER 20

I saw a story in the paper this week about a poor girl in the west of Ireland who got raped in church, in the confessional! A girl isn't safe anywhere, these days.

OCTOBER 23

The fragility and the precariousness of life came home to me last night in shock waves. Bill was already asleep and I was just getting ready to climb into bed. I reached for the bed-lamp switch and, at the same time, feeling that the room was too hot, I reached with my other hand for the metal handle of the radiator to turn it off. A wire in the lamp had come loose and was exposed to the metal base; if I had only touched it with one hand, to turn it off, I probably would have received a small shock. But with my other hand touching the metal cap of the radiator I literally grounded myself. The shock hit me full blast. I was instantly flung backward across the bed, two feet from where I had been standing.

I thought, for a split second, when the shock hit me, that I was dying. It was a hideous feeling that I'll never forget but don't like to remember. Bill awoke to my screams and saw my body flying across the bed. I couldn't speak coherently for a few seconds, and when I finally was able to explain what had happened, he was frantic. "I'm all right," I said. "At least I'm alive."

But he phoned Dr. Rutledge, who had to come out across the city at midnight to examine me. I was unharmed except for a small burn on my hand.

The electrician who came to fix the lamp this morning didn't make me feel any better when he said cheerfully: "You must have a strong heart. There's many a one who would have just dropped over."

OCTOBER 28: *Cork*

We're in Cork this week for our "official" three-day visit. Although it's a handsome town, Cork, which has not one river but two running through its center, would totally confuse a stranger. In Dublin, I get my bearings by turning right or left at the Liffey, but in Cork, how would you know? And you'd take your life in your hands if you slowed down to look for a street sign since the cars weave in and out of traffic like alpine skiers on a slalom course. But the city is clean and airy, and the small streets and lanes that rise sharply up into the hills are quaint and pretty.

We started on our rounds with a call on the Lord Mayor, Gerald

Goldberg, a scholarly, soft-spoken man with an encyclopedic knowledge of Ireland. We liked him very much and had dinner later with him and other Cork town fathers at the Arbutus Lodge Hotel, the only restaurant in Ireland with a one-star rating from the Guide Michelin.

We left the Lord Mayor's office to visit the Cork *Examiner,* where both of us ex-journalists felt at home. The operation of the paper is completely computerized and impressively modern. The typeset is clean and clear and the overall news coverage is excellent for a small city newspaper. Bill subscribes to it and gets a copy at his desk each morning, along with the Dublin papers we both read.

Once again, I couldn't remember whether a bishop is called "Your Grace" or "My Lord," so when we called on Bishop Lucey of Cork I had to mumble something that I hoped could be taken for either. We had an interesting visit with the elderly bishop, but I'm afraid that as a woman, a liberal and an American Catholic, my views and those of the bishop are very, very far apart. Under the circumstances, I kept my views to myself and praised the tea.

On to University College Cork, for a luncheon and a presentation to the University College library of two hundred books on American history, politics and economics, donated by the International Communications Agency.

At the end of three days, I headed back to Dublin on the train with Jean Rylands, from the embassy. Bill is coming home in a few days after a detour to County Clare, where he has a speech to give and a lot of cousins to see.

NOVEMBER 1

Three and a half months in Ireland. It seems like a week or a lifetime. I do wish we had a weekend cottage here, where we could escape to catch our breath and see what we're doing in some perspective. Both of us are putting our hearts and souls into this job, and I think we'll have to plan a trip out of Ireland for Christmas or we'll never slow down. We're worried about Christopher, too. He's making a slow adjustment and is very homesick for his pals and his school in Washington. Although he occasionally has a boy out from school to spend the weekend, it's an isolated, lonely life for him out here in the Park. David has many residence children to play with, and Liam can get on his bike and go see his own friends, so each of them has made a better adjustment. We thought it would be Liam, at fifteen, who would find the move difficult, but he loves his school and couldn't be happier.

We've had lots of minor illnesses, too, rare in our usually healthy family. Bill and I have had two or three severe intestinal upsets, but I think that is just a process of getting immune to different "bugs." Bill has had a series of bad colds, and we've discovered that he has nasal polyps, which have to be removed. I think our bodies most definitely reflect the stress of move and change and become more than usually susceptible to minor infection.

I'm still trying to "learn my lines" for the role I'm playing here. I try to be dignified without being pompous and to be informal without being fatuous. I've been interviewed frequently by newspapers, magazines, radio. They always ask the question: How do I know how to run this large household, manage a staff, entertain for hundreds, plan meals for formal sit-down dinners, and so on. But all that involves only a good sense of organization, a competent, experienced staff (which I have) and a real liking for social occasions. The real question is: How do you create a public facade that reflects your inner self honestly and effectively without confusing style and substance?

NOVEMBER 2

Our house is getting a new roof, an expensive, annoying but necessary project. It's at the stage now where the old slates are off and the roof is covered with heavy plastic sheeting while it is being prepared for the new covering.

There was a wild gale last night, blowing and howling across the Park, whipping against the back of the house, bringing limbs and small trees down like splinters and uprooting one of the two-hundred-year-old beech trees on the boundary.

The rain matched the wind in its ferocity. No gentle Irish mist tonight, but a torrential, pounding, uninterrupted downpour. Bill is out of town, so I sat alone in my bedroom, watching the storm through the tall windows facing the Park. The back lawn was illuminated under the bright glare of security lights, and the rain looked as if it were pouring from a vast Celtic cistern. The lawns, sodden after weeks of rain, are filling up and making small lakes.

I closed the wooden shutters against the noise of the wind and the beating rain and went to bed. I fell asleep immediately and was having a dream, prophetically, about tidal waves, when Liam burst into my bedroom, shaking me awake. "Get up," he said urgently. "The rain is coming in everywhere."

He had been awakened by the sound of gushing water, and had followed the noise to the room next to his, called the Blue Room, one of our guest suites. The carpet was already soaked and water was pouring in through the makeshift roof.

"Quick," I said to Liam, "go look for buckets in the laundry room. I'll get pots and pans out of the kitchen." We were soon catching the worst of the leaks with rapidly filling pots. I grabbed an armful of towels to try to blot the carpet but realized that it was useless.

"We'd better check the rest of the house," Liam said, and we prowled from room to room, flicking on lights and checking ceilings and windowsills. As we approached the ballroom, we heard the now-familiar gushing sound and dashed in to find another miniature waterfall pouring in over one of the pillars. More pots and buckets, a holding action against what we feared would be an onslaught. But those two leaks proved to be the only ones, and after an hour I sent Liam back to bed and stood watch over my pots until dawn, emptying them into bathtubs and sinks as they filled, feeling much like the poor little Dutch boy with his finger in the dike.

At dawn I woke the staff for reinforcements, but by then the rain had stopped and the wind settled, so the crisis was over.

The roofing men arrived this morning to assess the damage. The gale-force winds had torn away the plastic sheeting, leaving the unfinished roof exposed to the heavy rain. The damage in the ballroom is minimal, but the carpet in the Blue Room is destroyed and will have to be replaced. There are water marks on the beautiful blue and white French wallpaper, but I think they will dry. I don't want to replace it. The Blue Room is my favorite room in the house, decorated with great style and elegance by Mrs. Raymond Guest, whose husband was ambassador here in the mid-1960s. The matching wallpaper and fabrics are a blue and white peacock print and probably irreplaceable now.

NOVEMBER 7

Huge reception this evening at the Burlington Hotel for Russia's National Day. There was a group of about fifty people out in front of the hotel, holding placards, protesting the treatment of Soviet Jewry. Inside, smoked salmon and champagne.

NOVEMBER 8

I was officially welcomed into the American Women's Club this afternoon at a beautiful tea given by the president at her home in Wicklow. As the ambassador's wife, I'm the honorary president of the club, and I was surprised to meet so many American women, most of them wives of businessmen connected with American companies in Ireland. There are more than three hundred American businesses here, and the (Irish) Industrial Development Authority is working hard to attract more. The women, without exception, spoke of their fondness for Ireland and the good personal friends they have made.

We had to dash off to the airport this evening to meet Mrs. Lillian Carter, the president's mother, who has come to Dublin for ten days with the Iowa Friendship Force. Each of the Iowans will stay with an

Miz Lillian poses with the rugby team, the Lord Mayor, and Bill

Irish family (and so will Mrs. Carter), and "get to know the people." *Much* excitement in town about "Miz Lillian's" visit. She has made herself into a media personality, and people respond naturally to her exuberance. She stepped off the plane first, instantly recognizable. The band played "When Irish Eyes Are Smiling" and she did a little jig coming across the tarmac. Everyone loved it.

NOVEMBER 10

Our week is full of Miz Lillian's doin's. Today we went to a reception given for her by the Lord Mayor of Dublin at the Mansion House. She had her picture taken with a group of broad-shouldered giants who turned out to be the Irish Rugby team. Hearing them try to explain the intricacies of rugby to Miz Lillian was worth the price of admission.

NOVEMBER 11

I gave a luncheon party today for our Georgia visitor. A clutch of photographers came in before lunch, and one of them asked her to hold the picture of President Carter, which we keep on our hall table, in her hands for a photograph.

"I may be corny," she replied to the photographer, "but I'm not *that* corny!" She's a lady of incredible stamina, quick wit and a strong will. She's good press, and the Irish like her.

NOVEMBER 12

We went to the Marine Ball tonight at the Shelbourne Hotel on Stephen's Green. All my life, I've heard of the "Marine Ball" and never knew until tonight what it was. It's the birthday party of the Marine Corps, and all over the world they are having a party tonight to celebrate. Our small Marine contingent here, who guard the embassy (but not the residence, as some people think), put on a colorful affair this evening.

We ate, we danced, and I won a bottle of wine in the raffle. Midway through the dancing, someone came up to us and whispered: "You can leave whenever you wish."

"Thank you very much," we whispered back, and stayed until the last dance.

NOVEMBER 14

We sat still for an interview and a photo session this afternoon with *Image* magazine. We brought the boys in for a group picture and David was very naughty. He grabbed a cigarette from the box on the table, stuck it in his mouth, slumped over a chair, put a pillow over his face; he finally sat up straight, looked right into the camera, and crossed his eyes. The scolding I gave him was only a holding operation. I think he's a boy who's asking for time.

NOVEMBER 22: *Newry, County Down*

My parents are here visiting us and we went today to Newry, County Down, in Northern Ireland to look for our roots. My father's great-grandmother and great-grandfather, Owen McNelly and Katherine Killian, sailed from Ireland for America in 1832, and we're looking around Newry for eighth cousins. All we found was that our name, McNelly, had obviously been changed from McNally, since there are no McNellys to be found in Ireland.

My poor father had such a romantic, idealized picture of Newry that he wasn't emotionally prepared for the sight of barbed wire, saracens, and rifle-bearing soldiers, which is the picture of Newry today. It's been one of the hardest hit of the troubled towns in the North and has an unhappy history of communal antagonisms based on religious differences. My ancestors left because of those antagonisms in 1832. In 1977, the good citizens of Newry are still struggling to find the spirit of Christian brotherhood.

NOVEMBER 23

Despite all the eventful interludes, I am still a homemaker here and today I went off with Dennis to Musgrave's, a big wholesale food outlet, where we buy supplies for the house in bulk. I buy—and pay for—all the food we use—for parties, for ourselves, and for the staff. I'm reimbursed a set amount for staff meals, and I fill out a monthly report of the entertaining costs. We have a fixed reimbursement per person, varying for lunches, dinners, cocktails, teas, and receptions.

It's difficult to make it all come out even each month, but as all housewives do, I stretch it here, prune it there.

The reimbursement for our entertaining is called our representational allowance, and when we came here, it was ridiculously low, $10,500. Bill arranged to have it doubled to $21,000 for the year. The ambassador's percentage is two-thirds of that, with the remaining third divided among the other embassy officers for their official entertainment allowances. Even with the generous increase, I can tell that it will be hard to stretch it through the year.

We find Ireland expensive, particularly food, hotels, gasoline, and repair work. The children's school tuitions are far less than they would be in America, and lessons are very reasonable (piano, tennis, riding and so on). But on the whole, it is a costly country in which to live, and I often wonder how an Irish housewife stretches her pounds to feed eight, ten or twelve hungry mouths, particularly when one reads that one pound in eight is spent on drink.

NOVEMBER 28: *Galway*

Bill and I are making our official trip to Galway this week, but before we left we had a big birthday party for David, who turned six. We invited all thirty-four of his classmates. It poured steadily, so we couldn't take them outdoors to play; despite a magic show, games and food, the atmosphere grew from chaos to pandemonium so we finally just left them alone and let them dart about like fireflies, using up their massive doses of six-year-old energy.

In Galway, we are following much the same pattern we set in Cork, visiting the newspaper offices, the mayoress, the City Council, the very beautiful Church of Ireland church, St. Nicholas, and the vast, new, ornate Roman Catholic Cathedral built with the help of Cardinal Cushing and the many Galway Irish who went to Boston.

We went this evening to see a performance at the Druid Theatre which was created by a young and talented local group struggling to get established as Galway's community theater. It was a first-rate performance of a play about the life of Oscar Wilde. During the interval, a tiny nun, with bright, twinkling blue eyes, came up and introduced herself to me. Since it was *not* a play that a nun might ordinarily attend, I was interested in her even before she began to speak. She told me she was a psychiatric social worker running a training school in Galway for itinerant teenaged girls.

I had seen the itinerants strung out along the main road when we arrived; dozens and dozens of caravans and tents with the usual litter, trash, and garbage strewn about, and clothes drying on the hedgerows. I had also been following a story in the papers about an itinerant family in Galway trying to get housed. The residents of the housing development were objecting strenuously on the grounds that they would bring their trash and squalor with them into their new neighborhood.

Sister Brigid, the social worker, invited me to visit her training center tomorrow and meet some of the girls. I told her I had been curious about the itinerants ever since I had first seen them camped in the empty lots in Dublin, with their pathetic, ragged, filthy children begging up and down O'Connell Street, and the women, wrapped in blankets with babes in arms, begging around Stephen's Green.

"Come with me tomorrow, then," Sister Brigid said briskly. "We'll visit a camp site first, and then you can meet the girls at the center. We'll tell you about itinerant life in Ireland."

NOVEMBER 29

A bitterly raw day. The cold seems to come up from the ground and grab you around the ankles, holding on tight. Gerry and I met Sister Brigid this morning at her center and drove to one of the itinerant sites. En route, she talked to me about the "traveling people," as they like to be called.

"They aren't Romany gypsies, like so many itinerants are in Europe. They're Irish. Thousands of tenant farmers were evicted from their homes during the potato famines of the 1830s, and by 1840 there were two millon itinerants on the road without a home. They slept under hedgerows or in farm buildings.

"By the early twentieth century, many of them had colorful painted wagons and were traveling from town to town, doing tinsmithing, horse trading and chimney cleaning. Nowadays, of course, those skills are obsolete, and they have to depend on junk trading for a living. That's why you see so many used car parts around their camp sites."

I asked Sister about the beggars I had seen on the streets of Dublin.

"The women and children beg," she said. "The men would never lower themselves to do it, but a man is considered lucky if he marries a 'good beggar.'

"And don't call them tinkers," she warned me, as we pulled into the camp site. "That's a derogatory term. They like to be called travelers or the traveling people. Social workers call them itinerants."

Their camping ground was incredibly dirty and filled with rubble of every sort. A cheerful band of bright-eyed, rosy-cheeked children with runny noses, dirty faces and traces of impetigo on their skin came running out to look with amazement at our car. Women came to the doors of their tents and caravans and looked suspiciously and sullenly at us until they recognized Sister Brigid, then they broke into warm smiles.

Their children ran to hug Sister. She's obviously very high in their esteem and each of them pulled at her for attention. When I was introduced to them, they looked me over shyly. They were far more interested in the car than in me, and when Gerry showed them the push-button windows, their eyes opened wide in amazement.

We went inside one of the tents. It was really just a piece of green canvas stretched over poles. To my astonishment, the inside was immaculate. The dirt floor was swept clean, the crib and the one double bed were neatly made up with quilts, and a cupboard was filled with clean cups, saucers and plates. There was a small, pot-bellied coal-burning stove in the middle with a tea kettle hissing on top, but the bitter cold seeped in from all sides and came up through the earthen floor.

The mother of the family, a handsome, articulate, bitter-voiced woman in her mid-thirties, welcomed me sardonically. "Come into my lovely home," she said. "Wouldn't you love to live here yourself?" She went on to tell me how she and her family had applied for public housing, but had been turned down many times. She has eight children. The baby sleeps in the double bed between herself and her husband. The next two toddlers sleep in the crib, and the rest of them bed down on the dirt floor. Colds, bronchitis and pneumonia plague the family.

Sister Brigid also attested to the difficulty of finding housing. She said she had housed thirty-four families in Galway over the past five years, but there is terrific prejudice against them on the part of the settled community.

"Put a traveler in a street of houses and twenty years later they will still be called travelers. They are accused of bringing in numerous members of their families to live with them, of carousing all night, having noisy parties, drinking too much, fighting, littering. Sometimes it's true," Sister Brigid said, "sometimes it's not."

A group of women congregated outside the tent as we said good-by. They had seen my camera and wanted me to take pictures of them and their children, which I did, and promised to mail to them. "What's your address?" I asked, getting out a pen and notebook. Ripples of laughter broke out among them and they nudged each other.

"You can mail them to me," Sister Brigid said. She was laughing, too.

We drove back to the Fairgreen Center, where twenty to thirty teenage itinerants come each day for training. While the boys are doing metal- and woodwork, mechanics and welding, the girls are taught industrial machine work, crafts, cooking, dressmaking and child care. They all take hygiene and literacy courses. "There are five centers like this in Ireland," I was told. "The boys and girls are paid an allowance while they attend and even though their sporadic school attendance has left them semilit- erate, they are becoming proficient in their skills. But," Sister Brigid added, "they are immature and not ready to work in a 'settled' commu- nity."

The girls had prepared a lovely tea party for me, and they were warm and friendly once they lost their initial shyness. We had a good visit, and when I got up to leave and to thank them for the tea, I suddenly, on the spur of the moment, invited them back to Dublin to have a tea party with me at the residence. I thought they would accept enthusiastically. Instead, my invitation was met with a stunned, embarrassed silence. Fi- nally, one of them said: "I've never been invited to anyone's house in my life."

"Well," I said, trying to laugh off my own embarrassment, "now you can't say you haven't been asked."

"We wouldn't have the bus fare," another one pointed out.

"I'll take care of that," I promised them airily, not knowing quite how, and great smiles began to spread across their faces. I left them with shouts of "Don't forget! Don't forget!" ringing in my ears.

NOVEMBER 30: *Dublin*

We took my parents and our boys to Clifden on the weekend, way out on the edge of County Galway. Tony and Renée Rutledge loaned us their lovely restored home, The Schoolhouse, which is perched on the end of Sky Road in Ballymaconree. It's a glorious spot, overlooking Kingstown Bay and the hills beyond, and although there are houses nearby, it has an empty, end-of-the-world feeling about it.

No book about Ireland is ever complete without a ghost story to en- liven its pages and chill the reader and, while we didn't see a ghost in Ballymaconree, we did have an Experience. I'll tell it exactly as it hap- pened:

My parents slept in a room at the end of the upstairs hall. Bill and I shared another one, with David in a small room between us. The first morning we awoke in the house, my father came down to breakfast and said: "We heard David crying in the night and thought he had an ear- ache, so your mother asked me to get up and go to him. But he was sleeping soundly, and he seemed to be all right."

David assured us that his ear didn't hurt. I thought it was odd that I hadn't heard him.

The second morning, my father came downstairs again and said: "Your mother is going to give me pneumonia. *Twice* last night she heard David crying and made me climb out of my warm bed and check on him, but each time he was sound asleep."

I looked at Bill. "Did you hear anything?" He shook his head.

I told my father not to get up again. "David will come in to me if he has an earache," I assured him.

When we returned to Dublin, I phoned Renée Rutledge to thank her for the use of the house. "We loved it," I told her. "It must be one of the most beautiful spots in Ireland."

"I'm so glad you had a good time," she replied. "I didn't want to tell you before you went and disturb your visit, but a funny thing has happened to me there twice, each time when I've slept in the room at the end of the hall. (The one my parents had.)

"I was awakened in the middle of the night by a child's cry. The first time it happened, I thought I must have been dreaming. The second time, I knew I wasn't, and I got up and searched the house, even went outside with a flashlight and looked around the yard but saw nothing. When I came back, the crying continued, the poor, pathetic whimper of a small child."

I felt the skin prickle on the back of my neck as she talked, and then I related the story of David's "crying."

"I'm not surprised," Renée said. "You know, of course, that before the house was restored, it was a school for abandoned orphans."

December 1

The telephone system in Ireland is going to give me ulcers or else I'll be beatified and known as Blessed Elizabeth of the Dial Tone. I tried on and off for two hours this morning (are ye listening, Minister of Posts and Telegraphs?) to reach 190, the information operator. It would alternately ring busy or there would be no answer. Finally, it rang once, stopped, and loud music mysteriously began playing. Then a man's voice in a rich Dublin accent came on the line.

"Hallo? Hallo? Listen. I've been trying to get through to you for two hours. Is this the operator? Hallo?"

I was so rattled by this time that I just replied weakly: "Hello."

"Yeah, well I've been trying to reach you for two hours."

"I'm afraid we have a crossed line," I explained. "I'm trying to reach the operator, too."

"You mean this *isn't* the operator?" He sounded close to tears.

"No, it isn't," I sighed, and then, just to brighten up his frustrating day, I added gravely: "This is the wife of the American ambassador,

Elizabeth Shannon, speaking from the Phoenix Park."

There was a long silence, followed by: "Jaysus!"

As I put down the phone, I heard him shouting: "Brid! Will you ever come here and listen to this!"

DECEMBER 5

A cold, gray day with a fine, slanting mist that seems to cut into your face no matter which way you turn against the wind. With sad hearts, the entire embassy staff filed into the reception room of a small funeral home in downtown Dublin to pay our last respects to the youngest member of our embassy family, the baby son of our communications officer, who died suddenly three days ago of meningitis. Last week he was a healthy, bouncing two-year-old, his parents' "Irish baby."

There can be very few things on earth as heartbreaking as the sight of a small white casket, no bigger than the bassinet so recently left empty.

Tomorrow he will make the long journey back to Iowa with his family.

DECEMBER 8

I have finally established a routine that I follow on most weekdays when we are in Dublin: Up at 7:45 with the boys and Bill for breakfast and the mad rush for school. Teeth brushed? Hair combed? Lunch bags? A rose for David's teacher. Ten pence for the missions. A new shoestring for a rugby boot. Who stole my bookbag? I often wonder if the Bookbag Thief lurks around other houses as he does ours in the early hours before dawn, a crafty fellow who hasn't yet been seen by human eyes but who followed us to Dublin from Washington. One day the sly, sneaking, bold little rogue will be defeated. He'll appear through the mist, as he always does, and he'll cry out in pain; there won't be any bookbags around! All the boys in this house will have grown up and gone away, and he, the nasty little twit, will have to slink off into the darkness, undone, ruined, outcast forever. In the meantime, he seems to be on active duty around our house three nights out of five.

All the men pour out the door at 8:15. Liam speeds off on his new ten-speed bicycle through the Park to the Chapelizod Gate, where he leaves his bike with the gatekeeper and goes the rest of the way by city bus. I like to point out to Liam, and frequently do, that Dervla Murphy doesn't have *any* gears on her bicycle and she rode it all the way to India and back. But my efforts with my children to fight conspicuous consumption are met only with dark looks and sighs. "She's at it again."

Christopher, David and Bill climb into the car with Gerry and set off for Ballsbridge, with Bill reading a book aloud to them en route. Aside from their shared enjoyment of reading, it keeps the peace and saves Bill from radio pop music, for which Christopher is developing an alarming taste. They are currently reading *The Wind in the Willows*.

I retreat back to the dining room for my second, third and fourth cups of tea and read the three morning papers. I'm a newspaper addict who gets very shaky when the morning papers don't appear. I particularly enjoy the *Irish Times* coverage of the arts and literature.

I'm dressed and down at my desk in the library by ten or ten thirty to work with Maeve until lunchtime. We plan dinner parties, luncheons, receptions; make up guest lists; do seating plans; make lists of what house guests, if any, will be arriving during the week; bring our ORE (official residence expenses) and our "representation" (expense account) forms up to date.

I go through the mail and decide which of the many groups who ask to have a tour of the house I can cope with in the coming month. Then Bill and I talk over the phone about dinners, receptions, openings, speeches, appearances and trips we are going to accept. And then I initiate tours and receptions of my own, for handicapped children, old people, and now my itinerant girls.

Dennis and I discuss the current household problems: the new dishwasher we need, the freezer that's on the blink, the drain outside the drawing room window that leaks and is letting water seep under the floorboards, the intercom system that has broken down (again), the assistant cook who is leaving (again).

I write thank-you letters, send a note with a potted plant to anyone I know who is in the hospital, return telephone calls, speak to the staff if one of them has a personal problem, confer with Anne about menus for coming events (I leave the planning of our family meals to her; pizza, chili, spaghetti, chocolate chip cookies and brownies have been added to her already extensive repertoire).

I sign checks for the household and personal bills, balance my budget, write personal letters, talk to Michael about the garden and walk over some area of it that needs tending to, clip newspapers to keep up my scrapbook, write an occasional article for an Irish paper or magazine, and often write my journal.

If I'm going to give a speech, I write it out, word for word. I wish I had Bill's talent of standing up and talking off the top of his head, but unless it's a very informal setting, I like to know what I'm going to say in advance.

I usually have lunch at my desk and work away until two-thirty, when it's time to pick up the boys from school. It takes me thirty minutes, or longer, to drive through the Park and across town to their school, but I love to see their faces when they shoot out, and to listen to their stories on the way home: David told me the other day that he went to the headmaster to squeal on a friend.

"What a nasty thing to do," I remonstrated with him. "Why would you do a thing like that?"

"Because he peed on the pitch," David replied primly. (The "pitch" is the playing field.) "That's against the rules. When Father Rebeyro [the dean of discipline] comes back, he'll biff him."

"Maybe he'll forget," I said.

"I'll remind him," David promised darkly.

Every day we stop for a red light on Kevin Street, in front of the Good Times Bar, and every day David and I make a pact to go in there and have a good time. One day we will.

The late afternoons are spent with the boys. Each of them has a staggering load of homework, too much sometimes, but it's good discipline and it has to be done. David has to have help with his; Christopher sits down and works away, methodical and organized. Liam finds a thousand reasons for putting it off until the last possible minute, then works in energetic spurts. The afternoons are too short for them to play outside after school. Now, in December, it's almost dark as we drive home.

Most evenings, we are out or have guests here. "The night shift," Bill calls it, dashing in at six thirty, changing into evening clothes, plucking a fresh carnation from the vase, and hitting the road again by seven.

December 16

Christmas is upon us. What happened to November? Where's October? Help! Michael and his son Jimmy came into the house today laden with the woodlands—holly, fir boughs, pine cones; the smell of Christmas is entwined in the staircase, on the mantels, over the doors. When it permeates the house, it captures the spirit. The Christmas tree arrived today and had to be set up in time for the embassy staff party tonight. Dennis, the boys and I worked on it all day. It stands tall and impressive, two floors high, reaching right up to the skylight in the central foyer.

We unwrapped our own decorations brought from home, our crèche with its Barvarian carved figures that Bill and I bought in Oberammergau on our first trip together to Germany. The boys pounced on the boxes of ornaments, unwrapping each figure and each decoration, something from home and familiar. "This is *ours!*" "Oh, I remember *this!*"

By seven o'clock the house was transformed, the ballroom alight with silver and gold, tinsel and fir, hanging from the ceiling, adorning the fireplace, catching the eye wherever one looked. The drawing rooms were aglow with fire light, candles casting shadows on the wall, the smell of evergreen everywhere. Red ribbons tied into bows on wall sconces, my tiny angel choir singing in their new loft—the mantel of the drawing room fireplace.

71

A record softly played Christmas carols and Bill and I stood in the darkened foyer by the twinkling tree, greeting each guest with a handshake and—Irish-style—"Happy Christmas." The season has begun.

DECEMBER 17

The Embassy Wives' Club gives all the children of the staff—American and Irish—a Christmas party each year. Since our own chancery rotunda is out of commission with repair work (it's being made more secure), we had the party this year at the residence. Santa arrived with a gift bag over his shoulder, ringing his bells and shouting "Merry Christmas!" and the old magic was there. We still have one believer left in our family.

Nan Robertson of the *New York Times,* a colleague of Bill's and an old friend of our family, arrived to spend Christmas with us and to do a story about our house in the Park and our lives here. She and I spent thirty minutes today trying to decide what shade of blue to call the blue of the Blue Room!

Dublin doesn't dress up for Christmas the way London or New York does. Bright lights give O'Connell and Grafton streets a festive air, but the rest of the city keeps on its everyday clothes. The stores are jammed, and somehow the clerks manage to stay courteous and helpful and find the stamina to wish shoppers a "Happy Christmas," but not many decorations or lights brighten up residential neighborhoods or shop windows. Few of our American Christmas traditions—combinations of older European customs—seem to have come from Ireland or to have emigrated here. But there is one lovely custom in the countryside: A lighted candle twinkles in the window of each house to light the Holy Family on its way.

We had one of the best parties of the season this evening, a get-together of the residence staff, their husbands and wives and all the children.

Unlike last night's big party for the staff from the chancery downtown, this is strictly an Irish gathering. We Shannons were the only Americans present, and since we live with the residence staff day in and day out, it was much more a family affair. Bill served as bartender and made drinks for the people who wait on us all year. The boys and I passed around the food.

It got off to a slow start, but finally the ice began to melt and each of the adults and children in turn stood up and did his or her "party piece." It's a wonderful Irish talent, being able to stand up and recite, sing, dance, entertain in some fashion. It's a social requirement here and, alas, the Shannon family tonight were lumps of clay. Finally, in desperation, Liam got up and recited what he could remember of "The Charge of the

Light Brigade." Inspired by him, Bill recited "Sea Fever" by John Masefield, one of his favorite poems, and I finally chimed in with "Who's Woods These Are I Think I Know," by Robert Frost. But none of us could begin to compare with Gerry and his sweet, clear rendition of "Danny Boy," or Maeve bringing tears to our eyes with her beautiful voice singing "Let There Be Peace." And *no one* could compare to six-year-old Colm Buckley and his many-versed "Paddy McGinty's Goat."

Next year I will uphold the family honor.

CHRISTMAS DAY: 1977

We didn't have a white Christmas, but that would be rare in this mild, wet, maritime climate. We went to morning mass at Chapelizod after the boys had their "opening" under the tree. And then midday dinner, a huge, succulent turkey, ham, mashed potatoes, gravy, canned sweet potatoes (couldn't find fresh ones here), Brussels sprouts, mushroom and celery dressing, cranberry salad, and finally, the pièce de résistance: Dennis' dramatic entrance with the flaming plum pudding, served with Anne's brandy butter sauce.

We took a long walk around the grounds after dinner, and paid calls and shared a little Christmas cheer with all the residence staff and their families.

We're leaving on the twenty-ninth for a two-week skiing holiday in Switzerland. The boys are aglow with excitement. It's their first trip to the Continent, their first try at skiing. Christopher has had his bag packed since yesterday afternoon.

DECEMBER 29: *Switzerland*

The porter at the station in Zurich spoke to his customers in four languages. "See?" Bill pointed out to Liam, as we handed him our luggage. "Even he can speak four languages and you complain about learning French."

"So you want me to grow up and be a porter," Liam said. Fifteen-year-olds think they're so smart.

We got a train for Bern, changed for Interlaken (a mad dash with Liam laden down with bags, all of us running and panting like pack mules, dragging David by both arms). Another change at Interlaken took us to Lauterbrunnen. We're headed for Murren, but it's not on the main line, that's for sure. We were climbing all the way and we kept our noses pressed against the windows of the train looking for snow. Alas, we got out at Lauterbrunnen in the dark and cold, but there was still no snow.

We asked the stationmaster how to get to Murren, feeling by now as if we were chasing Shangri-La; he nodded curtly in the direction of a funicular stop.

We dragged our luggage across the road and stood, stamping our feet in the dark, hoping that sooner or later the funicular would appear and shoot us up the mountain that loomed in the dark in front of us. The boys kept pestering us about the snow. "Oh," said I airily, a noted alpinist of many years' experience, "there's always snow at the altitude we'll be. Just wait."

"What if there isn't?" Bill whispered.

"There *will* be."

Finally, the funicular clanged down the steep track and rattled to a stop in front of us. Our ascent would be nearly perpendicular.

"I'm not getting on that thing!" David muttered.

"Come on," I urged, feeling as eastern European refugees must have felt when they got to Vienna and were told it was only 5,000 more miles to New York.

"Who told us about Murren, anyway?" Bill asked. He always gets interested in the logistics and planning of our trips at about this stage.

"The Swiss ambassador told us," I said. "He said it was lovely and beautiful and family-oriented and promised me that we would love it."

"Did he tell you his brother owns an interest in the Swiss railway system and it's losing money?" Christopher asked dourly.

"Let's everyone try to be cheerful," I said desperately, to a most cheerless-looking group.

The conductor motioned us aboard, so we climbed in, numb with cold, fatigue and hunger. As we headed straight up the mountain, Liam suddenly shouted, peering out into the dark: "Look! It's snowing!" And it was, coming down in a thick white sheet. By the time we pulled into a station with MURREN written on the signpost, the snow was all around us, fresh, crunchy, deep.

A young man met us at the station with a sleigh and pulled our bags to the hotel. No cars are allowed in Murren, so we walked behind him, along the tiny, winding road, with snow piled up on either side, higher than David. Alpine chalets, shops, a tiny church with a tall, thin steeple lined the road. The brightly lit rink with ice skaters gliding to the sound of a waltz lay glistening against the dark backdrop of the mountains.

"Wow!" Liam said. "It's just like a postcard."

We were shown into our two small hotel rooms and told that we could have a late dinner in ten minutes. I pulled back the curtain of our window and stood transfixed. There, looming almost over our heads, silent, white, its peak hidden in clouds, its sides flashing in the moonlight, stood one of the kings of the mountains: the Jungfrau.

Bill came over to look out the window with me. "Well," he said, "at least we know we're in the right place," and we all went in to dinner.

1978

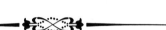

January 5

The boys came back from their skiing today, red-faced and frosty, and furious about two tiny German boys, half their size, who ski with Olympic skill, decked out in five-hundred-dollar outfits, and zoom past them time after time, calling out with infinite superiority as they flash by: "*Achtung! Achtung!*"

"I'm going to ach their tung if they keep at it," Christopher muttered.

"Stick out your pole and trip them," David suggested helpfully.

"Just keep your mouth shut and concentrate on learning to ski better yourself," advised their father, the diplomat.

This is a heavenly place. Every one of us loves it and is happy. The older boys are beginning to ski well enough to have fun. David has opted for ice-skating and sledding. We rented him a funny little old-fashioned wooden sled on which he careens down the hills in death-defying style. He and I go ice-skating every afternoon, and then Bill joins us for a long, snowy walk through the woods.

On Monday, we took a cable car up the Schilthorn Mountain (10,000 feet) to a restaurant called the Piz Gloria, where we lunched in spectacular fashion on a revolving platform looking out over a vast Alpine panorama. It was a brilliantly clear day, and the sun's rays bounced off the snowcapped peaks, making our high, white world glitter and sparkle.

By the time we made our descent, a fiercely cold wind had blown up, swaying the cable car from side to side as it creaked its way back down the mountain. Snow swirled in angry gusts on the floor of the valley below, closing in our view. The sun was lost behind the rolling, snow-filled clouds, and we shivered and huddled close to one another. It was a startling and whimsical change of weather, proving to us how frail we are when pitted against the ferocity and willfulness of these cold, shrouded mountains.

JANUARY 12: *Dublin*

Home again, suntanned, refreshed, and ready for work.

Commander and Mrs. William King came over from Galway to spend the night with us, and while we chatted at dinner I learned some wonderful stories from them about the history of our house.

Anita Leslie King's grandmother was Leonie Jerome, the sister of Jennie Jerome Churchill, Winston's mother. Leonie met her future husband, John Leslie, in this house, at a party given by Randolph and Jennie Churchill. They were living here while Randolph served as private secretary to his father, the Duke of Marlborough, who was viceroy at that time.

Winston Churchill was a little boy of five and six when he lived here, riding his donkey cart around the lawns and, no doubt, racing up and down the long back hallway as David does. What wonderful ghosts this house must have.

Anita, a writer and social historian, has vivid recollections of her grandmother's stories of the balls, dinners and flirtations that took place at the residence while the Churchills lived here. We tried to figure out the exact spot in the drawing room where Leonie met her future husband. "She always said she first saw him hiding behind a pillar," Anita said.

The house continued to nurture Leslie romance: Anita and Bill King spent their wedding night here as guests of Ambassador and Mrs. George Garrett. And they are back tonight on their anniversary. Anita has promised to look through her family papers to see if there is anything else about the house I can use in writing up a small memoir of it. I have begun to act on my New Year's resolution to write its history.

Bill King, a thin, handsome man with striking blue eyes and an athlete's build, has sailed around the world by himself. When I asked him, as everyone he meets must, if he didn't get lonely on his long and dangerous voyages, he simply said: "No, it wouldn't have occurred to me to be lonely."

Aside from the strength and skill required, I wouldn't have that kind of inner resourcefulness. I wonder how one develops it?

JANUARY 18

A congressional delegation arrived today, made up of members of the House Foreign Relations Committee. They had been on a long trip through the Middle East and were delighted to have an Irish stopover on the way home.

Bill briefed them in his office, and they met with various Irish officials. Tonight, the foreign minister, Michael O'Kennedy, and his elegant wife,

Breda, gave them a lovely dinner in Iveagh House, the Department of Foreign Affairs. It was chilly in the beautiful, high-ceilinged dining room, and Breda, who is always sensitive about the welfare of her guests, sent down for my coat without my asking. She can spot goose pimples at fifty feet.

Congressional delegations have a reputation in the foreign service for being extremely demanding in their requests for personal attention and frivolous in their interests. But I have entertained two delegations since we've been in Ireland, and I haven't found that to be true. The members of the delegations who have come through Dublin have all been, without exception, eager to learn what they could about the Irish situation, receptive to Bill's detailed and knowledgeable briefings, and responsive to the plans made for them. Their schedules in Dublin have not been frivolous; they have been tight and demanding, squeezing in as many meetings and briefings as possible in a short time.

JANUARY 20

With a quixotic unconcern, Irish attendance at social functions is based more on whimsy than on the clock. If we are invited to a dinner party at seven thirty, we look at the clock and say: "Right. Time to go." And we usually arrive on time.

Irish guests, I am convinced, sit at home not watching the clock, but listening to a mysterious inner voice which only they can hear. It guides them toward their destination by some mystical concept of time.

Since the inner voice is different for each guest, it gives its signal at different times. And so the prompt, seven-thirty arrival may stand and watch, fatigued and glassy-eyed, as gay, ebullient, unapologetic party-goers float in at eight, nine, or ten o'clock—whenever their voices have spoken. Maybe it's a carry-over from the fairies. Or druids. Or God-knows what.

With great good grace, hostesses never seem dismayed by their late arrivals. In fact, they often say to the prompt guests: "Aren't you *wonderfully* on time!" But are we? I sometimes wonder, are we just woefully early?

Anyway, I learned a lesson today. We were invited to the Shelbourne Hotel for an exhibit and luncheon to celebrate the tenth anniversary of the Gorey Arts Center, which Paul Funge, an energetic, red-bearded artist and entrepreneur has started down in Gorey, County Wexford. I was to meet Bill there, so I arrived alone, on time, and was puzzled to find the room empty. Thinking I might be in the wrong place, I went down to check with the receptionist, who assured me that the reception would be starting "anytime now."

I went back up and found some young men and women in blue jeans putting up exhibits. My offer to help was gratefully accepted, so I took off my coat, rolled up my sleeves and was soon hammering posters onto plywood. While we were working, a waiter came in and started setting up a bar, but he didn't seem to be working with any sense of urgency, so I put down my hammer and helped him set out glasses on the table. By this time, guests were trickling in. A very artistic young man whispered to me: "*May* I have a gin and tonic?" and then laughed uproariously, as if we shared an intimate joke over his liking for gin and tonics. I decided it was time to make my "official" entrance, so I slipped out to the ladies' room, combed my hair, rolled down my sleeves and reentered. I was greeted effusively by the committee who were all happily unaware of my earlier appearance.

Cyril Cusack was there, the actor I always think of as Fluther for his stunning portrayal in *The Plough and the Stars* (the first Abbey performance I ever saw), and we talked about his California moviemaking days in the early 1960s. "I enjoyed it," he said, "but I got terribly homesick for Irish accents, so I came home."

Paul Funge doesn't know yet that I helped mount his exhibit.

JANUARY 21

The boys seem settled into school after their Christmas holiday, and Christopher is happier and more contented now. He is writing blissfully away on a history project, which he has titled, "The History of the Roman Empire." After covering ten foolscap pages in his tiny scrawl, he said yesterday, "I think I started back too far."

"When did you begin?" I asked him.

"In 4000 B.C. I want to give the whole picture."

JANUARY 24

I discovered the Chester Beatty Memorial Library today; I'm ashamed to say I didn't even know of its existence, tucked away among the large, handsome houses on Shrewsbury Road. It has one of the greatest collections in the world of artifacts illustrating the development and history of calligraphy from the Babylonian, Islamic, Egyptian and Chinese cultures. It also has a stunning collection of jade books from China.

Chester Beatty was an American who made a fortune in mining as a young man, then devoted the rest of his life to collecting. He had no one special interest, so his collection is eclectic, which makes it all the more interesting.

He had planned to leave the collection to a museum in London, but became frustrated with English tax laws, so, to the great good fortune of the Irish, he gave it to Dublin instead.

I left the museum sooner than I wanted in order to dash over to the

Allied Irish Bank Headquarters to meet Bill for a luncheon with the chairman, Niall Crowley, and some of the bank executives. Una Crowley, Niall's wife, was there, along with "my banker" and good friend, Kay Costelloe. We were told that we three women had blazed trails: it was the first time women had ever, *ever* lunched in those sacred halls. Now that we've gained a toehold, perhaps it won't be the last time; we women are a very pushy lot.

JANUARY 26

The boys and I picked up Bill at the chancery this afternoon after we had run an errand to purchase a late Christmas present. As Bill climbed into the backseat of the car next to me, David couldn't hold in his giggles. "Don't you see anything, Dad?" he urged.

Bill looked around the car mystified and just then, a tiny black, silken Labrador puppy, eight weeks old, tail wagging energetically, crept out from under my coat and eyed the master of the new household.

"We've already named her," David explained. "She's Molly Malone." Molly seemed to approve of her surroundings, and settled down for a nap en route home.

JANUARY 27

HIGH TEA AND HIGH TIMES AT THE U.S. AMBASSADOR'S HOUSE, blazoned the *Irish Times* this morning, and there I am, smiling out of the front page, surrounded by my girls from Galway.

WELCOMING THE OUTCASTS, editorialized the Cork *Examiner.*

CARAVAN GIRLS TASTE THE HIGH LIFE, said the *Daily Mail,* from London.

"When the Galway Girls Went to Tea at the Embassy," captioned the picture in the *Irish Independent.*

I never dreamed my casual invitation to the itinerant girls would turn into an event that would reverberate around Ireland, but it did. Our house was swarming with television lights, popping flashbulbs, reporters busy scribbling down quotes for tomorrow's issues, while the girls, although slightly taken aback at all the publicity, were poised and calm, talking to reporters, drinking tea, eating chocolate chip cookies and enjoying themselves.

I had finally gotten their trip to Dublin organized with the help of Joe Malone of the Irish Tourist Board. He put me in touch with the owner of a fleet of buses, Mr. Maurice Jackson, who loaned us one of his buses for the trip. Sister Brigid said the girls had been looking forward to their outing for so long, they had arrived at the training center at 7 AM "so as not to miss the bus."

They looked pretty and fresh in slacks and jeans, sweaters and T-shirts,

The itinerant girls from Galway

with "mod" hair-do's and easy, sweet smiles. They were not at all shy or inarticulate once they began to feel at home. A reporter asked them if their training in dressmaking and cooking would help them get jobs. One of the girls smiled and said, looking around the ballroom: "I think I'll become an ambassador's wife," and that broke them all up.

A dark-eyed girl with long, brown hair sat alone during most of the party; she seemed remote and quiet, and didn't join in the bantering and jokes. I asked Sister Brigid about her. "She lost her baby in a fire in her caravan last winter," she said. "She's taking it so hard and still hasn't gotten over it." I tried to say a sympathetic word to her, but she just put her head down and large tears fell silently down her cheeks. I'm told that fires are not uncommon and that many itinerant babies and children have lost their lives while left alone in an untended caravan.

The girls sew well and brought me two beautifully embroidered pillows they had made. But the literacy classes have not been so successful. "Every time I try to read, my head dances a jig," one of the girls said. The rest nodded in sympathy as if they, too, experienced the same problem.

They left at 6 PM, after we had finished off the afternoon with a song-fest. I promised to go back to Galway and visit them again, and they have promised to return here one day. They are good girls; tough and witty, eager to share in the good things of life and to put an end to their strange, nomadic, unsettled existence. But the mark of an itinerant has left its emotional scar. I think they have an uphill road ahead of them. They are a breed apart in Ireland.

January 31

When we were up at Henry McIlhenny's house party in August, one of his guests said to me: "There's one woman in Dublin you simply must meet, Mab Moltke. I *know* you'll love her." And I do.

Mab is an American who has lived for many years in Ireland with her daughter, Vicki. They have a beautiful home in Monkstown, a Dublin suburb, where Bill and I have spent several pleasant evenings around the fire this winter. Among many other talents and professions, Mab is a skillful amateur decorator, so when she came to lunch today, I bounced some of my decorating schemes off her. I'm timid about my first project. We're going to paint the two front halls and the foyer a very pale yellow, with white woodwork and white plaster trim. I would prefer something more dramatic and vivid, but it's a vast amount of wall space so I'll play it safe for now.

The two boys' rooms are next. David is getting white walls with bright green woodwork and trim, to match his new green and white bedspreads and green woolen café curtains. (When the curtains were made and brought back to be hung on their new brass rods, I discovered to my dismay they weren't split in the middle to pull open on each side. "Oh," said the seamstress, "now that shouldn't be a problem, luv. Just pull the top one over on one side and the bottom one over on the other." I sent them back.)

Liam and Christopher's room will be painted a sand color, with dark brown woodwork and shutters. Their new spreads, made from a very dramatic blue, beige and gold "flame" print, are a success. We had picked out the material with Susan McQueen in Washington last May, and it is finally all here and in place. Bill and I are still waiting for our queen-size bed to arrive.

Dinner tonight at the Japanese embassy. The ambassador's petite wife is lovely in her traditional Japanese costume. I feel vast and clumsy towering over her. Everything seems so wonderfully subdued, calm and tranquil in her home, compared to my phone-ringing, dog-barking, boy-stomping house.

Dinner was a classic procession of delicious food, one small portion following another, each served in lacquered or china bowls, covered with a lid so that each dish was a surprise. We began with raw fish, sliced razor thin, and succulent. We continued through eight courses, of soups, tempura, shrimp, beef, pork, and vegetables, all accompanied by warm saki.

The Sidney B. Coulter Library
Onondaga Community College
Rte. 173, Onondaga Hill
Syracuse, New York 13215

(I'm a little bit afraid of saki, so I only paid it lip service, although several of the men seemed to be knocking it back like thirsty sailors. But everyone was able to leave the table upright.)

Death's Door Stories

One of the things that puzzles, amuses and gives me the shivers is the Irish preoccupation with illness and death. Never a week goes by without the morning papers featuring the Weeping Widow. The closer the camera can get to her grieving features, the better. A really big, important funeral will merit several pictures: "The Mourners at the Church," "The Famous Person Talking to the Bereaved Family," "The Graveside Scene."

A man's worth is measured by the size of his funeral, the bigger the better, and people will often attend services for someone they know only casually, as a mark of respect but also to swell the attendance. ("Sure, didn't his mother come to my Michael's funeral and they'd only met the once?")

The government will grind to a halt to attend, en masse, the funeral of a great sportsman or elder statesman, and if one local politican is there and another misses it, woe to him in the next election. The rituals of death always take precedence over merely mortal matters.

Illness merits the same close attention. If someone mentions that a friend is ill, he or she will immediately be asked: "Is it . . . ?" leaving the narrator with a choice of Being Discreet or Telling All. A favorite response, given in whispered tones, is: "They opened her up and just closed her again."

A friend of mine told me, just after we arrived here, about the wife of a politician who had been operated on. The nurse who assisted had told my friend that the doctor took one look and "just closed her up." Like a finished book.

The first time I met the dying woman, I gave her a long, mournful, "I know" kind of glance, thinking all the while: Isn't she brave, putting on a good face for her last few months, sitting here laughing and smiling while all the time. . . . But as the months stretched out, and her good health seemed chronic, I began to have serious doubts about the accuracy of the initial report. Last week at a luncheon, she told me she feels a thousand times better after having had her gall bladder out!

Another time, I was at a large party at the National Gallery talking to a very animated, charming woman, who suddenly broke off in mid-sentence, shifted her expression to one of deepest sorrow, and said: "I must dash off now, and sit with Lady X tonight. You know"—she lowered her voice to a conspiratorial whisper—"Lord X is dying."

Months later, I was introduced to Lord X at a party, and he seemed to be in absolutely peak condition. Looking him over quickly for signs of imminent departure from this world, and finding none, I started to ask: "Aren't you the one who . . ." but then I thought better of it and let the matter drop.

I'm kind of a fire safety nut. Well, no, not a nut. I just always believed everything that Fireman Friendly used to tell us when we had Fire Safety Week in grade school. Anyway, I discovered that there are no fire escapes or even makeshift escape routes in the residence. There are two staircases from the second to the ground floor, but this is a huge house with an old electrical system, fireplaces in constant use, and it's a long jump from the bedroom windows to the ground. So we had fire escape ropes installed in three upstairs bedrooms and smoke alarms put in all over the house.

The escape ropes are the kind that operate on a pulley. There are loops at either end of the long rope. You fasten one loop around your body and jump. You will glide slowly to the ground, leaving the second loop for another person. As that second person glides down, the first loop will come up again, ready for use. At least, that's what the men who installed the system told us.

We had a mock fire drill today, to show the staff and the children how to use the ropes. The big question was: Who is going to demonstrate? Liam said: "Stop looking at me." Bill suddenly remembered a telephone call he had to make. I explained I would have to change into slacks and that would take hours. But among all us cowards, a hero emerged. Dennis stepped forward, squared his shoulders, and said quietly: "I'll jump." And so he did, and just as the instructions said, he glided slowly and easily from the second floor to the ground and landed in the rose bed. We all leaned out the window shouting, "Oh, well done, Dennis! Let's hear it for Dennis.!" Heroes have to take a lot of guff.

I must remember to ask at the children's schools about fire drills. They say they haven't had one, but perhaps they have missed it. I must confess that I think there is very little awareness of fire safety in Ireland. But pehaps I'm a safety nut after all. (An Irish friend with a wicked tongue told me that contributions made to the Church in reprobate old age are known as fire insurance.)

FEBRUARY 2

Dinner tonight at the Royal Irish Yacht Club with Garret and Joan FitzGerald. The talk was all about Northern Ireland. Bill and Garret, and their other guests, were depressed and felt that the British were not really facing up to the situation in the North, that their heart and muscle were not in the right place, no matter what they said.

Everyone agreed that Ted Heath would have done something if he had remained in office. The bombings and killings are fewer now than they were five years ago, but there is a death of the spirit among a generation of boys and girls growing up in the North, whose energies are being dissipated because there is not a British political leader with the stamina, the charisma, the courage to say: This must end.

I met a most extraordinary woman at dinner this week. She told me she used to live in America, but had left because she felt that her children weren't being brought up properly there.

"Their manners are terrible," she said. "You know, American children are never taught to say 'please,' and 'thank you.' It's most annoying."

I had to admit that was true, sometimes.

She then went on with obvious relish and pleasure, to tell me that her eldest daughter, now fifteen, is having an affair with a forty-year-old man. I wondered, but didn't ask, if she says "please" and "thank you" before and after.

FEBRUARY 6–9: *Limerick*

We're off again this week, taking our "road show" to Limerick. We are staying with friends, the two Costelloe sisters, and that makes the trip more relaxed. Anne has worked for Aer Lingus at Shannon Airport for many years, and she has just recently brought a suit against the airline for discrimination against its women employees. Her case, one of the first of its kind in Ireland, is going to the High Court soon. Kay, whom I've already mentioned, is assistant manager and our "personal banker" at the Allied Irish Bank on Baggot Street.

We visited Moorepark Agricultural Research Center on our way here. They have had a long association with American agricultural research projects and have incorporated many American farming methods into Irish agriculture. We had a warm reception there and were then taken on a tour of the Center. It's the first time I have ever visited a pig husbandry station, and I fell in love with the tiny, squealing, pink, fat, warm little things. I cuddled one in my arms while its mother lay inside an immaculately clean pen, staring up at me with suspicious, beady little eyes. "It's adorable," I crooned, scratching its hairy little ears.

"I wouldn't recommend it for a house pet," Dr. Jim O'Grady, head of the Pig Husbandry Department, warned me. "In a very short time, they grow into that size," pointing to its vast, heaving mama. Nevertheless, I'd love to have one. I'm told they are both affectionate and intelligent.

In Limerick, we paid our official call on the mayor and his wife, Councillor and Mrs. Frank Prendergast, met the city and county managers, and then had a wonderful tour of the historical sites. Paul Funge and a local historian, Mr. Mannix Joyce, were our guides; we visited the tiny cottage in Bruree in which Eamon de Valera was reared, and the school across the road where he had been a student. We moved on to see the ruins of the Dominican monastery, John's Castle, and Old Town walls and the Old Church of SS. Peter and Paul.

Limerick City itself is to me something of a mystery, a dichotomy of passionate republican ideals and hyperconservatism, a society that I think an American would find hard to penetrate.

FEBRUARY 10

Despite its reputation for being a dark, remote and therefore potentially dangerous area at night, we've always found Phoenix Park quiet and placid. Tonight, however, was quite a different story.

Bill and I were driving home through the Park about midnight with Gerry. There was a dense fog and it was difficult to see many yards ahead, so Gerry was hugging the side of the road. Suddenly, through the swirling mist and gloom, we saw a figure lying in the middle of the road, waving what Bill took to be a white flag.

"Stop the car," Bill ordered gallantly.

"Lock the doors," I added prudently.

Gerry slammed on his brakes, and we skidded to a stop just feet in front of the prone figure. A man was bent over her, but she jumped to her feet and ran toward our car.

"Rape!" she screamed. "Help me! Open your doors!"

Gerry grabbed our car telephone, which is connected to the embassy, and tried to ring through to the guard.

"Rape," she screamed again, pounding on the window of the car. "Save me!"

Just then, a shadowy figure appeared out of the fog on the other side of the car, pounding on Bill's window.

"She stole my fifty quid, she did, and I want it back," a young man shouted to us. "She's a thief, she is!"

Gerry was having no luck ringing the embassy.

"What in God's name is going on," Bill asked, looking from one side of the car to the other, and rolling down his window.

I unlocked my door, and the girl jumped in beside me, sobbing loudly, and threw her arms around my neck. "Oh, save me, save me, mum," she sobbed, with all the emotion and skill of a frustrated Sarah Bernhardt. She wiped her eyes with the "white flag," which turned out to be a very dirty girdle.

"You're all right," I told her, trying to disengage from her steamy and malodorous embrace. "Just calm down and tell us what happened."

Meanwhile her attacker—or her victim, we weren't sure which at this stage—put his head through the open window on Bill's side and yelled:

"Don't believe her. She's a common thief, and I'm going to get my money off her. I picked her up in a pub and told her I'd take her home. We stopped in the Park for a little, like, ya know, cuddle. And then she got her f——— hand into me pocket and got me fifty quid."

"That's not true, mum," she said, sniffing loudly. Her lip was bleeding, and her eye was beginning to swell. "It was, like, ya know, we was in dis pub, just having a few, and he says he'll take me home, so I goes with him, and he stops the van here in the Park, and then he begins to . . . like, ya know . . . well, I'm a good girl, I am, and I wouldn't have none of him. So he begins to beat me up." At that stage she began to howl again. "I want me mum!"

"Oh, shut up," I told her, beginning to tire of her wails. "Let's drive on to the residence and call the gardai. They can straighten it out."

"Can I ride with you?" she asked.

"I'll follow in my van," the young man said, and disappeared into the fog.

Gerry headed slowly up the Main Park Road, and the girl sat back in the plush seat, suddenly forgetting her fright and looking around the big car.

"This is a grand car," she said, and put her arm cozily through mine. She looked me up and down and then sniffed again. "I just hate men, don't you?" she asked.

"No," I replied, "but then perhaps I haven't had your experience with them." That set her off again and I handed her a Kleenex.

When we got to the gate house, I took her into the small bathroom to try to wash the blood from her lip and put a cold compress over her eye. Her "assailant" drove up in his van. The guard called the gardai, and very soon one arrived on his motorcycle. After hearing her garbled story, he put the girl on the back of the motorcycle and the boy followed again in his van. They disappeared into the fog and mist; the last I saw of them, from the lights of our gate, the girl had the handsome young garda tightly entwined in her arms and her chin resting on his shoulder.

The next afternoon, Gerry phoned to the garda station to see what the outcome of the "investigation" had been. A ban garda (policewoman) had searched the girl at the station and found the fifty pounds stuffed into her bra. She confessed and was sent home. The young man, wiser and luckily no poorer, will no doubt think twice about a cuddle in the Park with his next pickup.

FEBRUARY 15

Dinner tonight with Mary Lavin and her husband, Michael Scott. Mary's first husband died when her children were small, and Mary and Michael were married a dozen years ago. He runs the School of Irish

Studies, where many American college students come to do a year in Ireland and to learn about Irish history and literature.

Mary is, of course, the Mary Lavin of *The New Yorker,* of "Tales from Bective Bridge," of "The Becker Wives"; a master of the short story, a writer whose work I read and loved in college and read again later; a woman who "understands the human heart" (to quote one of her colleagues) better than anyone writing in Ireland today.

I have to backtrack and tell how we met. I was eating a plate of lasagna with Kay Costelloe in the Unicorn Minor, a tiny Italian restaurant in a lane off Baggot Street one day. We had two stools and a counter to ourselves, which isn't easy in that popular, crowded spot, and we were shoving in the pasta and shoveling out the gossip when I noticed, through the grillework separating our counter from the rest of the restaurant, a remarkable-looking woman. Piles of thick, iron-gray hair pulled back into a knot, heavy black eyebrows, piercing blue eyes that seemed to see everything in the restaurant, enjoying what they saw. Also, everytime I wasn't staring at her, she seemed to be staring at me. Finally I said to Kay: "Who's your one over in the booth alone, with the gray hair?"

"That's Mary Lavin," Kay whispered. "I know her from the bank." Kay knows everyone from the bank.

I went straight over. "Hello," I said. "I know who you are, and I love your stories." She smiled a warm, natural smile and said: "I know who you are, too. Sit down."

Within minutes, we were friends, with a date to meet soon for dinner.

She and Michael have been to our house several times since, but tonight we did what we had been promising ourselves to do for months, to meet, alone, just the four of us and Caroline, Mary's journalist daughter, at their mews house in Lad Lane, and have an evening to ourselves.

We had a wonderful dinner in the kitchen, with Mary exclaiming at every biteful that she couldn't cook at all, and a marvelous evening filled with laughter and talk and the lively enthusiasm of new friends who have found soul mates but haven't yet heard each other's stories.

Michael and Caroline are natural "straight men" for Mary; her stories bounce off them and onto us like a three-way Ping-Pong game, all of us enjoying her, enjoying ourselves.

"You must meet Ben Kiely," she ordered. By chance, I had just finished *Proxopera,* his book about the troubles in the North, and I had been moved by its powerful indictment of violence, of men who maim and kill under the guise of "freeing Ireland." Then we talked about every Irish writer we liked, disliked, had read, hadn't read, must read. It was a colorful travelogue through contemporary Irish literature.

We left very late. It was just the kind of evening I had hoped for when we knew we were coming to Ireland.

Four women journalists from the *Irish Times* came to lunch today. Although the *Times* is very liberal about hiring women as reporters and feature writers, there is no female senior editor on the paper. It's the same old story: They can write well, God bless 'em, but decision-makin' is *man's* work.

The group today were bright and articulate. We discussed all kinds of things, from working mothers to the work of the Dáil, but I was particularly interested in their opinion of the Women's Peace Movement. They feel that it has expended the energy it once had, that its leaders are now indecisive, eager for publicity, and without a concise agenda for the future. "They just don't know where they want to go, or what they want to do, and they haven't any political muscle." I also wanted to hear more about their opinions of Northern Ireland, but they were obviously weary of the subject and far more interested in talking about the "beats" they cover here in the Republic: education, parliament, social issues.

Although they were all "liberated" single women, each said that if and when she married and had children, she would stop working to raise her family. They said that after seeing the frenetic lives of working mothers on the *Times,* they think it is too difficult trying to combine the two.

Nearly all young Irish women continue to work after marriage, but the majority still feel that mothering is a full-time, demanding job, and those who can devote themselves to it full-time do so. I was surprised to learn that it was only in 1972, when the first Report of the Commission on the Status of Women was published, that the public service marriage ban was lifted. Until then married women could work in their private businesses, of course, or on the farm, but they could not teach or hold civil service jobs, and most banks, businesses and corporations went along with that tradition.

The soaring rate of inflation in Ireland is, however, changing the work patterns of families here, as it is in America. Many young families suddenly find themselves confronted with bills that simply can't be paid on a single income.

I've been following the Train Robbery Trial in the papers for weeks, so I decided to go down and see the live show today. It's taking place at the Green Street Courthouse, which used to be reserved for murder trials but is now used only for trials of politically related crimes, principally those committed by IRA members.

Four young men have been accused of having IRA connections and of robbing a train in Tipperary two years ago. The courthouse is under very strict security; we had to telephone to ask if I could come in, and then Gerry was stopped at the gates by several uniformed guards.

The three judges who are hearing the trial invited me into their chambers for a cup of tea before the proceedings started. Their study is a wonderfully old, Victorian room, with fading red damask book-lined walls and a roaring fire; the judges, in their robes and wigs, made the nineteenth-century scene come alive.

In the courtroom, Mr. Seamus Sorohan, counsel for the defense, came over to say hello. He looked impressive and handsome in his robes, even under a rather lopsided wig. The courtroom is oval-shaped and wood-paneled, with the spectator seats banked steeply in the rear in a semicircle. The prisoners' dock is in the middle of this circle, and they enter it directly from an underground staircase.

The barristers and their assistants sit in rows in the middle of the room, with the judges high up on a dais in front. The witnesses take their seat in a box to the left of the judges.

One of the three judges in this trial has been accused by the defense of falling asleep during cross-examinations. Judging from the frigid temperature in the room, I would say the poor thing was suffering from hypothermia.

A hush fell over the courtroom as the four defendants were brought into the dock. They were all in their late twenties or early thirties and looked puny and slightly underfed. You'd have to stretch your imagination to picture any one of them having the derring-do to organize a train robbery. Three of them affected total boredom; one was alert and took notes throughout the proceedings.

Sorohan questioned two gardai at great length, trying to establish that the confession of the accused had been forced by brutal treatment. Neither wavered. They answered in a cool, straightforward manner which must have been difficult to sustain in the face of Sorohan's masterly performance of attack and retreat, cajole and needle.

Although the courtroom was jammed with gardai standing at each entrance and in the spectators' section, I seemed to be the only civilian there. When I discovered a small electric heater under my seat which I could turn on, I thawed out and enjoyed the drama. I stayed through the morning session and left when the prisoners were being taken back to jail. A French farce took place as they and I were leaving. I thought they would disappear as they had come, down the underground staircase below the dock, but instead, they were led out of the dock and around the back aisle between the spectator seats and the barristers' seats. I was leaving by the same route, going in the opposite direction, and suddenly we were all face to face, trying to pass each other in the narrow aisle. As I moved aside in one direction, one of the prisoners moved the same way. I sidled over to the other side and he sidled over at the same moment. As we both started to move back in the same direction, we burst out laughing and he stopped, gave me a little bow, and let me pass.

"That's McNally," the garda who was escorting me out whispered. McNally? My cousin, perhaps?

MARCH 2

Fifty members of An Taisce, the Irish conservation society, came to tour the house and gardens this afternoon. As they left, Anita Leslie King arrived for the night. She said she had brought us a "little house present," and asked Bill to come out and help her unload it. *Unload* it?

Minutes passed and I couldn't stand the suspense. I wandered out into the dark and there they were, unloading a small, kicking, braying, bad-tempered chocolate brown donkey out of a horsebox and into the meadow to join our own donkey, Brogeen.

Brogeen asking for a kiss

"He'll keep Brogeen company," Anita said. I bet he'll do a lot more than that with her.

Which brings me to the tale of the Big Donkey Switcheroo. I haven't told it yet, because I still haven't figured it out, but it will never be any clearer; in fact, as time goes by, it seems to grow more dense. This is what happened (I think). As the story unfolds, it is clear I'll never make it big in horse-trading circles.

We bought an old donkey named Pinkie from a donkey dealer. He was to be a holding operation until a livelier replacement could be found. We also bought a cart and harness, and a few weeks later, Yankee Doodle arrived to be traded, as planned, for Pinkie, although we had become very fond of him.

Soon afterwards, from another donkey source, we heard of a former resident of the meadow, Brogeen, long since put out to pasture in Kildare, when her previous owner, former Ambassador John Moore, left the residence. It seems that Brogeen was longing to return to the Park and if we could provide transportation for her, she would be ours.

Thinking that she would be a companion for Yankee Doodle, we asked our original donkey dealer if he would transport Brogeen to the residence. Which he did. Late one night, after dark.

The following morning we saw Brogeen, happily home again, but no Yankee Doodle.

"Where," I asked our donkey dealer on the telephone, "is Yankee Doodle?"

"I took her and left you Brogeen," he said.

"I know," says I, "but we *bought* Yankee Doodle, and now she has somehow disappeared in this exchange program."

"You paid for one donkey, and you've got one donkey," says he.

"But," I said, desperately trying to add two, subtract one, and divide by three, "we don't have the one we paid for. Brogeen belonged to someone else. Before we got her, that is."

"Brogeen is a lovely donkey," he said firmly. And that was that.

I used to wake up at night and squint into the darkness, saying to myself: Now let's get this straight. First, we decided to get a donkey. So we got Pinkie. Okay. Then we traded Pinkie for Yankee Doodle. Right. Then this fellow called about Brogeen.

Oh, well. We do have Brogeen. We don't have Yankee Doodle. Pinkie has gone into retirement. As the man said, we bought a donkey and we have a donkey. And I have to get some sleep.

MARCH 12

David made his First Communion today. The other boys celebrated their First Communion at home in our living room on Gramercy Street with our old friend Father William Clancy officiating. We thought it

David, much decorated, at his first communion

would be sad for David to miss this tradition, so we sent an SOS to Bill Clancy in Pittsburgh, and he was able to get away for a short Irish holiday.

Little girls in Ireland dress like miniature brides for their First Communion: white lacy dresses, white shoes and knee socks, little white gloves, parasols, tiny handbags, and a veil. They love it, of course, and they all look adorable, but one can't help an inward groan at the expense of these little outfits, which sometimes run as high as $150. Little boys have to settle for a somber dark suit, and David Shannon had to settle for his school uniform. However, he received not one but four white satin rosettes with a silver medal on each, traditional gifts from friends or relatives, and he insisted on wearing all four, two on each lapel. As he knelt at our makeshift altar in the ballroom, he looked like a miniature Idi Amin.

We invited the residence staff and their families to the mass. They are David's family-away-from-home and the ones he wanted to share his special day with. After mass, we had a little party to celebrate, and David was an attentive host.

When you see your own children making their First Communion, you understand what angels are all about.

I knew there would be pitfalls on this job, but tonight shouldn't have happened to anyone. All I can say is there will *never* be a social situation now that I can't handle, no matter how knotty, no matter how thorny, because nothing—*nothing*—can ever be quite so ghastly as what happened to me this evening.

We gave a black-tie, seated dinner for twenty-four, to honor the newly arrived French ambassadorial couple and to say good-by to the retiring Swiss ambassador and his wife. I wore a new dress finished by Thomas Wolfangel, the German-born Dublin designer, only hours before the party and I thought I looked terrific. The house was filled with pots of spring daffodils and tulips and has never looked more beautiful. The dining room gleamed with silver, candle light and white linen. Huge Simon Pearce glass bowls filled with flowers shone under the sparkling Waterford chandelier.

Dennis and I made our last-minute spot check with my faithful Labrador, Molly. Everything was perfect, no detail forgotten. We went over our scenario once again: dinner to be announced at 8:15, or ten minutes after the last guest arrived if that was after 8:15.

An hour later, we floated into dinner, I smiling graciously around my table which was lined with Dublin's diplomatic, literary and theater elite. I nodded to Ambassador Richard Aman from Switzerland, on my right, a tall, handsome, dignified man with a military-style mustache and a very straight back: I smiled at French Ambassador Jacques du Puy on my left, small and dapper, dark-eyed and charming. As we all sat down, I thought to myself: Now, isn't this just perfect, just the way an ambassador's dinner should proceed, everyone looking happy and animated, with lively conversations already springing up around the table. As I put my feet under the table, I felt something soft and spongy under my chair. Puzzled, I discreetly reached down to see what was there, and to my horror, I put my hand into a very large, still-warm, newly laid pile of Molly's droppings. Her full amount for the day, lovingly deposited under her mistress's chair, her contribution to my dinner party.

I straightened up with my soiled hand dangling at the side of my chair. The French ambassador was talking to me, telling me about living in New York in the 1950s. I stared at him wildly. What was he saying? New York. Oh, yes. I used to live there, too. Very changed since 1950, I believe. My hand was reeking, obviously, and both my feet were firmly embedded in the pile. I couldn't move. The Swiss ambassador was asking me about Liam's fishing trip. "Did he have any luck?" he inquired solicitously. Did Liam go on a fishing trip? I couldn't remember. I tried to smile. "Do *you* fish, ambassador?" I asked. My voice sounded weak. The ambassador looked puzzled. "But you remember, I taught Liam how to flycast last week," he said. Oh, that's right.

I think I'm hysterical. What am I going to do? Should I simply stand up and say: "I'm ill, you will all have to go home"?

Or, "Our cook just had a heart attack, there will be no dinner to-night"?

Or, "Will you all please go out and come back in again. That's an old American custom"?

Maybe I could start crying loudly and they would all be so embarrassed they would get up and leave, and I could clean up the mess and then go in to them and say, piteously, "I'm all right now."

But the waitresses were already moving into the room with the food. It was too late now to do anything. I would have to brazen it out.

Kitty came round with the first course, a beautiful, molded salmon mousse. I tried to dish it out just using my right hand, but it kept slithering off the spoon.

"Use both hands," Kitty whispered.

"I can't," I whispered back, and nudged Kitty with my elbow and rolled my eyes toward the floor. Kitty looked perplexed and moved on with the mousse.

The Swiss ambassador was telling me that he was looking forward to retirement. So am I—tonight! When Dennis came to pour the wine, I whispered for him to bring me some Kleenex, and I dropped them on the floor, over my feet, and tried to wipe off my hand. The dinner progressed: soup, entrée, salad, dessert. Talk about France, talk about skiing in Switzerland, about the current play at the Abbey. Ambassador du Puy seemed to have a head cold, thanks be to God. He probably couldn't smell anything.

Finally, champagne was poured and Bill got up to make a beautiful toast to our departing Swiss ambassador. We all had to stand up and toast Switzerland. I managed to look like I was standing, without moving my feet from where they were now glued.

Another toast to France . . . *Vive la France!* Once again, with the rung of my chair digging into my calves. I stood without moving my feet. At last, *at last,* it was over! I said, very loudly, "Let's go into the drawing room to have coffee," and I pushed my chair back, but remained seated. I planned to wait until everyone else was leaving the room, then make a mad dash for the kitchen, where I could get myself and my ruined shoes cleaned up.

But no, my evil genie had one more trick in store for me before the evening was over. My gallant Swiss dinner partner had not been an ambassador for two decades for nothing. He stood, rigid and unmoving behind my chair, waiting for me to stand. As I pushed my chair back, he saw the wad of white Kleenex on the floor. Mistaking it for my white linen napkin, he bent down to pick it up.

"No!" I screamed, grabbing his arm. *"Leave it!* It's all right."

"Aha," says His Excellency, flushed with wine and champagne, rampant with good manners, "I may be retiring, but I will never be too old to bend down and pick up a lady's napkin." He tried to wrest his arm out of my grasp as he leaned slowly downward, but I expanded my grip to a half nelson and tugged him away from the table, hissing in his face: *"Go have your coffee."* He looked quite startled this time, and meekly left the room without another word.

I fled into the pantry and took off my shoes and threw them into the wastepaper basket. All the tension of the evening broke, and as the maids and butlers were hurrying back and forth between the pantry and the dining room, I sat down on a kitchen table and laughed and laughed until the tears came.

"You're very lucky, madam, that it was under *your* chair, and not one of the guests'," Flanagan, one of our butlers, said.

"Oh, don't say that, Flanagan," I gasped. "Don't even think it!"

MARCH 17: *St. Patrick's Day*

You'd think that St. Patrick's Day in Dublin would be one of the grand celebrations of the western world, but that's just another American myth.

Bill and I got to the reviewing stand on O'Connell Street at 10:30 AM this morning, to watch the parade, excited to be spending our first Patrick's Day in Dublin. It was cold and gray, with a gusty wind blowing directly into the stand, but Bord Fáilte—the Irish Tourist Board—had thoughtfully provided blankets and hot tea for us all.

The Lord Mayor and his wife arrived at 11 AM in the ornate, gilded, horse-drawn carriage that is a glittering souvenir of vice-regal days in Dublin, and is now used for very special events. The streets were lined with spectators and the television cameras were ready to roll.

I, a lover of parades who need only to hear the roll of distant drums to feel charged with excitement and ready to march, was surprised and disappointed to see the parade get off to a lifeless start.

Endless commerical entries from a home security company warned us of Dublin's growing crime rate and urged us all to buy their product; not, I thought, a motif to make the heart beat louder or give the parade the lighthearted holiday touch one expected.

Endless troops of children walking forlornly in ragged lines, neither looking at nor responding to the spectators; little girls in drum majorette costumes, their poor bare legs and arms blue and mottled with the cold, trying to look cheerful as they passed the reviewing stand, twirling batons they hadn't been trained to use. And then a sad and somehow poignant sight: a group of elderly American tourists in their trench coats and plaid pants, carrying signs saying "Kiss Me, I'm Irish," walking in groups of twos and threes, waving to the crowd. Their companions who couldn't make the walk rode behind them in a tour bus, waving from their seats. They were so happy to be in Ireland to celebrate this most Irish of saint's days, and apparently no one had told them that New York, Boston, or San Francisco would have put on a much better show.

Finally we did hear the roll of drums and the blare of horns and a big, brassy United States Army band marched into sight. They had come over from their base in Germany to participate in the parade. They stopped in front of the reviewing stand and played three or four numbers. The crowd loved them; they brightened up the day and put some life into an otherwise dreary display.

I don't know; perhaps it takes a country with a more martial tradition than Ireland has to put on a good parade. Or perhaps they just need more practice.

APRIL 2

Bill left last week for a trip back to the States, so I said to the boys today: "Let's go to the races." Or, as we say in Ireland, Let's go racing.

Off we went to the Curragh, in County Kildare. It's a large, beautiful track, and the air today was electric with excitement when we arrived. The Grand National was being run in Liverpool on the same day, so we all kept running into the bar to watch those results on television, as well as keeping an eye on our own horses. Liam was in charge of the betting. I find the whole system of racing, betting and horse playing totally incomprehensible. For one thing, the track is so far away you can barely see the horses. You need binoculars, but it always takes me so long to focus them and see anything more than my own eyelashes that the race is finished before I can find the horses. I focused on a neighboring cow pasture for one whole race. As each race starts, everyone stands up to watch. At that point I always seem to drop my purse, or my hat blows off, or my betting stubs fly away, and by the time I get organized, the race is over.

I can appreciate the beauty of the horses and can imagine the thrill of breeding a winner, but I'm afraid my heart is not in racing. I love looking at the men watching the races with their thin-lipped, squinty-eyed intentness, wearing their well-tailored tweeds and brown soft hats; and the ladies, with their earth-colored, conservative suits, sensible shoes and serious hats. It's a style unique to an Irish racetrack. You might see the same face walking down Grafton Street on any afternoon and you would know the mind behind the face was thinking of horses.

APRIL 3

I'm taking a course in Irish history, "1800 to the Present," sponsored by the American Women's Club of Dublin and taught by a professor from University College in Dublin. We began with the dissolving of the Irish Parliament in 1800 by the Act of Union. Today's lecture was on Daniel O'Connell, the great Irish patriot whose statue presides loftily over the entrance to the street named after him, one of Dublin's leading thoroughfares. O'Connell first taught the Irish the tools of political reform through mass nonviolent protest. He also taught them how to organize, support and vote for candidates of their own choosing, lessons that the Irish country people brought to America and have been using effectively ever since. He opposed violence and, as a great orator and lawyer, tried to win Ireland's battles in courtrooms and in parliament. Today's responsible politicans such as Jack Lynch and Garret FitzGerald are following his example.

APRIL 7

A friend of mine, Consuelo O'Connor promised to introduce me to Harold Clarke, of Eason's booksellers and publishers. They sponsor the publication of the Irish Heritage Series, a beautifully produced collection of short monographs on different aspects of Irish culture, history, crafts, architecture, music, wild flowers—just about anything that seems to have photographic possibilities and to be worthy of several thousand words of explanatory text.

Consuelo, knowing of my interest in the history of the residence, wanted to talk to Mr. Clarke about the possibility of doing an Irish Heritage booklet about it. It seemed to be just the right vehicle for my project. So we met tonight at the O'Connors', and he was interested. We made a date to meet at the residence next week with his photographer and discuss it. If I have a firm prospect of publishing, I'll do the research I've been putting off for months.

APRIL 11

This afternoon I gave a party at the residence for the children from a school for the physically handicapped. Most of them have cerebral palsy or spina bifida. It seems to me, from the superficial knowledge I have, that care of the handicapped in Ireland is excellent. Although some facilities are lacking in equipment and space, the atmosphere seems to be unfailingly cheerful, kind and happy. I was astounded today, as I think most people are who aren't habitually around the physically handicapped, at how versatile they are, and how much fun to be with: witty, cheerful, keenly observant, cracking jokes and entertaining me far more than I "entertained" them. They spun through the house in wheelchairs, on crutches and in go-carts, on walkers and hands and knees. They made me realize how handicapped those of us are who have lost joy.

APRIL 13

Harold Clarke and John Brooks, the photographer, came out to the house today and closed the deal for the booklet I will write for the Heritage Series. I agreed to take my commission in the form of free copies, which can be given out to guests at the embassy. I also mentioned that I should get official permission from the State Department to write such a book and will contact their legal department next week. We didn't set a deadline but, as always, the sooner, the better.

APRIL 17

In history class today we covered that dark, tragic period, the famine years. In each of the four years 1845-48, there were partial or total potato crop failures in Ireland. For a country that had been in a financial depression previous to the famine, whose population had grown from three million in 1750 to more than eight million in 1840, and whose main source of food was the potato, the failures were a tragedy of immense proportion.

It is thought today that some sort of powerful virus blighted the potato. The plant would grow and seemingly thrive. Then suddenly, as if a poisonous wind had blown across the land, whole fields would wilt and be laid waste. The smell of rotting potatoes spoiled the air. People died from disease as much as from starvation. Tens of thousands of homeless families, burned out of their cottages by landlords when they couldn't pay their rents, roamed the roads, the precursors of the itinerant population in Ireland today.

Husbands buried wives; children buried parents. The lucky ones left Ireland on immigrant boats bound for America or England. In a decade, the population decreased by two million. Although the brunt of the tragedy was felt in the west, it was a hemorrhage of death and immigration from which it has taken Ireland a century to recover.

"Why," I asked our lecturer during the question period after class, "was all of rural Ireland so dependent on one crop? Why did the ruin of the potato spell certain starvation to poor farmers?" The answer lies partly in the fact that Ireland was in an economic crisis before the famine. Grain crop prices had plummeted, farm laborers were out of work, the population had grown too rapidly over the previous decades; as the economy grew poorer, the farmer had to sell the other foodstuffs to pay his rent, and then he began to plant poorer quality potatoes to get a higher yield. This in turn exhausted the land. So the farmer was in poor condition to face the catastrophe which would have been devastating in the best of times.

"But why were they so dependent on the potato?"

Simply because they could grow more potatoes on less land than any other crop. Fishing rights on the well-stocked rivers and streams were denied Irish farmers by the landlords. Seeds for alternative crops were expensive and hard to come by. The Irish seas, plentiful in fish, were dangerous; rocky coasts and steep cliffs made access to the sea difficult. One needed a boat to fish the seas. The Irish peasantry had come to trust and rely on the hardy potato to keep hunger at bay.

Although the British government instigated a program of famine relief, it was often mismanaged and ineffective. It was difficult to get supplies to remote farms because of the lack of an adequate road system. Stories are still told of Protestant "do-gooders" forcing the starving Irish Catholics to renounce their religion in exchange for a bowl of soup. "Soupers" is a term that lingers in Ireland as a distasteful noun for Protestant families who "turned" during the famine years. Memories are long in Ireland.

The tumbledown, roofless cottages that dot western hillsides, open now to wind and weather, the only life in them the tufts of heather that grow from their gray stones, are mute evidence of the famine's ravages.

APRIL 25

I've been a disappointment to the fashion industry in Ireland, I know. I'm not a clothes horse, and I don't attend fashion shows or browse through boutiques and showrooms. The truth is, I hate to shop for clothes. The only stores I really enjoy looking through are bookstores, antique shops, hardware stores and garden nurseries. I wish some fairy godmother would appear on my horizon each season with a new wardrobe created especially for me, and that would be that. Bill plays the role occasionally, and buys me beautiful, expensive and elegant clothes that I would never dream of buying for myself. After chiding him for his extravagance, I wear them and love them.

However, I made an exception to fashion shows today and held one at the residence, sponsored by the American Women's Club, to raise money for a school for handicapped children. Thomas Wolfangel put on the show, and I ended up buying one of his well-cut suits.

APRIL 26

We're all atwitter this week because the Royals are coming. Queen Margrethe and Prince Henrik of Denmark are paying an official visit to Ireland. Since not many kings and queens include Ireland in their stately rounds, a royal visit is an exciting interlude for all of us.

The ambassadors and spouses are invited to a diplomatic reception at Luttrellstown House, owned by Mrs. Aileen Plunkett and rented to the queen for the duration of the visit. Apparently the president's house in Phoenix Park isn't big enough to host a royal visit. The time of the reception has been set for five o'clock, and by noon today my phone was ringing: "What are you wearing?"

I haven't the faintest idea what one wears to a royal reception at 5 PM. Someone mentioned hats. Someone else said that a long dress was de rigeur. If I wear a hat *and* a long dress, I'll look like my grandmother going downtown to shop.

The men are just as bad, and seem to be in a tizzy over whether they should wear morning coats, tails with "decorations," or (I love this expression) "lounge suits." I asked Maeve to phone the Protocol Office at Foreign Affairs and ask them, but Protocol had no word on what the women should wear.

I decide on a short dress and a hat. If I curtsy, will my hat fall off? Maybe. *Can* I curtsy? I practice in front of the mirror and look funny. Should I sweep to the floor (and perhaps not make it up again?) or should I just put one foot in back of the other and dip? I decide to play the curtsy by ear.

We were told to be "in line" at Luttrellstown at 4:30 PM. That seems like a long time to stand in line, *even* for a queen. But we obey and for the festive occasion we put the flags on the car before we pull out of our gates. Luttrellstown is on our side of the city; we have only to drive through the Park, go through White's Gate, and we are on a very pretty little country road leading to Mrs. Plunkett's beautiful country home. The cottages that line the road are festooned today with Irish and Danish flags. Children and grown-ups stand in the doorways and lean out the windows to watch the procession of officials make their way to the reception. They all smile and wave as we pass by, and I wave back, in my most queenly fashion. Bill laughs at me and says: "*You* aren't the queen!"

"Never mind," Gerry says, "she's the Pretender."

We are ushered into the vast main hall of Luttrellstown with the rest of our colleagues, and lined up according to our length of service in Ireland. Bill and I are still near the back, between Argentina and Greece. Everyone is busy consulting with ambassadors from royalist countries about the curtsy. The Dutch say they don't curtsy to their queen. The Spanish say they do.

The Russians say they won't.

I'm still undecided. Finally, we are all put in order by a very tired, overworked protocol officer. The big doors of Mrs. Plunkett's drawing room open, and we begin to file in.

Each of us is introduced to the queen, who stands—young, blond, tall and stately—next to her very handsome, smiling husband. He looks more relaxed than she does. I shake hands and don't curtsy. She is wearing a hat. I'm glad I wore mine.

After the receiving line, we all go into the dining room for champagne and very good hors d'oeuvres. I want to ask the queen, who is a serious archaeologist, if she will be taken to Dublin's Wood Quay. It contains ruins of a Viking village recently uncovered during excavations for a building foundation. The future of the ruins has been a very controversial issue here. *I* think that the taoiseach should announce that the site has been made a national monument in honor of the queen's visit and that the ruins, with the striking vista from the Liffey up the hill to Christ Church Cathedral, will remain intact forever. I suggest that to the queen and she smiles.

"They could name it the 'Queen Margrethe Viking Village,' " I suggest and she laughs. My allotted time for chatter is over and I move on.

APRIL 28

We met again briefly at a huge reception at Dublin Castle. The poor woman must have stood for two hours in the receiving line. I wonder if she enjoys it? Or hates it? Or just puts up with it. Being an elected or appointed public official is one thing; the strains of office are temporary and one knows one can always quit or retire. A queen is forever. I wouldn't like it. Her face is impassive, neither smiling nor frowning, looking neither interested nor bored; but she gives immense pleasure to the hordes of people moving slowly through the receiving line, whose everyday, mundane lives are brightened for a moment by shaking hands with a real, live queen.

APRIL 28–MAY 1: *The Burren, County Clare*

Almost the only thatched roofs one sees in Ireland these days are part of an Irish Tourist Board scheme. The pretty, white-washed cottages, quaint on the outside and modern within, dot the countryside all over western Ireland and can be rented on a weekly or monthly basis. So many people have written to ask about them that we decided to try one for a week and see for ourselves what they are like. The cottage we chose is in the "Burren," that peculiar, rocky, barren area in north County Clare.

The Burren is a fascinating place for geologists, spelunkers, and wild-flower lovers. Unique to Ireland, its strange, moonscapelike appearance evolved from an ice age formation of flat limestone boulders that covers the land for miles. Rare arctic and alpine plants, dependent on the intense degree of light they receive in this treeless region, bloom in the cracks and crevices, making splashes of bright blue, mauve, purple and yellow on the flat, monotonous stretch of gray stone. "Kissing is out of favor when the gorse is out of bloom" goes the old song, but the Burren blooms in all seasons.

I find it eerie and slightly spooky. Only a few narrow, empty roads cross the Burren, and one can easily imagine the whole gamut of Irish ghosts, fairies, banshees and leprechauns having nightly conventions on this lonely, uninhabited land.

The wet Irish spring has followed us west. Wind and rain are lashing across the land in a never-ending gray, wet sheet. The children, who have become so used to rain they don't even notice, are out exploring the dozens of small caves in the area, their ears ringing with warnings about the dangers of going too far into any openings.

Mrs. O'Dea, the farmer's wife who manages our cottage, brings us delicious, freshly baked soda bread and pitchers of goat's milk each day. Yesterday I walked up to the farm to have a cup of tea with her and arrived at milking time. (She had earlier nearly flattened me with the casual remark that she was going up the hillside to round up her nineteen kids, and I, for a wild moment, thought she had set some sort of new record for Irish motherhood. It turned out, of course, to be her flock of goats.)

Since I had never milked a goat—which is not to say I have spent a great deal of time milking anything else—I decided I might as well have a go at it. As I'm always saying with boring repetition to the boys, "a learned skill is never wasted." So under the giggling guidance of the O'Dea daughters, I pulled up my stool and bucket and eyed the bulging udder uneasily.

"Sure it's just like milking a cow," one of the children said encouragingly, "only you do it from behind, and the milk comes out easier."

I pulled my stool to the backside and gingerly took hold of a rough pink tit. The goat couldn't have been more cooperative, and stood patiently in the rain while I pulled, tentatively at first, and then with more authority. All the other goats in the herd, curious about the newcomer in their midst, gathered round to watch. One old fellow with a long beard and menacing horns looked like he might be a troublemaker, but fortunately he kept his distance. My bucket filled with warm, white, pungent milk. The O'Deas' goats feed on all kinds of wild herbs and their milk smells and tastes like a bouquet garni. Contrary to popular rumor, it isn't strong or bitter or foul-tasting.

Each evening we lit a turf fire in the cottage and played cards or read. Night falls quickly and totally in the Burren, and with the rain pelting against our windowpanes, we felt the remoteness, the loneliness and the isolation of the west of Ireland farms in the "olden days," before roads, cars, electricity and television brought in the world. No wonder they used to reach for the "poteen" jug on dark winter evenings. And no wonder they learned to sing and dance so well and to tell wonderful stories to shut out the darkness that crept around their hearths.

MAY 3: *Cork*

We sent the children home on the train from Limerick and headed down to the Cork Choral Festival, a gala event that brought most of the diplomatic corps, President Hillery, and choral music lovers from all over Ireland to Cork City. Dozens of countries were represented in the festival, and this year the eastern European countries and Russia walked away with all the prizes. They were marvelous, full of verve and life, singing with beautifully trained voices and direction, wearing colorful, exotic costumes. My only complaint was that the singing went on endlessly. I was enthusiastic at eight o'clock, interested at nine, listening at ten, bored at eleven and frantic at midnight. I had worn a long silk skirt that fastened around the waist with a drawstring that tied in a bow at the front. As the hours went by, I began to fidget so much in my seat that I managed to break the drawstring, leaving me with a voluminous full skirt and no way of holding it up except to gather it firmly in my fist and hang on.

When the curtain went down on the last chorus at about 12:45 AM, and we VIPs in the front rows prepared to exit, I pulled my skirt tightly together, put my fur stole over my other arm, and stood, waiting for President Hillery to leave. As he passed me, standing at the end of our row, he smiled, and then, to my horror, offered me his arm. My smile froze; if I let go of my skirt, it would billow to the floor around my feet. If I didn't take the president's arm, I would surely be committing a diplomatic faux pas. All I could think to do was to crook my elbow in his direction, hold my skirt and pray. He put his arm through mine, and the two of us made our way from the hall, the president chatting amiably to me while I prayed all the way up the aisle.

MAY 5

We had a mini–Kennedy Administration reunion in Dublin this week when Mortimer Caplin who had been head of the Internal Revenue Service, his wife, Ruth, and their daughter, Kathy, came to stay with us. We were joined one evening for dinner by Newton Minow, who had been Kennedy's chairman of the Federal Communications Commission, and his wife, Jo. Newt Minow was the author of the once famous phrase describing American television as a "cultural wasteland."

We all went out to dinner in Dun Laoghaire, and since we had made plans to meet Joe and Imelda Malone at their house in Foxrock later that evening for coffee and dessert, we left the restaurant much sooner than we normally would have. We also forgot to tell Gerry of our plans, so he wasn't there when we got ready to leave.

As we were standing in the foyer of the restaurant, about to call a cab,

I spotted Bill's colleague, the Russian ambassador, Anatoly Kaplin, seated at a table with a half-dozen of his countrymen who were in Dublin for an agricultural show at the Royal Dublin Society.

I brought the Washington Caplins over to meet their namesake, and it took them only twenty seconds to discover that they had a mutual distant cousin from the same tiny village in some far-off corner of Russia. Two Irishmen meeting in a bar on Third Avenue in New York couldn't have dredged up common ancestry any quicker. Ambassador Kaplin, warmed by this discovery, insisted that we take his car and driver to the Malones'.

"We have just begun on our lobster," he explained, waving his arm across the laden table, "and we have many courses to go. My driver is sitting outside. Tell him where you want to be taken. He knows Dublin very well."

We piled into the small car, the Caplins and Minows in the backseat, Bill in front with part of me on his lap and the other part hanging over the stick shift. I smiled at the driver who did not smile back.

"We're going to the Malones' house on Westminster Road, in Foxrock," I told him. "Do you know where that is?"

"No."

He pulled out an enormous map of Dublin and spread it all over the dashboard. He stared at it glumly for some moments and then announced: "It's not on the map."

"Well, head off in this direction," I told him, pointing the way. "I think I can find it."

I gave directions while Bill kept a running commentary on the sights of Dublin for our friends in the backseat, who peered in vain into the night. With many jerky starts and stops and much use of the stick shift, we made a circuitous advance toward Foxrock. When it became apparent that we had traveled down the same street several times, I suggested that we stop at a garda station and inquire. One of the backseat guests hopped out and was back in a flash.

"We're near. Go straight down this road about a mile and watch for the turning on the left. We can't miss it."

"What he say?" our monosyllabic driver asked.

"Straight on," I interpreted. "Can't miss. Very near."

He sped off, while we all watched for nonexistent road signs, and after several miles, Bill said we probably weren't heading in the right direction after all.

"Turn around," I told the driver. By this time, my derrière and his hand on the stick shift had become . . . how you say in Russian—*intime?* He made a quick U-turn in the middle of the road and we retraced our steps. As we approached the same garda station, I suggested we stop again and this time I went in.

"Sure, Mr. Malone must be having a party tonight," the cheerful garda said. "Someone else was in just a while ago, asking directions."

I didn't bother to tell him we were one and the same.

"Just go straight down the road and look on your left. You can't miss it." That had a familiar ring to it.

"Which way?"

"That way," he said, pointing. We had, of course, been traveling in the wrong direction.

"Right," says I heading for the door.

"You wouldn't be traveling with the American ambassador, would you?" the garda asked. "Seems he left a restaurant in Dun Laoghaire over an hour ago, headed for Mr. Malone's with the Russian ambassador's driver, and he hasn't been seen since. His own driver is looking for him, and so is Mr. Malone, and the Russian ambassador is looking for his driver."

"If you get any more calls," I said, with my hand on the door, "just say the ambassador was last seen heading out on the dual carriageway for a big night out on the town in Naas." I left the puzzled garda and ran back to the car. We found the house this time, and Gerry was standing outside, flagging us down as we approached.

"We were beginning to worry about you," Joe said, as we all filed into his house.

"Oh, we were just giving our friends my 'Dublin by Night' tour special," Bill explained.

MAY 21

The sun shone for my birthday and we all went to the Trinity Regatta, a slow-motion afternoon of boating, cream cakes, strawberries, tea and pretty girls in lawn dresses and big floppy hats—a sweet Victorian scene replayed each year on the banks of the Liffey in twentieth-century Dublin. I was so fascinated by the setting, the languid atmosphere, so satiated with cake and tea, and so lulled by the warm sunshine that I forgot to watch the boat races. I spent most of the afternoon having a very long conversation with a man whom I had been told, last week, was "dying." He had rosy cheeks and bright eyes, and ate copious amounts of strawberries. Leaving this world seemed to be the last thing he had on his mind.

MAY 24

I'm one of those mothers who cause school principals to hide and teachers to prepare their defense when they see me coming. Having served on everything from the head-lice committee to president of my children's parent-teacher association, I have only to walk into a school building to start forming committees. Although some schools in Ireland have parent-teacher associations, they haven't been part of my experience here. I find teachers very reluctant to meet with parents, especially upper-school teachers, and most of them never do on an informal, after-school basis. The teacher unions in Ireland seem extraordinarily powerful and militant, and one of their pet grievances is time spent "for free" talking to parents about their children's progress. What American teachers do routinely, Irish teachers expect to be paid for.

Anyway, I was dismayed one day last autumn to peer into the "library" of St. Michael's and to find boys sitting at long tables doing their homework, but not a book on the empty shelves. I was told that the school could not afford to stock a library. I phoned up my good friend Phil Keaveny, another St. Michael's mother, and we discussed the situation. By the time we hung up, the St. Michael's Library Committee was formed. One of our first fund raisers took place tonight at the residence, a dinner-dance with all the profits going to the library. It was a great success; the parents were generous and giving, and I can just envision rows and rows of new books lining those bare shelves.

MAY 31

The directors of the American Irish Foundation are in town again. They are giving this year's literary award to Paul Smith, author of *The Country Woman, Come Trailing Blood,* and *Summer Sang in Me.* Mr. A.W.B. "Bill" Vincent, the president of the foundation, and Bill Shannon presented the award to Smith today in Listowel, County Kerry, during their annual Writers' Week.

Paul Smith, an eccentric and shy man, is out of the mainstream of the Irish literary establishment, and he seems to have done very little to try to endear himself to his colleagues, so the award to him this year evoked some surprise around Ireland. But Bill and I have both read several of his books, and found in them beautiful, touching descriptions of life among Dublin's poor in the early part of the century.

The presentation of the award was followed by a reception at Glin Castle hosted by the Knight of Glin and Madame Fitzgerald, his beautiful, vivacious wife. There are several legendary knighthoods in Ireland, dating back hundreds of years. There are the White Knight and the Black Knight, who was our host this evening. One of my favorite titles is McGillicuddy of the Reeks. I'd love to see that go into a Visa card computer. Then there are The O'Grady and The O'Malley, heads of their respective clans. The wives of these legendary figures are known simply as "Madame." I've been urging Bill to call himself "The Shannon" and aspire to knighthood so that I can become "Madame," but he says we would only start getting calls asking for plane reservations if he did that.

We wished we could have lingered in Listowel to attend the poetry readings, workshops, art exhibits and plays put on during Writers' Week, but we had to go back to Dublin for the annual diplomatic dinner hosted by the Irish government at Iveagh House.

JUNE 1

It was a marvelously warm summer evening when we arrived at Iveagh House. The light in Ireland on a clear evening illuminates the landscape with such dazzling clarity that one's sense of vision is immediately sharpened and one reacts to the brilliant colors of the sky and the land with a heightened sensitivity. The clear outlines of form and shadow, blurred on so many gray, cloudy days, and the rosy hue of the waning sun give the country the look of a pretty woman whose natural beauty is suddenly enhanced by an artful application of makeup.

I wore a sleeveless, backless jersey dress, and for once I didn't shiver or have gooseflesh. Our Irish hosts, on the other hand, were absolutely "destroyed" by the heat (which had soared to 70 degrees) and tried to pry open long-sealed windows in the high-ceilinged dining room.

We were seated at individual tables for twelve, with the diplomatic corps mixed in with members of the government. All of us regard this kind of dinner as an official duty, and the fun or interest of the evening depends entirely on one's luck in the seating arrangements. One of my closest friends in our ambassadorial circle called me up this afternoon to tell me about a new red taffeta dress she had just bought and was going to wear this evening. I saw her when she came in, and she looked smashing. She was seated between two bishops.

I have found myself solemnly discussing the price of pork with a member of the Pigs and Bacon Commission, or farm price ceilings enforced on Irish exports by the EEC. But I have also had a better time by introducing some provocative questions such as: "Are Irishmen truly puritanical and sexually inhibited, or is that just a false rumor spread by generations of Irish mothers to protect their sons against the dangers of Other Women?" Sometimes I take one side of the question, sometimes the other, but I have never found an Irishman who doesn't rise to the occasion, relish the discussion, and forget the price of pork.

Tonight I had a lucky draw and enjoyed my dinner conversation. We got onto the subject of Irishmen in general and their inhibitions in particular, and I said I found it ironic that with all their gifts of language and love of talking, so many Irishmen found it difficult to convey any real emotion verbally in their relationships. (This information is gleaned more from my women friends than from personal experience.) My dinner partner agreed with me. "If an Irishman is deeply in love with a girl and wants her to become his wife, he just might mutter, after a few pints, 'Will ye be buried with my folks?' " The girl who accepts *that* proposal must know from the start that her wedded life is not going to be garlanded with poesy.

I personally have come to believe that Irishmen aren't puritanical at all, quite the opposite. They are often shy and cruelly inhibited, but that's quite a different thing. Underneath the protective armor of their shyness and the tragedy of their inhibitions, lies a deeply imaginative, often wildly romantic soul, more akin to the vivid, extravagant lustiness of the inhabitants of some faraway Mediterranean island than to their thin-blooded, reserved northern neighbors. I often think that one would understand Ireland far easier if it were located somewhere in the Mediterranean Ocean, off the coast of Sicily, rather than sitting where it does, atop the cold Atlantic, buffeted by the chill winds and cold rains of northern Europe, which dampen but don't extinguish a truly warm and passionate spirit.

JUNE 3

Senator Alan Cranston of California, an old friend from our days in Washington, came to Ireland on his honeymoon this week. He brought his bride to spend the weekend with us at the residence. It was a pleasure to entertain a couple who enjoy Ireland as much as they do and who are so interested and enthusiastic about seeing the sights.

Once we had a member of Congress staying with us who got up early one morning and began his day by asking: "Where's my car?" Since the embassy doesn't provide cars for our houseguests and since Bill had already left for the office, I offered him my own car.

"But where's my driver?" he asked plaintively.

"You're looking at her," I replied, so he graciously allowed as how he could drive himself.

I pointed him in the right direction and with warnings about staying on the left side of the road I waved good-by as he disappeared down the drive. I did yell after him that the gas tank was on "empty," but I don't think he heard me. After he had to hitch a ride back to the residence, leaving a stalled car out of gas on the grassy verge of the Main Park Road, he stuck to taxis.

JUNE 5

I spend many of my spring afternoons this year taking groups around the residence and the gardens. Irish women's clubs, residents of old people's homes, itinerant children, visiting Americans and, often, "chapters" of the Irish Georgian Society who have come from the United States on tours sponsored by the society. Desmond Guinness organizes their itinerary and I offer to include a tour of the residence for members when I can because I admire their hard work and dedication to the preservation of the Georgian legacy in Ireland, an uphill battle if ever there was one. I also enjoy the Georgian Society tours because generally the people on them are well informed about Ireland, interested, curious, and involved in historic preservation back in their home states in America. The exceptions, however, make the good stories:

I had a group in last week. We had tea and cakes in the drawing room, took a tour of the house with my usual fifteen-minute talk on its history, architecture, paintings and furniture, and then went outside to take a walk through the gardens, which are looking exceptionally beautiful right now.

As we finished our walk and had congregated in front of the house for some picture taking before the group went back on their tour bus, a stout lady with radiant golden curls and makeup to match came lumbering up to us, provoked in the extreme and panting heavily. She was a latecomer on the tour and had arrived at the house after we had left for the gardens.

"Where's the ambassador around here?" she demanded. When none of her embarrassed colleagues answered, she turned to me, whom she didn't know, of course. "Have you seen the ambassador around?" she asked.

"No," I murmured. "I don't think he's here."

"Hmph!" she said, looking angrier than ever. "We were promised that we would meet the ambassador and be given a drink." She turned to me again. "Did they give you a drink?"

"Tea," I muttered, apologetically.

"Tea? *Tea!* I didn't come all the way out here in the midst of this god-forsaken park just to get a cup of tea. I want to meet the ambassador. What kind of a place do they run here, anyway?"

At this point, a terribly embarrassed and ill-at-ease tour leader came up and introduced our frustrated guest to me. "This is *Mrs.* Shannon," she began.

Happily my name meant nothing to her, and with a curt acknowledgment of the introduction, she climbed on board the bus, her blond curls still shaking with rage. God help Bill if she ever finds him.

She reminded me of another incident out here in the Park a few weeks ago. A member of Congress was in Ireland on a private visit, but had stopped by Bill's office to pay his respects, and had asked if he could invite his traveling companions out to the residence for a little tour. When he was assured that they would all be welcome the following afternoon, one of the women at the embassy whom I know well phoned me up: "Watch him," she warned me. "He's very jolly and nice, but when he gets a few drinks under his belt, he starts pinching fannies. And he likes a few drinks."

Forewarned, I asked Anne to make one of her super-duper de luxe teas.

The guests arrived promptly the next afternoon, and within seconds of getting them seated in one of the drawing rooms, Dennis, on cue, rolled in an absolutely groaning tea table: hot scones dripping with butter and raspberry jam, currant cake, tiny egg salad and watercress sandwiches, butter cookies, apple tart, and a big pot of tea. I honestly thought the congressman was going to burst into tears as he watched Dennis's retreating back.

"Milk or lemon?" I asked him brightly, as I poured his cup. I don't think he'd been asked that question for twenty years.

"What? Oh. Milk, I guess," he replied glumly.

I urged the scones on him. "Anne makes the best ones in town," I bragged. He demurred.

"You must try the currant cake," I insisted.

He just stared at it.

"You'll never have another apple tart like this," I said, pouring lashings of thick cream on it and putting it on his lap. I thought he was going to throw up.

The rest of his party threw themselves into the tea with gusto, and we chatted about the house and about Ireland. Finally, my guest perked up, glanced at his watch and said, with a broad wink aimed in my direction: "My goodness gracious. Five o'clock. I guess the old shadow has gone over the yardarm!" He gazed at me with a sort of desperate intentness.

"Oh, dear!" I exclaimed, jumping to my feet. "How the time flies, and I'm not minding my manners at all."

He looked sublimely relieved.

"Here it is already five o'clock, and I haven't taken you all on a tour of the garden," I announced.

He bowed his head in defeat.

We did every path on the estate; I pointed out varieties of shrubs, bulbs, hedges, trees, borders, vegetables, fruit. I was a walking botanical tour, and he panted along by my side, his spirit at rock bottom. Once he was able to interrupt my flow of ceaseless garden chatter, he announced that the group really must be heading back to town, and he didn't linger over his farewells.

When I got back to the house I phoned my friend at the embassy. "How'd it go?" she asked solicitously. "Fine," I replied. "I gave him tea."

"Tea?" she exclaimed. "I bet he hasn't been given tea in twenty years. How'd he take it?"

"Like a man," says I.

JUNE 8

Liam began his intermediate examination today, his "inter," as it is called. All high school sophomores in Ireland are nervously bending over their desks today, opening up the same standardized exam, and the poor boys and girls who are unprepared or unacademic or just poor exam-takers will be literally shaking with fear as they stare at the unanswerable questions.

For the teenagers who are leaving school after their inter, the results of the exam will help them get into trade school, apprenticeships and jobs. For those who are going on to finish high school, the exam is a dry run for the all-important "leaving examination" which they will take two years later, in June of their final year. The results of the leaving determine their future schooling and job placement. The exam is graded by the point system; so many points for an A,B,C or D in an "honours course," fewer points for the same grade in a "pass course." The total number of points, if high enough, will ensure a place in a university, a teacher-training college or the equivalent of a vocational college. More unusual from the American standpoint, the points accumulated in the exam also decide the course of study a university-bound student can enter. Irish students go directly into their professional studies, such as medicine or law, after high school. Therefore, one needs so many points for medicine, so many for law, fewer for history and the social sciences, and so on. Medicine demands the highest number of points. So the results of the leaving examination are all-important. It is possible for a boy or girl who does not achieve a desired score on the exam to attend a cram school which is designed specifically toward retaking the leaving exam. The results of these cram courses are mixed. If a student has come *very* close to his desired score, missing only by a point or two, the year's cramming may very well put him over the top. But if the results are poor the first time round, his chances of making it up in a year are dim.

There are many critics of the leaving examination system in Ireland, and I'm among them. It makes the high school curriculum extremely exam-oriented and standardized. And I think it is unfair to determine a child's future on the results of one examination. Important qualities of personality such as leadership, vitality, energy, creativity, compassion, ability to relate to others, and so on, are not valued and judged in the exam. There is a certain kind of intellect which is "exam-oriented": a good memory, a passion for facts, and a computerlike ability to spew out what one memorizes are all faculties that make a good exam-taker. There are, however, equally important and sound intellectual abilities, such as problem solving, intellectual curiosity, and inventiveness, which may not come through on an examination paper.

I realize, of course, that there has to be some method of choosing students for a university career, and that it is also unfair to train a teacher, an engineer or a doctor for a job that isn't available. The exam method, however, disqualifies potentially capable members of those professions.

While I was showing a group of Irish women through the residence this morning, I mentioned that Liam was doing his inter today. One of the women immediately responded: "You should be down on your knees in church instead of showing us through your house." And many an Irish mother will be in church today, praying for her child's success.

JUNE 9

Today Bill and I went to Auginish Island, outside Limerick, to witness the taoiseach, Mr. Lynch, break the ground for the building of a large factory for converting bauxite ore into alumina, the chief component of aluminum. A Dutch, Canadian and American multinational organization is building the factory, which will give much needed jobs in the area, although the potential pollution of the Shannon estuary from the factory's waste has been a controversial subject among conservationists in Ireland.

At the dinner celebrating the occasion this evening, Paddy McCormack, the general works manager of the project, stood up and predicted that quickie wildcat strikes would plague the project unless the government did something about them. (In Ireland, they are called "unofficial" strikes.)*

JUNE 19

We left today for our three-week holiday in France. The boys have never been there, and Bill and I have never traveled through Normandy and Britanny, so that's our destination. We went over today on the car ferry from Rosslare to Le Havre, on a big, comfortable ship with a pleasant dining room, bars, shops and a game room. I'm sitting in one of our bunks now, writing on my steno pad. We have four bunks for the five of us, and we've just tossed a coin to see who would get David for the night. Guess who won? Move over, David, your mother is trying to write.

JUNE 20: *Le Havre-Falaise*

Within minutes of leaving the ship at Le Havre, we were cruising along the French countryside, scouting for a bakery shop. We soon found one and loaded up on strawberry tarts and eclairs. At the first filling station we saw we filled the tank with gas for $40. Our budget is unbalanced already, one hour into the country.

Bill decided to take the boys to a one-star restaurant on their first night in France. He looked through his guide and found one nearby, than sat

* Although some of the guests at dinner that night thought his remarks inappropriate in the circumstances, he has turned out to be prophetic. The project has been plagued by recurrent labor disputes.

by the telephone in the hotel for five minutes, saying over and over to himself aloud in French: "Good evening. May I reserve a table for five for eight o'clock?" We all laughed so hard that when he finally made the call *he* began to laugh and had to hang up and start all over.

JUNE 23: *Normandy*

After visiting the cathedral and the tapestries at Bayeux, we drove to Omaha Beach, one of the sites of the invasion of Normandy during World War II. I have never seen it before, and I wasn't prepared for the very strong surge of emotion I felt when I stood, in a biting wind and under scudding clouds, and stared at the row upon row of plain white crosses, stretching as far as one could see. Many were named, but others were simply inscribed "To an Unknown Fallen Comrade." The beach is wide, wind-swept, lovely, but standing on the cliffs above, staring out at the gray Atlantic, one can hear the echo of the roar of battle in the howl of today's wind. David came up to me as I stood staring out over the ocean and tucked his head under my coat. The wind was blowing even more fiercely. He asked me why I was crying, but I told him the wind stung my eyes. Little boys don't understand the horror of war. Too many big boys don't either.

JUNE 29: *Locmariaquer*

Today, purely by accident, we found the perfect village. Locmariaquer is small and pretty, with narrow, winding streets, doorways and windows spilling over with geraniums, small gray stone houses with polished brass knockers, painted shutters, fresh white curtains that blow out of opened windows. Sunlight and shadows make patterns on the cobblestone lanes and walkways. The village rolls downward toward the sea, skirting an eleventh-century church and ending up on a wide walkway along the water's edge.

Everyone loves it here, and the boys even cleaned out the car after dinner, to atone for their fighting and squabbling during the afternoon.

JULY 1

Today was the kind of day that happens to a family now and then, unexpected at the start, unremarkable and unremembered by children since nothing remarkable happened, yet filled with an atmosphere too elusive to hold for long.

We spent the day on the beach, under a warm sun and cloudless sky. We have discovered our best cove so far, lined with boulders and secluded by a pine-covered hill. There was a tiny island, just visible on the water's horizon, with a small, white lighthouse on it. Liam made a good pencil sketch of the island and presented it to me because I am reading Virginia Woolf's *To the Lighthouse*.

David dug happily in the sand for hours, singing "We Three Kings of Orient Are," over and over. Christopher sunbathed and read another of James Herriot's books about his life as a veterinarian; he laughs loud and long every few pages. Bill is deep into Boswell's *Life of Johnson*. Not just minutes, but hours passed in this sunny, uninterrupted, peaceful cove. Everyone got hungry at once, and we ate what I had brought along from the car: cheese, bread, peanut butter and jelly, apple tarts and orange juice. By midafternoon we were tingling with the start of sunburns; a wind had sprung up and the air quickly became chilled. We packed up and walked along the narrow path between the pine trees, with the sea on our right, calm and glittering, tiny whitecaps breaking the surface. A dozen sailboats are skimming along smartly in the bay, aroused from their afternoon's stillness. The lighthouse on the island is more visible with the afternoon sun slanted against it. The boys are brown, happy, cheerful. No one argues, no one teases or pushes. Bill is rested and content.

Back in our small hotel, everyone showers off the sand and sea water, and the boys come bouncing into our room, starving, ready for dinner: Liam, taller than I am now, with his wet hair a tumble of dark blond (a problem to him, he says, because it is "fluffy" and not "flat." I wish mine were not flat, but fluffy). Christopher, tall, brown, and broad-shouldered, his hair dark and shiny. David, flying out of the shower, singing, laughing, hugging, wet, brown, skinny, shaking water on everyone.

At dinner, Bill promised Christopher that if Christopher ate all his fish, he, Bill, would grow a beard. The fish was choked down, and Bill's beard will start growing tomorrow. After dinner, Bill and I took a long walk through the village and out on a country lane. The two big boys played *boule* behind the hotel, and David swung on the swing set. When we returned we had a brandy in the hotel bar and finally went upstairs to bed. A good day. A day to be brought out and savored, like a favorite photograph, on days that aren't so good. Besides the sun and the sea and the beach, a day full of the particular closeness a family feels when traveling together in a foreign country. "They" speak a foreign language. "They" eat strange food. "They" look funny. "We" are bound together by our comfortable familiarity. And that makes us more aware of our need for each other.

JULY 6: *Chartres*

En route to Paris, via Chartres, arriving there in midafternoon, in time to see the cathedral before finding our hotel. We had tried to tell the boys something of its glory without overselling it, but we needn't have worried; they, blasé as ever, were stunned into respectful silence as we entered its vast doors.

We had a beautiful dinner in a one-star, three-fork restaurant with everyone good and enjoying his meal except when Christopher kicked David under the table for saying "Mercy buckets" for *"Merci beaucoup"* for the 110th time today.

JULY 12: *Paris*

We've "done" Paris, cramming what we could into four days. The boys like the new Pompidou Museum. I neither liked nor disliked it. I don't know what to make of it. They loved Montmartre and going to the top of the Eiffel Tower with Bill. (I sat in the sun in the park below and read my book while they went up, and a man tried to pick me up, which brightened my spirits enormously.) When Liam went to the Louvre, he sat and drew a sketch of the Mona Lisa and someone took a picture of him drawing a picture of *her,* and that brightened *his* spirits enormously. David liked the carousel in the Tuilleries best of all. Liam ordered frog's legs one night and *ate* them. Christopher liked Les Invalides museum the best. We're on the boat now, headed back for Ireland. I'm tired, elated, and filled with the peculiar kind of energy that "foreign travel" always instills in me. Ready for new things, and with an openness of spirit and a sense of adventure reawakened. It's been a lucky trip; no car trouble, no illness, a few quarrels but not too many; lots of laughs. We're fatter and poorer and we've had a good time. I'm *determined* to improve my French.

JULY 13: *Dublin*

We missed the Fourth of July in Ireland this summer by being in France on our holidays. The old diplomatic tradition of having an open house at the embassy or residence on the Fourth, and inviting every American in town to stop by and have a drink was instigated before the advent of jet travel and the hordes of tourists who now flock to Europe each year. Over a quarter of a million of them come to Ireland each summer, not to mention the thousands of American businessmen and women, students, and retired people who live here.

A few embassies have a big celebration on their national day, and invite hundreds of guests into one of the hotels for drinks and canapés. But most of them simply invite the other ambassadors to their home for a glass of champagne, a *vin d'honneur,* a toast to their homeland.

JULY 19

Bill went out to University College Dublin last night to lecture to foreign students attending summer school. When he had nearly finished his talk, which was about Irish immigration to America, he was interrupted by a group of young hecklers, accusing him of giving a biased account of relations between the United States, Ireland and Britain. He waited patiently while Maurice Manning, chairman of the course, tried to restore order. After a few moments, the hecklers gave up and left, and Bill continued with the lecture.

This morning the incident is reported in the *Irish Press,* which describes Bill as "visibly shaken." Oh, the dramatization of a nonevent.

JULY 31

Took the boys to their dentist in Stillorgan. He did his postgraduate work in the United States and takes good care of the boys' teeth. One day, and soon I hope, the Irish will take the care of their teeth more seriously. "When Irish Eyes Are Smiling" is a beautiful song, but more often than not, an Irish smile is a disaster area of vacant lots, nooks and crannies, black holes and brown craters that were never intended for public display. The minister for health in Ireland once told Bill that he thought Americans were "obsessed" with the care of their teeth. Oh, that the obsession would pass to our Irish friends. I stood the other day at a cocktail party and became so fascinated with the loose front tooth of a gentleman guest that I totally lost track of his conversation. The tooth, alone and near defeat, would wobble back and forth as he talked, clinging to its rootless position only by an act of faith. One bite into a tart apple would have sent it the way of its lost companions.

AUGUST 4

We drove out to Blessington in County Wicklow this evening to attend a ceremony at Russborough House, the home of Sir Alfred and Lady Beit. Russborough is one of the great houses of Ireland and contains the Beits' magnificent art collection. It is an awesome experience to be chatting away in someone's drawing room and look up to see the originals of paintings one has studied and looked at in art books all one's life. Gainsboroughs, Goyas, Vermeers, Velasquezes adorn the walls at Russborough. Many of those paintings were stolen in the early 1970s in a famous IRA robbery carried out by Rose Dugdale and her cohort and boyfriend, Eddie Gallagher. They slipped into the house one evening, tied up the Beits, and made away with as many paintings as they could take. All of them were eventually recovered, the criminals were caught and are now in jail in Limerick and Port Laois.*

* The two criminals eventually got married while in prison. Dugdale was released in 1980 and, when last heard from, was running a pub in Donegal.

Russborough was built in 1741 by a wealthy Dublin brewer named Joseph Leeson. Richard Cassells, the German architect who had designed Carton and Leinster House (the home of the Irish Parliament) and who introduced the Palladian style to Ireland, drew the plans. The great Francini brothers, Italian stuccodores who brought their skills to Ireland, were responsible for the magnificent ceilings in much of the house. It is said that Russborough has the finest plasterwork in all of Ireland.

Tonight the Beits gave Russborough and its contents to the Irish nation. In a very moving ceremony which took place on a small, makeshift platform in the hall, Sir Alfred, tall, distinguished and handsome, stood next to his wife, whose white hair framed her strikingly beautiful face and deep blue eyes. Each of them made a short and eloquent speech about the house, its contents, and their plans for opening it up to the public (they will continue to live in one wing). Then Sir Alfred handed the taoiseach, Mr. Lynch, a white envelope which presumably had in it the official document containing the legalities of the gift. People have said that Clementine Beit is the most beautiful woman in Ireland, and she looked it this evening as she stood next to her husband during the ceremonies.

AUGUST 7

We had a "literary" evening tonight with some of Ireland's most illustrious writers. But even illustrious writers can't resist gibes at each other (or perhaps particularly illustrious writers), and one of them whispered to me of another: "Someone was doing a dissertation on X's book and was puzzled by his use of five adjectives in a row, describing a character. He looked up the first adjective in the thesaurus and found the following four words in *that exact* order." The teller of this story glanced over at his subject and grinned maliciously. "Of course, he'd just die if he thought anyone knew." I heard the same story again later that evening. It has obviously become one of Dublin's legends.

AUGUST 8

Horse Show Week again. Last year, everything seemed so strange, so foreign to us; the show, the people at the parties, even the guests in our box. This year we feel at home. I like the stillness when the horses are taking the jumps, the lovely flowers that line the green jumping field, the riders in their different uniforms—red and white, green and white, salmon pink and white; the glistening coats and brushed tails and manes of the horses; the skill of the riders, the band of Irish pipers in their rust-colored kilts, the huge ginger-haired baton twirler who leads the pipers and throws his baton dozens of feet in the air and always catches it, to the gasps and delight of the crowds. I love the Irish-ness of it all. Ireland did well today, with Paul Darragh and Eddie Macken taking a first and a second place.

AUGUST 10

Dennis phoned us in our bedroom very early this morning to tell us of the death of Pope Paul. Bill had the flags up at half mast, and a message came in this afternoon that a funeral mass for the pope would be held in Dublin in the Pro Cathedral, with the nuncio officiating.

AUGUST 11

Ireland once again won the Aga Khan Cup at the Horse Show. Paul Darragh was the hero of the day, and Eddie Macken gave us a breathtaking fast ride on Boomerang.

We went straight from the show to the Pro Cathedral for the funeral mass of the pope. The church was filled to capacity and the steps outside were lined with people. One realizes on such occasions how sad it is that this most Catholic of countries doesn't have its own Catholic cathedral in the capital. The "Pro" (provisional) cathedral was built to serve as a temporary cathedral for Dublin until a permanent one could be built. That has never happened. The two Church of Ireland cathedrals in Dublin, St. Patrick's and Christ Church, are magnificent thirteenth- and twelfth-century Gothic churches, vast and handsome, and largely empty. I think it is unimaginative on the part of the Church of Ireland and Roman Catholic churchmen in Ireland not to arrange for shared use of the space.

AUGUST 17

Our neighbors from Washington, the Staceys, with their two boys, Cyrus and Mark, are here visiting. We took them today to see Castletown, the most glorious of the eighteenth-century Georgian homes in Ireland. It was saved from destruction by Desmond Guinness and the Irish Georgian Society just as the wrecking ball was about to descend. The Staceys, as are all tourists on a first visit to Ireland, are dismayed at the poverty of the house and the vast amounts of money desperately needed to restore it to its original grandeur. But as I explained to them, just the fact that it was saved and is being restored is a triumph in this country. I think it is wrongheaded to accept the excuse given by many that Georgian Ireland is simply a symbol of hated British oppression. Georgian Ireland is Irish. The workmen who built those houses and cared for them and the people who lived in them were Irish. Americans should tear down every pre-Revolutionary building in the country if we were to follow the same philosophy.

After Castletown, we drove across Dublin to County Wicklow for lunch at Hunter's Hotel, one of my favorite country inns. The sun was shining (we're actually having summer!) and the small, colorful garden at Hunter's looked inviting. After lunch, we drove off down the fuschia-lined back lane from Hunter's to Mount Usher, one of Ireland's most extensive and loveliest gardens. It is owned by the Walpole family. (I used to buy linens and towels at Walpole's in Washington and have been told that it's all the same family, originally a Belfast linen-making dynasty.)

The gardens of Mount Usher are open to the public, and it is one of my favorite spring, summer or autumn walks. Hundreds of species line the wooded walkways. The little Vartry River is dammed, with swinging bridges across the water, to make a still pond behind the house before it drops into a tiny waterfall to run freely again. Formal gardens give way to woodland; rhododendrons bloom early here in the spring. Azaleas of many species, colors and hues, spring bulbs, summer perennials, flowers of autumn keep the garden a plant lover's delight for eight months of the year. Trees and shrubs from South America, Tasmania, New Zealand, China and North Africa offer visitors to Mount Usher a spectacular variety and rarity. It isn't the first place in Ireland that I have coveted, but every time I visit here, I imagine the fun and excitement of taking over the garden and adding to what the Walpoles have already created.

AUGUST 19

A tearful good-by to the Staceys. Mark, aged six, and David's friend since both were in the baby carriage, pulled his mother aside and offered her ten pence if she would let him stay longer. We had to dash home from the airport to greet thirty Japanese scholars who are in Dublin for the first time, visiting the Chester Beatty Library. Most of them have never been out of Japan before, none of them speaks English. Their guide translated what Bill and I told them about the house and our role in Ireland. As we toured the house, they were able to tell me that the handsome painted leather screen that stands in our dining room is a Victorian reproduction of an Oriental sixteenth-century screen with Korean motifs. No one here knows who found it or bought it for our house, but it is universally admired.

I was curious to see if our Japanese visitors would enjoy our American-cum-Irish hors d'oeuvres, and they did. They also enjoyed our Scotch whiskey. They left in a very cheerful mood, chatting to each other and offering us prolonged and gracious thank-you's for their little party.

Our second annual embassy picnic at the residence today. The sun shone and I pitched seven innings of softball. (Last year's victorious team captain was "threatened" by the ambassador with an impending tour of duty in Uganda as his score mounted against my team's. This year's opposition team captain came with a mock telegram postmarked "Chad," from last year's captain, saying: "For god's sake, let her win!")

The veterinarians posted to the embassy in Dublin brought charcoal grills and made barbecued spareribs. As the aroma wafted over the green lawn I wafted toward the vets and managed to extract a plateful off each one of them. Eight vets are assigned to Ireland to supervise the sale of Irish beef to American military bases throughout Europe. The US Army buys more than ten million dollars' worth of Irish beef each year.

In the evening—with my muscles beginning to say: You pitched too many innings of softball, you idiot—we took the boys and drove out to Castletown for dinner. We ate in the Castle kitchen, which has been turned into a restaurant, and stayed for the evening's *Mellowdrama,* a performance put on by D. Guinness and Co. to raise money for the Irish Georgian Society. It was a roaring, wacky, hilarious performance, with villains, heroes, and a maiden in you-know-what. The children sat in the first rows and booed, hissed and threw paper wads at appropriate times, which was *all* the time.

I drove home, remembering, too late, that the Knockmaroon Gate in the Park would be locked, since it was past eleven, and got hopelessly lost trying to find my way to the Castleknock Gate. We finally spotted a lone garda sitting in his car by the side of the road, and he set us straight.

I phoned a friend the other day, and misdialed his number. When a woman answered, I asked for John O'Loughlin-Kennedy, and she said: "No, you have the wrong number. But I think I know who you want. I went to a dance with him twenty years ago. Call me back if you can't find his number, and I'll help you locate him." The telephone system in Ireland may be deficient, but the family-friend network still operates.

I'm enjoying a collection of letters written from Ireland by Mrs. Alvin Owsley when her husband was American minister here in 1935–37. Her children were the ages ours are now, and their lives here forty years ago not so different from ours. Mrs. Owsley, who is widowed and lives in Dallas, Texas, is still a frequent visitor to Ireland. She wrote to me when she saw an article about us in the *New York Times:* "I loved reading about your family there. It brought back such lovely memories. Those years we spent in Ireland were among the happiest in our lives." As these are ours.

"We asked about you before we invited you, and you'll be glad to know you passed inspection," were the words with which our American host met us at the door this evening. I didn't know whether to turn around and walk out or burst out laughing. Since no devastating riposte came immediately to mind, I simply smiled and said: "Thanks."

"Oh, don't take him seriously, he's a real joker." His wife smiled as she took our coats.

"That's right," he said. "I like to try people on for size." I didn't dare look at Bill.

"Come on in and meet the gang. We brought our friends over from stateside with us. You never know who you'll meet when you take a house abroad."

Introductions were made; we recognized a few Irish faces among the imported houseparty.

My host took my arm in a tight grip and pulled me over to the window. "Just look at that view," he said. "When I do something I do it with class. This house is class. Just look at this room. There's a million dollars in this room, just in paintings, rugs, furniture and jewelry. 'Pounds,' as you folks say over here. Ha. Ha. Honeybun"—he called his wife over—"show Mrs. S. here your necklace."

"I pick out all her jewelry," he said, fingering the diamonds. "Like it? Sure you do."

"It's beautiful," I agreed.

"See, Lizzie—you don't care if I call you Lizzie, do you?—people who are into mega-bucks tend to look down on diplomats. I mean, real power is where the money is, right? When you're into mega-bucks, you don't have time for ambassadors. Usually. But never mind, we're on holiday over here, and we're glad to have you guys here with us tonight." (I wondered if I was going to be asked to sit on the table during dinner and be the centerpiece.)

"Now you take me," he went on. "I'm what you might call a *real* American."

"What tribe?" I asked.

"What's that? Oh, yeah, I get it. That's good. You're a joker, eh? I like a sense of humor. Where was I? Oh, yeah. Now, I'm a real American. No one talks down America to me. Wait'll you taste the champagne, you're gonna love it."

As we chatted with the Irish guests, we discovered that they didn't know our hosts, either, and were told when invited that it was a party in *our* honor. *We* were there because we were told it was in honor of a visiting American political VIP. The VIP never showed up, nor was he ever mentioned during the evening.

I spotted an elderly friend, a man crumbling into his eighties, deaf in one ear, blind in one eye, but full of irrepressible wit and charm. He was a welcome sight as I fled from my egregious host.

"What in the world are *you* doing here, my dear?" he asked.

"Haven't you heard? The party's in our honor. What are *you* doing here?"

"Oh, my goodness. When you get to be my age, you accept any invitation that comes your way."

"We were told that Mr. X was supposed to be here tonight," I explained.

"The oldest ploy in town," my friend responded. "That was just their way of making sure you showed up."

"But," I replied, nodding in the direction of my host, "he said he didn't particularly care for the company of diplomats. In fact, he made that crudely clear." I felt like I was swimming in murky waters.

My friend laughed so hard he spilled sherry down his white ruffled front. "Oh, you *are* naive. He'll start every conversation he has for the next two weeks by saying: 'As the American ambassador said to me last night.' He's just *thrilled* that you are here, you poor thing. And I suppose you'll have to sit next to him at dinner. *I* will turn off my earphone, put on my monocle, and slurp my soup noisily. That way, I will be happily ignored by the ladies on my left and right and can enjoy my dinner in peace."

My host came over and took my arm again. Did he always hold women's arms as if he were afraid they were going to run away? Had experience taught him that, at least?

"In to dinner, sweetie," he announced.

"I'm Lizzie," I reminded him.

"Sure you are, Lizzie sweetie." He winked. "Wait'll you taste the wine. Dublin's finest. Like it? Sure you do. Wait'll you taste the champagne. That comes later."

Pour away, I thought. The only way to get through this evening is to get drunk.

"As I said," (and he said it again), "I'm a real American," and served himself six slices of roast beef to prove it.

"But sweetie," I said to him, "you just said you don't care for the company of diplomats and after all, they are representing your beloved country for you around the world. Aren't you being just a teeny-weeny bit unpatriotic?"

Like most bores, he didn't hear or listen to anything anyone else said, so that remark just slid off the table.

Dinner progressed, and the conversation never rose above the level at which it had begun. I tried subtly to look at my evening watch to see if we could possibly make a courteous departure, but looking subtly at the tiny face of my evening watch is hard. I have to appear to be smelling my wrist to get close enough to see the minute hand. It was only ten o'clock.

We adjourned to the drawing room to have coffee, my incubus still hovering by my side. "Let me show you the pictures in the library," he whispered.

"How much are they worth?" I asked, trying to fall into the spirit of the evening.

"Lots," he answered.

I followed him into the darkened library, so mesmerized by his specious, graceless, garish personality, by the total vulgarity of his spirit, that my defenses as well as my antennae were at low ebb. I should have known better. He would *have* to make a pass before the evening was over. He had nothing else to offer a woman.

As I felt for the light switch at the library door, he grabbed me by both arms—his "hold her, she might run" grasp—and pushed me up against the wall. "I've been waiting for this moment all evening, baby," he muttered into my ear.

"I'm Lizzie sweetie," I said, squirming out of his grasp. " 'Baby' is somewhere in the other room, waiting for you. Good night and thank you for dinner." I fled and he didn't follow. I never saw him again. If I ever do, I'll scream first, then run like hell.

AUGUST 23

Bill and I took the boys for a tour of the Guinness Brewery today. We live very close to it up in the Park. Its vast, old, red-brick warehouses and factory smokestacks in St. James Gate, by the Quays, are on our route from the Park into town. The smell of hops (far more pleasant than the occasional unspeakable smells emanating from the Liffey) is often in the air. We were shown a movie about the history of the brewery, then toured some of the buildings where enormous vats turn the hops and the yeast into Ireland's most popular drink.

Arthur Guinness ("Uncle Arthur," as he is fondly remembered in Dublin) founded a small brewery in Leixlip, County Kildare, in 1748. Three years later, he moved with his brother into St. James Gate and took over a small, unused brewery.

In the eighteenth century in rural Ireland, whiskey, gin and poteen (that fiery home brew made of potatoes) were more popular drinks than beer. Arthur's brew, which had become known as "stout," was made from roasted barley (this gives it its dark color). Gradually it grew in popularity, and by the time Arthur's son retired from the brewery, it had become Ireland's best-selling drink. His grandson, Benjamin Guinness, made Guinness the largest brewery in the world. Benjamin's town house on Stephen's Green in Dublin was given to the Irish government in 1939, and now houses the Department of Foreign Affairs.

The brew that has made the Guinness fortune is simple in its ingredients: water, yeast, malt and hops. The water for the Guinness made today is taken from the St. James Well in County Kildare. It is filtered and taken by pipe to Dublin, where a one-day supply of two million gallons is kept. The mixture of the other three ingredients and the fermentation process are unique. They're what make Guinness so special . . . and so beloved around the world.

Working for Guinness is a way of life in Ireland. They house their employees, provide medical services, sports clubs, and trips. Son often follows father and grandfather into the brewery.

The old flatboats that used to carry the beer up and down the waterways in Ireland are no longer used. A friend of ours (a brother of the same John O'Loughlin-Kennedy!) has turned one of them into a comfortable houseboat which sleeps ten people and goes on cruises up and down the Shannon. Nowadays, the beer is loaded into heavy metal containers, put on Guinness trucks and delivered via the country's highways, or put aboard ships headed for foreign markets. Guinness aficionados will tell you with total conviction that the Guinness you get abroad isn't the "real stuff." I'm no judge because I have never developed a taste for it, despite the fact that I've been told it is a staple of life, will cure everything from hives to hiccups, and make a mother's milk more plentiful. Bill likes it, though, and whenever we visit a pub, usually with an American visitor in tow, he has a pint or two (or a "jar" in Dublin jargon). It's always on tap in Dublin's pubs. There is a mysterious ritual connected with the filling of a glass. You have to fill, wait for the foam to subside, fill, wait, fill. Sure, it takes a skilled artist to do the thing properly.

Pubs in Ireland are still the great meeting place for young and old; once sacred ground for men only—if women did venture in, they sat hidden away in tiny "snugs" at the back of the room, divided by a partition, and served through a sliding door from the bar—the pubs are now frequented almost as much by women.

I shall never forget going into a tiny country pub in County Clare in 1963 on my first visit to Ireland. It was filled with old men, sitting comfortably around a peat fire, smoking and drinking and looking as if they had been planted there sixty years ago. They talked in that start-stop, whispery way that country people have, with lots of eyeball rolling and lifted brows doing the descriptions. The atmosphere was smoky, and the light dim. When I walked in and sat down on a bar stool, all conversation ceased. The men looked down into their pints with expressions of sorrow and embarrassment. I had come into sacred territory, the last place where a lad could go for a little peace and quiet, away from the responsibilities of home and hearth, where, God save us all, there would be no nagging woman around, asking for a little work to be done, when all that was clearly needed was time to think, talk, sip, smoke and relax.

I ordered a Harp lager at the bar. Bill sipped on a Guinness. We spoke in whispers to each other. Not one of the regulars opened his mouth, and the bartender kept his eyes averted. He looked as if he would burst into tears if we ordered a second round.

AUGUST 25

I flew out of the Fitzwilliam Tennis Club in such a flaming rage my ears were literally buzzing. The club very generously gives ambassadors honorary membership. Their wives and children have "lesser privileges," which, as far as I could make out from reading the regulations, mean that we can swim there from 3:15 to 3:45, unaccompanied by husbands. Women can also use the "lounge" but not the bar. (I have never mastered the art of sitting in the lounge after a swim and ordering a Coke from the bar, since there is no waiter in the lounge. I usually glance furtively right and left to make sure no one is glaring at me, quickly duck into the bar, whisper: "One Coke, please," and then dash back to my Proper Place.) Anyway, it's a nice swimming pool, and the boys and I enjoy stopping in after school or on a holiday afternoon.

Today my friend Libby Donahue from Washington was visiting, and after we took the boys swimming, we decided to go up to the lounge and watch a tennis competition that was in session. I crossed over the Sacred Portal into the bar, and got us each a Coke, then we decided to sit out on the balcony overlooking the courts and soak up the warm sun. Since the balcony was attached to the lounge, it didn't occur to me that it would be off limits. I should have known better.

After we had been seated there a few minutes, a thin, rather dough-faced man with a brown mustache and teeth to match, looked at me frostily and said: "I hope you women aren't going to take up all the chairs."

Thinking it was his crusty old way of making a joke, I joined in the merriment. "Oh, you've got to watch us all the time," I bantered. "Or else we just take over."

"That's exactly what I mean," he snapped. "You aren't a member of this club. You shouldn't even be here. Why," he added, his final insult, "you probably parked your car in the Members Parking Lot!"

"Well," I began, and stopped, insulted, rebuffed, embarrassed and outraged. "It just so happens that I *am* a member of this club (forgetting that a husband's membership doesn't apply to his wife).

"You certainly are *not,*" came his reply. "No women are. You are"— and he bared his brown teeth—*"trespassing."* And with that he stared stonily in front of him, watching the pat-pat of the tennis ball on the court below.

127

Libby was already on her feet, picking up her purse, sweater, Coke, and other belongings. She was furious, and her face was mottled with red anger spots.

"Let's get out of here," she said, and I more than readily followed her.

As we headed for the stairs, I told her to wait, and I ran up to the manager's office, where I recounted to the secretary what had just taken place. I thought an apology from the club was in order.

"Were you seated on the balcony?" she asked.

I said I was. "Right off the lounge, where the regulations clearly state women can sit."

"Oh, but they can't be on the *balcony*. That's for Members Only. I'm afraid you were in the wrong, and in all fairness, the man who spoke to you was in the right. There *is* a sign posted by the door of the balcony, saying: 'Members Only.'"

If there was I hadn't seen it.

As I walked back downstairs, I returned to the lounge, and looked again at the door leading to the balcony. There, lying upside down on the floor, where it had fallen off a small standing easel, was the sign.

I left the club, realizing that it was the first time in my life I had ever been told to leave a place, and not for being unruly, noisy, improperly dressed; just for being me.

AUGUST 31

We left Dublin four days ago for a short, end-of-summer holiday in the west. We stopped off at Glin Castle in County Limerick to stay overnight with Joan and Maurice Tobin, friends from Washington, who are renting the castle for a few weeks. We went on the next morning to the Waterville Lake Hotel, far down on one of the five "fingers" of Kerry. It's owned by an American, John Mulcahy, who also owns the lovely Ashford Castle Hotel in Cong, County Mayo. Waterville is not "quaint" or Irish in its style or appearance, but it is handsome, spacious, extremely comfortable, and has an excellent dining room. We enjoyed fresh salmon the night we arrived, and the next day went out in a boat with a gilly to try catching one of our own. Actually, I sat in the boat and did needlework while the rest of them fished. Not a bite. Jack Mulcahy says that the Irish government has given out too many commerical fishing licenses and that the net fishing at the mouths of rivers has ruined sport fishing around here. He put in thousands and thousands of fingerlings, but there's not a fish to be caught in the lake. Still, it was a lovely day for a boat ride. We stopped at a little island and sat on the soft, green, spongy bank while we ate the lunch put up for us by the hotel. Although it was warm and sunny, there was a mist moving toward us over the mountains that I think means, as the Irish say, we shall "lose the weather."

Dennis, trying to decide if it will rain

SEPTEMBER 6

Our good friends Sean and Paula Donlon are moving to Washington. Sean has been appointed Irish ambassador to the United States. I can't think of anyone who would be better for the job, but, selfishly, we hate to see him leave Dublin.

We gave them a farewell reception at the residence this afternoon from 6 to 8 PM. Dennis and I wavered back and forth about using the garden. The sun was shining, and he began setting up the bar in the marquee we had erected in the Pretty Garden. At five o'clock the rains came, and we all dashed madly around to set up an alternative bar in the ballroom. At six o'clock, the sun was shining, bright and innocent in a cloudless blue sky, as if to say: "Doesn't the party begin at six? What did *I* do?" I glared up at the sky and sun, that elusive and whimsical friend, and it shone benignly all the rest of the evening. Our guests, sipping wine among the roses, said the garden had never looked more beautiful.

SEPTEMBER 8

A group of Friends of the New York Public Library is in town and came out for tea this afternoon. I gave them my house and garden tour and chatted with them. One of the men in the group finally said: "When we were in China, the ambassador met with us and gave us a briefing. Isn't the ambassador going to see us here?"

They always feel shortchanged if they don't get to "meet the ambassador." Fortunately, Bill arrived home from the office a few minutes later. He joined the group and gave an impromptu briefing. They went away pleased.

SEPTEMBER 10

Just as soon as the Friends left, we departed for a weekend on the Shannon River. The O'Loughlin-Kennedys invited us and the boys for a weekend on their brother's boat, the old Guinness barge.

"It will be a beautiful cruise if we get the weather," Kay promised, and I was eager to get out on the river.

Alas, it poured steadily the entire weekend, which wasn't too bad for the adults, since we could sit inside and read and visit, but the boys were restless and bored and wanted to be out on deck, or off in the little dinghy that we pulled behind us. But the downpour was steady, relentless and heavy.

Nevertheless, the river was beautiful, even in the rain. We went through several locks en route, and the boys could jump out and help manuever the big, heavy barge through the narrow passage, getting soaked in the process but not caring. At one stop, the lockkeeper had gone home for lunch, and the boats lined up, two deep and six or seven long, before he returned down the wooded path on his bicycle, his rain cape flying out behind him. A German tourist in the boat just behind ours had become more than impatient with the hour's wait; he paced up and down the dock, swearing under his breath, looking at his watch every few minutes, asking of us: "When do you think he will return? This is unheard of. Imagine, going off for lunch and leaving the lock unattended. I have never myself personally heard of such a thing."

The poor man was working himself up into a right lather when the cheery and well-fed attendant returned. The tourist immediately began bombarding him with loud complaints:

"Where were you?" he bellowed. "We have all been waiting here over an hour, just to get through this lock."

The attendant, not at all swayed from his good humor by the aggressive manner, asked: "Where ye going?"

The German tourist glowered. "I am going up this river," he said pompously, "if you ever open up the lock."

"Have ye got a date up there somewhere with the Chairman of the Board?" asked our lockkeeper. "'Cause one part of the river is just like another, and it will look the same at two o'clock as it did at one o'clock.

Ye should calm down now, and have a bite of lunch yourself, and sure you'll get to where ye are going in plenty of time."

The German stomped off to his boat. The lock began to fill up and soon enough we were all easing our way out into the waters of the lough. Of course, the lockkeeper was right. Time stands still on the river.

I've been admiring the "print room" at Castletown ever since I first saw it. It was designed and put up by Louisa Conolly, the mistress of the estate from 1758 to 1821. Print rooms were an eighteenth-century decorative innovation, popular in large houses in England and Ireland as a rainy-day occupation for the ladies.

Prints depicting any motif or theme could be chosen, trimmed to the desired size and shape, and attached to the walls of a room with wallpaper paste. They were decorated with paper borders, bows and ribbons, which were printed on sheaves of paper for such a purpose. The ladies cut out the bows and borders and fitted them to their prints to achieve whatever pattern they desired. The end result was an interesting, personal and unique decorative effect. Several of these eighteenth-century rooms are extant in England, but Castletown's is the only one surviving in Ireland.

Desmond Guinness has had one made in his library at Leixlip Castle. It was designed by a most talented Englishwoman named Nicola Wingate-Saul. I met her through Desmond and she agreed to "help" me make a print room at the residence. Since she is the expert, she will be the designer and maker, and I will be the helper.

We began planning today. I'm going to put it in the downstairs ladies' powder room, which is a large, bright room off the main entrance hall. Its high, white walls are ideal for prints.

Nicola brought fifty black and white antique prints from an old print shop in London. They represent Old Testament scenes; we will leave some of them in their original rectangular shape, and cut others into octagons. Desmond has donated sheets of border and bow prints from the National Trust in England; my job—meticulous and time-consuming—is to start cutting out bows. We can tell already that the fifty prints won't be enough and we'll have to send for more.

We entertained a congressman and his wife at dinner tonight. He was on his first trip to Ireland and was loving it and eagerly soaking up Irish history. However, when Bill began explaining Ireland's World War II policy of neutrality, this burly ex-Marine jumped to his feet. "Are you trying to tell me that Ireland ... *Ireland!* ... was neutral during the War?" he demanded. Bill backtracked and began again explaining the

The Print Room

history and reasons for Ireland's stance, but our newly converted Irishman would have none of it.

"Well, I'll be damned," he said more than once, shaking his head in disbelief. I really thought he was going to pack his bags and fly out of the country tonight.

SEPTEMBER 16

Off to Waterford early this morning, where Bill will open the annual Waterford Light Opera Festival. An American company from Pleasantville, New York, is participating this year, doing a musical I have never heard of, called *She Loves Me.* The festival goes on all week, with companies from Ireland and Europe participating. The winning performance is rewarded by the presentation of a beautiful Waterford vase, designed especially for the occasion. There is a story floating around town that one of the previous years' winning companies had celebrated their victory long and fully, and, upon going back to the hotel, the member entrusted with carrying the invaluable vase dropped it and smashed it to smithereens. If I did that, I think I'd just keep on walking until I was out of town.

I sat in our Waterford hotel room this afternoon, cutting out bows for my print room. The maids were curious and kept finding excuses for coming into my room. Finally, one of them got up her courage and, watching me snip and cut, said: "Did you ever think of taking up needlepoint, luv?" I can hear the stories at home this evening: "God bless her, she's a sweet little thing, but she just sits there hour after hour, cutting out paper bows."

SEPTEMBER 28

Maybe all the cutting out of bows has got to me. On the one hand, I don't think I'm dotty . . . on the other hand . . .

I woke up this morning and immediately began thinking how grand it would be if we had turkeys. We could fatten them up and have them ready for Thanksgiving and Christmas. Eight of them would feed our family and those of all the residence staff.

It wasn't difficult to locate a turkey farm out in Kildare, so after lunch today Gerry drove me out. We were shown into a vast barn that had hundreds—probably thousands—of young, gobbling white turkeys milling aimlessly around, looking for all the world like the crowds at any airport when a flight has just been canceled.

"Just grab whichever ones you fancy," the turkey breeder said cheerfully and started to go out of the barn, leaving me and a thousand turkeys staring at one another.

"Hey, wait a minute. How do I grab them?"

"By the tail," he said, and shut the door behind him.

"I'll go hold open the door of the boot," Gerry announced quickly and followed the turkey breeder.

I looked them over. "Come here," I coaxed a nice, plump-looking, motherly sort of bird. She immediately gobbled loudly and dashed off with surprising agility to a far corner of the barn. Sensing that I would have to be more assertive and self-confident, I swooped down on the nearest turkey I saw and aimed for its tail. It was off like lightning, flapping its wings and rolling it eyes, and its fright caused a general uproar among the masses. They knew now that trouble was brewing. Their contented gobbles changed to a higher pitch and they began talking shrilly to each other, probably planning their counteroffensive.

I grabbed again, and this time I was left with a dozen tail feathers in my hand, and a semiplucked, tailless turkey headed for safety among her feathered friends. Every turkey in the place was staring at me reproachfully. Why am I doing this, I began thinking, instead of striding gracefully up the aisle of the supermarket, plucking frozen butterballs from a bin, like any sensible woman?

I sighed. "Come on, Gertrude," I said, lunging at a white blur of feathers, and wrestling it to the ground. I got both feet in one hand and her tail in the other, and bore her out triumphantly to Gerry, who was standing patiently by the open trunk.

"Nothing to it," I told him, as I flung her in. He slammed the door down quickly, and I went back for more. The second one was easier, and by the time I caught the third I had the knack of it. We filled the trunk with eight squawking, gobbling, flapping turkeys and sped home, hitting rush hour traffic on the dual carriageway leading from Naas to Dublin. We could hear the turkeys squawking over the din of the rain on the roof of the car. Then, suddenly, they were still. Not a peep.

"Gerry," I whispered. "They're all dead."

"They couldn't be," he answered.

"They are. Stop the car and let me take a look at them. They might have died from fumes."

Gerry pulled over and we jumped out into the rushing traffic and pouring rain to open the trunk. We peeped in. They were all settling down for a nice roost, gabbling softly and looking quite contented. As I slammed the door shut, a car pulled into the emergency lane behind us, and a young man got out to see if we needed help.

"No," I said, thanking him. "I just stopped to see if my turkeys are alive," and I jumped into the car to get out of the pouring rain.

Poor fellow, I can here it at the pub now: "Ah, come off it, Paddy. Now, what did she *really* say?"

"I swear to God she said 'turkeys.' "

My postscript to anyone foolish enough to buy fresh turkeys at a turkey farm: line the trunk of your car with newspaper before you bring them home. We generated enough fertilizer between Naas and Phoenix Park to enrich our garden for the next ten years.

OCTOBER 3

With popes dying and popes being invested at an alarming rate, we seem to drive down to Shannon Airport on a weekly basis to greet the planeloads of VIPs stopping over to refuel on their way to and from Rome.

How many times since we have been in Ireland have we wished that the planes stopping for fuel would land at Dublin Airport and save us the long, tiring trip down to Shannon and back. But the Airport Authority has a firm commitment from the airlines to stop at Shannon, and so they do, and when a VIP comes through Ireland, the big, black car heads west.

Mrs. Rosalyn Carter had led the delegation to Pope Paul's funeral back in early August. We had met that group on their return from Rome. Today, Miz Lillian is on her way to Pope John Paul's funeral. As she stepped from the plane for the hour's refueling wait at Shannon, she spotted Bill standing at the foot of the ramp, and with her usual quick wit and insouciance, she quipped: "Well, ah know we're getting gas in Ireland, 'cause there's Bill Shannon waiting for me at the bottom of the steps."

OCTOBER 12

Bill is touring around Ireland for a week with two of his sisters and their husbands. I met Terence de Vere White this evening in front of the Gate Theatre, to join a group of his friends and see *Proxopera,* a play adapted from Benedict Kiely's powerful novella about the IRA. It didn't receive good reviews, but I enjoyed it nevertheless, and was glad to see Terence, whom we've missed since his move to England.

We all went to dinner afterwards with Hilton Edwards, who directed the play, and Peter Luke, its author. Hilton, who looks like a taller, fat version of Jimmy Durante, was vibrant and amusing, telling us anecdotes about his many decades in the theater in Ireland and reminiscing about his longtime friend Michael MacLiammoir, one of the great figures of the Irish theater, who died last year. Everyone was in high spirits, despite the failure of *Proxopera.* We stayed until well after midnight, and I drove Terence back to his hotel through dark and deserted streets.

OCTOBER 19

I began a course on James Joyce's *Ulysses* today. I have started this novel before and failed to get through it, but if I can't do it here, surrounded by Joyce's Dublin, with every landmark in the book now familiar, and the rhythm of Irish speech sounding natural to my ear, I will never succeed. Americans, I have discovered, are far more interested in Joyce than the Irish seem to be. So many of our visitors from the States want to visit the Joyce Tower in Sandycove, and, when they get there, feel like they are walking on "sacred ground." Michael Scott, the architect who codesigned the American embassy in Dublin, purchased the Tower and gave it to the Irish government to be kept and restored as a national monument. But except for the Tower, there are few designated *Ulysses* landmarks in Dublin. Many of the houses, pubs and shops have been torn down or put to other use.

OCTOBER 20

The whole Fitzpatrick clan, our neighbors from Washington, arrived in Dublin yesterday. They have been living in London this fall, and took the boat crossing from Holyhead, in Wales, to Dun Laoghaire, in Dublin. I took Jim and Sandy this morning to the Green Street Courthouse. The Train Robbery Trial is still going on, and I knew Jim, a lawyer, would enjoy it.

It was, as always, freezing in the courtroom. I'm surprised that Irish justice isn't meted out by all the defendants' dropping dead of pneumonia before their trial is over.

OCTOBER 22

The Fitzes and the Shannons piled into the car today and headed off for County Kildare to see the Irish National Stud, with a side visit to its neighbor, the Japanese Gardens. The Stud is a marvelous experience and shouldn't be missed by any visitor to Ireland. Dr. Osborne, the personable and hospitable director, was there to meet us and show us around. The horses are magnificent, each one immensely valuable, each possessing certain characteristics that horse breeders all over the world are searching for, to create that elusive mine of gold, an international racing winner.

The fees for a stud vary according to the value of the horse and its record of winnings, but they can run as high as $10,000 per servicing. Artificial insemination is never used in the breeding of thoroughbreds to avoid any likelihood of fraud. A birth at the Stud is an exciting event, followed and overseen by vets and owners alike. One never knows when a wet, shaky, big-eyed foal will turn out to be another Arkle, one of Ireland's all-time greats.

OCTOBER 25–28: *Belfast/Derry, Northern Ireland*

We've just come back from four days in Northern Ireland. It was our first trip to the North except for the day's outing to Newry my parents and I made when we were looking for "roots." And, for the first time in all my travels, I felt a misapprehension about going to the North, leaving the boys behind. Feeling sheepish about doing it, I nevertheless wrote down some family instructions, put them in an envelope, and gave the envelope to Maeve to hold for me, "just in case." As Dervla Murphy said about her travels in Northern Ireland: "Never before had I embarked on a journey that required courage." Her mountain journeys would certainly have required more courage than I could ever muster, but I shared her foreboding about Northern Ireland.

I've been reading Irish political history in preparation for our trip, trying to sort out the political origins of the Troubles. It's a sad history, filled with bitterness, bloodshed and long memories. The tensions between those who try to solve the nation's problems by political and legal methods and those who believe in violence have been a recurring theme in Irish history for many centuries.

The two traditions run like twin streams through the past two hundred years. The great political leaders such as O'Connell and Parnell were aware of the potential for violence, but they usually kept their distance from it and used political debate and agitation, oratory and the force of their personalities to lead Ireland toward independence. Even they, however, used the *potential* of violence as one of several levers to persuade successive British governments to make political concessions while nonviolent settlements were still possible.

Then along came John Redmond, the leader of the Irish Party in the House of Commons just before World War I. He was less forceful and less skillful in walking the narrow line during the Home Rule Crisis of 1913–14. By relying totally on British goodwill and parliamentary methods, Redmond lost the political initiative, and the forces advocating violence—the Irish Republican Brotherhood (which is the precursor of the Irish Republican Army), and the Ulster Unionists—moved into the forefront of political activity. The IRB, who were the heirs of the Fenians of Parnell's time and the rebels of 1798 and 1848, believed independence could be won only by armed force.

They organized the 1916 rebellion that began in Dublin on Easter Monday. At the same time, the hard-line Unionists in the North showed that they were willing to resort to rebellion themselves and to defy an act of Parliament, if Parliament granted home rule to Ireland.

Redmond should have used the possibility of armed rebellion to compel a home-rule settlement; when he failed to do so, the Easter rebellion fatally undermined his political position. The rebellion was a fiasco in military terms, but the execution of its leaders—Pearse, Connolly, McDonough and a dozen others—converted them into martyrs (as Pearse knew it would) and gave the violent approach prestige and moral legitimacy. (Two leaders of the rebellion, Eamon de Valera and Countess Markiewicz, were spared their lives, de Valera because he was an American citizen, having been born in New York City and brought to Ireland as an infant, and the Countess because she was a woman!)

The moment those Irish patriots were shot in the courtyard of Kilmainham Jail, the two streams of Irish political effort—the violent and the constitutional—flowed together. The new Sinn Fein party, the political arm of the IRA, fought and won the general election of 1918, but its winning candidates, instead of going to London to take their seats in the House of Commons, met in Dublin and acted as the government of the Irish Republic, which had been proclaimed at Easter 1916. For two and a half years, from 1919 to the summer of 1921, the British tried to crush the nascent Republic, but without success. Ireland, as it had never been before, had become a nation in arms. The whole country supported the rebellion, either openly—sending its sons to fight—or covertly, hiding men on the run, lying to British troops, tricking, conniving.

The secret of its tactical success was that Michael Collins, one of the leaders of the rebellion, avoided pitched battles with the British Army and used the hit-and-run tactics of urban terrorism and guerrilla warfare.

In the summer of 1921, the British arranged a truce and intensive negotiations began. These resulted in the peace treaty of December 1921, which, in effect, gave Ireland its independence, but as a self-governing dominion, not as a full-fledged republic. There was to be a governor-general appointed by London, and there was still to be an oath of allegiance to the crown.

The third and ultimately most significant provision of the settlement, although it was not generally realized at the time, was that the Irish had to accept partition, with the six northeastern counties becoming the separate entity of Northern Ireland and remaining within the United Kingdom.

The exclusion of this part of northern Ireland from the Irish Free State led to the outbreaks of recurrent violence. It has plagued the North without a break since 1969, but in 1922 it was the oath of allegiance to the crown and the substitution of the "Irish Free State" for the "Irish Republic" that seemed more menacing to the Irish people.

Michael Collins, the military chieftain of the Irish war for independence, led a narrow majority of the Irish parliament in accepting the terms of the treaty. But Eamon de Valera, the president of the Irish Republic, and a large minority refused to abide by its terms. As a result, the new Irish Free State had to establish itself by crushing a "Republican" rebellion. Michael Collins was murdered in an ambush near Cork, and by the summer of 1923, the rebellion was over.

In 1926, de Valera led his supporters into the Irish Free State Parliament as a legal political party.

But even when we arrived in Ireland last year, the wounds of the civil war were still healing. Collins, who had been killed in the war, is still commemorated in a partisan way, and de Valera, who died in 1975 after a long career as prime minister and then as president, is still a figure of fierce controversy. Worst of all, however, the fact that independence had been won from the British by force rather than by negotiation meant that there would be fresh occasions for the use of violence.

As we drove across the border into County Down on Wednesday and were stopped briefly by soldiers at a roadblock, their uniforms and rifles brought the reality and the immediacy of the problem home to us. But the roadblock turned out to be the result of an accident rather than a police maneuver; a grain truck had careened around a curve, mowed down twelve cars, killed a passing pedestrian, rammed into a house, overturned and spilled grain over half of Newry.

We arrived in Belfast in time for lunch with Charles Stout, the energetic and knowledgeable United States consul posted to Northern Ireland. Two members of the British foreign service stationed in Belfast joined us and gave us a briefing on their views of the Troubles. Their concern seemed to be solely with security; they were fighting the enemy in the North and their mission was to put an end to the guerrilla warfare. Politics was someone else's business.

Our lunch took place in a quiet country pub outside the city. From our entry into Belfast, out to the pub, and back to the Stout home, there was no sign of bombings, soldiers, tanks, rubble, barbed wire, or any of the trademarks of the Troubles. We were to see all of those later.

That evening, the Stouts gave a dinner party for us at which a mixture of Unionists and the opposing political party, the SDLP (Social Democratic Labour Party), Protestants and Catholics gathered and conversed amicably throughout the evening.

The Lord and Lady Mayoress of Belfast were there, both young and attractive, she Catholic, he Protestant, proving that "mixed marriage" *is* possible, and respectable, in Northern Ireland; Harry West, the red-faced leader of the Unionist Party, a farmer by profession and affable in conversation; Lord Melchet, wealthy, handsome, a political activist and, so I'm told, chased by all the single women in Northern Ireland; Paddy Devlin, Catholic and SDLP, with his rotund body and little snub nose looking like an Irish elf; Colonel and Mrs. Tony Wilson, of the British military forces in Belfast. (Of all the people I spoke to that evening, he, ironically, seemed to have the most sensible and compassionate view of the problems facing Northern Irelanders.) There were other guests, making a lively, talkative, scintillating party, enhanced by Mrs. Stout's magnificent Italian dinner, but one knew, as the genial talk flowed back and forth, and social graces covered long-held animosities, what deep and bitter feelings animated the two groups in the Stouts' home that night.

On Thursday, Bill, Charlie Stout and I drove to Derry. En route, we stopped in Armagh to visit John Taylor, another Unionist leader who is running for the European Parliament this year. At few years ago, he was hit in the face and neck by IRA machinegun fire while seated in his car. With his jaw broken into numerous pieces, it was only by a miracle of modern surgery that he was saved. One might think such a close brush with death (and the reality of violence) would have set John Taylor on the path for peace among his fellow Irishmen, but he seemed hard and unmoving politically, telling us that violence always was and always would be a way of life in Northern Ireland. Surely, such an outlook builds walls as treacherous as the high barbed wire strung along the streets of Belfast, separating Catholic from Protestant neighborhoods across the city.*

From the Taylors' home, we made a short tour of the city, so lovely and proud and gray, sitting high on a hill overlooking the green, rolling countryside. We visited the Protestant and Catholic cathedrals, both magnificent churches built to honor Christ and to glorify the Christian spirit, a spirit now defiled by the hatred and divisiveness that religion has "inspired." The red hats of former cardinals hang in solemn rows from the ceiling of the Catholic cathedral. To me, they symbolize the bloodshed spilled in Northern Ireland under the name of religion.

We drove on through the lovely countryside toward Derry, admiring the neat farms, the well-maintained roads, and the clean, fresh, unlittered landscape.

Much is made in Ireland of the contrast between the well-maintained farms of Northern Ireland, with their small, manicured gardens, freshly whitewashed cottages, sturdy barns and air of prosperity, hard work and care, and the general neglect, weedy, straggling yards, mucky barnyards and rusting machinery that litter some of the farms one sees in the Republic. While it is a pleasure to see those farms in the North—the result of all that good, Calvinistic dedication, duty, thrift and hard work—one can only wonder if there is something in that same strict spirit, a frowning soul perhaps, that has contributed to the unyielding, uncompromising political attitude of northern Unionism.

The road led us at lunchtime into Derry, a sad, beleaguered city perched on a steep hill overlooking the River Foyle. In January 1972, the

*John Taylor was elected to the European Parliament in July 1979.

infamous "Bloody Sunday" took place in Derry, when British troops opened fire on unarmed demonstrators, shooting and killing thirteen Catholic youths. (A few days later, as the young men were being buried in Derry, an enraged mob burned down the British embassy in Dublin to protest the massacre.)

The wounds of Bloody Sunday are slow to heal, and the people in Derry have paid for that wanton act of killing through a dark decade and more of bloodshed, bombings and military occupation. It has become a broken city; its "Bogside," the Catholic neighborhood of Derry, is a vandalized ghetto where suspicion and hatred have replaced community care.

A soldier had been shot the night before we arrived, so the Bogside was teeming with military trucks, saracens, armed foot soldiers, and the general air of a city at war. A large sign posted at the entry into Derry reads ominously: "If you have any information about MURDER OR EXPLOSIONS, ring . . ."

We met John Hume, the indefatigable and tireless leader of the SDLP, in a restaurant on the city's outskirts. He, too, is running for the European Parliament in the next election.* His fair and honest voice, his willingness to conciliate and compromise, and his total dedication to seeing a Northern Ireland free from bigotry and ancient prejudices make John Hume one of Ireland's most respected politicians. He and those like him work bravely, in the shadow of fear and impending violence, risking their personal safety for the cause they believe in. Alas, there aren't enough like John Hume in Northern Ireland.

On the road back to Belfast, we stopped to see the "Giant's Causeway." One of the most famous sights in Ireland, this unique rock formation of 37,000 columns jutting out to sea off the coast of County Antrim was made by volcanic action some sixty million years ago. As the lava flow slowly cooled, the many-sided columns were formed. At least that's what scientists say today. I tend to go for the older explanation: Finn McCool, the famous Irish giant of legend, wanted to walk to Scotland. Not wanting to wet his feet en route, he built the steps himself.

Leaving the Causeway behind us, we drove around the Port na Spaniagh, which takes its name from the wreck of the Spanish galleon *Gerona,* the flagship of the Spanish Armada, which was blown to this small bay during a raging storm that scattered the fleet after Drake's victory. All hands went down at sea on the *Gerona* in 1588. In recent years, pieces of the wreck have been uncovered by divers.

The entire coast of Northern Ireland is breathtakingly beautiful. It should be—and one day will be—a natural and lucrative tourist attraction and a place where Irish and foreigners alike can come to admire its beauty and peace.

*John Hume also won a seat in the European Parliament.

                                    * * *

On Friday morning, Mrs. Stout and I went to the offices of Sidney
Stewart, who runs the Volunteer Services of Belfast. He has served as the
Belfast connection for Ireland's Children, a small American foundation
on whose board I serve. Its energies and money are devoted to projects
involving children in Northern Ireland. It is a nonpartisan, nonsectarian
foundation that tries, with limited funds, to give help where it is most
needed.

Mr. Stewart took us out to Turf Lodge, a predominantly Catholic
housing estate in Belfast which had been especially hard hit by violence.
The IRA have a training center there, and although one of the nuns who
works as a social worker in the flats told us that the center isn't as active
as it was a few years ago, it still attracts the restless, angry young men
who make up the roll call of IRA Provos.

The blocks of flats, which, if well-maintained, would be a passably attractive housing development, are defiled with broken windows, Provo
graffiti, and litter. We went inside one of the flats to visit a woman friend
of our guide. She was beset by family troubles (a teenage daughter constantly in trouble, a retarded son, a husband who can't find work . . . the
themes of women all over Turf Lodge). Her flat would have been a pleasant home if she had gone to work on it with pail and mop, duster and
broom. But constant worry, money troubles and fear use up one's energy
and leave no incentive for mundane housework.

As we walked back to the car, the nun asked if I was afraid to be in
Turf Lodge, and I answered truthfully that I had no sense of fear there.
"That's good," Sister said. "You shouldn't have anything to be afraid of.
The only thing that could happen to you would be to find yourself
caught in a crossfire."

"Gee, thanks, Sister." I laughed and we climbed into our car. She told
me that the children in Turf Lodge have been emotionally maimed by
the decade of violence that has been their daily sideshow. Now, during a
relatively peaceful period, they are too "hyped up" for usual child's play,
and resort to vandalism and destructive pranks.

We visited a small training project, organized by the nuns, whose aim
is to teach the young wives and mothers of Turf Lodge the fundamentals
of cooking, housekeeping, child care and sewing. Most of these young
women married as teenagers (there's nothing else for a teenager to do in
areas such as theirs), and they are woefully lacking the skills and training
they need to run their homes. They enjoy their mornings at the project
(their babies are cared for at a day-care center funded by Ireland's Children), but sadly, their frustrated, out-of-work and immature young husbands, for whom life offers no such diversions, often resent their participation in any activity that takes them out of their homes and "betters"
them. When one young wife learned how to make a casserole at the
project and proudly brought it home to feed her family, her unhappy

young husband threw it out the window, telling her she was getting too "uppity."

We left Turf Lodge and drove across town to the Ardoyne, another Catholic ghetto, and the site of some of the worst bombings, shootings and murders. The narrow, cobbled streets crisscrossed a devastated area of burned-out houses, broken glass, litter and boarded-up windows. Rows and rows of identical brick housefronts, so tiny they looked like grubby dolls' houses, lined the streets, their small doorways opening right onto the sidewalk.

Bridie Maguire was waiting for us outside her door when we drove up. "You're late," she said. "When I heard there was a bombing across town I thought you might have been involved. Come on in my wee home." For once that overused Belfast adjective furnished an apt description. Wee it certainly was, but it was warm and cozy and filled with her handsome children.

Bridie and her husband, with the help of their Ardoyne neighbors, founded the Herbert Street Youth Club when the Troubles began. They took over an empty house on the block, turned it into a miniature disco, sports club, craft center and general meeting place for the area's youth. "We had to keep them off the streets," Bridie explained, "and try to give them something to do."

The club was pitifully inadequate; its four tiny rooms, two up and two down, were crammed with Ping-Pong tables, sporting gear, crafts, records, games and an old record player. An American teenager, coming out of a well-equipped community center or youth club, would have been stunned at the lack of space and facilities. Money and jobs are scarce commodities in the Ardoyne. But Bridie Maguire, indomitable, enthusiastic, and caring, was not dismayed.

"Sure it's too small, but we're going to build a proper one," she told us. And we walked down the street, past her house, and turned into a littered alleyway that led into a big, vacant lot.

"Right here," Bridie said, waving her arm toward the empty, dismal site, encircled by rolled loops of barbed wire (the visible barriers that separate Catholic from Protestant neighborhoods in Belfast are called "peace walls"). Bridie's brown eyes sparkled in the cold, gray mist of the autumn afternoon, and she hugged her torn cardigan closer around her. "Somehow we'll get the money, and we'll build a fine wee center here for the kids. We'll have basketball courts and games rooms; a place for them to dance and a place for the wee ones to play." I believe she'll do it. I don't know how, but I know she will.

Later, at dinner, we met with the secretary of the Alliance Party, the nonsectarian party in Northern Ireland that appeals to middle-class liberals and university people. In theory, it sounds so reasonable, so right and so fair. But is has very little support across the country. The North of Ireland is not a reasonable or fair place.

Boys from the Ardoyne outside Bridie's club

Bridie herself, on the site of the new club

Across town again and into the center of the city, where the streets are cordoned off and everyone entering or leaving the area must submit to a thorough search of his person and his car. Announcing to the young British soldier at our entry station that we were the American ambassador and his wife made no difference. We were politely ordered to get out of the car and were searched thoroughly, as was our car. We were on our way to meet with some of the city's leading businessmen, journalists and publishers. Their conversation did nothing to dispel my deepening gloom about the country's future. One of them said: "Anyone caught carrying a gun or making explosives should be shot *on the spot.*" He then went on to say, with chilling enthusiasm, that if he ever came home and found that his wife had been "molested" he would take a gun and personally shoot her attacker.

"But then you would be carrying a gun," I pointed out. He looked annoyed at being interrupted by a member of the sex whose virtue he was so enthusiastically defending, so I sank back into my tea and wee biscuits.

We drove home at the end of our fourth day, weary, disheartened, bewildered, and very happy to be back in the "Republic" of Ireland. Or the Twenty-six Counties, or the South, or the Free State, or Southern Ireland, or Ireland or (so dear to the hearts of BBC announcers) "Eire."

NOVEMBER 12

Arthur Schlesinger, one of Bill's professors during his graduate school days at Harvard, his wife Alexandra, and Jean Kennedy Smith are all staying with us this weekend; they are enjoying Ireland and are fun to have around because they're so enthusiastic and interested in the things we show them and tell them about Ireland. We drove Alexandra by the square where her ancestor Robert Emmet, the Irish patriot, was hanged, drawn and quartered in 1803. The American Irish Foundation is planning to have a plaque erected on the site to mark the "occasion."

We took them to a drinks party at the home of Harold Clarke and Iain Maclachlan this morning. Harold and Iain have lovingly restored a Georgian house on North Great Georges Street, doing much of the work on it themselves. The party was in honor of Colleen McCullough, the author of *The Thorn Birds,* this year's enormous best-seller about life in Australia. I've read it and enjoyed it, so I was eager to meet her. She's full of talk, big, vivacious and exuberant; my own parochial idea of an Australian.

Another guest at the party, one of Bill's ambassadorial colleagues, sidled up to me, gave me a little poke in the ribs and said: "I think we

145

both enjoy the same things, no?" *I* thought he was talking about *The Thorn Birds,* and said enthusiastically, "Oh, yes, I just loved it!" But he winked broadly, as they say, and said: "That's not what I mean." What do you say to that?

I just smiled and said: "You're in love with life, Excellency," and left him sipping his champagne.

NOVEMBER 20

I went to a luncheon party today hosted by Senator Gemma Hussey, a political activist and feminist whom I have met on several occasions. She had ten of her friends, all feminists, all attractive, intelligent, amusing women. I felt very much at home with them, almost like being back with my old Gramercy Street friends. They talked about women in Ireland, about the feminist movement here, about men's relationships with women, the role of women in Irish politics and about current political gossip. One of the women told me she felt very much out of the mainstream of Irish life, and judging from the range of her interests, her staunch feminist views, and her very liberal attitudes on social issues, I would think that she would feel more at home in Washington or New York than in Dublin. I enjoyed myself enormously, laughed a lot, learned much and am looking forward to attending the Women's Political Seminar on December 2, which they talked of today.

THANKSGIVING DAY: 1978

The turkeys aren't plump enough. We have to wait for Christmas. I made a brief talk about the history of Thanksgiving on the Gay Byrne radio show this morning. I had a terrible cold but my voice held out. Just at the end, I remembered to wish all Americans in Ireland who might be listening to the show a very happy Thanksgiving. It is always a lonely feeling to celebrate a national feast day in a country away from home. We celebrated at the residence by having fifty American students from the School for Irish Studies to our house for a wine and cheese party before they all went on to a real Thanksgiving dinner. When they left, we sat down with the boys to Anne's turkey and dressing, and all the trimmings.

NOVEMBER 24

We left this morning for a weekend near Cashel, in Tipperary, to stay in the lovely Georgian country home of our friends Bill and Joan Roth. En route, scarcely out of Dublin, our car broke down. We invaded a small farmhouse to ask if we could use the telephone to call the local garage. We didn't want to say "who we were," so we just sat and chatted with the farmer and his wife while we waited for the repair truck. Our host, however, had a very keen ear, and I hadn't said more than two sentences when he said: "I heard your voice yesterday on the Gay Bryne Show. You must be the wife of the American ambassador."

NOVEMBER 29

Bill is in Dundalk for a few days, so I went by myself to Charter Day at King's Hospital, Liam's school, to hear Archbishop Simms, the Anglican Archbishop of All Ireland, give the Charter Day address. There was not a single woman on the platform, among the trustees and school officials, although it is a coed school. I must write a note to the headmaster, Dr. Magahy, and point that out. It isn't a good example to set for the girls.

Dr. Magahy took Irish mothers to task during his speech to the parents. "Twelve-year-old boys and girls come here to begin their secondary education," he said. "The girls do well and seem to manage their personal lives efficiently and easily. The boys are hopeless. They lose their socks. They forget to brush their teeth. They can't keep track of their sports' gear. They have no idea how to sew on a button. Their mothers have coddled them, and made babies of them, and waited on them hand and foot, so we end up with a class of young adolescents who can't care for themselves."

That is *so* true. I've been in many an Irish household where I've seen the little girls of the family running errands, cooking, cleaning up, and generally assisting a great deal in the running of the place, while their brothers sit in the corner and grin and the Mammy seems to think that's a wonderful contribution to make.

During Magahy's speech, I saw many a father nudge his wife and roll his eyes, while the mothers all smiled sheepishly at one another.

I reported on that speech later in the evening, when I was attending a farewell party for Eleanor Ridge, the embassy consul who is leaving Dublin this month. An Irish friend at the party said: "Oh, he's absolutely right. I remember being at university as an architecture student with my brother. We both took the same course of studies. We would come home together, and my mother would say to me: 'Make the tea, dear, for your poor tired brother,' while she would sit him down in front of the fire, all but wagging her tail with slippers in hand." It was told as a funny story, but it had bitter overtones.

Another friend who had been listening, chimed in: "Oh, that's nothing. I have six brothers. My mother used to drive them home from rugby matches, let them out at the front door, carry their muddied rugby boots and gear into the house herself through the back door, scrub off the muck, wash the jerseys, and dash upstairs to have their tea ready when they got out of their hot baths. *I* was ironing my own dresses by the time I was eleven."

DECEMBER 2

I was out early on this Saturday morning to attend the Women's Political Association's annual Seminar. I went with Renée Rutledge, and she introduced me to many of the women there. The WPA is an organization of politically oriented women who came together several years ago and formed the association to create and sponsor more political activism among Irish women. Senator Gemma Hussey; Mavis Arnold, a journalist; Hilary Pratt, who, with her husband, runs the Avoca Weavers; Tricia Crisp, an American woman living in Dublin and working in real estate; Audrey Conlon, who is active in public relations work, are a few of the women I've met who are active in the WPA and have drawn me into their circle of friendship. "The Sisterhood," as they laughingly call themselves, fight a gallant—and uphill—battle for women's rights in Ireland. Although men in Ireland will give lip service to the cause of equal rights for Irish women, I don't think most of them, in their heart of hearts, believe in it. They have been spoiled by their mothers, separated from girls as children in single-sex schools, watched the examples set by their own fathers, felt threatened by women entering their world and succeeding in it, bothered by having to take on domestic chores at home and encouraged by the Catholic Church, which, despite what it says, still, in Ireland, makes women second-class citizens.

But the women of Ireland play into the roles created for them by their menfolk. Far too many of them are passive, loving, hardworking creatures, serving the physical needs of husband, family and home, not giving themselves the opportunity to enrich their lives outside of their homes, not feeling secure enough to have an opinion on matters outside the domestic sphere, not taking the trouble to inform themselves about issues that directly shape their lives: political issues, economic policy, farm policy, education, religion. Too often, they "leave it to the men," and the men are happy to be their caretakers.

Women such as those who are active in the WPA and in other women's groups are the exception to this generalization. But in Ireland, as in America and elsewhere in the world, a growing number of younger women, just out of school, beginning their careers or their families or both, are reaping the fruits of the movement for the liberation of the spirit of women and for their equal rights in the world. They have strong opinions about what they want from the world, what their roles should be, and what kind of roles their husbands or boyfriends should play in their lives. And it is a far different role from that their fathers played with respect to their mothers.

A newspaperman in Dublin recently wrote a funny column about seeing a young father pushing his baby in its pram down Baggot Street one sunny morning. "I never thought I would live to see the day," he said, "when a young man in Ireland would be seen pushing a pram for all the world to see!"

In 1970, the Irish government established a Commission on the Status of Women. They published their report in 1973, and it was a far-reaching survey on the needs and aspirations of women in Ireland. In 1977, Gemma Hussey, newly-elected to the Irish Senate, and a strong advocate of women's rights in Ireland, reappraised the Report, and evaluated the progress which had been made since the original report was published. She found that real steps forward had been achieved since the publication of the report in 1973; she also found a great many areas in which women's political, social and economic life in Ireland was stultified. For instance:

Although it is no longer possible for a husband to put his wife and family out of their home (both spouses must consent to the sale of the house), a wife might find out that she is not entitled to the money from the sale if she has not been co-owner.

The sale or advertising of contraceptives is still illegal in Ireland, although the Supreme Court ruled in 1974 (in the McGee case) that the *importation* of contraceptives is legal. The dilemma presented by those two conflicting laws is usually solved by a customer leaving a "donation" at the door of a Family Planning Clinic where contraceptives may be fitted or obtained.

Although the majority of schools in Ireland are still single-sex, coed schools are increasing rapidly. In January 1976, there were 371 coed secondary schools as against 466 single-sex schools.

Girls are still offered far fewer honours math and science courses in their schools, and are therefore still far less qualified to go into engineering, science, or medicine when they prepare for university.

Only about 11 percent of married women in Ireland work outside their homes. There has, nevertheless, been an increase over the last few years of working married women, although it is frowned upon in many areas. (When we first arrived in Dublin, there was a protracted exchange of Letters to the Editor in the *Irish Times* on the pros and cons of "working wives." A majority of the contributors seemed to feel that, so long as there was unemployment of any kind in Ireland, a working wife, presuming she is supported by her husband, has no right to "take away" a job from an unemployed "head of household.")

Working couples are taxed as a unit, which gives an unfair advantage to unmarried people who share living quarters. (A new organization called the Married Person's Tax Reform Association, led by Mairead Ui Dhuchain, a Dublin teacher, and Yvonne Scannel, a young lawyer who lectures at Trinity, is preparing a case to take to the Supreme Court to change the country's present system of taxing working wives.)

Participation of women in elective politics is small; 6 women serve in Dáil Eireann (the House of Representatives in the Irish Parliament) alongside 142 men. In the Seanad (Senate) 6 women serve with 54 men.*

Divorce is illegal in Ireland. The financial and emotional strain of a broken marriage more often falls on the woman, and many an Irish scoundrel still takes the boat to England and begins a new life there, leaving his wife and children behind to cope as best they can. Even though Ireland has a Reciprocal Agreement with Britain to order a husband to continue paying maintenance, it is a difficult law to enforce.

There are organizations working to change these conditions. The Dublin Well Woman Centre opened this year, and although it was picketed by the League of Decency, it seems to be thriving. About 150 women a week are served there through family planning counseling, cervical smear tests, breast examinations, the pregnancy testing service, and a premenstrual tension clinic. They also perform thirty to forty vasectomies a week on men in the under-forty age group.

Although I never see advertisements for the Centre in the papers, word of mouth is a powerful communicator in Ireland, and women who need its services have found out about it.

Earlier this autumn, five thousand women took part in a march organized by the Rape Crisis Group. Plans are being organized to set up a rape crisis center. Anne Kavanagh, chairwoman of the Council for the Status of Women, presented a Submission on Rape to the minister for justice, who said he would "study it carefully."

We have an American senator spending a few days with us in the Park. He inadvertently turned on our alarm system this afternoon by pushing the wrong button. As Dublin gardai pulled up the driveway, he appeared at the top of the stairs, resplendent in a silk paisley bathrobe, and said: "Did I do that? All I wanted was a cup of tea."

DECEMBER 9

We gave a big fund-raising party here for the Irish Georgian Society. Ten newly published Irish authors came and signed copies of their books, which the society sold to the guests. It was an enormous success, and a wonderful way to get through a lot of Christmas shopping in a hurry. It was also a pleasant party, except for one bizarre incident:

Kitty Horgan, one of the residence staff, called me away from a group

*In the autumn elections of 1982, a record fourteen women were elected to the Dáil. Gemma Hussey was re-elected to her seat in the Dáil and was named minister of education in the new Fine Gael government. She is the first woman to serve in this position.

of people in the drawing room and whispered: "There's a woman in the ladies' cloak room who is *very* upset. She says her mink coat has been stolen!"

I hurried with Kitty into the little sitting room adjoining our ladies "loo," and there she was in a good fit of near-hysteria. Her husband was there, too, comforting her, but as soon as I walked in, he said: "I think you should have a special room for the furs, and keep them under lock and key."

"It's brand-new," the guest wailed. "I'll hold the embassy totally responsible."

"Of course," I soothed her, wondering at the same time if this might not be a new kind of con game. Respectable-looking couple slips into large embassy party, reports stolen fur, collects insurance.

I looked questioningly at Kitty. "I remember it, all right," she confirmed. "I hung it up right here. I'm sure we'll find it if we look again more carefully." The room was overloaded with wraps of all kinds.

"I tell you, it *isn't* there. I've looked and looked, and so has my husband." She began to weep.

"Let's look again," I said to Kitty. "You start at that end, I'll start here." Everytime we came to a mink coat, we pulled it out and showed it to our guests, but put it back when they shook their heads.

Finally Kitty said: "This is it," and took a lovely, long mink from a hanger. The woman's eyes widened and she turned on a beatific smile, grabbed the coat and held it to her as if it were a long-lost child.

"Sorry for the trouble," her husband muttered. "She's very fond of that coat."

Stranger things than that have happened at the embassy with fur coats, though. Someone left a beautiful blond mink stole at our chancery downtown during a large function and never did claim it. As weeks passed, a member of the staff telephoned as many women as she could who had attended, but we never came up with the owner.

DECEMBER 11

After a black-tie dinner for twenty-four guests tonight, we had a round-table discussion on the pros and cons of Wood Quay, the most controversial local issue in Ireland at the moment.

Sparks were soon shooting round the table.

Wood Quay is a site along the River Liffey, between Winetavern Street and Fishamble Street, which has been designated for a new municipal office building. In 1974, before the building began, a group of archaeologists from the National Museum began to dig there, looking for artifacts. Their enthusiasm grew as they began to unearth the riches of an early Viking settlement, dating back to the eleventh century, filled with the remains of village life: jewelry, articles of clothing, pottery, bronze, hair combs, gold adornments, bones, the prow of a Viking ship jutting out one side of the wall of the site.

As the digging continued, outlines of the houses and streets of the settlement became apparent. Valuable knowledge of the era was gained as relic after relic was brought up, much of it totally preserved throughout the centuries by being covered in mud and water.

From the quality of the craftsmanship in many of the items, it became obvious that the Vikings of that era had much more sophisticated skills than had previously been believed.

A crew of archaeologists worked against the clock to complete their excavations and stay one step ahead of the bulldozers, which were coming in to start digging for the building's foundation. Finally, a citizens' group called Friends of Medieval Dublin, led by Father F. X. Martin, a professor of history at UCD, began exerting pressure both on the Museum to continue their search and on the Dublin Corporation to give up Wood Quay as a building site and allow it to remain an archaeological park. They took their case to court, and in June of this year Justice Liam Hamilton of the High Court declared a portion of the site a national monument under the terms of the 1930 National Monuments Act.

Preservationists were elated and thought they had struck a victory for conservation, history, archaeology and Dublin's past. They were to be sorely disappointed, however, when they realized that Justice Hamilton's decision stated he was not "expressing any view on whether other interests, commercial or economic, might not require the site to be destroyed. Such a decision was one for the Commissioners of Public Works under the same National Monuments Act of 1930." And so the commissioners gave permission for the corporation to go ahead with the work. Father Martin is trying once again to get an injunction to stop the bulldozers. The Friends of Medieval Dublin and all of those who are dedicated to the cause of conservation are devastated by the decision. Others believe that the site is not valuable enough to be saved. ("Who wants to look at someone else's eight-hundred-year-old garbage," is how one city councilman put it.)

The anti–Wood Quay viewpoint was expressed at our table tonight by Harold O'Sullivan, who is the president of the Irish Congress of Trade Unions and is also head of the clerical workers union that includes many municipal workers who would have offices in the new building. The pro–Wood Quay position was defended by Carmencita Hederman, a city councilwoman and, along with her sister, Consuelo O'Connor, a tireless defender of the city's heritage.

It was a lively discussion; people are not unemotional about the Wood Quay issue. But we all parted amicably at the evening's end.

One of the things I find most frustrating about being an ambassador's wife is that here in Dublin, as in Washington or anywhere else I have ever lived, I soon get deeply involved in the community of which I am a part, its political, cultural and educational life, and it doesn't take long for me to have opinions and sometimes strong emotions about one side or another of an issue.

On Wood Quay, for instance, I am appalled that any city would even dream of letting such a fascinating, historic and valuable part of its heritage be destroyed by an office building. Dublin has many empty sites that could be used just as well. Once Wood Quay is covered up, it is lost forever, a part of Ireland's history that every schoolchild, every adult and every tourist should visit. The site alone, even if there were not archaeological ruins on it, should be left as it is to maintain the magnificent, uninterrupted view from the river of Christ Church Cathedral.

But as a diplomat's wife, I can't voice opinions on these local issues or take one side against the other. So I have to egg the guests on to battle, while I sit on the sidelines, and, after they have all gone home, I make Bill my captive audience while I rant and rave. And keep this journal.

DECEMBER 18

The Christmas season is here again. Went to a wonderful party tonight given by the Lord Mayor and Mrs. Paddy Belton at their mansion on Dawson Street. The house looked wonderful, lit up magnificently and decorated for Christmas. After an elegant and sumptuous dinner, we all danced in a makeshift disco, with strobe lights and good music. The entire diplomatic corps was there, and I knew each of us appreciated being entertained by the Lord Mayor. I have heard a few foreign diplomats here say they feel that Dublin doesn't do a lot for its diplomatic corps. Never having served anywhere else, I have no basis for comparison, but I do think that an Irish version of THIS, that wonderful organization in Washington (headed at one time by our good friend Paula Jeffries) would be a useful project in Ireland. "THIS" stands for "The Hospitality and Information Service"; it is entirely run by volunteers and dispenses just what its name says to hundreds of diplomatic families in Washington. Cooking exhibits, classes on how to shop in a large American supermarket, talks and lectures by men and women prominent in many fields of American life, small family brunches, large dinner dances are all part of the services dispensed by THIS. I have often heard diplomats in Washington express deep gratitude to the women in the organization for enriching their stay in that city. Here in Dublin, the American Women's Club plays that role to some extent, but of course it embraces only the American community in Ireland.

Ambassadors and their wives have the way paved for them, but younger, less-well-paid and less-experienced foreign service personnel can find life in a new country and strange city bewildering indeed.

I invited Mrs. Patrick Hillery, the president's wife, and their eight-year-old daughter, Vivian, to tea this afternoon, not as "official" visitors, but simply as neighbors. The tree is up in our house and all the Christmas decorations are out, and it's the season for neighborly visits.

Since I can't provide any small girls of my own, I invited the daughters of some of the residence staff, as well as a few friends with young girls.

After a rather stiff beginning, while the little girls all sat in a row and looked at one another, I decided to break the ice for them by taking them to see all the decorations, leaving their mothers behind in the drawing room to visit.

The dining room, freshly painted this very week, looked especially beautiful. A log fire blazed in the fireplace, the mantel was covered with holly and fir boughs, and a large, golden, papier-mâché Christmas bell hung from the Waterford chandelier.

As we left the dining room, I pulled the enormous, heavy double wooden doors closed behind me. The girls were all in a cluster by my side. Just as I closed the door, I heard a terrific ripping, tearing sound, and one of the doors, put back onto its hinges that day, came ripping away from the wall, falling foward and finally landing with an almighty crash flat on the floor of the drawing room, missing Vivian and the other little girls by inches.

The dust settled and our screams subsided; staff came running from all directions. The girls thought it was marvelously funny and exciting. I was limp with fright. My hands were still shaking as I rejoined the ladies for tea, but at least we had accomplished one thing. The girls were giggling together like little magpies in the corner; nothing like a shared near-disaster to create instant friendships!

One of our favorite evenings of the year, the residence staff party. This year I was prepared and didn't shame myself by my pathetic lack of talent. I wrote a long series of verses about "The Night Before Christmas" at the residence, working in the names of all the staff. Gerry, Maeve, Willy, and Margaret all sang. Christopher recited a poem, Colm did "Paddy McGinty's Goat" again, without which it wouldn't be Christmas. David sang "The Day Delany's Donkey Won the Half-Mile Race," Siobhán Noctor played the piano, little Michael O'Donohoe sang and recited, Rosemary and Ursula sang a duet. Oh, what a talented lot we are. Before the evening was out, we were all on our feet, doing a rather cock-eyed version of "The Siege of Ennis," the Irish answer to the Virginia reel, with Maeve's mother pounding out the piano for us.

The papers say this has been the wettest December in Ireland since 1930. When a large lake began forming in our backyard a few weeks ago, I believed it. It's also been one of the coldest months: ice and snow, zero temperatures, high winds, sleet, hail, and now, more snow.

The day arrived when we had to make a decision about the turkeys. Michael O'Donohoe came in yesterday with a long face and a woebegone expression replacing his usual cheery smile. "I can't do it, Mrs. Shannon," he said, looking almost ready to cry. Michael had taken care of the turkeys since their arrival. When he lets them out of their pen for a "stroll in the garden" they follow him everywhere. "Sean Smith says he'll do it."

So Sean, who also works here at the residence, was busy at it all morning. No one dares venture into the farmyard. We hear the noises from afar. David suggests that we put the flags at half-mast.

Finally, the deed was done. Sean brought two fine, plump birds into the kitchen to show Anne. She thought we should send them out to Mr. Gogarty, our butcher, to have them cleaned, but *I,* with all the confidence of the unskilled, said: "Nonsense! We'll do the job ourselves. It's easy. It's all written down right here in *The Joy of Cooking,* step by step." Anne looked doubtful, but I rolled up my sleeves and tried to infect her with my enthusiasm.

" 'First,' " I read, " 'grab the bird firmly, and break the leg at the knee.' "

I looked at Anne. "Where's the knee?"

Anne peered at the scrawny leg. "I didn't even know turkeys *had* knees," she said.

"Well, never mind. Just break it anywhere. We have to pull out the tendons."

"How do I break it?"

I read on. "It doesn't say. Maybe Dennis knows." Dennis had wandered into the kitchen to see what we were up to, and we grabbed him before he could escape. He put the leg on the edge of the table and gave it a mighty wrench. It broke clean off.

"There you go!" I cried. "Nothing to it. Now. 'Pull out the tendons.' "

"With what?" Dennis asked.

"Try the pliers," I said, fishing them out of the tool box under the sink.

Dennis stared at the leg. "Which are the tendons?"

I read again from the book. "It says there are four of them, so whatever looks like a matched set of four must be tendons," I replied. Dennis got hold of something stringy, and pulled. It came out easily.

"There you go!" I was triumphant again. "Now pull out the

other three." They wouldn't move. I went upstairs and got my eyebrow tweezers and we got one more out, but the last two remained firmly in place.

"Never mind," I said. "Let's move on." I picked up the book.

" 'Cut off the head, immediately tie up the two main veins so they won't drain, and pull out the neck.' "

I looked around the table. Brian and Kitty had joined us by this time. There were no volunteers.

"Okay. I'll cut off the head. Dennis, you be ready to tie up the two main veins immediately. Anne, you get set to pull out the neck. All set. Let's go."

I took our heaviest kitchen knife and gave a mighty whack to the head. It came off, and blood spurted everywhere.

"Dennis, quick, tie the veins," I cried, holding my hand over the gaping, bleeding hole. Dennis looked green.

"Where are they?" he asked in a whisper.

"Never mind. Let's just pull out the neck." Anne took hold of the neck and pulled as hard as she could. Her hands and arms were covered with blood. "It's stuck or something," she said. "It won't move."

Brian and Kitty both grabbed on with Anne, and all three tugged. Dennis was slowly edging toward the door. Brian's foot slipped in a pool of blood on the floor and he sat down heavily, pulling the turkey down on top of him. Kitty, Anne and I began to laugh helplessly, as the poor massacred turkey lay face down in Brian's lap.

"I've got a good idea," Anne began.

"Never mind. I know what it is," I said, and picked up the telephone.

"Hello, Mr. Gogarty? This is Mrs. Shannon. I was just in the process of cleaning our turkey for Christmas, but I've been called away on urgent business. Do you think you could finish up the job for me?"

DECEMBER 24

We took the boys and our house guests, Bill and Natalie Gorman from Santa Barbara, California, to the Christmas Eve service and carols at St. Patrick's Cathedral. The Cathedral's boys' choir sang gloriously. Natalie, a voice coach and former soprano with the Metropolitan Opera, joined in the hymns with her own special harmony, to the astonishment and delight of the people sitting near us. The singing ended with a magnificent performance of "Hark, the Herald Angels Sing" to the music of Handel's *Judas Maccabeus*. The spirit of Jonathan Swift, who was appointed dean of St. Patrick's in 1713, must have been pleased with the glory of the music on this festive Christmas occasion. The church was packed and overflowing. It is always one of the loveliest nights of the Dublin Christmas season.

CHRISTMAS DAY 1978

We woke to a steady, cold downpour. It lashed against the house and across the lawns all day.

The boys unwrapped presents after breakfast. David received lots of toys and clothes and books, but when Liam and Christopher both opened the boxes with their cowboy boots, and there were none for David, he put his hands on his hips and said petulantly: "Nothing for me, *as usual!*"

We went to mass at the Augustinian Church on Thomas Street and heard Mr. McNulty's boys' choir sing, sweetly and tenderly. At our Christmas dinner, we took pictures of Anne's magnificent, golden turkey (late of County Kildare and decorated for war wounds in the line of duty), and of Dennis bringing in the perfect flaming plum pudding.

Then we put on our rain gear and sloshed around the residence grounds, visiting the Noctors, the O'Donohoes, and the Byrneses, to wish them Merry Christmas. We ended our rounds with Maeve and Dennis, sharing a glass of Christmas cheer in their apartment, and finally we invaded the staff room to wish everyone a Merry Christmas before they sat down to their own turkey dinner.

By four o'clock, it was dark. We drew the drapes in the library, lit a roaring fire, and started a game of Monopoly that seemed to go on forever. The wind howled in the Park all night.

NEW YEAR'S EVE 1978–1979

Liam was the only partygoer among us tonight. Bill and I sat home with the other boys, watched "The Late Late Show," and toasted each other with a glass of champagne at midnight.

"Tell us your funniest joke of 1978," David begged his dad.

He thought for a minute. "Pat and Sean met on the 'El' in New York, after having left County Mayo together nine months before.

" 'How are ya, Sean? Are ya married? Well, I am, so come to us for dinner Monday night. Now listen, here's what you do. You come up a short flight of steps and push the button with our name with your elbow. Back in when the door opens, and look for our name on a line of bells in the lobby. Push our bell with your other elbow, then hop in the elevator and push "4" with your elbow. I'll be outside our flat waiting for you.'

" 'That's grand, Pat, I'll be there. But what's all this elbow business?'

" 'Sure, you're not coming empty-handed, are you?' "

Happy New Year.

1979

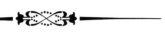

JANUARY 3

Liam and Christopher have gone off to London for a week to visit the Fitzpatricks and Bill and I are spending our holiday doing the sights of Dublin, visiting all the shops and galleries and museums that he hasn't taken the time to see since we've been here.

We met yesterday for lunch at the Rotisserie in the Royal Hibernian Hotel, then just meandered around streets and shops. We finally went into the Shelbourne Hotel Bar about 5 PM to have a drink before we went home. I thought that was *the* place to meet, but maybe the hour was wrong. The only other occupants were a dreary-looking, bedraggled prostitute, smoking and knocking back brandies, and two inexpressibly vulgar young men sitting at the bar and discussing the various methods of sexual intercourse. The prostitute, overhearing the conversation, perked up and combed her long, straggly hair, but to no avail. They left after two quick drinks.

We went back downtown again this afternoon to the Dawson Gallery to look at pictures. We each decided to buy one, he, an aquatint of Yeats's head by Louis le Brocquy; I, a small self-portrait by a young Irish artist named Patrick Harris. We went to celebrate our pictures at the old Wicklow Hotel lounge, and that turned out to be a very cozy and pleasant place, with a fire in the grate and lots of people streaming in and out, meeting friends for a drink.

JANUARY 5

I met the new Indian ambassador's wife this evening at a reception at the nuncio's, and cemented our friendship by whispering to her confidentially that she had a tiny speck of mayonnaise on the side of her nose.

Her thin, graceful fingers quickly rubbed a nostril, and she smiled faintly.

"That is a diamond, my dear," she said.

I wonder if I should try contact lenses.

January 26

A titled guest said to Dennis the other night, at a reception in the residence: "Why in God's name do you serve such *ghastly* tonic water here? The next time I'm invited, please see to it that you serve Schweppe's. It's the *only* thing I can drink with my gin!"

February 2: *Kilkenny*

We've just returned from three days in and around Kilkenny. While we were there, we stayed in Butler House, the former Dower House of Kilkenny Castle, where widowed mothers of the earls of Ormonde retired after the reigning earl took a wife. It's now used as a guest house for the Kilkenny Design Workshop.

We had trouble finding Butler House when we arrived in Kilkenny and went up and down the main street several times. Finally we stopped at a small grocer's shop to ask directions, and his answer to our query could have come straight out of a John B. Keane play about Irish country life:

"Do you know where Butler House is?" I asked the grocer.

"I do."

"Could you tell me where it is?"

"I could."

"Where is it?"

"You just passed it."

"Where?"

"Directly across from the hotel."

"Thank you," I said, and headed for the door.

"You passed it twice," he added, with the sure knowledge that every Irishman has about what happens in his town, even before it takes place.

We both find Kilkenny one of the most vibrant and interesting towns in Ireland. Its citizens have been very active in restoring some of their historic buildings, including, of course, the enormous and handsome Kilkenny Castle in the middle of town.

The founding of the Kilkenny Design Workshop here has focused attention on arts and crafts; a group of Irish people a decade ago decided to organize the skills of Irish craftsmen and women into a profitable business. They brought European craftsmen from Scandinavia to observe what their Irish counterparts were doing and to share their own skills.

The result of the Workshop has been a flowering of artistic and skilled craft activity in and around Kilkenny. Glassmaking, ceramics, weaving, basketmaking, leathercraft, gold and silver smithing—all are done either at the Workshop or in private establishments in the county. Foreign craftspeople from all over Europe have come to work and live at Kilkenny. The Workshop sells their products, both in the town and at the much larger Kilkenny Store in Dublin.

We went to dinner that night with Jim and Maeve King; Jim is the young, attractive director of the Kilkenny Center. He and Maeve represent to me exactly what the Center is all about ... the solid, sound craftsmanship of Ireland plus the new, young, outward-looking generation.

We called upon the Catholic bishop of Ossory, Dr. Birch. His house is so modest that we drove by it twice before we finally realized where it was. I found him a wonderfully sensitive and caring person, deeply involved in helping the itinerants and others in need of social services. He lives very simply himself and has often shared his home with those in need. I admired the fact that, instead of wearing the usual heavy, ornate gold and bejeweled ring of a bishop, he wore a handsome, simple silver ring of modern design made for him by one of the silversmiths at the Design Workshop.

We had a very easy and pleasant visit with him. His simplicity and innate kindness made him a most gracious host. At an official dinner given for us last night, I began to tell a government minister sitting next to me what a wonderful man I thought Bishop Birch was. But before I could utter more than two words, the minister, who is not from Kilkenny, put down his fork impatiently, looked at me with a deep frown on his face and said: "Birch is a crackpot." Sometimes in Ireland, there is a very thin line between being innovative or different and being a "crackpot."

FEBRUARY 6

Sometimes a certain look, a turn of phrase, a smile can captivate you. Today, a one-line announcement in the *Irish Times*'s "Social and Personal" column simply tilted my heart.

"Mr. Brendan Stephens has returned to town."

What a wonderful announcement! It could be the title of a song, the first line of a novel. Had he been away long? Months? Years? Was he away on a holiday? Was he residing in a foreign jail? Will he stay home, once returned? Does he often leave and announce his return? Is he a bachelor alerting hordes of eligible young women of his whereabouts? Does he have debts which he is now ready to face? Is there a duel he has promised to fight upon his return? Is his announcement a warning or simply a glad announcement?

Mr. Brendan Stephens, how I wish I knew you so I could say "Welcome back!"

Despite pessimistic reports from America that marriage is a dying institution, I can happily report that an article in the *Independent* this morning assured us all that marriages arranged by the Knock Introduction Bureau are flourishing.

The Bureau has "200 introductions in progress, and has had 10,790 inquiries." 10,790!!! That's a lot. If you consider that all of Ireland has only about three million people. You can take it from there.

So people are still interested in tying the knot, and the Knock Introduction Bureau is probably as good a way as any (better than some) of getting acquainted.

The story went on to say that there was only "one of each sex in the 60-plus group." That's a relief; I wouldn't want to hear about the Knock Introduction Bureau engaging in any kinky stuff.

Friends have told me about the big marriage market that goes on in Lisdoonvarna each year after the harvest comes in. I think it's mostly a farmers' market, but I'm told that many an eligible catch from the west of Ireland shows up in County Clare's "premier spa" for the festival, and many a lass goes home with an engagement ring in her dreams if not exactly on her finger. I've always wanted to go there for "the crack," but haven't managed it yet. The one time I did get to Lisdoon, the entire tourist population appeared to be in their eighties and holding. They had come to take the mineral baths and drink the waters. Perhaps, though, given Ireland's proclivity for late marriages, they were also there for the marriage market.

I've become a fan of the Wills columns in the newspapers. They say a lot about the personal state of an Irishman's finances, but even more about his life-style and saving and spending habits. Until recently, Ireland was a very poor country with a per capita income higher only than those in Greece and Portugal in Europe. Now that the Irish have joined the Common Market, and with the new industrialization of the country (American, German and Japanese factories are opening up all the time), prosperity has arrived. Even so, I'm amazed by the large legacies. Today's column was headlined: COUNTY MEATH FARMER: £282,773. That's approximately $565,546. And he was a bachelor! Why didn't some Meath spinster land him? On the other hand, he may have had a house full of maiden sisters who would have viewed any inclination on his part to take a wife with the same happy anticipation they might reserve for news of an epidemic of bubonic plague.

Another item today read: SHOP OWNER, DONNYBROOK: £226,000 (or $453,398). Then we come to poor Mrs. X., who died intestate leaving a tidy £5,936 for her family to quarrel over for the next five generations and fatten up a few solicitors in the process.

Andrew, a "factory employee," left £61,580. About $100,000. Andrew had to have been a teetotaler, that's for sure, and probably a tightwad to boot.

A fascinating item closed the Wills column today: COUNT MICHAEL TOLSTOY, RETIRED LANGUAGE TEACHER, COUNTY WICKLOW: £28,990.

FEBRUARY 15: *Kerry*

Despite a snowfall last night, which has left the roads glazed with ice in places, we went off this morning for our official tour of Tralee in County Kerry. We visited the huge power station on the Shannon River, near Tarbert, en route, then stopped in to visit the *Kerryman*, Tralee's own newspaper, and ended our day with Bishop McNamara, in Killarney. We're staying at the Aghadoe Heights Hotel, with a magnificent view from our room of the lake and the misty mountains in the distance.

FEBRUARY 16

Our first stop this morning was at the Burlington Mills factory for a tour and lunch with the managers and their wives. I'm always impressed when we visit American factories in Ireland because the manager who takes us around invariably knows each employee by name and will stop and chat one up, or ask a family question of another. The atmosphere seems unfailingly cheerful. One apparent result of this style of manager-employee relationship is the lack of strikes at American factories in Ireland. Although the country as a whole has had many strikes while we have been here, most of the factories run by US firms seem to have been exempt.

After lunch, I went off alone to visit the Convent of Mercy elementary school. The nuns and the children knew I was coming and they gave me a really rousing, endearing welcome. All the children lined up on the front walk leading from the sidewalk to the school, holding little American flags and singing.

After a beautiful performance in the auditorium, I made a quick stop in each classroom, where I asked the children questions about Ireland and America. One tiny boy of kindergarten age, with more than his share of freckles and deep blue eyes that already had a twinkle in them, replied, when I asked him where Dublin is: "Sure, isn't everything in Kerry?"

FEBRUARY 20: *Dublin*

Bill and I avoided the "night shift" this evening and slipped out to the Oscar Theatre to see Rosaleen Linehan and Des Keogh, two of Ireland's best comedians, in a musical review with political overtones, called *Just Good Friends*. It was hilarious; I laughed so hard my face hurt. In Ireland, where newspapers and the rest of the media are extremely discreet and cautious about public figures and their private lives, comedians find them fair game and show no mercy in their satiric reviews. Several Irish politicians were "murthered" in the show tonight, including one who was satirized in a song about giving up smoking, giving up drinking . . . but when it came to girls . . . ah well, sure two out of three sacrifices is a good record.

As everyone already knows, the Irish telephone system would curdle a mother's milk, make a nun turn to drink, and drive a saint to grand larceny. But there's compensation, nevertheless, and stories to be told, thanks to the very vagaries that have created the skittish, whimsical, temperamental instrument in Ireland they call the telephone.

The other day Patrick Wall, a young man who was visiting us from New York, decided to pay a visit to his aged uncle on a farm near Kilmihil, a tiny village in northwest Clare, a place where terms like "urban sprawl" and "industrial pollution" are unknown. Since the uncle doesn't have a car or a telephone, I was worried about Packy getting off the bus in Kilmihil and never finding the farm. I decided to phone the local pub there and ask the owner if he knew the whereabouts of the uncle's farm. Chances were almost certain that he would.

I asked the local operator in Dublin to put me on to "the pub" in Kilmihil.

"Which one, luv?" he asked.

"It's just a tiny village. There's probably just the one."

Loud and incredulous laughter floated over the line. Then he plugged into the local operator in Kilmihil.

"How many pubs you got down there, luv?" he asks.

"Nine," says she.

"Well," he said, coming back to me, "which one will it be?"

I explain my problem to him. We get the Kilmihil operator back on the phone and ask her if she knows Packy's uncle. She doesn't but says that one of the pubs acts as sort of a bus stop, so why not begin with that one. She gets through to the owner, and he does know the uncle. I get on the line and tell him about Packy. Sure he'd be glad to run him out, it's only a matter of a couple of miles. And won't the uncle be pleased to see his young nephew all the way from New York. We chat for a bit and then I thank him and tell him my name and he's thrilled and says won't I say a few words to the daughter and son-in-law, he'll run and get them, so I chat with them, and then I say isn't it too bad that I didn't get the name of the Dublin operator to thank him for helping me out, and a voice comes on the line, unmistakably Dublin, to say to tell the truth he has stayed on the line to make certain that everything worked out all right, which it seems to have, so we all say good-by.

Then there was the time my friend Kay was in hospital last summer and put in a call to her sister in Limerick.

"Hurry up," she says to the operator. "There's a mile-long line here waiting to use the phone."

"Where are you, luv?"

"Vincent's."

"Oh, you're not well, is it?"

"Better," she says.

"And you're calling the sister in Limerick? So you're up from the country then?"

"Right."

"Well now," he says, "I pass by the hospital twice a day on my bicycle, and I could bring you any little thing you might need. Fierce lonely there in the hospital, isn't it?"

"Not so bad," says she, looking at the long line behind her.

"I was in Vincent's two months ago," he continued. "I was in a pub, just off the Green, and there was this fierce fight broke out. I didn't have anything to do with it, mind you, but before I knew what happened, this fellow hit me over the head with a bottle and half broke my skull in two. They left, with me bleeding to death on the footpath in front of the pub. All your fancy folk just stepped over me.

"Finally, these two prostitutes came along and picked me up and put me in a taxi and took me to Vincent's, where I got my head stitched up. If it hadn't been for them, I'd still be bleeding. I've been looking for them ever since, to thank them like, you know."

Kay says that's a grand story, but the line is now two deep and the old woman behind her keeps kind of nudging her in the shoulder.

"I'll put you through now, and don't be thinking about paying for this call. Just talk to the sister as long as you want to. That's better for you than your medicine. When you're sick in hospital, you shouldn't have to pay for phone calls."

When Ann comes on the line, a full minute later, she says to Kay: "The operator says I'm not to worry about you, you sound chipper and they take grand care of you at Vincent's."

FEBRUARY 22

I visited a counseling center for teenagers this morning on the grounds of the Mater Dei Institute. I had coffee with the staff during a break from their appointments and had a chance to talk to them about the kinds of problems they deal with. Although most of their patients are referred from schools, a few simply come in off the street and say: "I need help." Drinking, school truancy, pregnancy and family fights are the common problems. Drugs are not yet a serious problem among teenagers (although I hear more talk of it now than when we first arrived), but chronic and excessive drinking is almost epidemic. The legal drinking age is winked away in many public places. Over and over again, I've seen very young teenagers, scarcely out of childhood, leaning against the side of a pub door, hopelessly drunk, vomiting, then staggering back inside for more. The mother of a fourteen-year-old boy said to me the other day: "We're so proud of our son. He's been on a drink-control program and hasn't touched a drop in three months."

Drinking and sports are so intertwined in Ireland—creating the "macho" image of the burly, two-fisted athlete-drinker—that even the scrawny fourteen-year-old who has never held a hurley stick or kicked a soccer ball gets the message: drinking is manly. To be masculine is to be drunk.

FEBRUARY 23

The itinerant girls from Galway arrived this afternoon for another visit. Many of them were here last year, and I am so impressed with the improvement in their general style. They are much more poised and articulate, better dressed and more at ease. One of the brightest among them is married now and expecting a baby any day. Any hour, from the look of her! She said she really shouldn't have come on the trip but hated to miss it, and anyway if her baby decided to make his arrival today, right here in the residence, it would be an American citizen, born on "American soil."

After tea, they sang songs they had prepared for the occasion, accompanied by a guitar-playing priest who came with them. They have lovely voices, untrained but very clear and true, and they know the words of endless songs. They've continued their sewing and cooking courses with Sister Brigid and brought a white woolen banner they had made for me, embroidered in red and green lettering with "Cead Míle Failte" (A Hundred Thousand Welcomes), the motto of the Irish Tourist Board. I told them I would hang it over the front door whenever they came to call.

Then I told them about a letter I had received after their well-publicized visit the previous year. A man from the midlands had taken a very dim view of my having entertained itinerants and thought I was quite naive about having them in my house.

"The next thing!" he wrote, emblazoning his letter with exclamation points, "you'll have them camped out on your lawn! Stealing from your garden! Letting their horses trample your flowers!" and, he finished darkly, "even worse!"

The girls had a good laugh over the letter, and I assured them I had been spared the predicted evils.

In the evening, we took David and Christopher to the Gaiety Theatre to see one of Ireland's great natural resources, Maureen Potter, whose annual Christmas Pantomime is soon closing. She's a tiny package of talented dynamite whose expended energy during a single performance could launch a rocket to the moon. We went backstage afterward to meet her; she's about as big as David, and she was chipper and fresh and gave no sign that she had spent the past two hours belting out song after song, dancing, high kicking, joking and generally hurtling herself around the stage like a dervish, entertaining everyone from babes to grannies. Christmas wouldn't be Christmas in Dublin without Maureen Potter.

FEBRUARY 26

The taoiseach and Mrs. Lynch came to dinner tonight, our "official" dinner in their honor. We gave them tomato and cheese tarts for starters, followed by beef stroganoff, noodles, peas, salad and *crème brûlée* for dessert. Pasta dishes really haven't gained a foothold in Ireland, and I think tonight must have been the taoiseach's introduction to noodles. He eyed them warily at first, but, once tried, enjoyed a second round of them enthusiastically. He told me that he, not Mrs. Lynch, is the chief cook of the household and although he has no time for cooking now, he enjoys it as a vacation hobby.

He looked tired this evening. The Fianna Fáil "Ardfheis," which is the equivalent of his party's annual convention, was held in Dublin over the weekend and was no doubt a strenuous exercise in party politics. The last three minutes of his major address to the party at the Ardfheis had been cut off television to fit into RTE's (the national broadcasting organization) own program schedule. I was astonished that the television station would cut off the prime minister in an address to the party and the nation, and I should think Mr. Lynch would have been furious.

After dinner, one of the guests, Sean O'Siochain, the head of the Gaelic Athletic Association, gave us a song at my request. Then I asked the taoiseach if he would sing. He has a lovely voice, even though Mrs. Lynch gives him a hard time about his singing. So he said he would dedicate a song to me, and he stood up by the mantel and sang "The Rose of Old San Antone." After he had broken the ice, *everyone* wanted to sing. Archbishop O'Fiach got to his feet and sang "The Old Orange Flute," a Northern Ireland Protestant song. (His driver, out in the kitchen with Anne, said, when the singing began: "He'll be on his feet in no time with 'The Old Orange Flute.' ")

Tom Murphy, the president of UCD, gave us a song, and finally we ended with Mrs. O'Siochain's beautiful and touching "Ireland, Mother Ireland."

The evening sped by. It was midnight before we realized it. I took the Lynches out to the kitchen to meet out staff, which they did with great simplicity, warmth and charm.

Giving an official dinner for the head of government of their host country is a necessary part of the diplomatic function for all ambassadors and their wives. There can be very few countries in the world where such an evening, filled with cabinet ministers, an archbishop and various VIPs could pass with such ease and informality, such warm guests, and such fun. I wonder ... does Mrs. Thatcher have a party piece? Is Indira Gandhi a bundle of laughs? I don't know. But I can imagine many a hostess in many an embassy around the world, kicking off her shoes when the last guest has left, and saying: "Wow! I'm glad *that's* over." This hostess, however, stood in the doorway, waving good-by and wishing that the party could have gone on and on.

MARCH I

All right, lads. Shape up. I just read in the *Independent* this morning that the Law Reform Commission has recommended that "playboys" (I had thought that playboys went out with Porfirio Rubirosa) who get unmarried teenage girls pregnant pay damages to *all* the members of the girl's family, not just to her father, like in the old days. The commission said that the old law, which allows a father to sue a seducer for "loss of his daughter's services," should be scrapped and replaced by a "single family action." (The old law also stipulates that a mother—e.g. "widow"—cannot take an action for seduction of her daughter. What "services" might this little pregnant teenager provide for her father but deny her mother? And who ever thought up such a law in the first place?)

However, as with every proposed social change, these timid recommendations were looked upon with suspicion by some farseeing realists, who said, in effect, never mind what those playboy lads might be up to, the proposal could "encourage impoverished parents to send teenage daughters out on 'gold digging' missions where they allowed themselves to be seduced by wealthy 'playboys.' "

These are the same realists who, when the lads are on the streets at 2 AM, say they're "going home," but when the girls are on the streets at the same hour, say they are "looking for trouble."

MARCH 8

Kay Costelloe brought her aunt to lunch today, a very spry and bright retired Dublin schoolteacher, now into her eighties, who had wonderful stories to tell about her long career. She'd taught Brendan Behan in elementary school and enjoyed reminiscing about him.

"I always knew he was something special," she said. "He used to get in trouble at school, but he could always talk his way out of anything."

I asked her if he wrote anything for her while he was a boy.

"No," she said. "I don't think he ever wrote anything then. But he had a way with words. You wouldn't talk to him for five minutes and not notice it. They just seemed to pour out of him."

I dashed downtown at 6 PM this evening to meet the noted Irish artist Cecil King at the Hibernian Hotel to plan a reception we are going to give at our house for the Contemporary Arts Society. Bill and I are eager to meet more artists and to learn what is going on here in contemporary art. Our old friend Nancy Balfour, who used to be the American editor of the London *Economist,* is president of the British Contemporary Art Society and is coming to Dublin this weekend. We want her to meet some of her Irish colleagues in the arts while she is here.

Cecil and I had a drink in the lobby and planned our party. Then I had to meet Bill at the embassy, where he had been visiting with another artist, "Patrick Ireland" (whose real name is Brian O'Doherty). He wants to open a small museum here in Dublin to house his own private collection of contemporary art, and wants Bill to be a trustee. Their first concern now is to find a suitable site to house the collection.

And then, off to dinner with yet another artist, Gary Trimble, the sculptor and architect responsible for planning and overseeing the work on Charles Haughey's contemporary-style house on one of the Blasket Islands, off the coast of Dingle. Gary and Carol have become good friends of ours during the past year, and although Bill doesn't know it yet, I have commissioned Gary to sculpt a head of Bill for me.

MARCH 20

I was giving Elaine Greenstone, a friend from Washington, a tour of Trinity College this afternoon when the enormous PAYE (Pay As You Earn) demonstration passed us on Nassau Street. The unions organized this demonstration of workers who have income tax deducted from their wages. They are furious because the farmers put so much pressure on the government this year over a proposed farmers' tax, that the government had to back down and ease some of the levy. Farmers have a reputation among the city folk in Ireland for being less than accurate in reporting their income. Since salaried people don't have the opportunity to manipulate their taxes, they naturally feel some resentment of the farmers' ability to do so. In protest, they marched today, 250,000 strong, across Dublin. It was one of the largest demonstrations in the history of Ireland, and as they passed endlessly in front of us, we were struck by the quiet, serious good nature of all the marchers.

During the years of the Vietnam War, the embassy in Ballsbridge, like American embassies across the world, was the target of numerous demonstrations protesting our involvement in the war.

Now the war is over, and for the moment at least, no one is staging a protest. All is quiet and peaceful . . . except for Siobhán.

Siobhán is a woman in her early twenties, a Dubliner. Not unattractive, not politically oriented, not anti-American. She's clean, neat and well-spoken. She just has this one bad habit: she likes to cut down the American flag from its pole in front of the embassy. When asked why, she swears it's not a political protest. She says she just can't resist: "It's like, ya know, takin' dope or something."

In despair, the Marines put the pole on the roof of the building. Siobhán can't reach it, but it's awkward getting up there to raise and lower the flag.

She was warned over and over again, first by the Marines and the security guards, and finally by the gardai, to leave the embassy alone. "If you do something destructive again, it's the courts for you," they warned her.

So she broke the swinging wooden arm that controls access to the parking lot from the driveway. The judge sentenced her to three months in jail.

One morning, I had a phone call from a social worker at the jail, who began by saying: "I know this is an odd request, but it's an odd case. Siobhán doesn't belong in jail. She's not a criminal type and she is associating here with women who are a bad influence on her.

"I was thinking that maybe if you gave her a job at the embassy, it would satisfy her craving to be hanging around there and would be a constructive solution to her problem."

"First of all," I began, "I have nothing to do with hiring people at the embassy. But I can't imagine that anyone there would want to have her. She has created endless trouble for everyone for months and months. Why not get her into a good psychiatric hospital for a while? That would be far more constructive than a job at the embassy."

"She won't go," the social worker explained. "And no psychiatrist thinks she is serious enough to commit against her will."

Siobhán is out of jail and this afternoon, as I passed the embassy on my way to pick up the boys from school, I saw her out in front, swinging upside down on the iron railings around the entrance and making faces at the Marine guard at the door. As she said to the judge who sentenced her: "You should keep me in jail because if you let me out, I'll go right back to the embassy. I just can't resist. It's like, ya know, a magnet. I just love it there, cutting down the flag and all."

This has been a spring of discontent in Ireland. The countrywide post office and telephone strike, which began in February, shows no signs of ending. It's a strange world in which one cannot mail a letter or place an operator-assisted phone call.

Since the dustbinmen are also on strike, garbage is piled high all over town. I assumed they were striking for more money but, as is so often the case with strikes in Ireland, it isn't money they are after, it's better working conditions. I heard a radio interview the other day with the leader of the strike; he said they don't want to work in wet weather (he didn't say whether he had seriously considered immigration to a drier climate) because the raincoats they are issued make them sweat, and that in turn causes chest troubles.

The switchboard operators at the Department of Foreign Affairs are also on strike, making it difficult to reach anyone at that office. The taxis had a one-day strike on March 16; the buses had a slowdown in March as well. The airport joined in with a slowdown on March 16 and 17. All incoming and outgoing planes ran two to four hours late.

Despite the winter doldrums, the strikes, and the cold, wet, gray March weather, my days are brightened by the national debate on the Family Planning Bill that has been introduced in the Dáil by Charles Haughey, the minister for health.

AN IRISH SOLUTION TO AN IRISH PROBLEM, the *Irish Times* headlined. I needed more than the *Irish Times* to clarify the situation for me, so I attended the Dáil to hear the debate.

The *importation* of contraceptives was made legal by a Supreme Court decision, provided they were not being imported for subsequent sale. Mr. Haughey's Irish Solution is to legalize the *sale* of contraceptives, "to control the availability of contraceptives and restrict effectively their supply to certain authorised channels for family planning purposes."

As I understand it, they will have to be authorized by a physician and will be sold only by chemists (pharmacists) when the valid prescription is presented. Only married persons will be authorized to buy them.

The chemists have been polled: "Will you sell contraceptives?" One headline warned: CHEMISTS MAY STEP IN IF DOCTORS OPT OUT. Another reassures: MOST CHEMIST SHOPS WOULD SUPPLY CONDOMS.

In the meantime, the students took the issue into their own hands and installed a contraceptive vending machine in the student union concourse beneath the library at University College Dublin. (Fifty pence for a packet of four. I heard that the most "macho" line among male students on the campus these days is: "Anyone got fifty pence in change?") However, mindful of student morality, college authorities removed the machine. The students didn't take the infringement of their rights lightly: "We regard this incident as an attack on the principle of student union autonomy," a spokesman said. The student government will discuss the matter when it meets next week.

The medical profession, however, has another view: GYMSLIP PREGNANCIES WORRY TOP DOCTORS, warned the *Independent*. I had to phone my friend Renée Rutledge today to ask: "What are 'gymslip' pregnancies?" I had put them in the same category as tubal pregnancies, but I was way off the track. Gymslips are the costumes teenage girls wear for gymnastic classes, and although they are hardly a costume designed to inflame the passions of young males (not that it takes much to inflame any teenager's passions), this is the code name used in Ireland for teenage pregnancies. "The number of abortions done in the UK on Irish girls was 2,287 in 1977," the same article stated. Most of the girls going to England don't even give their correct names or country of origin. The doctors suggest better sex education in the schools. The League of Decency demurs.

Inside the Dáil, Dr. John O'Connell, Labour Party spokesman on health and social welfare, said: "It is only here that we can solemnly discuss not means of helping people to live responsible and happy lives, but a way of limiting their chances of doing so." He reminded his colleagues of Yeats's remark to an Abbey Theater audience that had disrupted a play by O'Casey: "You have disgraced yourselves again."

Mr. Oliver J. Flanagan (the Fine Gael TD* from Laois-Offaly) blamed the whole thing on "wildcat crazy journalists." What, he asked, was the Dáil coming to? Had they all lost their senses? They were wasting the time of the House legislating for what they knew was morally wrong, and for what the wisdom of the Church told them was morally wrong. He quoted some Polish bishops and a recent speech by Pope John Paul II. He hoped that every God-fearing Catholic doctor would wash his hands completely of this.

Ruairi Quinn (Labour member, Dublin South-East) said he thought the state should get out of the bedroom.

The Irish Catholic Doctors' Guild asked the minister of health to "think again" on his proposed family planning bill that would make contraceptives available. They said the Supreme Court ruling on the McGee case (which made the importation of contraceptives legal) was based on a "dubious legal concept imported from America." They suggested that Mr. Haughey should "grasp the nettle" and give Ireland a world lead in natural family planning ... as if they don't have that already.

As the controversy raged, the anticontraception lobby intoned the Rosary outside the Dáil.

* "TD" are the initials in Irish for the phrase "member of Parliament."

It is all very much like controversies in Boston when contraception used to be illegal in Massachusetts.

MARCH 25

Even though it's a Sunday, Dr. Oliver McCullen, the ear specialist, saw David in his office this morning. The poor fellow has had an endless series of ear infections all winter, and they have affected his hearing and his schoolwork. He seems to go right out of one infection into another. Dr. McCullen is going to put him on cortisone for two weeks, and if that isn't effective, we'll put him in the hospital to have ear surgery.

MARCH 26

I have nearly finished researching my booklet about the residence. The State Department has no historical background on the house at all, but the material I was able to collect from the Public Record Office in Belfast, and at the National Library here in Dublin, has given me a fairly complete history of the house, its origins and its uses.

It was built in 1776, by a flamboyant Swiss diplomat named John Blacquière. He had come to Ireland to serve as chief secretary to the viceroy, Lord Harcourt. As well as carrying out his administrative duties for the government, he was also named bailiff of Phoenix Park and commissioner of the Paving Board. These sinecures gave him possession of a few acres and a modest four-room cottage in the Park, which he quickly enlarged to sixty-nine acres (despite legal proceedings taken against him by irate citizens who accused him of "encroaching on the public demesne"). He then built a handsome Georgian home for himself on his newly acquired estate at a cost of £8,000. He spent £2,000 more to fit out the wine cellar, and sat back to enjoy life in eighteenth-century Dublin.

Soon realizing, however, that a government salary couldn't cope with the financial strain of lavish entertaining and high living suitable to a gentleman of his proclivities, he gave up the house in the Park. (He later solved all his financial problems by marrying an heiress.)

Successive chief secretaries had been urging the British government to provide them with a permanent home in Dublin. They had been living in quarters in Dublin Castle, and as one of them, William Eden, complained in 1780: "Confinement in the Castle air will soon destroy both me and my family." So the British government bought the house in the Park from John Blacquière in 1782, and it served as the official residence of chief secretaries until the last one, Sir Hamar Greenwood, left in 1922. The list of tenants is impressive: Sir Arthur Wellesley, who later became the Duke of Wellington (1807-9); Lord Castlereagh (1798-1801); George Otto Trevelyan (1882-84). Trevelyan succeeded poor Lord Frederick Cavendish, a victim of the famous "Phoenix Park Murders." Cavendish had been appointed to succeed William Edward "Buckshot" Foster (nicknamed for having introduced the use of buckshot into the British army) as chief secretary. Foster was intensely disliked by many Irish nationalists. A group of extreme nationalists called the Invincibles planned to murder him when he left Phoenix Park on his last day in office. Fortunately for Foster, he left for England earlier in the day than expected and escaped their plot. Unfortunately for Lord Cavendish, he arrived on the evening of Foster's departure to take up his new duties as chief secretary. He and his assistant, a man named Thomas Burke, left the chief secretary's lodge in the evening to walk up the Main Park Road to the viceregal lodge, a quarter of a mile away. As they left the gates of their residence, four members of the Invincibles set upon them, mistaking Cavendish for Foster, and murdered them. Their bodies were brought back to the residence and were laid on the floor in front of the fireplace in one of the drawing rooms. Their murderers were eventually caught and brought to justice.

By 1813, the house was in need of extensive repairs. Sir Robert Peel planned and carried out a modernization during his tenure, and also seems to have kept the wine cellar up to the standards of John Blacquière. His inventory in 1813 shows £2,300 worth of wines.

Edward Short was appointed chief secretary in 1918, and his daughter, Mrs. Doreen Ingrams, came to call on me at the residence a few months ago. She hadn't been back in the house since she left it as a girl, but she had a vivid memory of living there:

"When the viceroy came to dinner, he would be seated in the middle of the table, facing the two large double doors leading out into the drawing room. After dinner, the ladies would get up, one by one, to 'withdraw,' and they would each stop at the doorway, turn, and make a deep curtsy to the viceroy before leaving the room.

"My sister and I used to hide behind the curtains in the ballroom, which gave us a direct line of vision through the two drawing rooms into the dining room. We would record each of the curtsies, scoring the ladies for their grace or their clumsiness."

The house stood empty from 1922, when Ireland became independent, until 1927, when the first American envoy, Mr. Frederick Sterling, arrived to open a ministerial legation in Dublin. The Sterlings decided the big white house in the Park would make an ideal home for the new American residence. The property was rented from the Irish Board of Works, and until 1948 it housed both the residence and the chancery. In 1949, a new, ninety-nine-year lease was signed with the Board of Works. The post of minister was raised the following year to an ambassadorial post, and Mr. George Garret, serving as minister, was named the first American ambassador to Ireland.

The structure of the public rooms on the first floor is unchanged since Peel redecorated in 1813. I had lunch today in the residence with Mrs. Veronica Rowe, the great-granddaughter of Buckshot Foster. Mrs. Rowe's grandmother, Florence Vere O'Brien, was a serious, scholarly woman, interested in politics and very involved in her father's work. She kept a detailed diary of the political and social climate of Dublin during her years in the Park and illustrated it with charming pen and ink drawings. Mrs. Rowe brought the original diaries with her to lunch today, and we sat in the drawing room and compared the sketches made in 1880 with the room today. They were startlingly similar.

MARCH 28

I spoke for a long time at dinner this evening with the wife of the Swedish ambassador. She is a psychologist and is working on a project here in Dublin involving the effects of hormones and adrenaline on males and females. She is one of the few ambassador's wives—perhaps the only one—I have met here who can actively pursue a career of her own. For women who have professional interests, diplomatic life is a frustrating experience; frequent moves allow no time to establish oneself in a city. Language difficulties are often a barrier; the difficulty of obtaining work permits in some countries makes it hard for foreigners to find employment.

APRIL 2

I had to go into the hospital today for a very minor surgical procedure. I was out again in the evening. Irish hospitals are wonderfully kind, warm places, very unlike my scanty experience with American hospitals. The nurses, many of them nuns, are patient, humane and understanding. Doctors have time to talk to patients in a reassuring and unhurried manner. I think I shall come back to Ireland if I ever need to be hospitalized. The medical care is excellent, the nursing care superb, and the rules . . . well, relaxed enough to make recovery filled with laughter, surely a good medicine for everyone.

A few weeks ago, I was visiting a friend who was recovering from surgery. When I saw her in the hospital, she was up and about and feeling well again. Not only feeling well, but having the time of her life! Her floor was filled with women recovering from female operations. As they regained their strength, each was taking full opportunity of her enforced holiday. Every evening, as soon as visitors' hours were over, they congregated in each other's rooms for a little prebedtime liquid cheer, thoughtfully provided by a visiting husband.

The other night, one of the women, just up from a hysterectomy, ran into a priest friend in another ward. He was from down in the country and feeling lonely in hospital, not having had many visitors to cheer him up.

"Come to our room tonight, Father," the lady told him. "We meet about ten and have a little chat. Perhaps you could lead us in the Rosary."

So the priest joined the patients that night for their party but, alas, the "medicine" went right to his head (being weakened from his illness and all). By the time he was ready to return to his room, the poor fellow could hardly tell a Hail Mary from an Our Father. He insisted, nevertheless, on making his own way, so the women bade him good night and returned to their own rooms, leaving the good father to weave his way down the dim hallway.

In his befuddled condition, he entered the wrong room (all hospital rooms looking alike) and climbed into bed. He may have thought that hospitals give a man more pillows than he ever needs. He pushed and shoved and arranged his bed. He pulled the sheet up over him and as he was drifting into sleep, a low moan broke the silence of the room. But then all was quiet and he fell into a deep sleep.

Sometime in the middle of the night, as she was making her rounds, a young nurse burst into the matron's office. "Come quickly, Sister," she whispered. "Father O____ is in bed with Mrs. Mc____!"

The two of them hurried through the darkened corridors and found the unconscious twosome, the priest softly snoring while his poor, drugged bedmate moaned and groaned in her sleep. She, just recovering from surgery, was pushed precariously to the edge of her narrow bed, her arm dangling from the side. The two nurses frantically got the priest up and half-walked, half-dragged him down the hallway to his own room. Then they settled the innocent lady back into the center of her bed, and continued on their nightly rounds.

The next morning, the patient, more alert and recovering from her drugged state, called in the nurse.

"You know, Sister, I had the most vivid dream last night of someone climbing into bed with me. I know it's ridiculous, but I could swear it really happened."

"Don't worry your head about it, luv," replied the nurse soothingly. "It's a very common postsurgical hallucination."

Except for a bit of a headache, due of course to his illness, the priest had no recollection at all, hallucinatory or otherwise.

APRIL 18

The Speaker of the House, "Tip" O'Neill, and Mrs. O'Neill, accompanied by a congressional delegation, arrived in Dublin today. We'd been expecting them for several weeks, and I've been busy with the staff at the residence planning a dinner party. The last thing I want to give them, at the end of their tour through Eastern Europe, is a stiff, formal "diplomatic" dinner. So I've tried to organize an evening that will be fun and interesting and will allow them all a chance to meet our Irish friends.

We went to the airport this afternoon to meet their plane. The foreign minister and his wife and several people from the Protocol Office were there. They had arranged for the Irish Army Band to play and for the Speaker to review the troops as he got off the plane. But the plans for carrying out the formalities of the welcoming ceremony didn't seem too tightly knit.

When the plane landed, Bill and I and the Irish delegation went on board to say hello to the Speaker before he disembarked. We all walked back down the steps with the Speaker leading the way. Someone from the Protocol Office lined us all up as we descended so that we could shake hands with members of the delegation as they disembarked. The Speaker found himself in the receiving line and was soon shaking hands with his own delegation, whom he had just left on the plane.

"Welcome to Ireland!" He beamed at them.

"How the hell did you get *here?*" one of them asked in bewilderment. "I thought I just saw you on the plane."

The Irish foreign minister had stayed behind on the plane to let the delegation get off first, and as he came down the steps he ended up going through the receiving line, also being welcomed to Ireland by the Speaker, and I was laughing so hard by this time I could scarcely shake hands with anyone. The band struck up "When Irish Eyes Are Smiling," and pretty soon everyone just mingled together and headed for the waiting cars and buses.

I entered a car with Mrs. O'Neill, and we followed the lead car to the hotel where the delegation was staying. With a motorcycle escort, we made the trip, which usually takes thirty-five to forty minutes, in a breathtaking twelve. We clung to our arm straps and tried to make polite conversation as the car raced through red lights, swung around corners, bounced across concrete traffic islands, and roared through the city.

The dinner this evening was a great success. After dinner, we congregated in the ballroom to hear a concert by Robert White, the American tenor who has become enormously popular in Ireland. John O'Conor, Ireland's leading concert pianist, accompanied him on the piano.

Then another friend, Pat Campbell, who has helped me orchestrate the entertainment so many times at the residence, got up and acted as an informal master of ceremonies, calling on our guests to perform. Some of the entertainment was prearranged, just to "prime the pump," but after that it was spontaneous. Kathleen Byrne, née Watkins, brought her harp and played and sang. Rosaleen Linehan sang some of her own songs, including one rearranged especially for the Speaker. Maurice O'Sullivan played his guitar and sang. Foreign Minister Michael O'Kennedy sang.

Gay Byrne told some good Irish stories. Finally, to everyone's special delight, the minister of finance, George Colley, a man not usually associated with song, got up and sang for us.

The American delegation, who seemed to be enjoying the evening hugely, produced their own talent, and finally the Speaker stood up and told several of his stories. Since he has a professional sense of timing and delivery, he was a big hit with the audience. Mrs. O'Neill whispered to me: "He *loves* it; no one here has heard his jokes."

Reluctantly, at least on my part, we broke up about 1 AM. The congressmen have a full round tomorrow of appointments and meetings with Irish government officials. The taoiseach and Mrs. Lynch are giving them a dinner tomorrow night at Dublin Castle.

It's been a long day. David went into St. Vincent's Hospital this morning at 8 AM for his ear surgery, and Bill and I took turns sitting with him in the hospital until we brought him home just before leaving for the airport to meet the Speaker. His ears are sore, but we hope the operation will prove a success and put an end to his troublesome infections. He was a very good patient.

APRIL 19

Dublin Castle looked beautiful tonight. After a reception in the "Throne Room," the taoiseach and Mrs. Lynch and their guests of honor were piped in to the dining room by an Irish piper. The Irish Army Band, seated in the balcony overlooking the dining room, played during dinner. Mr. Lynch made a rather long and formal toast, and the Speaker responded with a formal speech of his own, in which he referred to himself as an Irish nationalist and accused Britain of using Northern Ireland as a "political football." The moment I heard him use that phrase, I knew the headlines were made for tomorrow's papers.

We stayed late. The American guests were having a good time and enjoying the informal Irish hospitality. They have come to Ireland after an arduous tour of several European countries and I think they find the warmth of their welcome here and the ease and friendliness of their Irish hosts a relaxing and rewarding sequel to their Eastern European reception.

APRIL 21

Bill and I drove in our own car, and followed the congressional bus from Dublin to Galway, then on to Dromoland Castle for the weekend. After a stop at the Galway Crystal Factory, we went for lunch to Paddy Burke's in nearby Clarenbridge. Several delegation members asked me about the itinerant campsites they had seen by the side of the road as we drove into Galway. Although they had heard of Irish "tinkers," they didn't really know who or what they were or what kind of life they led. When we reached Paddy Burke's, I phoned Sister Brigid and asked if she could bring a carload of "my girls" to the restaurant to meet with the congressmen and their wives. She and the girls were there within thirty minutes. I introduced them around and they all had a chance to talk to and question one another. The Americans were astonished that such poised and articulate girls could live in conditions as appalling as those we had seen by the roadside coming into town.

MAY 2–3: *Cavan and Meath*

The Marx Brothers would have loved us in County Cavan yesterday morning. We began our official tour with a welcoming ceremony in the County Manager's Office in Cavan Town. I was presented with a beautiful bouquet of flowers and as I stepped forward to receive them, I tripped over the wastebasket and fell into the arms of the county manager. Bill smiled and leaned back in his chair and the back fell off. He looked startled but grasped the arms and maintained his balance. No serious casualties yet. We still had the pig factory ahead of us.

After a marvelous lunch at a charming inn in Belturbet, we went to visit St. Patrick's School for Boys. Bill spoke to them in an assembly: most of their questions were about Speaker O'Neill's trip to Ireland and his intentions, if any, to intercede with Great Britain about the problems in Northern Ireland. The best question of the day was that of a boy of about twelve, who raised his hand and asked Bill: "Why exactly did you come to Ireland?"

This morning, after a visit to the Cavan Crystal Factory, we visited a local bacon factory. *I* thought we were simply going to see big slices of ham being cut into strips of bacon, packaged, and made ready for retail sales. But no. As we neared the factory, I heard the unmistakable squeal of pigs. Lots of them. The sounds were clearly cries for help. Pigs are *not* stupid. As the large vans backed into the unloading ramp and hundreds of pigs were herded into long, concrete shower stalls, they *knew* they were in serious trouble.

We donned white coats and helmets and entered the factory in the rear, where the pigs were being unloaded. After their showers, which our guide said keep them from fighting, they were put on a conveyor belt and sent into a gas chamber. Quick and painless. Good-by, pigs.

Their throats were slit, their stomachs opened and they were bled. Then they were hung on overhead belts by big hooks and passed through an open fire, where they sort of sizzled for a few minutes until a pig barber came and shaved them with a huge razor. Some of our party deserted the tour at this point, but I decided to hold out until we got to the bacon stage. I might never have another opportunity. (I might never *want* another opportunity.) I followed our guide out of the barbershop toward the cutting room where the pigs, still on big overhead conveyors, were being shuttled. Just at the moment that I heard someone yell "Watch out!", I was knocked on the head and shoulders. I staggered forward. As I turned to see who had smacked me, my attacker passed overhead, pink tail still neatly curled and dainty little toes sticking straight out in front of him. Before I could duck again, the next pig came along and whacked me sharply on my right shoulder as he passed by. Someone pulled me to the side and said: "You're right in the path of the pigs, luv," and I gladly stepped aside and let them have the right-of-way.

After we visited Kells and Trim today, we had lunch with the manager and officials of the Tara Mines, a large zinc and lead mine outside Navan. They had arranged a tour of the mine after lunch and gallantly invited me to don boots, light, helmet, and oilskin coat and join them. After my encounter with the pigs, I was hesitant, and besides, I really hate mines and caves. Or anything small, dark, confined and underground (like subway stations when the lights go out). But on the other hand, one doesn't often get the opportunity to tour a zinc mine 1,900 feet underground, and when I was assured that there were no bats on the premises, I agreed. The wife of the county manager of Meath, who was lunching with us, said she was game if I was, so the two of us put on our costumes, which were, of course, comically large.

The elevator went down and down. And down. It seemed to take a very long time. I thought when we got down it would be like a scene from *How Green Was My Valley,* and we would crawl through narrow, dank, creepy tunnels, with perhaps a small donkey leading us. To my astonishment, when the doors of the elevator opened, we stepped out into a brightly lit, spacious underground cavern, with lots of men walking back and forth, lights hung on walls, and plenty of room for us to walk four abreast, upright. It *was* dank and cold and the floor of the mine was wet, often deep with puddles of water. But the air was clear, and it wasn't claustrophobic as I had feared. We passed lines of men coming from smaller passageways off the main concourse. They were carrying picks and the little lights fastened onto the front of their helmets twinkled in the dark. I thought it would be fitting if I sang a couple of verses of "Hi Ho, Hi Ho, It's Off to Work We Go," but the thought of what Christopher would say to me if he were along restrained me. I did, however, ask for an ax, and took a swipe at the side of a wall. Nothing happened.

After the mines, on to New Grange to visit another small underground passage: the prehistoric burial grounds. And then home again.

The postal strike has gone on for fourteen weeks. Everyone is used to it by now and no one seems to mind anymore. The Irish are very accepting of things and have little sense of outrage. I actually heard *myself* say to someone the other day: "Oh well, the postal strike is a nuisance, but on the other hand, it saves writing thank-you notes." We should all be down at the General Post Office on O'Connell Street, picketing the picketers.

The petrol shortage has everyone more upset than the postal strike. There are long lines now (up to three hours' wait) to get petrol. The filling station where most of the embassies buy petrol has just announced to all the diplomats that from now on we must each put down a fifty-pound deposit if we want to charge our petrol (which we do, in order to get our tax rebate). The diplomats are furious, and we have all decided to quit patronizing that station.

And if postal and petrol strikes aren't bad enough, the Dental Health Foundation has just announced that Ireland is in the throes of a major epidemic of tooth decay! "Forty percent of unskilled and semi-skilled workers over 16 have no natural teeth! Thirty percent of professional and managerial workers over 16 have no natural teeth! Fifty percent of the entire population have gum disease!! Not more than 10 percent of the population under 25 have a full set of uppers and lowers!!! Toothpaste consumption is 11 tubes annually per head, compared with 16 in the UK, 24 in Western Europe and 36 in the United States." (We're always the most conspicuous consumers.)

MAY 11

I've been dying to go to a fortune-teller ever since we've been in Ireland, and today a friend of mine arranged for me to have a session with a woman from Waterford, supposedly one of Ireland's best.

She reads tarot cards. We settled down in my friend's office, and she began dealing the cards. She told me an impressive number of facts about myself, some of which she could have learned from newspaper or magazine stories but some of which surprised me. She concentrated furiously. Her face began to sweat, and her hands trembled as she dealt the cards again and again, reading their faces, trying to interpret their meaning.

She predicted a "huge professional" success for me "in the arts" within the next two or three years. At first she said music, changed it to "literature." She also predicted a "small accident," nothing serious. "Be careful," she warned. And she told me that I was going to receive a beautiful gift "very soon."

We had the St. Michael's Library dinner dance at our house this evening, and Phil Keaveny, chairperson of the committee, gave me a beautiful gift—a handwoven cape from the Weaver's Shed, a factory owned by one of the committee members. I am now awaiting professional success while driving carefully and walking with trepidation.

MAY 17

One of the frustrations of our job here is that social and official functions don't leave us enough time to enjoy the variety of theater and musical events that Dublin has to offer. But we managed to get to a piano concert tonight at St. Catherine's Church in the "Liberties" to hear John O'Conor play a Beethoven program. St. Catherine's is a lovely old church on Thomas Street that had been let fall into a derelict condition. People in the neighborhood used to throw garbage and trash into its broken windows. Finally, before its total destruction, Lord Moyne, Desmond Guinness's father, came to its rescue and organized its restoration.

Bill spoke there last winter when he dedicated a plaque in front of the church to Robert Emmet. The church stands on the corner where Emmet was hanged, drawn and quartered.

It was a beautiful concert tonight. John is an international concert pianist, well on his way to becoming one of the leading pianists in the world. We sat next to President and Mrs. Hillery and had a chance for a short visit with them during the intermission. We brought John and Mary O'Conor back to the house with us for a small party after the concert.

MAY 22

We spent a fascinating morning and early afternoon doing something Bill has wanted to do since we arrived here. We had a guided tour of Georgian Dublin, with Desmond Guinness. He and Penny came by at 10 AM and, with Gerry driving us, we went all over town, popping in here to see a ceiling, there to see a staircase. He is an efficient, fast guide. He knocks at the door and asks in the most polite manner: "*Could* we just pop in and take a quick look at your plaster?" Or your ceiling? Or your doorway? The host, although sometimes taken by surprise, is always pleased to see Desmond and shows us in. We dash from place to place, no lingering allowed. We saw more this morning than we had seen all year.

For all the destruction of Georgian architecture in Ireland, Irish builders are always ready to attribute a bit of Georgian prestige to their new buildings. Housing estates called "Georgian Village," Georgian Manor" and "Georgian Townhouses" are going up all over Ireland while authentic and irreplaceable Georgian buildings fall under the wrecker's ball.

MAY 23

Susan McQueen, the head decorator from the Department of State in Washington, is in Dublin this week to look at the residence and a few of the other homes the embassy owns here. She and I are planning a rather extensive decorating job for the house, recovering furniture and getting badly needed new rugs for the public rooms.

I have discovered that if I work through her office the cost is charged to her own budget. If I work on my own, it will come out of Embassy Dublin's budget. Since ultimately it all comes out of the same US government pot and goes for the same ends, I can't see the reasoning for this policy, but I am perfectly willing to go along. It will make our own embassy budget-keepers happier.

We've had a wonderful three days going through the house room by room, planning, talking, making lists, exchanging ideas. When I go home this summer on home leave, I shall spend a couple of days in her office and we'll pick fabrics and look at furniture samples. The old house is going to have a beautiful new face this time next year.

MAY 29

Bill and I went to Dunganstown, County Waterford, today, to lay a wreath in the John F. Kennedy Memorial Park on a hill called Slieve Coillte; JFK would have been sixty-two today.

After the ceremony, we went to a pretty cottage a few miles distant where Mary Ryan, Kennedy's cousin, lives with her daughter, son-in-law and grandsons. We had a quiet visit with them, and each one reminisced about Kennedy's triumphant visit to Ireland in 1963. The Irish adored John Kennedy. His visit is talked about still, his death still mourned. Nearly all of the farm homes I have visited in Ireland have a picture of Kennedy on their wall; nearly everyone takes enormous personal pride in his accomplishments, regarding him as "one of our own" who made good in America. The recording of his speech to the Irish Parliament is still sold in Irish record shops.

Bill and I had been in Ireland that same summer, but after Kennedy's visit. Banners welcoming him were still flying in each village. When we returned to Washington in the autumn, we received an invitation to dinner at the White House, in honor of the then Irish prime minister, Sean Lemass. After dinner, we stood for a few minutes chatting about Ireland with the president. He had stayed at the residence during his time in Dublin, and he had been enchanted with it.

"Bill," he said, "when I finish the presidency, I'm going to get myself appointed ambassador to Ireland. I can't think of anything I'd rather do more." He laughed and pointed a finger at Bill. "And when I'm finished, we'll get *you* appointed!" Three weeks later he was dead, and fourteen years later, Bill went to Ireland to live in the residence.

We recounted that story today to Mrs. Ryan, and she smiled. "Yes," she agreed, "he loved it here. He had a way with the people. They'll never forget him."

JUNE 11

This evening we went to a concert at Carton, one of the great country houses of Ireland, in County Kildare. The concert was part of the Music in Great Houses series. I had never seen Carton before, and although we were only in the Long Hall for the concert, it was warm enough to stand outside during the intermission and look out over the beautiful expanse of softly shaped hedges and rolling hills. The mist was hovering tentatively at the bottom of the garden, as if waiting to roll in after the concert was over. We stood on the back lawn with a glass of wine and watched the light fade, turning the green hills purple, then gray and finally black. And I fell in love with Ireland's beauty all over again, as I do about twice a week.

One of the most enjoyable things about being an ambassador, or The Wife, is to meet interesting people from all walks of life and, if you like them, to invite them to dinner. *Almost* everyone comes. (So far, only one government minister has refused consistently on the grounds of being too busy, a newspaper editor has refused on no grounds, and a very nice lady I would like to know better has refused on the grounds that she heard on the grapevine we didn't allow smoking in our house, which isn't true.)

If there is a writer, a painter, a musician, a sports figure . . . anyone . . . we want to meet, we just get on the phone and, sooner or later, we meet. The same with parties we attend; if there is a specially interesting or amusing guest that either of us is taken with, we will sooner or later lure him up to the Park. Maeve can track anyone down. I once accused her of being able to rouse someone from the dead if we wanted him for a dinner party.

So . . . I met the most fascinating, handsome, charming, intelligent man this evening. I just knew it was in the stars that we should expand our acquaintance. Such boyish charm combined with such mature judgments! Such wit combined with such elegance and style! I sat with him for half an evening, being entertained and doing my best to entertain. At the evening's end, I said: "You must come soon to the residence," and he promised he would.

The next morning I said to Meave: "When is our next big wingding?" and she reminded me about the black-tie dinner we were giving the following week.

"Great!" I said. "I've got another guest, a man. I think he's got a wife, but I'm not sure. See if you can round them up and invite them."

Maeve's face fell. "We've got twenty-four already," she said. Twenty-four is our limit at a seated dinner.

"Oh, well," I said optimistically, "someone will get sick. Someone usually does." I gave Maeve the name of my new-found friend, and she looked him up in the phone book and issued an invitation.

The night of the dinner arrived. I spent hours reconstituting myself and stood by the fireplace greeting each guest as he or she arrived, with one eye on the doorway.

One by one they came in, cabinet ministers, politicians, musicians, bankers, just plain friends, but still no "Mr. Murphy," as I shall call him. Finally, when twenty-two of the twenty-four guests had arrived (one couple had had to drop out; I could always count on it), Dennis appeared at the doorway, looking apprehensive. (For Dennis, looking apprehensive meant he had a slight frown between his eyebrows.)

"Mr. and Mrs. Murphy," he announced; my heart skipped a beat. I smiled radiantly. And in walked a very elderly lady, all dressed in black, her hair freshly waved, her cane brightly polished. She was followed by a tall gentleman, even more elderly, slightly stooped and with a pronounced limp. He *was* handsome . . . in about 1914. My smile froze. I stared at Dennis and then at the "Murphys," but I recovered quickly enough to make my way to them and shake their hands warmly.

"So good of you to come," I said.

"What?" said Mr. Murphy.

"So good of you to come!" I shouted. As I shook his hand, he winced and pulled it away quickly.

"Arthritis," he said.

"Sorry," I said.

"What?"

"Come in and meet our guests," and I led them into the crowded room.

"You're so sweet to invite us," Mrs. Murphy said. "We seldom go out anymore. You know how it is when you get old; people tend to forget you."

"Not at all," I said, smiling and lying. "We were just delighted that you could come."

As soon as I had introduced them around, I fled to find Dennis. He was in the front hall, conferring with Maeve. "Who are they?" I whispered. Maeve was almost in tears. "They were the only 'Murphy' in the phone book with those initials," she explained. "And when I spoke to her, she seemed delighted to come and said they had been here before."

"Well, see if you can find out who they are," and I went back to the party. Within minutes, Dennis handed me a note. "He used to be so and so, and then he was appointed so and so . . . ." Maeve had gathered up his entire biography. He *had* had an illustrious career, and of course it would have appeared only natural to them to be invited to an embassy where they had previously dined. Years ago.

We all went in to dinner. A government minister sat on my right. "How kind of you to invite old Murphy," he said. "I haven't seen him around in years. But that's just typical of you and Bill."

I thought of trying to explain my mistake, but thought better of it and just smiled. "Yes," I said. "We like to remember the old folks."

JUNE 17: *Dublin–Washington, D.C.*

We left Dublin this morning for home leave. Foreign service personnel and their families are allowed six weeks every two years with their return fares paid to visit the United States. Home leave has to be taken because the government wants its diplomats to stay in touch with the American scene. For us, it's a blessing to see family and friends again. But for some foreign service families it is a dubious perquisite. They have been posted abroad for years, have no home in America, few friends there, and perhaps a family who wouldn't welcome relatives with children arriving to live with them for six weeks. Many of them have to stay in hotels or resorts for the duration, which is an expensive summer vacation.

We arrived back on Gramercy Street this afternoon about 5 PM, to stay for a week with friends up and down the street. Our old house looked warm and inviting in the sunlight. It seemed strange not to walk up the familiar flagstone walk and in our own front door.

All the neighborhood congregated this evening to welcome us back. Except that all the children were a foot taller and a few had dropped their voices an octave, it was as if we had never been away.

JUNE 18

Since we have to have physical examinations at the State Department while we are on home leave, we decided to get them out of the way promptly. We went down this morning to begin the tests. As I was being shuttled from room to room, my engine and all my parts checked for faulty operation or poor maintenance, a nurse handed me fifteen little white boxes.

"These are for stool specimens," she told me briskly. "Each of you has to give me a sample for three days in a row. There are five of you in the family, right? Bring them all back to me on the third day. Store them in the refrigerator in the meantime."

I could only stare at her. "What?"

"These are for stool specimens," she repeated, and told me the whole thing over again, still cheery but a shade less patient.

"But we're posted in Ireland," I told her. "There aren't any tropical or intestinal ailments in Ireland."

"Regulations, my dear. Three boxes apiece. Three days in a row. Be sure and return them before five PM on Thursday. Next, please."

"But each of my children is staying with a different friend," I began. "And we're house guests, too. I can't go around to all our hostesses and say: 'Excuse me, could I just move over the milk and mayonnaise and put my stool specimen in the 'fridge. And don't mistake it for a goody from the deli! Ha ha.' And anyway, for five people to have five stool specimens for three days in a row ... I mean, what if one of us doesn't perform?"

"Are you trying to tell me that your children are constipated?" she asked me frostily. "Is that what you're trying to say?"

"Well, no. Not that I know of." The truth is, once they got out of diapers, I ceased taking any interest whatsoever in their stool specimens and just trusted to nature.

"But they're traveling and they may be off schedule." I grasped at any straw. I was *not*, repeat NOT going to fill up the refrigerators of Gramercy Street with Shannon Stool Specimens.

"Look, dear," she said wearily. "It's regulations. If you want to talk to someone about it, go ahead, but I've got people lined up out in the hall-way."

I meekly took the brown paper bag she handed me, filled with fifteen tiny white cardboard boxes, and made my way out of the Medical Department and down to the cafeteria, where I was meeting Bill

"What's that?" he asked me, as I sat down with my paper bag.

"You're never going to believe this." I told him.

"Oh, for God's sake," he said. "Throw them away."

"I can't. She said we have to do it to pass our physicals. Anyway, what if it turned out later that we all have worms?"

"We do *not* all have worms. None of us has worms. Throw them away."

"No," I said morosely. I'm more obedient about some things than he is. "I'll have to figure out something."

As it turned out, not I, but my friend Sandy Fitzpatrick figured out a brilliant solution. I was sitting, a few hours later, on her back porch. Christopher was staying with her boys. I told her about my boxes.

"I mean," I said to Sandy, "here we are supposed to be on vacation, forgetting our responsibilities, having fun, renewing old friendships. If there's any way to break up a friendship, it's putting you-know-what in someone's refrigerator. Here I come each morning, running up and down Gramercy Street like the Town Crier, shouting as I approach each house: '*Don't flush! Hold it!*' and here I come with my little white box and my wooden spatula [which came with each box], gathering up what I can."

"Look, babe," Sandy said. "It's simple. When do you have to take them back?"

"Thursday PM. Or after the fifteenth stool. Whichever comes first."

"Okay. Here's what you do. On Thursday, when nature calls, take all your little boxes into the bathroom. Line them up. Open their little lids. Do your thing. Hopefully, you'll have enough to go around. Get your spatula and fill each tiny box with a tiny little sample. Label them. Take them back. That's it. Simple. Who's to know?"

"Brilliant," I agreed. "But what if it shows that I have worms?" (I was convinced by this time that it would.) "Then we'll *all* have to be treated."

"Nonsense," Sandy said. "You don't have worms. You don't look wormy. Anyway, it's those dread tropical diseases they're looking for. And you haven't even been to the tropics."

"Right," says I. And that's what I did. So the Shannon Stool Specimen Caper ended happily. No worms. No dread disease. At least I don't have any. As for the others, well, they'll have to take their chances.

JUNE 24: *Washington-Texas*

We all departed for Texas on the same day, but to different destinations and on *four* different planes. Because Bill didn't want all three boys to fly together (talk about Irish pessimism), Christopher and Liam flew together to San Antonio via Dallas. David and Siobhán O'Tierney (who is with us on our trip home) flew via Atlanta. Bill and I were going first to an American Irish Foundation meeting in Houston, so he flew with Sean Donlon, the Irish ambassador, to Houston in the morning, while I followed in the late afternoon after my third trip to the airport.

"Dear," says he, "I'll just pop on down with Sean, and you follow later in the day . . . with the bags . . . after the boys all get their planes." Sean's black limousine came for Bill at noon. I stood in the front hall, surrounded by sixteen pieces of luggage, and waved good-by to him, feeling not unlike my great-grandmother back in Virginia must have felt when *her* husband said: "I'll just mosey on down to Texas, dear, and find us a spot of land, and you follow later with the children and the goats." (And she did, too, by boat, all the way from Virginia to Galveston, and when she got there, she rolled up her sleeves and started fighting Indians.)

JULY 21

We have had a wonderful month in Texas. It was as hot as everyone wanted it to be (except Bill, who is the only person extant who thinks Irish weather, is "wonderful"). We swam in the Gulf of Mexico, visited near and distant relatives, achieved magnificent suntans, and tried to store up sun and energy for the months ahead.

JULY 30: *Dublin*

I heard about a program for taking children from city homes to a farm for a few weeks during the summer vacation, to give them a taste of country life. We can't claim to be a real farm, but we are in a countrylike setting, with our sixty-nine acres in the middle of Phoenix Park, so I signed up to take a boy between David's and Christopher's ages. A woman phoned a few weeks ago to tell us we were to pick up John Peate, age eleven, in Coolock, a section of north Dublin, today.

We drove up to his house this morning, and saw lots and lots of round blue eyes staring at us from behind the curtains. John, blue-eyed, brown-haired and handsome, with a deep dimple in each cheek, came down the walk with his small bag, ready to go. He's a delightful, poised and handsome boy. All of us were immediately taken with him and my fears about his feeling strange and unaccustomed to life at the residence turned out to be completely unfounded. He's totally relaxed and acts as if he has lived here all his life. He has nine brothers and sisters at home, so he has found it easy to make friends with the residence children of all ages.

AUGUST 10

Aga Khan Cup day again at the Horse Show. We sat in the president's box, edging closer to the front row this year as our predecessors are beginning to leave Dublin for posts elsewhere. Seating in the box is arranged according to one's length of time on post.

The afternoon began warm and sunny. Breda O'Kennedy (the wife of the foreign minister) and I decided we were dressed too warmly, but, as Breda said, you never know from one minute to the next in Ireland, and sure enough, a heavy downpour began soon after the show started.

Despite the bad turn in the weather, today is exciting. Everyone breathlessly waits to see if Ireland will bag the cup again this year for the third time. They ride well and steadily, and although without the spectacular finish of last year, they do win. The hero of the day is Con Power, the tall, lanky army officer on the Irish team. Ireland has retired the cup, and I hope the Aga Khan can afford a new one.

AUGUST 17

At a dinner party this evening I met a gentle, soft-spoken doctor who does a lot of marriage counseling in his practice. "For couples who haven't consummated their marriage," he explained to me. I must have looked startled, because he laughed and said: "You look as incredulous as the members of the seminar I spoke to in London last year. It was a conference of medical marriage counselors. They gave papers on the most ex-

191

traordinary sexual problems you could imagine, but when I stood up and gave my paper on the problems of consummation, they all gaped at me as if I had dropped down on them from the Victorian age."

"Do you have many of these cases a year?" I asked him.

"Ten to twenty," he replied. "And they aren't all, as you might expect, very young and naive, nor simple, backward country people. Some of them are educated, relatively sophisticated couples. But they are shy, inhibited, uninformed; just totally ignorant of what sex is all about."

"Don't they even read a book before they go to the altar?" I asked. "Or have a talk with a friend?"

"Not usually. And if they do, I think their reaction might be: 'Go away, I don't believe it!' "

"What do you say to them?"

"They usually come in to see me, not because of their real problem, but because they want children and aren't achieving a pregnancy, obviously. When I examine the woman and find out the cause of her infertility is nonconsummation, I speak first to the wife alone, then to the husband alone. I use diagrams and simply tell them the facts of life. Then I speak to them several times together. I encourage them not to touch each other for a month, then to take a long weekend and splurge, go to a nice hotel somewhere, away from their hometown, relax, enjoy each other, have no distractions and just let nature take its course. And nine times out of ten, that simple solution works. To their delight and surprise, a pregnancy usually ensues, also!"

I found it hard to believe. But then I remembered talking to another friend, a most open and witty man and the doting father of four boys. I think he devotes more time to his boys than anyone else I have met in Ireland. One night at dinner, we were talking about sex education and I asked him if he, and most Irish fathers, took their boys aside and told them the facts of life.

"Good God, no!" he said, reddening.

"Then how do they find out?"

"Like I did, from other boys."

"Would you be uncomfortable talking to them about it, if they came to you with questions?"

"Yes."

Since sex education is a taboo subject in most Irish schools, it is hard for boys and girls to learn the facts with any accuracy. I've been told hilarious stories by women friends about what they *thought* was going to happen, and how startled they were to find it wasn't *that* way at all. On the other hand, when I talked to a young friend of mine who, with her husband, lectures on the "physical side" of marriage to engaged couples, she told me that everything is discussed openly, easily and without embarrassment, and that each of the young men and women feels free to ask questions about subjects on which they are uninformed. Those premarriage conferences, however, are held in Dublin; my doctor friend is from the country, which makes a difference in people's social attitudes and mores concerning sex.

AUGUST 18

I decided a few weeks ago that it would be *fun* and *educational* for the boys and me to go on a camping trip through the west of Ireland. "She's at it again," Christopher said. I used the boys as a pretext, since they aren't at all keen on the idea, especially going with their mother, but I thought it would look funny if I went by myself, and anyway I couldn't erect a tent alone, so they at last agreed . . . reluctantly.

The summer before we came to Ireland to live, we spent a holiday here, going on a week's horse-drawn caravan trip, meandering at a speed of three miles a day around Clew Bay in County Mayo. It was a grand adventure, and I think my idea of a camping trip with the boys this summer is to experience those sights and smells and sounds again. I'm not really an outdoor person, not the kind who would ski cross-country for twenty miles and sleep in a mountain cabin, or backpack across France. But I do like to hear country sounds at night, to see the stars from a sleeping bag, to smell the vegetation and feel rain and wind and sun. Happily, in Ireland one doesn't have to worry about snakes, mosquitoes, chiggers and all those small things that can plague a camper in America. Or big things, like bears or raccoons. On an Irish camping trip, rain is the only enemy.

We went to a camping equipment warehouse the other day and rented our gear. A "complete set for four." It all fits into the trunk of the car. We packed jeans, sweaters, "Wellies" (those wonderful high-top rubber boots that Irish children and country people live in) and many cans of ravioli, beans, fruit, cheese and bread. There is also an enormous tin of chocolate chip cookies, so that Christopher won't succumb to starvation in the wilds of Galway or Mayo.

My friend Dervla Murphy would *not* be proud of me. When I was planning this trip, I saw Dervla one day and asked her what we should take.

"A sleeping bag and a pan," she said.

I waited, my pencil poised, ready to jot down all her suggestions.

"Yes?" I said.

"That's it."

I looked at her and laughed. "Come on, Dervla. I mean, we've got to have a tent. And air mattresses. At *least*. And a stove to cook over. Lanterns for night. Food."

Dervla shrugged. "Why not stay in a hotel, then?"

Someday I am going to go on a camping trip with Dervla just to see if I survive.

AUGUST 20: *By Lantern light in a tent on the west coast of Galway*

We're here, believe it or not. We hit the Vintage Car Festival in Birr en route, and arrived in Galway in late afternoon. I'm sitting here by lantern light, writing in my journal. Liam and David are playing a card game called Switch, David's current favorite. C. is reading a book. Our air mattresses are blown up, our sleeping bags spread out, and we've finished dinner.

The day began with sad news. We heard this morning that our dear friend Gary Trimble had been killed last night in a car accident in Dublin. He was going to sculpt a head of Bill for me; it was still a secret between us. We were going to tell Bill about it on his birthday and then he would start sitting. Gary was a blithe spirit, good-hearted and generous, such a loss to his family, his many friends and to art in Ireland.

We checked our camping gear before starting out and discovered to our dismay that there are only three sleeping bags instead of four. David instantly was on the defensive, remembering last summer in France when he so often had to share a bed with someone, usually me.

"I'm not sharing a sleeping bag with *no one*," he repeated several times for emphasis. "No way."

"We'll stop in Galway and buy a new one," I promised.

The route to Galway was familiar. We took back lanes and country roads. The weather was terrible; fog and rain, and we passed a terrible auto accident at a small country intersection, with two cars completely demolished, one of them upside down and squeezed into folds like an accordion in the ditch by the side of the road. I drove slowly and carefully through the rain, but the children's spirits were high and we felt a sense of adventure steal over us.

I had to pull over to the side once and climb into the back seat to pull one of Christopher's baby teeth. It bled and bled. I began to think we would have to stop in a village and have it attended to, but eventually I forgot about it. When I remembered it again, the bleeding had stopped.

We arrived in Clarenbridge, just outside Galway, at noon and stopped at Paddy Burke's pub for lunch. When we came back outside, to our delight and surprise, the sun was shining, the sky was cloudless and the road already dry.

We drove through Galway City, Oughterard and Clifden, and headed out the Sky Road toward the Rutledges' country house. We had decided, back in Dublin, that our first night "on the road" we would camp on friends' property, just to get the hang of it and not feel quite so isolated.

Tony, Mark, and Rebecca Rutledge all helped us erect the tent in their front field, a few hundred yards from their house and looking out toward the sea, just another few hundred yards down the slope. Renée, as dubious about the delights of camping as Christopher is, once again offered us the hospitality of their house. C.'s face lit up, but fell immediately when I said, "Oh, no, that would spoil all the fun!"

"Not even dinner?" Renée suggested.

"Not even dinner."

C. sighed.

So we lit our two-burner stove (only one burner works), opened our ravioli, and had bread and cheese, and grapes for dessert. I opened the bottle of wine that Dennis had put into our food box, and poured a cupful into my tin mug.

"I'm going to tell Dervla that you brought French wine on our camping trip," Liam said.

"You do, and I'll tell her that you brought a pair of pajamas," I retorted.

David raced down to the sea and brought back a pan of water to wash the dishes, then we all four went for a long, long walk down a small, hilly, twisting road, lined on either side with a low, rocky fence. The sea was on our left, down a gentle drop of a hundred feet. Heather and fuschia are both in bloom and line the road. We passed one car and no pedestrians in two hours. Peter O'Toole, the actor, lives on that small remote road. We, nosy fans, went to his door and knocked, on the pretense of borrowing eggs, but alas, no one was at home.

We watched the sun fall into the sea. As the last, lingering shades of pink and red left the Irish summer sky, it was nearly 10:30 PM. We headed back up the road in the dusk, and by the time we crept into our tent, the sky was black and the night had fallen. Night, in the Irish countryside, is all-enveloping. Renée had left their back-door light turned on ("just in case you change your minds," she had said) but as we passed by it on the way to our tent, I turned it off.

We lit our small gas lantern inside the tent. The boys took off their boots and climbed into sleeping bags. Liam read Kipling's "Rikki-Tikki-Tavi" aloud for thirty minutes until I turned off the lamp and we all snuggled down in the dark. Liam and I slept on either end of our row and we put C. and D. between us. The boys were asleep instantly, but I lay awake, listening to the rain making a soft pitter-patter on the canvas tent top. The wind had come up again, and I could hear the waves in the bay start to lap the beach. I felt wonderfully peaceful, contented, and happy there, on that wild and rugged Irish coast.

I think I had just drifted into sleep when I awoke, trembling in fear. I had to restrain myself from screaming, then whispered to Liam:

"Wake up! Something is lying against me outside the tent!"

195

Liam and Christopher outside our tent

Poor Liam, deep in sleep, woke groggily and muttered: "Wha'?"

"Something outside the tent is on top of me, pushing against me and breathing heavily. Quick, put on your boots and take the flashlight and go outside to see what it is."

"*What?*" Liam said, fully awake now. "In this rain? Listen to it come down. I'll get soaked."

"Liam," I said in my "do it now or else" voice. "Something is out there in the dark trying to get into this tent. It's up to you to see what it is."

Liam, muttering about whose idea was this camping trip anyway, pulled on his Wellies and disappeared into the darkness and the rain. I stood hovering at the tent flap, ready to come to his rescue if need be, but only if his life was in *immediate* danger. He began suddenly to laugh. Not a very cheerful laugh, but amused, all the same. "Look," he called to me, pointing his flashlight toward my side of the tent. There, curled up, brown and wet, its two big ears pointing straight to the sky, lay Rebecca Rutledge's pet donkey. It had come from the field below us, seeing our light in the tent and looking for warmth and companionship on this wet, blowy night. It had found my body a comforting source of heat, and softer, no doubt, than the rocky walls it usually called home.

Liam came back into the tent, shook off his wet mac, and we crawled back to bed.

"Thanks, Liam," I whispered in the dark.

"Don't mention it," came the reply. "I always knew I was cut out for heroic deeds."

AUGUST 21

One of the rewarding things about camping, of course, is going to bed with the sun and arising at dawn to enjoy nature's fresh awakening. We got up at 10:30 this morning and then only because David woke up and began to hum.

"I thought you all had died," Renée said, when we came up to the house after breakfast. "I begged Tony to go see, but he assured me you would be all right. Did you hear the storm last night? It was desperate. Howling and blowing and the rain coming down in torrents. I woke up at three and couldn't go back to sleep for thinking of you poor things."

We poor things had slept through it all.

Tony wanted to take us out in his sailboat to Innisturk, one of the small islands that dot the bay near their house, but it was too windy and he feared to risk it. We went instead to a nearby beach, walked along the water's edge and collected coral.

The Atlantic Ocean, with its many bays and inlets off the coast of Galway and Mayo, is dotted with islands. Some of the larger ones, like the Aran Islands, are still inhabited. Others are empty now, their population having dwindled away with immigration or government schemes to resettle the inhabitants on the mainland. These schemes have been met with varying degrees of acceptance by the people involved. Some islanders are glad to leave their lonely, rocky homes and make a new life on the mainland. Others have acted on their own initiative, following sons and daughters, knowing how difficult it is to make a living or enjoy the amenities of modern life on the islands.

But a few old-timers—set in their ways, and their ways not always compatible with life outside the narrow confines of their island—have refused to go. Not only that, they don't welcome intrusions by "strangers" who might find the islands "picturesque" or "charming" and try to buy a plot of land and move in.

There was one unfortunate lady, an artist, who, inspired by the magnificent views from one of the islands, bought a small farm from an islander who was leaving, and moved in. She proceeded to build a fence to keep in her dogs. She didn't realize that, by doing so, she had cut off a right-of-way that had been in use on the island for centuries. The locals communicated their displeasure with her fence and her presence on the island

197

in a simple, direct and effective method: they poisoned her well. The lady took the hint and moved.

AUGUST 28

We stayed two more days with the Rutledges. Renée said it would become a legend in the neighborhood that she was so inhospitable she wouldn't let the wife of the American ambassador sleep in her house but made her sleep in a tent in the field. I said good, I'd like to be part of a legend.

The weather continues in its whimsical Irish fashion. The days are lovely and sunny; at night the rains begin and the wind howls. On the third night, toward dawn, our tent began to leak. I awoke to find water in my sleeping bag, but given the choice between an early rising and a wet sleeping bag, I would always choose the latter, so I just rolled over and went back to sleep.

When we left Clifden, we headed toward Letterfrack, Tully Cross and Westport. We stopped long enough to go through Westport House, which is open to the public in the summertime. It has some beautiful pieces of furniture and good silver and china on display, but it is highly commercialized, with an amusement park in the basement complete with go-cart rides, a scary dungeon, a used-book store and—of course,—a tea shoppe. Still, we all enjoyed seeing the house, and the boys enjoyed comparing some of its architectural features with those in the residence.

Generally, the boys have been cheerful, cooperative and helpful, C. less than the other two because he isn't naturally an outdoor person and also because Liam, competent and in charge of our campsite, is imperious with his comrades. David, as ever, is sweet and cheerful, and he hasn't had an earache.

We camped around County Mayo, staying a couple of days at Rosyvera, the home of former Ambassador and Mrs. Curley, near Newport. Their caretaker, Michael Chambers, a kind and genial man, was obviously bewildered by our wanting to pitch our tent in the Curleys' walled garden instead of sleeping in the large, gracious and empty house. In fact, although his innate courtesy would never have let him show it, I'm sure he thought we were dotty.

The rains continue and we are often damp. David said last night that we are all going to get "rhismtuam," and it took us a full five minutes finally to translate that into rheumatism.

The boys had a good time exploring the castle of Grainnè Mhaol— Grace O'Malley—the Irish pirate queen who ruled the seas around Clew Bay in the sixteenth century. The stories of her exploits are legend in Ireland. She had several husbands, and it is said that when she tired of one she lured him to the parapets of the castle and simply threw him into the cold, deep and treacherous waters of Clew Bay.

We left our comfortable walled garden and the peace of Rosyvera and headed straight west for Achill Island, which can be reached by a causeway. It is beautiful and remote, its bogland dipping away from rocky terrain. Pink and purple heather cover miles of hillside, and high, rocky cliffs drop sharply into the sea, which today was calm and blue. Small white cottages, all looking freshly whitewashed, neat and pretty, dot the hillsides and cluster together at crossroads.

There are few tourists. People say the petrol shortage has scared everyone off the roads, and I think that must be true out here in Achill.

David wanted to play in the sand, so we stopped at a glorious, wide, clean and empty stretch of beach and sat, bundled up against the wind. He was wrapped up in thermal underwear, jeans, a turtleneck shirt, sweater, winter jacket, hood, and Wellies.

One little boy of about ten came across the beach wearing swimming trunks and a heavy Irish sweater. To our astonishment, he walked to the water's edge, took off his sweater, and plunged in. He swam and played in the water for about twenty minutes, ran out and put on his sweater over his wet body and walked away. We were simply in awe of him.

We walked up the side of Slieve Mountain to see the remains of a deserted village. The tumbledown walls of two dozen small cottages dot the hillside; I don't know the story of its devastation, but it isn't an uncommon sight in Ireland, simply another reminder of the harsh and tragic history of this island.

Although the weather has improved, the wind on Achill is fierce. I wouldn't be at all surprised to see a small orange tent flying westward, heading for Boston, high over the Atlantic, while three boys and a woman peer out of its flap, and a voice in the wind cries: "Liam, I *told* you to hammer those pegs in deeper!"

SEPTEMBER 4

The boys are back in school, summer is officially over, and we are beginning plans for the pope's visit to Dublin on September 29. He is expected to land in the Phoenix Park in a helicopter, and to say an outdoor mass here for one million people. The altar is being built on the "Fifteen Acres," just a few hundred yards from our back lawn. Since we will have a spectacular view of the entire celebration, we have invited six hundred guests, including the entire embassy staff and their families to come to the residence and observe the mass from our lawn.

It's a vast undertaking. Ron Tallon, the architect who devised the master plan, visited us this morning to explain where the altar will be, where the choir will be, how the seating will be arranged, and the myriad of logistical nightmares he is trying to anticipate.

The congregation for the mass will be grouped according to parishes. Each parish has a fenced-in "corral" which separates it from the next one.

The altar will be covered with a one-acre carpet and lined on each side with papal flags. There will be a five-thousand-voice choir singing a high mass, which one hundred bishops will concelebrate with the pope.

Our main worry at the residence is security during the mass. With one million people just yards from our five-foot ha-ha it would be very easy for anyone to scale the wall and enter the residence grounds. Our own small embassy in Dublin is not equipped to deal with such vast numbers of people, so the American embassy in London is going to send over some security men to help out.

Dennis and I are working on the outside plans. In case of rain, we shall have a marquee set up where we shall serve our guests wine and cheese after the mass. (We are suggesting that everyone bring a picnic lunch.) We shall set up twelve portable toilets, a small tent where babies and toddlers can be changed and cared for, and a first-aid tent. Several of our guests are doctors and have promised to bring along their little black bags, should they be needed.

Michael O'Donohoe and the gardening staff are busy clearing away two hundred feet of shrubs, trees and bushes along the path to give an unobstructed view of the altar. We had thought about renting bleachers for guests to sit on, but decided against it when we were quoted a price of £10 ($20) per seat. We have two hundred folding chairs at the embassy and everyone else can sit on blankets, or stand.

During the mass, one thousand priests will give out Communion. Every potter in Ireland is busy making small bowls to carry the Communion hosts from the altar into the crowds. Two priests who will be our guests during the mass, Father Flood from St. Michael's and Father F. X. Martin, will give Communion to our guests.

Maeve and I are organizing the guest list, the invitations, the instructions. Since the area of the Park which includes the residence is going to be closed off to the public from 6 AM onward, our guests will have to show the guards their printed invitations and identification to be let through the police barriers. Because the Park will be closed entirely at 10 AM, that will be the deadline for guests to arrive at our house. We have arranged for buses to shuttle from the embassy in Ballsbridge at 6 AM and 7 AM to carry our embassy staff and their families. Other guests will get here as best they can. There will be buses and trains running to the Park gates; from there to our house is another two miles, but no cars other than "official" ones are allowed in the Park that day.

We are supposed to go to the airport that morning with the rest of the diplomatic corps to greet the pope when he steps off the plane, but I doubt if we will be able to get out of the Park.

Dublin talks of nothing else. Little yellow and white papal flags are being sold in every shop. The men in the Park are literally working day and night (I see them!) to erect the altar and get everything ready for the mass. I have never seen such industry, such devotion to work, such *efficiency*! Motivation, you are the magic ingredient.

SEPTEMBER 5

There are new faces in the diplomatic corps these days; friends have departed and new arrivals come to take their place. I have had several calls to make this week, and one, today, was *not* a triumph of diplomatic finesse. I shouldn't even tell it on myself, but how can I resist such a good story?

My hostess served me with delicacies of her country, many, many of them, insisting that I try one of each, explaining to me in extraordinary detail how they were made, what the ingredients are, how difficult it is to find those ingredients in Dublin, how she had them sent from her own country. Finally, after eating six or seven, I realized that I was simply not going to be able to eat another one. "No way," as David would say. She, with alarming hospitality, urged me. I demurred. She pressed. I mentioned my waistline. Since she weighs about a hundred pounds more than I do, she only laughed. Then she frowned. "You don't like?" The whole scene was beginning to sound like the breakfast table when I was six.

"I love them," I said, defeated, and took another. I nibbled. She watched anxiously. "This one is served only at weddings and funerals," she explained. "I make especially for you."

I knew that I was going to throw up very soon. Suddenly, there was a discreet knock at the door, and her maid entered to call my hostess away; it seems there was a minor crisis in the kitchen.

I was saved! I took the pastry, wrapped it carefully in my handkerchief and shoved it into my purse. When she returned, I was delicately wiping my lips with a napkin, murmuring: "Delicious." She was satisfied.

We chatted on about our families, about living in Ireland, about life in her own country, until it was nearing time for me to leave. As I gathered up my gloves and my purse, I sneezed. I quickly reached in my handbag to pull out my handkerchief. And you know exactly what happened.

The pastry rolled out of the handkerchief, onto my lap and lay there, looking extremely uneaten.

"Oh," I said. And in the horrible second of silence that followed, I thought: Aren't the boys going to think this is a funny story? And that saved me.

"They were *so* delicious I had to bring one home to my children," I gushed. "They have *such* a sweet tooth."

Her face brightened immediately and she jumped up. "Of course," she said. "They must have more." And she ran to the kitchen and came back

201

with a small bagful which she kindly pressed on me, and I took it, reeking of enthusiasm.

I fled out the door and down the walk, into the waiting car, where I dissolved into tears of laughter.

SEPTEMBER 6

For two nights in a row, I have had nightmares. It's the first time since we've been living in Ireland that I've thought of physical danger. I'm sure that the murder of Lord Mountbatten* has brought it on. His funeral was held today in London.

Last night I dreamed that I was in the backseat of the Mercury with Gerry driving. Christopher and David were with me. We were flagged down by three people standing in the middle of the road. They wore beige gloves. Gerry said: "Oh, oh." He stopped the car and the people made the boys and me get out, and they got into the backseat. Gerry was about to drive off when I realized that the road was covered with snow and ice and I didn't have on any shoes. I rapped on the window and said: "Could you please give me my coat and shoes? You are sitting on them." The woman rolled down the window and threw them at me. Then they drove away. I raced to a ship nearby, where I knew I would find Bill, and said: "Come quickly, Gerry has been kidnapped by Madame Pavlova!"

Bill took my hand and we raced across what seemed to be a dimly lit stadium. We were running very fast, when suddenly people hiding on the edge of the stadium began to fire bullets at us. I said to Bill: "Run as fast as you can, weave in and out and try to keep your head down." As we ran, with bullets whizzing overhead, I woke up, sweating and with a pounding heart. Madame Pavlova?

SEPTEMBER 7

Foreign Minister O'Kennedy put on a spur-of-the-moment luncheon party today for Jane Byrne, the mayor of Chicago, who is visiting Ireland on her way home from Lord Mountbatten's funeral. She's Irish and wants to visit her roots.

She has never been to Ireland before and was surprised, she said, at how "modern" everything is. She said she had expected to see horse-drawn carriages in the streets. I told her she should be on the Naas dual-carriage way on a Sunday evening at 6 PM if she wanted to see something really modern.

* Lord Mountbatten was blown up in his boat off the coast of Sligo; several others in his party were killed or severely wounded. A fifteen-year-old Irish boy who helped out on the boat was killed in the blast. One man connected with the murders has been found, tried and convicted. In January 1982, the ballistics expert who testified at the trial was blown up in his car in Dublin and lost a leg as a result.

When I left Iveagh House, I took my car to a garage to have it looked after. It's ailing seriously, perhaps fatally. Everyone agrees that the bearings are gone and it needs a new engine. Since I love it and couldn't possibly part with it, old and decrepit though it is, I'll probably get a new engine.

SEPTEMBER 8

A wonderful Saturday with absolutely nothing to do. No birthday parties to drive David to, no rugby games for Christopher, no parties, dinners or receptions for us. No house guests. Nothing.

After dinner this evening, I took a long, long bath and fell asleep in the bathtub. A friend told me that ten people a year drown in bathtubs in Ireland. Can that be true? Of course, the Irish aren't good swimmers. I climbed into bed at 9 PM, read *The Year of the French* for twenty minutes, and am falling asleep again.

SEPTEMBER 11

Had lunch today with Tricia Crisp and the rest of the "sisterhood," at Tricia's house in Monkstown. The big news is the announcement that Senator Edward Kennedy will run for the presidency against President Carter. I spent a good deal of time explaining to the women about the American system of electoral primaries, a system so complicated that, as I talked, I realized I didn't totally understand it myself.

SEPTEMBER 12

Our Labrador, Molly, became a mother today. She produced a beautiful litter of nine, two yellows and seven blacks. She began her labors at 11:35 this morning and at 5:35, she gave birth to the ninth. She's a calm, attentive mum, even with so many people peeking in on her, and seems to be totally in charge of the operation despite having Kathleen and me hovering over her like attentive midwives. Nevertheless, Jimmy O'Donohoe, Molly's best friend at the residence, says he is going to sit up with the litter all night just in case she should accidentally harm one of them.

We had an American governor and his party here for dinner tonight. Over coffee, he asked me if I am a feminist. I was surprised; most men don't bring up that subject and if it's brought up in their presence, they sigh. However, I replied that I am. He said his wife is, too, and she doesn't like playing the role of the governor's wife.

I told him I would far rather be the ambassador than the ambassador's wife, but I've been trying to do my own thing here, and create a role for the wife that has a validity all its own. I think I am succeeding to some extent, and although I sometimes find it frustrating, I am never made unhappy by it. We talked about the roles of wives in different occupations and professions. He was concerned and sensitive about the issue and far more interested in it than any man I have spoken to recently. So many women who find themselves having to "play" wife would feel better if they could talk about the frustrations they feel, rather than having to pretend that there are no problems and no frustrations, that all is rosy and that since their husbands are working hard to provide for them financially, they shouldn't complain. Talking it out with a sympathetic husband doesn't make the problems go away, but it helps. Many men, I think, regard such feelings on the part of their wives as somehow a criticism of themselves.

SEPTEMBER 13

Responses are coming in to our invitation to the pope's mass. *Everyone* wants to come. And to bring Granny, or their aunt the nun, or their uncle the priest. We're trying to accommodate everyone, but I fear a cast of thousands. I asked Dennis to order four more portable toilets.

SEPTEMBER 17

Breda O'Kennedy and Máirín Lynch, the wife of the prime minister, came to lunch today. We talked about our forthcoming trip to the United States in November. The Lynches are making an official visit to America, and Bill and I will travel with them. (Actually, Bill has to go on ahead, to be there to meet them when their plane lands. I'll travel from Ireland with the official party.) Mrs. Lynch told me some of the things she especially wants to see while she is there, such as the Picasso exhibit in the National Gallery. There will be one "free" day during the week's tour, and I encouraged them to include New Orleans on the itinerary. They have never been there, and I think it is a unique and charming city. Mrs. Lynch seems receptive to the idea. The other cities on the tour include Washington, Boston, Houston, Chicago and New York. I'm excited just thinking about the trip, but I have to put it on my back burner until after the pope's visit.

As soon as the luncheon guests left, I dashed down to the Bank of Ireland to open an American quilt exhibit in the bank lobby. There was a wine and sherry reception afterwards and quite a large crowd turned out. The quilts, which belong to a collection formed by a young American couple named Hamilton, are exquisite.

SEPTEMBER 18

The weather, as it so commonly is in September, has been glorious. Warm and sunny and more like summer than August was. I entertained forty guests from the Cheshire Home for the severely handicapped at tea this afternoon. They were all in wheelchairs; some were blind. One dear soul who was stone deaf talked loudly throughout my little speech about the history of the house. Several of her friends tried to shush her up, but she rattled happily away. One of the young men is a poet and promised to send me copies of his poems. We took them on a tour of the gardens after tea. Everything looked glorious in the sunshine; I took the blind members of the group with me so I could describe the Pretty Garden to them. They were all extremely kind and receptive and had an intense interest in everything around them. I don't think I'd be that way if I were seriously handicapped; I'd be horrible and depressed and feel sorry for myself all the time. I wonder what gives them the special grace to be such extraordinary people?

SEPTEMBER 19

We went to dinner tonight at the beautiful Georgian home of Sybil Connolly, the grand dame of Irish dress design. I couldn't resist a quick peep into her salon before we went up to the second-floor drawing room. Blouses, long, billowy skirts, ball gowns were on display there, each one so beautifully constructed, so stylish and timeless, so elegant and so *pretty*. Sybil's clothes are works of art, and would be just as much at home in a museum as at a party.

Long before the current batch of talented young Irish designers hit the market, Sybil was designing clothes for the world's beautiful people, putting Ireland on the fashion map. She uses lace and fine linens, poplins, and wools, that are uniquely Irish; her famous handkerchief linen, folded into thousands of tiny, delicate tucks (taking ten yards of flat material to make one finished yard of tucks) has become one of her international trademarks.

SEPTEMBER 20

I'm beginning to think I'm co-hosting the pope's visit with the Irish hierarchy. I had a terrible dream last night, that on the day of the pope's visit the entire city was shrouded in a dense fog. Not a soul could stir. No one could see a foot in front, but the mass was said anyhow in the Park with the mist swirling overhead and the pope completely hidden from view. I was the only one there, sitting alone amidst the thousands of wooden benches. Suddenly I heard the pope's voice call out through the curtain of fog: "Is there no one here to serve the mass?" I started up to the altar, but I couldn't find it and ran back and forth, around in circles, shouting: "I'm coming, Your Holiness!" Then I woke up.

The diplomatic corps has been invited to meet the pope at a reception at the nuncio's. There is much discussion now about what to wear. The days of the long black dress and the mantilla are over, but most of the women are going to wear black, anyway. My only black daytime dress plunges down the front to an alarming depth. It will never do. I have a navy blue, high-necked, long-sleeved dress that will be all right. Do we kneel and kiss the pope's ring? The Spanish ambassador's wife says she will. I think I will be more comfortable shaking hands.

SEPTEMBER 28

We were sitting at dinner this evening, at the round table by the windows in the dining room. The evening was still bright, promising fair weather for tomorrow. As we were chatting with the boys and lingering over dessert, we suddenly heard the most beautiful music waft across the lawn and fill the house. It sounded like a thousand voices joined in song. We all jumped up and lifted the tall windows to see where it was coming from. It *was* a thousand voices, five thousand voices! It was the choir for the pope's mass tomorrow, rehearsing with Frank Patterson and Bernadette Greavy, two of Ireland's leading singers.

It sounded like a choir of angels, coming out of the evening air so suddenly like that, floating across the still Park. We gathered up all the residence staff and went out to the edge of our back lawn and opened the heavy, iron gate that leads into the Fifteen Acres. We never use that entry, and the old gate creaked and grated as we pushed it open. We walked the few hundred feet to the edge of the altar and sat down alone in the empty rows of VIP seats.

Workmen were putting last-minute finishing touches on the altar, working by spotlight. One of the priests in charge of the arrangements was standing on the altar, and beckoned for us to come up and see it at close view. The tall, slim white cross, soaring into the pale evening sky, was in place in the center of the altar, dominating the scene, and visible for miles around. A few early birds, mostly teenage boys, had come into the Park with sleeping bags, planning to spend the night and have a front-row view.

"Sure the auld Park will never be the same after tomorrow," a cheerful workman assured us.

And I thought of that spot in the Park and all it had seen over the centuries, since the days when poachers used to steal quietly up at twilight in search of the pheasant that roamed there. And of the deer, who still wander freely over the Acres but have been removed for the festivities tomorrow; won't they be glad when it's all over, and they can return to the stillness of their Park?

And of the day John Kennedy's helicopter took off from this very spot at the end of his glorious visit in 1963, the echo of his promise to return still lingering over Ireland.

And of the thousands of soccer players, spending their Sunday afternoons on the soft, green grass, forever kicking their ball toward a goal.

And of the days and nights, throughout Ireland's history, when thousands and thousands of British troops, called in to quell yet another Irish uprising, camped on this spot. And of all the past residents of our own big white house, those British politicians sent to Ireland to administer to a people who didn't want them. What would they have thought about a million Irishmen hearing mass celebrated by the *pope* in *Phoenix Park?*

Darkness had fallen but the choir was still singing as we walked back home, and I could hear them from the house as we prepared for an early bedtime. My brain is reeling. I feel like General Eisenhower must have felt the night before D-day.

SEPTEMBER 29: *The Day the Pope Came to Dublin*

This is the day.

It's difficult for a non-Irish person to grasp the feelings of joy, of enthusiasm; ecstasy, almost, that the Catholic population of Ireland feels about the pope's visit here. The Irish are a deeply religious, devout people. The Catholic Church and its doctrines are still the guiding force in the life of every Irish Catholic. The pope, as head of the Roman Catholic Church, is more revered here than any other world figure. The inaccessibility of the pope, until John Paul II came upon the scene, has lent centuries of mystery and glamour to the papacy. To have a pope come to Ireland, to travel around the country, meet the leaders of government and the Church, to smile and wave and to bless the population, is an event that will outshine all other national events for decades to come. One has to remember the dark days of Irish history, when the Penal Laws forbade Catholics to hear mass, when they had to gather secretly in a clandestine spot, perhaps the remote side of a mountain, with a stone serving as an altar, to practice the rites of their Church. They were willing to risk severe punishment rather than to quell the spirit of their faith.

Those days are over and belong to Irish history now, but it was a long, hard road from a tiny "mass rock" in the wilds of Mayo or the mountains of Kerry, to the tall white cross in the middle of Phoenix Park.

Old men told the young about those days in Ireland. They can tell another, happier story now, of how they were brought as babes to the Phoenix Park and held up high over their da's head to receive the papal blessing. Grannies will tell toddlers how, as young girls, they walked with their families through miles of darkened streets in the middle of the night to get a good position in Phoenix Park for the mass. It's a day of national jubilation, a rare auld day.

The first bus from the embassy arrived at the residence at 5:30 AM, filled with husbands and wives, kids, grannies, and the aunt the nun, the uncle the priest. It was dark and chilly, with a stiff wind, but the rosy dawn promised a sunny day ahead.

Bill was up and dressed to meet the first arrivals. We had put out coffee, tea, hot chocolate and biscuits for them. I had asked Dennis to call me at 6:30, and when the phone rang I ran to the windows to open the big wooden shutters that stretch from floor to ceiling in our bedroom. The windows look out over our back lawn and the Fifteen Acres beyond it. I had expected to see people drifting into the Park this early. I did *not* expect to open my shutters and to see a half million people, their shapes and figures blurred in the dim, dawn light, quietly milling around just a few hundred yards from my window. There was no sound at all; just a mass of humanity. It was a stunning sight.

I dressed hurriedly in a warm sweater and heavy woolen suit, and dashed down to join our guests. Everyone was shivering in the morning chill and with the excitement of the day, and everyone was smiling. Grown-ups were sitting around the grass on blankets, sipping hot coffee, while the kids played on the wide, green expanse of lawn, still wet with the heavy dew.

All our logistics seemed to be working perfectly. By nine o'clock, the non-embassy guests began arriving. Clearly, no one was having trouble getting through our complicated maze of security. At 9:15, Bill, the boys and I left the residence grounds in the Mercury to go to the nunciature. We flew our small American and ambassadorial flags from our bumpers as identification, and eased our way through the thousands of people flowing steadily into the Park. Buses came from all over Ireland, with nuns and priests, invalids, the handicapped, the elderly, the lame and the halt.

Streams of families, the very young and the very old, carrying camp chairs, blankets, picnic baskets, cameras, binoculars, walking slowly and quietly in lines as far as the eye could see, thousands and thousands and thousands of them, came pouring through every entrance to the Park. I will never forget the sight of them, or the strange, pervasive silence. Everyone spoke softly, as if a loud noise would break the spell that was cast over us all.

We finally got out of the Park through White's Gate and drove back up the Navan Road toward the nuncio's. The pope was to make a quick stop there before coming to the Park, and the nuncio had very kindly told us we might bring the boys to the back garden to catch a glimpse of him as he entered the house. (The diplomatic corps has been invited to a formal reception later in the evening.)

Flags were flying everywhere, Irish flags and papal flags, gold and yellow bunting draped across house fronts. David had a small papal flag on a stick and had stapled a tiny American flag on it. He brought them to wave for the pope when he arrived at the nunciature.

Police lined the road and we were stopped and checked twice on the short ride. When we arrived at the nunciature, we were lined up with about a hundred other guests in the back garden and told to wait there.

It was windy and cold and the boys, dressed too lightly, became chilled, then restless. Suddenly, we all looked skyward and saw a big green jet, the shamrock of Aer Lingus unmistakable on its tail, flying across Dublin toward the airport. Six Irish Army jets accompanied it. It was a thrilling sight. I was told that when the crowds in the Park first saw the jet in the sky, a massive roar went up that lasted for a full five minutes.

At last, after another very long wait (the pope was being officially greeted at the airport), two small army helicopters hove into sight, followed by two large blue and white KLM copters, one of them carrying the pope.

They landed in a pasture just beyond the nuncio's back garden and as the door opened we could see the pope come to the threshold, then descend the steps. He was dressed all in white, with a small white biretta on the back of his head. He made his way across the field, his entourage following at a slight distance, up into the garden and along the path where we stood. He walked slowly toward the house, waving to the crowd, smiling, but not stopping or breaking his pace. Suddenly, he spied the two little flags David was waving, and the American flag caught his eye. He stopped and bent toward David: "You must be a little American boy," he said softly, in accented English. David had been drilled all morning to say "Yes, Your Holiness" if he should be spoken to, but he was simply wide-eyed and awed into silence. The pope squeezed him in both his arms, then continued along the pathway toward the house. He turned for a moment to wave to the crowd, then quickly disappeared through the double doors of the nuncio's drawing room. David's had been his only greeting, and one that David will remember all his life.

We dashed back to our waiting car to get through the crowds in the Park in time to be back at the residence when the pope made his appearance in the Fifteen Acres. Luckily, a garda we know outside the nunciature gates assigned us a motorcycle escort and we made it back in record time. All of our guests had arrived, about seven hundred in all; they were lining the edge of our back lawn and had spread down our little path in the woods which looks out over the Park. Within minutes of our return, a cavalcade of limousines arrived, bringing the pope to the back of the altar. From where we stood, we could see him enter through a small door, where he changed into his vestments for the mass. He finally emerged into sight of the congregation on the high front steps of the altar. The sun was shining brilliantly and the forty-eight white and gold flags snapped in the strong wind. The gray carpet which covered the acre of altar looked like rough-hewn stone in the sunlight. The wind fluttered the bishops' red vestments as, walking in pairs, they filed slowly out on the altar. The crowd roared and roared, waving their tiny papal flags, shouting, smiling, laughing with the pleasure and excitement of it all, with the joy of seeing him at last.

No one could doubt the rapturous display of love and devotion. John

Paul II, the big Pole with the crinkly eyes and high cheekbones, responded with a wide smile. He held up both arms in a salute. And then the mass began.

The music throughout was magnificent. The choir and the soloists were supplemented by the Chieftains, one of the country's best traditional Irish music groups. The program was filled with Irish music as well as with the more traditional hymns of the church. Lay people from different walks of life had been invited to ascend the steps of the altar and read the lessons. The pope delivered his sermon in English. It was a very long sermon, nearly fifty minutes and, I thought, somewhat difficult to follow at times. At Communion, our two priest-guests served our group, standing under an enormous beech tree at the edge of the back lawn. The sun poured down through its leafy branches and made a kaleidoscope of moving patterns on the grass below.

When the mass was over, the pope climbed into the "popemobile," a strange-looking yellow vehicle resembling an open-air tank, and was driven slowly through the Fifteen Acres, smiling and waving to the crowds, so that people in the far back could get a closer look at him.

Liam and several of his friends had been sitting on the wall of our ha-ha during the mass. When the pope returned to the altar after his tour on the popemobile, one of the boys, Michael Murphy, leapt off the wall and ran across the intervening several hundred feet to the bottom of the altar steps, where the pope was coming down. Despite the multitude of security that surrounded him—the police, the guards, the priests and bishops—and with all the world watching on TV, Mick Murphy, fast as quicksilver, was suddenly standing in front of the pope, holding out his hand and saying: "Hi! I'm Mick Murphy." He was gone again before anyone could realize what had happened. His pals on the wall were enchanted with his boldness. It was a move neither Mick nor his friends will ever forget.

We stayed on the lawn after the mass was finished, while our guests nibbled cheese and crackers and ate the picnics that most of them had brought. It was nearly six o'clock when the last one left, and Dennis and I and the boys began collecting the empty glasses and filling trash bags. The first-aid tent, happily, had gone unused (although one young woman in the Park, nine months pregnant and unable to resist attending the mass, had given birth in the crowd to a healthy, eight-pound baby boy. You can imagine what he was named). Our loos had stood firm in the strong winds that prevailed all day. The buses rumbled back through the crowds to the embassy, but most of our guests left on foot, the way they had come, tired, elated, with a memory to last them a lifetime.

We had a quick dinner, a bath and a change, and left once again for the nunciature where the diplomatic corps was being presented formally to the pope. We were ushered into a very small, airless room where we were served drinks and told to wait.

The papal reception at the nuncio's

The "Judiciary" was in another room, and the "Government" in yet another. Obviously, we were not supposed to get mixed up and appear with the wrong group. Each of us was having our own little formal reception.

We waited and waited. The pope had been put through an exhausting day. After his mass and tour in the Park, he had flown to Drogheda, north of Dublin, to give a major speech where he had asked the IRA ("on my knees") to give up violence; on his return to Dublin he rode in a motorcade all through the city, paid a formal call on President and Mrs. Hillery, and then returned to the nuncio's, where he had all of us waiting for him. His face was glazed with fatigue when he came through our receiving line. He shook hands warmly with Bill (each of us was introduced by the nuncio), and mentioned that he was going to America when he left Ireland. When he shook hands with me, however, his eyes avoided mine and I received only a most perfunctory handshake. I was disappointed but, as I said, the poor man was exhausted.

And then, at the end of a very long day, we went home. The boys were still up and we all sat around in the library for a while, talking about the day. Although it was nearly lost in all the excitement, today was also Christopher's twelfth birthday. While we were out at the nuncio's, a reporter called the house to ask about our large gathering for the mass. C. got on the phone and told him that the whole thing had been arranged for his birthday. "One year they gave me a bowling party, then they gave me a magic show, and last year they gave me a theater party. So there really wasn't much left for them to do, until they got the idea of having the pope say mass in our backyard." C. thought it was a wonderful joke and was still laughing at his wit when we came home. He thought it even funnier when he saw it printed in the papers the next morning!

OCTOBER 22

My booklet on the American embassy residence is finished and published, and we had a party this evening up in the Park to celebrate. It's a handsome publication; the quality and variety of the illustrations are excellent. Harold Clarke, of Eason's, who publishes the Irish Heritage Series, gave me two copies of the booklet bound in red leather to present to President Carter and Secretary Cyrus Vance when we make our state visit to America next month.

One of the more enjoyable sidelights of researching the booklet was discovering the origins and history of Phoenix Park, one of the oldest urban parks in Europe. The name "Phoenix" is an English corruption of the Irish words "Fionn Uisge," which mean "a spring of clear water." There is a spring that runs underground in the Park, closely parallel to the Main Park Road.

Plans for the Park began under the vice-regency of the Duke of Ormonde in the seventeenth century. Ormonde, who returned to Ireland after his exile in France, was the first duke in Irish history. His common sense, vision and understanding of Ireland made him an outstanding viceroy. In 1662, King Charles II authorized the purchase of about four hundred acres of land in the middle of Dublin. By the end of Ormonde's term of office in 1669, over £30,000 had been spent on the Park, and half again as much was to be spent before it was finished.

It was envisioned in the beginning as a royal deer park, filled with game. Deer were imported from England, partridges from Wales, pheasants from the Ormonde estates in Ireland. The temptation for poaching was irresistible, and the deer and the birds were reduced drastically each year. To discourage poaching, the Park, which by now had grown to two thousand acres, was enclosed by a wall, designed and built by William Dodson. Why Mr. Dodson was chosen as the builder is unclear, since he had recently constructed a church that promptly fell down. Perhaps he had a brother-in-law who issued contracts. Alas, his building skills had not improved, and his park wall also soon began to crumble. A new wall was finally built by Sir John Temple, but the poachers were unfazed by any of these constructions and poached happily away.

Some of the land had to be withdrawn from Park use when the Royal Hospital in Kilmainham was built, and that reduced its total area to

1,752 acres, which it is today, making it the largest city park in Europe.

The wild game is gone now, although we do see an occasional pheasant on our lawns. But the deer still roam freely, and one of the loveliest sights from our residence is to see them, on a soft summer's evening, steal quietly up to the edge of the lawn and stare shyly at us while their huge antlers bob gently up and down, up and down, in silent, unexplained assent.

When Lord Chesterfield became viceroy in 1745, he interested himself in the landscape architecture of the Park and designed the straight rows of chestnut trees that line the Main Park Road. In the spring their pink and white blossoms decorate the road in lavish color. In the fall, the Park is thronged with small boys collecting a supply of "conkers" from under their broad, spreading branches.

In 1751, a Park ranger named Nathaniel Clements built a handsome house in the Park, which the British government bought in 1782 to become the official residence of the viceroy. The other two homes in the Park were the chief secretary's lodge (now the American residence) and the under secretary's residence, which for many years has been the home of the papal nuncio in Dublin. The nuncio has moved to new quarters in the Navan Road, and the future of his lovely old house across the road from us is uncertain.

The Park is maintained in excellent condition by the Board of Works, but the density of traffic on the Main Park Road is growing at an alarming rate. New suburban housing estates springing up on the far side are bringing thousands of commuters into Dublin through the Park. The speed and carelessness with which they make their morning and evening circuit on the Main Road are frightening, and the plethora of accidents is tragic. Each morning, as Bill and the boys drive to school and office, they watch out for the Shaver, as David calls him. One of the commuters coming into the Park through the Castle Knock Gate is a gentleman who obviously doesn't get up in time and does his morning ablutions in his car as he speeds down the road at sixty miles an hour. He plugs an electric shaver into the lighter on his dashboard, and with one eye on the road and another on his rearview mirror, he shaves. One day recently, when the traffic had backed up, the boys found themselves stopped right in front of the Shaver. David quickly scribbled a sign which he held up from our rear window: "Have You Brushed Your Teeth?" The Shaver laughed uproariously while he combed his hair and tied his tie.

The Dublin Zoo is also located in the Phoenix Park. It is our neighbor one mile down the Main Park Road, and the first summer we were here, David and I were frequent visitors. Although it isn't an extensive zoo, the grounds are lovely, with natural, charming landscapes, pretty ponds and interesting man-made habitats. The tiny Victorian gatehouse at the entrance to the Zoo is worth a visit in itself.

The Park is filled with sights that will stay forever in our memories as part of our Dublin heritage.

Old men with their caps and pipes walking muzzled greyhounds, three or four to a leash, in the evening twilight;

Sleek thoroughbreds being raced across "The Gallops" in the early morning dew;

The white mist rising over the Fifteen Acres, hovering waist high until the morning sun burns it off;

Joggers—panting, sweating, groaning—stretching their endurance one more mile;

Elderly men and women sedately walking small dogs on a midday afternoon;

The Sunday bicycle races and soccer games;

The slow, dignified cricket matches that seem to go on forever across the road;

Polo ponies racing each other down a soft, green field;

Little girls walking slowly and primly in their fluffy white dresses and tiny veils, brought to the Park for a Sunday outing after their First Communion;

Young men and old sitting in their cars reading Sunday newspapers;

Families picnicking on a warm summer's day;

Lovers, walking arm in arm, pausing to look at each other, to kiss, and to move on slowly under the broad, protective branches of Lord Chesterfield's chestnut trees.

OCTOBER 24

I had to give a speech tonight at the Shelbourne Hotel to the Ireland America Society. As we finished dinner and I was about to deliver my speech, "A Day in the Life of an Ambassador's Wife," the lights went out. At first we thought it was just a fuse, but a waiter came to tell us that there was a blackout staged by striking workers of the Electricity Supply Board and we would be in darkness for some time. Candles were brought, and I read my speech by their flickering light, Abe Lincoln style. I very seldom read a speech these days. Practice has given me the confidence to speak either from memory or with a few notes, the way Bill always does, but this was the first time I had given this particular speech, so I had to read it.

I'm asked to speak about twice a month, in Dublin or out in the country. I try to accept, particularly if it is for a group who want me to talk on a specific subject with some substance, such as the status of women in America or the American electoral system or (the one I enjoy the most) the state of education in America. I find that many Irish people have only a vague understanding of our educational system. They base their opinions on the sensational news stories and television series they see here, which picture American public high schools either as places of siege where guns have replaced books, policemen have replaced teachers, and athletes have replaced scholars or as adolescent country clubs where insipid girls with long blond hair hold inane conversations with handsome, vapid young men.

At the same time that I make my rounds in Ireland, talking to professors, teachers, principals, school inspectors and students, trying to inform them about American education, I'm learning more about the Irish schools.

There are many things about Irish education I admire, the depth, for example, in which subjects are taught, with the children made to learn dates, places, names . . . *facts!*

Irish children also memorize poetry, which I think is a good skill as well as a wonderful source of pleasure; I regret it has been abandoned in most American schools. Irish schools give homework each night and although some of it for the younger children is make-work, it nevertheless instills study habits that can be carried into secondary school. They are assigned essays to write and their written work is carefully and thoroughly checked by their teachers. The classrooms I have visited are disciplined and orderly, and there seem to be fewer fights on the playgrounds than one sees in America.

But one aspect of Irish education does trouble me. Corporal punishment is still used in Irish schools, usually meted out by the principal or a dean of discipline. The rod or stick used to punish is usually given some euphemistic name. It is called "the biffer" at St. Michael's, where it is used sparingly, but I have heard stories from other schools of serious physical abuse to children. Yet many people in Ireland still believe it is the right way to control a classroom. "Spare the rod and spoil the child" is the common child-rearing philosophy, and I know few parents who would be upset if their child was hit with a rod or stick in school, unless he was injured. Parents tend to take the teacher's side and assume that the child had it coming to him.

Teachers tend to demand unquestioning obedience and academic acquiescence from their students. I think this creates an attitude of passivity that is carried into adulthood and makes people far too accepting when they should be outraged, assenting when they should protest, conservative when they should be imaginative. The Irish don't stray far from the accepted rules of behavior, whether they're raising a child, planting a garden, building a home, cooking a meal, or decorating a house. It seems that all the extraordinary creativity in the Irish national character is channeled into the arts—theater, literature, music and painting—and few venture to use their imagination in mundane, everyday activities.

There are very few nondenominational schools in Ireland. The vast majority of private schools are Catholic or Church of Ireland. There is a "national" (that is, tax-supported) Catholic school system and a "national" Protestant school system. There are also community schools, comprehensive schools and vocational schools. And of course there is in Ireland, as there is everywhere, the snob element in schools. Whether you were taught by the Jesuits at Clongowes, Gonzaga or Belvedere, or by the Holy Ghost fathers at Blackrock, St. Michael's or Rockwell, whether you were a "Loreto girl" or a "Sacred Heart girl" can be very important in your professional and social life. But I've noticed something incongruous about school name-dropping: women drop their husband's schools into conversation far more frequently than their own—or than the men do themselves. Perhaps women care more about those things than men. Certainly some nuns can be great snobs; I heard a wonderful story about a Dublin convent which once imported a group of English nuns from across the water to make ladies out of the Irish girls. When one of the students was overheard addressing the old gardener as "Tom," she was immediately and firmly reprimanded: "Ladies *never* call gardeners by their first name," she was instructed. "Nor are they called 'Mr.' You simply say: 'Dooley,' as in 'Prune the roses, Dooley.' "

Free secondary education for everyone is a relatively new concept in Ireland. In 1966, the minister for education, Donough O'Malley, announced, somewhat to everyone's surprise including his own, that from then on there would be free, comprehensive postprimary education in Ireland. Until that time, there were only fee-paying academic secondary schools that were church-run or free vocational schools. Although there were a few scholarships available to the gifted, no child was guaranteed a secondary education unless his family could pay for it.

The Catholic Church did not look with favor upon this new turn of educational events. They saw that the power of the Church in education could easily slip out of their hands and into those of lay educators. When Ireland asked for and received a loan from the World Bank to finance the new education scheme, the Bank made two stipulations for the loan: the schools must be coed, and they must be nondenominational.

The Church didn't like those requirements at all and sent speakers around the country denouncing the whole scheme and telling parents about the inherent dangers.

The Department of Education, meanwhile, also sent speakers around the country telling parents what marvelous opportunities were going to open up for their children, with free secondary schools available to one and all. Finally, fourteen comprehensive secondary schools were built, with various concessions made to the Catholic Church:

1. The government would pay the fees of children who opted to stay in Catholic schools;

2. Each bishop could appoint two priests of his choosing to the Board of Trustees of the school. Two parents would also be on the "Board" but not on the Board of Trustees;

3. Religion would be taught in the schools;

4. The government would pay for each school to have its own chaplain;

5. Religious orders who had teachers in the community had the right to have some of their members teach in the schools. These teachers were appointed without going through the "due process" which lay teachers have to go through. (The unions objected strenuously to these clerical appointments.)

The Church reluctantly accepted these concessions.

One of the schools I visited recently was the Greendale Community School in Kilbarrick, Dublin. It has 828 pupils, and a very active evening Adult Education Program. The school is only four years old and takes in children largely from the middle-class housing developments that have sprung up in the area during the past decade. The school's interior is handsome, with bright-colored carpets, plants hanging from ceilings, vividly painted walls and large classrooms.

The teachers dress informally; the boys wear gray sweaters and the girls wear green, but that seems to be the limit of their dress code. There is a strict code of behavior, however, and the principal told me that there have been only two instances of drinking on the school premises. There have been no cases of drug selling or taking on the school grounds.

There is an eighteen to one pupil-teacher ratio, but because pupils must go to school twenty-eight hours a week and the teachers only teach twenty-two, the average class size is twenty-four. The minimum beginning salary for teachers is £4,000 a year, with the maximum salary going to £9,500. Principals make £3,000 more. (With the current rate of exchange at about $1.80, that would be from $7,200 to $17,100, with the principal's salary about $22,500.) It's very similar to the salary range in the District of Columbia public schools.

Anton Carroll, the young and energetic principal of Greendale, would like to see lower pupil-teacher ratios, more remedial work and more pastoral programs, to teach good citizenship to the students. And, he added, "more innovative principals who would light candles instead of cursing the darkness."

"But," I persisted, "are you happy about your school and the way it works?"

"Oh yes," he replied. "We turn out a wonderful bunch of kids, and isn't that the best way to judge?"

NOVEMBER 7: *Across America*

Every minute for weeks has been spent getting ready for our state visit to America with the taoiseach and Mrs. Lynch. I ran from one dressmaker to another, hating every minute of it, squirming through fittings, deciding at the last minute that I should have another hat to go with a coat, remembering that I need a long black strapless slip and not finding one, putting all the clothes for the trip out on my bed, checking off the functions we will be attending (twenty-six of them on my schedule to date), and carefully going over each outfit for each function, choosing shoes, underwear, jewelry, purse, gloves and hat, and—finally!—putting on a complete dress rehearsal, with Kitty zipping me in and out, making sure everything "works." It was a far cry from my usual "throw it in and hope for the best" attitude toward packing. A last-minute hitch: I have no hat box. No one travels with hats anymore, so of course no one buys hat boxes. What am I going to do with my four hats? Dennis, as usual, comes to the rescue and makes one for me. He covers it with black suede cloth, ties a red cord around it, and prints in tiny letters on the side: "Yves St. L." It's so stylish I hate to put my hats into it. I'm all set.

I have a beautiful new black-lace dress, strapless, with a matching jacket, to wear to the White House dinner. I have a ten-year-old white-lace jeweled dress from my London days, and three other long formal gowns. Three short cocktail dresses, two suits, four daytime dresses, a skirt and sweater and two coats make up the rest of my wardrobe.

Bill went ahead to be on hand to greet the Lynches when they stepped off the plane. He got a flight home with Zbigniew Brzezinski, whose official plane was refueling at Shannon last week. Our flight left Dublin this morning at 11:30 AM. I let the boys have a holiday from school so they could come to the airport to say good-by. Maeve came along, too, as well as several of the embassy staff. We had a gala send-off. The official party consisted of the taoiseach and Mrs. Lynch, the minister of foreign affairs Michael O'Kennedy, and his wife, Breda; the secretary-general of the Department of Foreign Affairs, Andrew O'Rourke, and his Danish wife, Hanne; Dermot Nally, deputy secretary-general; Frank Dunlop, the government press secretary; Walter Kirwan, assistant secretary-general; Commandant Christopher Leaney, aide-de-camp to the taoiseach . . . and myself.

There are seven other government aides accompanying the taoiseach and nine members of the press.

I kissed the boys good-by before getting into the little bus that would take us out to the runway. They stood in a row and waved for as long as I could see them. Soon after we boarded, the stewardess poured us all glasses of champagne, and the taoiseach, who was sitting with Mrs. Lynch in the seat in front of mine, turned around and toasted the success of the trip.

We landed at Shannon for the layover and everyone got off the plane to stretch. Mrs. Lynch slipped on the slick floor going back out to the plane and hurt her wrist, but she made light of it. Thank God she didn't break it, just at the start of our trip.

We were served a *delicious* lunch, a far, far cry from the fare one usually receives on airplanes, and after lunch I wrote for a while in my journal, then visited with Breda O'Kennedy; we exchanged stories on how we'd met our husbands. And suddenly we were landing in Newport News, Virginia. I couldn't believe the time had flown by so quickly.

State visitors to America are often taken to Williamsburg, Virginia, to spend their first night in the States and rest from their journey before they begin their arduous rounds. Newport News was the closest airport for our big Aer Lingus jet to land. The rest of the passengers on the plane had been told in advance that there would be an unscheduled landing there before the flight continued to its New York destination.

As we stepped off the plane, I immediately saw Bill standing with Sean and Paula Donlon at the bottom of the steps, waiting to greet us. Mr. and Mrs. Abelardo Valdez (he is chief of protocol) were there also, along with a half dozen Protocol staff members. We all climbed into waiting limousines and began the twenty-mile ride to Williamsburg. It was a beautiful fall day, sunny and crisp, with autumn foliage still lingering on the trees.

Everyone was free this evening. Bill and I had dinner alone and caught up on family news. He soaks up stories about the boys like a sponge, wanting to hear every detail, laughing uproariously at every antic, frowning at misbehavior, worrying about problems.

After dinner we walked into town and bought an Ace bandage for Mrs. Lynch's wrist, which looks as if it is swelling. I am ready for bed at 9:30 and expect to sleep soundly.

November 8

We awoke for an early breakfast at the Williamsburg Inn, and were ready, with bags packed, for the trip back to Newport News. The big, silver Air Force II was sitting on the runway waiting for us, "The United States of America" painted on its side. It was to be our official plane throughout the trip. The captain and all the crew came out to say hello and to welcome us aboard. We took off immediately and were at Andrews Air Force Base in less than thirty minutes. It was another beautiful day, chilly, sunny, clear and windless. A perfect day for the outdoor reception awaiting us on the White House lawn.

We transferred at Andrews to a helicopter, which took us on a bumpy flight and put us down twelve minutes later on the Mall, just south of the White House. We changed again into waiting limousines, and drove in a group to the back lawn of the White House, where hundreds of waiting Washingtonians and members of the press had gathered to watch Mr. Lynch being greeted officially by President Carter.

The big crowd ("far bigger than we usually get for foreign dignitaries," a member of the Protocol staff whispered in my ear as I was being placed in line) was roped off from the "official party." The press and photographers, along with TV cameras, were in the front of the crowd, and a large platform had been erected in the middle of the lawn, from which the president and the taoiseach would make their formal speeches of welcome and response.

Each of our cars stopped directly under the "Truman balcony" at the back of the White House. As we left our cars, we were shown our "toe cards," slips of paper with our names on them, placed on the ground to show each of us where to stand. I was wearing a red, green and black checked dress, with a matching Kelly green fitted coat and a small black velvet hat with a band of my dress material around the edge. I knew we would be received on the lawn of the White House, and I decided that the green coat would show up on color television and look well against the green lawn. Also, I was schmaltzy enough to want to wear green on this day.

When each of us was in place, the president walked out alone from the back door of the White House. (Mrs. Carter had flown to Thailand the day before to tour the Cambodian refugee camps.) The president stood by the driveway, ready to greet the Lynches as their car drove up.

Mrs. Lynch got out first, looking absolutely lovely in her brilliant coral suit and matching hat. The taoiseach followed her, and the president shook hands with each of them, then took Mr. Lynch with him to the platform. Mrs. Valdez, the wife of the chief of protocol, took Mrs. Lynch to her place at the side of the platform.

There was a nineteen-cannon salute; the band, made up of all the branches of the military, played both countries' national anthems, then the president and the taoiseach reviewed the troops. Back on the platform, President Carter gave his speech first, followed by Mr. Lynch's response. Since Bill had written a draft of the president's speech, much of which Mr. Carter used, I knew in advance what he was going to say, but it still sounded eloquent and meaningful hearing it in that setting.

I found the ceremony deeply moving; it was an oft-repeated ritual which succeeded because it was kept simple and dignified and, on this occasion, had just the right note of sentiment. I looked out across the lawn at the Washington Monument rising high into the cloudless blue sky and felt happy at being home, at showing off my country to our Irish friends, and showing them off to America.

When the ceremony was over, we went into the White House for coffee and a short visit. Then the officials in our party disappeared for meetings with the president while the rest of us left for a luncheon at Woodlawn Plantation, just outside Washington, given by the wife of the secretary of state, Mrs. Cyrus Vance.

The luncheon was very pretty and informal, with music by a Marine Corps string ensemble from the White House. After the lunch, Mrs.

Vance stood and made a toast to Mrs. Lynch. She also said some very flattering things about Bill and me, and mentioned the booklet on the residence that I had presented to her and the secretary earlier in the day.

Mrs. Lynch had to respond to the toast, and although she hates public speaking, she carried it off well.

After the luncheon, we were driven back to the White House, where Mrs. Lillian Carter was waiting on the front steps to greet us. Since the president's wife was in Thailand, his mother was to be our official White House hostess. Her blue eyes twinkled and a broad smile spread across her face as she spotted her old Irish friends pouring out of the limousines. She took us in to tea—which no one wanted after our enormous luncheon at Woodlawn. We nibbled dutifully—and then we were taken on a tour of the White House. All of us admired the portrait of Jacqueline Kennedy wearing a dress made for her in Ireland by Sybil Connolly.

We sat for a while in the East Room and listened to the singers rehearsing for tonight's program after the state dinner.

"I think the preparations are just as much fun as the dinner," Mrs. Carter said. "Let's go into the dining room and see what they are fixing up in there." The decorator who was "doing" the room for the dinner was there. He showed us the exquisite birds handpainted on the place cards that would be on every table, and the matching table skirts and linens.

We left the White House by the front door. I was standing on the steps talking to Mrs. Vance while waiting for my limousine to pull up, when suddenly all the doors of the limos snapped shut and the line began to pull out of the drive.

"Hey, wait for me," I shouted, but it was too late. The entourage was moving and I was left behind.

"I'd better watch more carefully the next time," I said to Mrs. Vance. Or better yet, I thought, I'll keep my eye on Hanne O'Rourke. She and I always ride together, and she can spot our car in line the minute it pulls up. When I see her move from now on, I'll move. But I wasn't stranded because Mrs. Vance gave me a lift back to my hotel.

Bill and I are staying at the Hay Adams hotel, just off Lafayette Park. The Irish members of the official party are staying at Blair House, the guest quarters for presidential visitors. We went there this evening to meet our party and to go together to the White House. We waited a few minutes in the drawing room of Blair House, admiring the eighteenth-century antique furniture and the pretty dried flower arrangements that fill the house. Even though Blair House is just across Pennsylvania Avenue from the White House, we once again climbed into cars and drove the short distance.

On the evening of a state dinner, the White House looks like . . . like what? Like the movies filming the evening of a state dinner. You are

With President Carter and the O'Kennedys before the state dinner

transported into a fairy tale, a land of spotlights, red carpets, champagne and flowers, and, even more heady than the champagne, the company of people of great power.

We walked up the brilliant red carpet laid out on the White House steps, through the glare of TV lights and flashing bulbs, and into the foyer, where the Marine orchestra was playing. Before we could stop to savor any of this, we were whisked through the foyer and into an elevator to take us to the second floor to the private apartments of the president. "Miz Lillian" and the president were waiting for us there, she a familiar friend by now, he impressive with his kind, friendly and simple manners. He gave the impression not of a politician who has lost his real self to the office he holds but rather of a man of genuine strength and integrity.

Vice-President Mondale joined us and teased Bill about a very flattering article that had recently appeared about him in the Los Angeles *Times*. "Who's your press agent?" the vice-president asked. "I could use him."

After a glass of sherry, we were directed down the staircase and into the East Room, where the other guests had congregated. We were each announced at the door of the East Room as we entered, and the ladies were escorted in on the arm of a Marine officer in full-dress uniform.

We were served champagne and stood around chatting until the president and the Lynches arrived to make their official entrance to "Ruffles and Flourishes" and "Hail to the Chief." Does one ever see or hear that moment and not tingle with the drama of it? I have stood in that room and watched other Irish statesmen come through that door with other presidents: Eamon de Valera, blind and nearly ninety, came in with President Johnson; Sean Lemass, taoiseach from 1959 to 1966, came in with President Kennedy. To me, they were impressive but remote figures, part of the pageant of history. I was thrilled to be a privileged spectator but I felt in no·way personally involved. Tonight, to watch Jack and Maírín Lynch come through the door with President Carter was a moment filled with the pride of friendship. I have come to know them so well that I shared vicariously in this moment of high drama in their lives.

Both men went to a platform in the center of the room and made their toasts before dinner. This is an innovation that President Carter has recently made to enable his guest of honor to enjoy his dinner in a relaxed manner, without worrying about what he will get up and say afterwards.

The president's toast was short, flattering and charming. Mr. Lynch followed with a longer response, which ended up with the story about the Irish lady who had six children and, when asked when she was going to have her seventh, replied: "Sure, haven't I heard that every seventh child born in the world today is Chinese?"

I was standing directly behind the speaker of the house, Thomas O'Neill, when the taoiseach told that joke, and all I could see in the room were the broad shoulders of the Speaker shaking in silent mirth.

The Lynches and President Carter then formed a receiving line and shook hands with their guests as we filed in to dinner. I was fortunate to be seated at a table between Millie O'Neill, the speaker's wife, and Sean Donlon, the Irish ambassador, both good friends. It was a delicious meal, beginning with striped bass with oyster sauce, and going on to stuffed saddle of lamb served with cauliflower and artichoke hearts niçoise, Bibb lettuce salad, Brie cheese and, for dessert, pineapple mousse "surprise" with petits fours. The wines were a good mixture of foreign and domestic vintages: Louis Martini Johannisberg Riesling 1977; then Simi Cabernet Sauvignon 1979; and Chandon blanc de Noirs with dessert. The pineapple mousse was the best thing of all.

After dinner, violinists came into the dining room and strolled around, playing while we had coffee. Then we retired to the East Room where we listened to a concert of operatic arias by nine young American vocalists. I sat just to the left and behind the president during the concert and I could see that he was transfixed by the music, totally relaxed and enthralled by it. He is clearly a music lover, but I could not say the same for all the VIP guests, a few of whom squirmed and fidgeted throughout.

When the program was finished, more champagne was served. By 11

PM, the guests gradually and reluctantly began to say good-by. Breda O'Kennedy took me over and introduced me to her dinner partner, Leonard Bernstein, who seemed so taken with the guests that he was trying out a not-very-plausible Irish accent and making plans to come to Ireland soon.

It was finally time to say good night and to end this most glorious, memorable of days. We said thank you, first to the president, then to Mr. Mondale; they had been genial, kind, attentive hosts during the evening, and had managed to do so while facing the worst crisis of their administration. Just three days earlier the American embassy staff in Teheran had been taken hostage. Little was said of the event during the festivities, but it was in the forefront of everyone's mind as we went through the elegant rituals of the day. The only time the president alluded to it in my presence was when we were having sherry in the upstairs drawing room. One of us mentioned it and he said: "These have been the worst three days of my presidency."

We said good night to our Irish friends in front of Blair House, and Bill and I continued on to the Hay Adams. Like Eliza Doolittle, I couldn't begin to go to bed, so we went down to the bar of the hotel and had a nightcap while we talked about the day. Bill told me about what he had done after I left him at the White House that morning; the talks with the president had centered around the continuing crisis in Northern Ireland. As he does back home in Ireland, Mr. Lynch stressed the need for a peaceful political solution, and he found Mr. Carter a sympathetic listener.

Later, at a working luncheon at the State Department, Secretary Vance had given his Irish guests a briefing on the Camp David Agreement and the progress being made toward a Middle East settlement. Since Ireland contributes troops to the peacekeeping force in Lebanon, it is deeply interested in the prospects of war and peace there.

Although Mr. Lynch is making this official visit in his capacity as head of the European Economic Community (each member nation of the EEC takes a six-month turn acting as head of the Community), the interest on Capitol Hill is overwhelmingly on Northern Ireland, on the part that gun running and money raising in the United States contribute to the violence, and what the US can do to bring peace. Since some members of Congress are well-informed on the issues while others are ignorant or confused, Mr. Lynch had to answer the same questions over and over again, and provide explanations of the basic facts. Fortunately, he is patient and good-humored.

NOVEMBER 9

I had it easy this morning, but the taoiseach had to be ready to face the "Today" program on NBC at 7:15 AM. His television performance was followed by a breakfast hosted by Speaker O'Neill on Capitol Hill at 8:30, which Bill also attended. That was followed by a meeting with William Miller, secretary of the treasury, an interview with editors and publishers at Blair House, and a luncheon at the National Press Club, where the taoiseach made a major speech and answered questions. In the question period, answering a query from the floor, Mr. Lynch indicated that an air corridor along the border between Ireland and Northern Ireland was part of the improved security arrangements that he had worked out with Mrs. Thatcher following the murder of Lord Mountbatten in August. Those in the official party who heard the speech found nothing new in the prime minister's guarded remarks, but they were to create a flap back in Ireland where his political enemies greatly exaggerated the importance of the so-called air corridor.

I met the women at Blair House, and we went to the Kennedy Center, where Paula Donlon was giving a luncheon for us. I managed to excuse myself from the concert that followed in order to dash out to Gramercy Street and see my friends. Mark Sullivan met me, by prearrangement, under Kennedy's bust at the Center, and drove me out. We gathered at Nevzer Stacey's house, across the street from ours and, although the visit was short, it was sweet and wonderful to see them all and to catch up on everyone's news.

The Iranian situation is very rapidly ballooning into a major world crisis. Nevzer, with her Persian looks, was coming home this afternoon by taxi. The driver asked her: "Are you Iranian?"

"No," she replied. "I'm Turkish."

"Your neighbors won't be able to tell the difference," he retorted. "They'll hate you."

We all gossiped nonstop for two hours and then, reluctantly, I had to hurry back into town for a reception at the Irish embassy and a dinner at Anderson House, given by the Irish government.

Bill arrived back at the hotel just as I did, having attended a wreath-laying ceremony at the Tomb of the Unknown Soldier and a meeting with John Sawhill, deputy secretary of energy, at Blair House. We had to make another quick change and hurry right out to the Irish embassy. The embassy residence has just had a complete overhaul: The work ran far behind schedule, as all renovation projects do, and the last of the workmen were putting on finishing touches just hours before the party. The house looks handsome, filled with all the best examples of contemporary Irish furniture, fabrics and art.

After the reception, the taoiseach and Mrs. Lynch were hosts tonight for a dinner in honor of the vice-president and Mrs. Mondale at Anderson House, the magnificent, ornate home on Massachusetts Avenue which is the headquarters of the Order of the Cincinnati (descendants of Revolutionary War officers). As we drove up to the door of the house, we saw pickets lining the street outside, holding up signs which read:

"Free the Americans." These angry reminders of the Iranian hostages were presumably directed at Vice-President Mondale and the other high officials attending the dinner.

I've been to many functions at Anderson House over the years, but I don't think I've ever seen it looking as beautiful as it did tonight. The flower arrangements were stunning; the crystal chandeliers, the French tapestries, the marble floors gleamed and glittered in the candle-light.

The dinner was superb. The Irish had flown over many of the ingre-dients on the plane with us: smoked salmon, Irish veal, "real" Irish soda bread. I sat at a table with Ethel Kennedy, Mrs. Peter Jay (the wife of the former British ambassador to the United States), Congressman John Brademas and former Postmaster General Larry O'Brien. We talked mostly of the Iranian crisis, but then the talk turned, as it always does, to Northern Ireland. I'm beginning to feel like so many of my Irish friends: fatigued and frustrated with the very mention of the subject.

Vice-President Mondale responded to the toast that was given by the taoiseach and said some warm and funny things about Sean Donlon and his work here as Irish ambassador. Then he went on to praise Bill and his work in Ireland, saying that his appointment as ambassador had been "made in heaven."

NOVEMBER 10

We left Blair House this morning for a short ride to the Washington Monument grounds where our helicopter was waiting to take us back to Andrews Air Force Base. Our Washington trip is over and we are head-ing out today for Boston.

When we arrived in Williamsburg two days ago, the protocol officers who accompany us gave us each a small green spiral notebook, embossed on the cover in gold letters: "The Official Visit of His Excellency The Prime Minister of Ireland and Mrs. Lynch to the United States: Novem-ber 1979." Inside, on the first page, it says: "Detailed Scenario," and every move that we make during each day is outlined in this little booklet. I open it up first thing in the morning while I'm still in bed, and a short review tells me exactly what I will be doing, when, how, where and with whom. I know what to wear and when to be ready.

I think the protocol people have done a fantastic job programming us, organizing us, helping us out of mini-crises along the way, answering a hundred questions a day. Just to get forty Irishmen in and out of hotels, planes, cars, dinners, receptions, and up in the morning for early depar-tures is a miracle in itself, and they do it all with grace, skill and good humor. We are the first state visit that the new, young chief of protocol has managed, and although he seemed somewhat nervous and tense on the first day, he is by now totally relaxed, and enjoying the trip as much as we are. "This is such a wonderful bunch of people," he has said to me on several occasions.

"They are," I answered. "You were lucky to get the Irish for your first state visit. You'll never have as much fun on an official trip again."

The dinner given in Boston tonight by the American Irish Foundation was elegant and fun. Bill has been a director of the foundation for many years and we knew many of the guests. But there was one secret embarrassment. The Irish delegation had brought a Waterford vase with them on the trip, inscribed to William Vincent, the president of the foundation, to be presented to him at the dinner. Alas, it was brought along to the reception prior to the dinner and apparently put down in too conspicuous a spot; it was never seen again.

NOVEMBER 11

In the original planning, this day in New Orleans was supposed to be a "free day" without any official obligations. But it turned out the people of New Orleans were far too hospitable to let our visit go unnoticed, so we ended up having a wonderfully gala and well-fed twenty-four hours here.

The brass band at the airport set the tone for the visit. They were dressed in costume and played jazz numbers as we walked off the plane. All the Irish members of the group were enchanted with them. They are determined to hear some good jazz before we leave.

Mayor and Mrs. Morial and twenty dignitaries of the city welcomed us, and we were whisked off to the Hyatt Regency, a big, modern glass and stone hotel, with a glass-sided elevator ascending through the domed lobby. We went up to the top, but our rooms weren't ready, so we milled around in a small top-floor foyer waiting for our luggage and our rooms. Anyone in the party who was interested was taken next door to the enormous Superdome to see a football game.

New Orleans has an Irish neighborhood, known as the Irish Channel, and the residents there had planned a big block party for the taoiseach. Bill, Breda O'Kennedy, Mrs. Lynch and I went together and arrived late; it was a wild scene, with surely every Irishman in New Orleans there, and some whose claims to Ireland might be dubious. It was fun, loud and dotty. An enormous black lady, with a star-spangled vest and a green sequined hat, came up to Mrs. Lynch and flashed a neon "Kiss Me, I'm Irish" badge in her face. "I may not be Irish, honey," she said, with a bubbly, infectious laugh, "but I'm the next best thing to it." She was washed away in the crowd before we had time to find out what the next best thing was.

Another woman, with a bonnet fashioned out of a huge green shamrock, came up to shake hands. "This is nothing," she assured us. "You should see us on St. Patrick's Day."

We all loved it and would gladly have spent another couple of hours there, but the word went around that the cars had arrived and it was time for us to make our way to the French Quarter and the civic reception in the Cabildo, once the town hall of New Orleans.

We were in the receiving line by six o'clock and didn't leave it till eight. Hundreds of New Orleaners passed through our line; black and white, nuns and priests, civic leaders, politicians, the local Irish. There was a jazz band playing at the top of the grand staircase, where we were greeting our guests. Perhaps they created the air of gaiety and excitement. Perhaps that is just the everyday atmosphere of New Orleans. But there was something there, something that made the air electric with excitement, that moved the most staid of us to animation. We shook hand after hand with zeal. We laughed, we smiled, we made jokes, we tapped our feet to the rhythm of the music. When the receiving line finally broke up, we joined the masses of people in the reception rooms and saw the most sumptuous buffet table that I have ever seen. There were ice carvings at both ends and a fantastic variety of hors d'oeuvres: oysters Rockefeller, crab, shrimp, beef tartar, pâtés of a dozen different kinds, and beautiful cheese platters. It was a demonstration of the famous New Orleans cuisine at its finest, and we all hovered over the table savoring each delicacy.

Before the night was over, we heard some very fine jazz. Our day in New Orleans was complete.

NOVEMBER 12

I read in a magazine somewhere about "flying exercises": how to stay fit and rested during long flights by doing certain exercises and by drinking lots of fluids to make up for the loss of moisture our bodies undergo at high altitudes. On an ordinary flight one might be somewhat conspicuous, if not immediately handcuffed and arrested, if one suddenly stood up in the aisle and started doing pushups or jumping jacks, but I thought that today, on the way from New Orleans to Houston, our plane, which has become like a second home by now, might be just the place to try out these airborne theories.

I enlisted an assistant instructor, and we led the group in knee bends, jogging in place, arm swings and other games to get our blood pumping and hearts beating faster. While we paused to gasp between exercises, we drank copious amounts of water. The stewardess watched our antics without comment. They've probably seen stranger things. It seemed to work, but maybe it was only the Texas sunshine that gave everyone a special lift when we reached Houston.

We were taken to a "ranch" to have a Texas barbecue and to see a rodeo. The ranch was a commercial tourist attraction, complete with dancing Indians in costume, a group of energetic tap-dancing square dancers, and a very poor version of a Texas barbecue; it was the first time in my life I've been served barbecued hot dogs! And worse, no cole slaw! But everyone enjoyed the rodeo and the warm sun that shone on us all day.

There was an official dinner tonight at the Petroleum Club, hosted by the Industrial Development Authority of Ireland. Houston is the center of the petrochemical industry in the United States, and the IDA is interested in wooing as many of these firms as possible to open branch factories in Ireland.

In addition, because of the rise in oil prices, Houston has become a major financial center and a source of investment and risk capital for ventures of all kinds, and, of course, the bankers and financiers of Houston serve on the boards of many corporations. From an economic standpoint, therefore, the taoiseach's speech and his private meetings with the Houston businessmen constituted the high point of the trip.

NOVEMBER 13

We flew into Chicago today and were met at the airport by Mayor Jane Byrne. It was a cold, windy, Chicago sort of day. As we stood in the open air on Daly Plaza, where the troops were reviewed and the welcoming ceremonies took place, the wind whipped around and chilled us all. I put my hand into Bill's pocket, trying to stay warm, and he leaned over and whispered to me: "Is that flame burning in the middle of the plaza for Mayor Daly?"

"No!" I whispered back. "It's for the Unknown Soldier."

"I wouldn't be too sure," he responded.

The taoiseach was busy with press interviews and radio/TV shows all through the day. This evening the mayor gave a lavish dinner at the Palmer House Hotel; she wore a beautiful strapless top and a long, full skirt, but she didn't give the impression that she was enjoying herself at her own party. She and the other guests at the head table were seated so far apart that they had to lean across their places to exchange a word with their neighbors. For most of the meal, the mayor stared out over the dining room, drumming her fingers on the tablecloth in rhythm to the show tunes played by the strolling violins.

NOVEMBER 14

And so we end up in New York City, of course; all the Irish are mad to get to New York. They love it, as do all Europeans, and made plans on the plane to visit their favorite stores, museums, restaurants. The Lynches and the O'Kennedys were whisked off to lunch with the Waldheims at the United Nations. Bill and I went walking and window-shopping. I bought two feathers to sew on my hat.

The Irish consul general in New York gave an enormous reception this evening at the Hilton. The street entrance of the hotel was lined with IRA pickets, so we drove up to a garage entrance in the rear. The reception room was mobbed, but we made a halfhearted attempt to form a receiving line. A young woman whom I hadn't seen before stood next to me in the line. At first I thought she was from the Irish consulate in New York, but then I realized that as she shook hands with the guests coming through the line she was saying: "Hi. I'm Jane Smith from Amtrak." I told her to get out of the line, but she wouldn't budge. She stayed with us to the end and, when she finally disengaged herself, she said: "It's the way I meet people. I just love receiving lines."

Mr. Lynch made a short speech to the crowd, and they responded enthusiastically. They roared and clapped and cheered. I whispered to him from the speaker's platform: "They really love you in New York," and he quipped back: "They haven't heard the results of the Cork by-elections!" (The election was held in the taoiseach's native city while we have been in America, and they were not encouraging for Mr. Lynch's political party.)

The dinner this evening was given by the American-Irish Council for Industry and Trade at the Metropolitan Club. Robert White, who had sung for us in Dublin when Speaker O'Neill was there, sang a concert of Irish songs and later joined us at the Pierre Hotel for a last farewell party. Tomorrow night the Lynches and the rest of the Irish delegation will fly back to Dublin. Bill and I are staying over in New York; the day after tomorrow, he is being presented with the Gold Medal of the American Irish Historical Society at its annual banquet.

NOVEMBER 15

We drove out to the airport to see the group off to Ireland. We shall see them soon again in Dublin, of course, but there is an air of sadness and of anticlimax in the air, and we all bade each other good-by as if it were final.

It has been a unique and wonderful trip, one that few of us ever get to experience. And it will be unforgettable. My first reaction, as the trip got under way, was that it was *mad* to schedule so many things in so short a time. But upon reflection, I can see that the "hurry hurry" atmosphere gave the trip some of its special glamour and intensity. Everywhere we went, we rushed: arriving in cities behind a motorcycle escort with sirens and lights flashing, dashing into hotels, looking frantically for a hairdresser or someone to press a dress, in and out of a shower in two minutes, making up and dressing in two more. Standing for hours in receiving lines, being vivacious, saying things over and over, each time with feeling, being friendly with strangers, enthusiastic with friends. Packing and unpacking. Packing again. The plane was our haven, a time to take off shoes, put curlers in our hair, chew gum, tell funny stories; time for the official members of the group to go over speeches, prepare toasts, talk to the press, review the day's schedule and then, ties tied, shoes on, smiles straight, to carry on. It was the very pace of it that kept us slightly manic and pitched high enough to carry it off.

Credit for the logistics goes to the US Protocol Office. But traveling with Jack and Maírín Lynch turned an official tour of duty into a relaxed, informal and pleasant journey. Their unflappable good manners, their undemanding patience, their wit and good nature set the tone for the trip and helped each of us follow their good example.

NOVEMBER 18: *Dublin*

Bill and I flew home this evening on separate planes; he arrived at the airport in Dublin before me, and was there waiting when I arrived. And so, home again, Cinderella. Well, hardly Cinderella, coming back to the residence! Exhausted! Would I do it again? Tomorrow! I'd know what to expect, do it better and more easily. But one thing is for sure. It would never, never be as much fun again, without the Irish.

NOVEMBER 24

I appeared as a guest on the "Late, Late Show." Ireland's most popular evening talk show. Gay Byrne has been the emcee of the show since its inception sixteen years ago, interviewing politicians, artists, writers, lady wrestlers, visiting American VIPs, rock singers, priests and men posing as priests. He and his guests have discussed the pros and cons of nuclear power plants, contraceptives, and women's liberation; the reasons for child molesting, the means of detecting breast cancer, the results of plastic surgery, and the sale of a latest best-seller. My appearance was non-controversial and bland. I just talked about what it is like to be the wife of the American ambassador. I thought I might be nervous doing a live TV show. I've done TV before, but always when I was talking about a subject I had also been writing about and could speak on with assurance. Not knowing exactly what Gay was going to ask me, I felt a few twitters as I stood ready to go on, but I'm a natural ham and once I saw the television camera I relaxed instead of tensing, and enjoyed myself.

NOVEMBER 30

The Women's Political Association annual Seminar has come around again. I had suggested to the committee earlier in the year that perhaps we could help them arrange for an American speaker. I had my good friend Barbara Watson in mind. She is the assistant secretary of state for consular affairs. Being black and a female, she is a good example to foreign women of what accomplishments are possible for women in

America today. Besides that, she is a powerful speaker and a brilliant, vivid personality. She agreed to speak at the Seminar, although she had just returned to Washington after a month's visit to China, where she negotiated the opening of five new American consulates. She arrived today with her assistant, Cathy Geraldi. Typical of Barbara, instead of taking a nap, she wanted to go straight to the embassy and meet our small consular staff. Later in the afternoon she attended a reception at the embassy given in her honor by the American Women's Club.

DECEMBER 1

Barbara's speech at the Seminar today was very enthusiastically received. She spoke to a full house. With her deep, sonorous voice and her accomplished style, she delivered her message—basically one of love and understanding between men and women, between nations of the world—with unusual depth of feeling and grace.

There is much misinformation and misunderstanding in Ireland about America's race problems. I think Barbara's speech at the Seminar and her appearance this evening on the "Late, Late Show" went some way to dispel a few misapprehensions.

DECEMBER 2

We had a small dinner tonight for Barbara, with Garret and Joan Fitz-Gerald, and the Alexis Fitzgeralds (no relations). It was a fascinating evening, full of American and Irish political talk. Barbara told us that the hostage crisis is building up to alarming proportions in America, with much anti-Iranian feelings spreading around the country, particularly on college campuses, where there are so many students from Iran.

The talk in Ireland these days is all about the possible resignation of Jack Lynch as leader of his party. Everyone expects that he will step down before Christmas. Who will be his successor? Some say George Colley; the tanaiste—deputy prime minister—has the votes. Others say Charles Haughey, the minister of health, will pull it off.

DECEMBER 9

Bill had just lit the fire in the library and was closing the heavy drapes for a quiet evening at home when the telephone rang on my desk. It was Dennis on the intercom.

"Gerry and Paul have been in an accident on their way to evening mass at Chapelizod. A taxi apparently went out of control and smashed into them. Their car is demolished. Orla was in the backseat but is unhurt. Gerry and Paul have been taken to hospital."

We spoke first to the hospital and then to Sheila, Gerry's wife, who was still reeling from the shock of hearing about the accident, but who assured us they will both be all right. Gerry escaped with facial lacerations. Paul, the Noctors' seventeen-year-old son, took the brunt of it, with a badly fractured leg and serious facial cuts and bruises. Gerry, the most careful and skilled driver imaginable, has passed on his driving ability to Paul, who was at the wheel when the accident occurred. There was nothing he could have done. The taxi was knocked into them by another car. We're all grateful it isn't worse.

December 10

We went to a "thank you" dinner tonight, given for us by the Lynches in gratitude for their trip to America. As we walked through the big double doors at the top of the ornate stairway, Mr. Lynch handed me a bouquet of yellow roses ("for the Texan," he said with a smile) and Mrs. Lynch embraced us both. All the members of the delegation were there. What a wonderful reunion, but what a bittersweet evening. Mr. Lynch is going to step down from the leadership of his party, as was expected, so this is his last official function as taoiseach.

I sat next to Mr. Lynch at dinner; he got up to make a toast to Bill and me, but everyone was having such a good time, and it was all so informal, he could scarcely get through his toast for all the kidding and teasing.

We went into the reception room off the dining room for our coffee after dinner. I sat down in a chair by the roaring fire to chat with some of the ladies; when the waiter brought around the coffee and handed me mine, I thought he still had it in his hand. He, alas, thought I had it securely in mine, and disaster struck. The cup overturned onto my white lace dress (my ten-year-old London job) and all over the little satin chair. I fled into the ladies' room, which was fortunately nearby, pulled off the dress and soaked the skirt in soda water. Mary Rushing, the wife of the deputy chief of mission at our embassy, poured the soda and I soaked it up with towels. We kept at it until the stain disappeared, except of course I was left with a very cold, wet dress (it's covered with "jewels" and sequins, and it's cold to put on even in its *dry* state). But I went out to the party again and stood by the fire, and except for the fact that little whiffs of steam arose from me, I don't think anyone noticed.

We put records on the phonograph and began dancing. That soon warmed me up. About midnight, I began to teach everyone how to do the Virginia reel, and since I had only a dim memory of it, we all ended up doing an Americanized version of an Irish reel. On that gay and breathless note, Bill and I left, so that everyone else could leave and go home to bed. I felt very sad saying good night to Mr. and Mrs. Lynch. Bill and I have both admired him very much as the leader of his country.

People in all political parties respect and like him. He is accessible to people in every walk of life and open to every viewpoint. Although he is intensely loyal to his political party, Fianna Fáil, he has united his country and is universally respected for his integrity and his kindness.

During the years that he has led his government, he presided over a period of rapid economic expansion, and under his leadership the government made an ambitious effort to win the unending Irish race between young people entering the work force and the creation of new jobs for them. And although Jack Lynch has not found a prescription for curing inflation—who has?—he has shown courage in facing up to the issue of wage ceilings for government employees. This is a particularly important issue here in Ireland, because many more people here work for the government than in the United States.

Although the Lynches entertain formally at Dublin Castle or, like this evening, at Iveagh House, they often have friends to their home for informal supper parties (with much joshing between them about Maírín's purported lack of cooking skills), and these evenings are filled with warmth and gaiety. As Kipling said in another context, they have walked with kings and not lost the common touch.

DECEMBER 13

I went to Leinster House (the Irish Parliament) for lunch today with Senator Gemma Hussey. It was the first time I had eaten in the Members Dining Room. It was an interesting experience, seeing so many familiar faces on their home ground.

While we were eating, Jack Lynch came in to lunch with friends. Gemma said it was the first time she had ever seen him there. He has resigned as taoiseach, and Charles Haughey has been elected in his place. (He beat George Colley by a very close margin in the Fianna Fáil caucus.)

DECEMBER 14

Mr. Haughey is forming his new government, and Breda O'Kennedy gave a small luncheon party today to say good-by to all the ambassadors' wives; she introduced Anne Lenihan, whose husband will become the new foreign minister. Breda made a very graceful, short speech, telling us how much she had enjoyed being our official hostess in Dublin during her husband's tenure as foreign minister. She has worked hard at her job, carrying out her official duties with great charm and tact, and making even the shyest among us feel welcome and at home at the functions she has hosted. We shall see much less of her now that Michael O'Kennedy has been named minister of finance in Mr. Haughey's new cabinet, and we shall miss her slim figure, her stylish manner, and her warm smile. No politician could hope for a more gracious helpmate.

There were lots of jokes and laughter at the table during the luncheon (most of us are quite good friends by now), but there were tears also. No change of government can be accomplished without losers as well as victors, and we shared the sadness of our friends who were defeated.

DECEMBER 18

Gerry made his first appearance since his accident tonight at the staff Christmas party. He was a little wobbly, but still able to give us his sweet rendition of "Danny Boy" before the evening was over.

I've been working with all the residence children for a month, directing them in a "Mellowdrama" I wrote with a special part for each one, fitted to his age and talents. The children have been wonderfully faithful and enthusiastic thespians, learning their parts, coming to rehearsals, organizing their costumes. David as Sherlock O'Shannon and Christopher as Dapper Dan McGrew rescue a fair maiden in distress (Siobhán Noctor) with all the rest of the supporting cast performing without a flaw. We gave our opening performance tonight to a full house.

Paul Noctor is still in hospital, but he's making good progress and will be home soon. Agnes, our laundress, has retired, so we missed her husband Willy's accordion tonight, but we sang and danced, and Liam and Brian between them dragged out every old and new Kerryman joke in the book.

DECEMBER 20

Today is the shortest day of the year, the winter solstice, when the sun has no apparent northward or southward motion. We got ourselves out of warm beds in the cold predawn darkness to travel up the misty Boyne River Valley to Newgrange, in County Meath, in the hope of witnessing an extraordinary phenomenon that takes place in the "passage grave," one of Ireland's megalithic burial tombs. Built 4,500 years ago, 36 feet high and 280 feet in diameter, this Stone Age burial site is an amazing feat of construction. The entrance to the tomb is decorated with an ornately carved stone, said to be one of the most beautiful in the prehistory of Western Europe.

Passing through the narrow opening at the entrance of the tomb, just barely wide enough for a human form to squeeze through, one goes along a low, narrow, curved passageway, about 30 feet long, and enters the main burial chamber, which is the size of a small room.

235

Each year, on the winter solstice, as the sun rises over the waters of the Boyne, a ray of the sun's light hits directly on the entrance of the tomb and penetrates the narrow passageway into the burial chamber. Some years, when the cloud cover is too heavy or when a dense fog covers the surrounding valley, this occurrence doesn't take place. One never knows until the moment of sunrise. As we drove along the road from Dublin, pink snatches of sky began to appear and it promised to be a fair day.

Arriving at the site, we discovered that a BBC camera crew had arrived before us and were busy setting up their equipment in the tiny burial chamber. One of our guides said he thought we were in luck; the sun's rays were beginning to shine across the broad expanse of the valley.

We positioned ourselves inside the chamber, pressed against each other in the tiny space. The cameras were ready to roll and the guide turned out the light in the passage. We stood huddled in the cold and dark, scarcely daring to breathe, watching the opening through which the light would appear. One of the archaeologists present got on his knees and pressed his cheek to the floor of the cave, so he could see down the narrow passage.

"It's coming," he whispered. And slowly, like a thin golden rapier, the light pushed its way into the cave, coming slowly down the passage and entering the chamber where it illuminated our faces. It lay on the dirt floor at our feet, taut and almost alive. No one spoke, and the only sound was the thin whir of the camera. After a few minutes, less than five, it receded, leaving us in darkness.

It was an incredible experience, eerie, supernatural and very moving. I felt exhausted when I walked back out into daylight, as if I had undergone a deeply religious experience. The fact that the phenomenon takes place each year on the same day shows that the builders were aware of the calendar and would also suggest that they were sun worshipers. Our guide told us that tomorrow, which is the "official" day of the solstice, there would be crowds of sun worshipers and other eccentric religious groups, who gather at the site each year on that day and perform their own mysterious rites.

DECEMBER 23

We left Dublin this morning on a nonstop flight to Rome, where we will spend two weeks staying in the flat of our friend Eoin O'Brien, on the Via Guilia. I love Rome and haven't been back since I was eighteen and went to stay with a schoolgirl friend, Marcia Bourgin, who was living there for a year with her parents. This year, by an odd quirk of fate, Marcia is back with her husband, a physicist from the University of Washington, and their own three children. Her parents will also be there for the holidays, so we shall have a Roman reunion.

1980

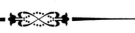

January 6

Our marvelous Roman holiday has been a great reviver for each of us, but various domestic crises awaited me upon our return. Siobhán O'Tierney, David's baby-sitter, has decided to leave us to live on her own. She has been a wonderful addition to our family since we have been here. We've loved her insouciance and her vitality, and her going will leave a gap in our lives. And Finula Bryce, the assistant cook, is leaving us to get married, so we must find replacements for them both. Along with filling those two positions, I am also involved once again with decorating projects. The plans I made with Susan McQueen last spring are beginning to fall into place.

My biggest outdoor project has been the front entrance, just as one drives through the main gate. It was overgrown and weedy, with bamboo and straggling holly bushes choking out the lawn. We stripped it all away and had a smooth, grassy lawn put down, filled each side of the entrance with rose beds, rhododendron bushes and holly. I tried to plant azaleas and wisteria on the outside of the gate, against the walls of the two small gatehouses, but the cows that graze freely in the Park during the summer and fall soon discovered them and had them for dinner one night.

The grounds of the residence, during the years that it was the chief secretary's lodge, were used as kitchen gardens for Dublin Castle. Acres of fresh fruits, vegetables and flowers were grown for the dinners and balls given by the viceroy at the castle or the chief secretary at the residence: strawberries, raspberries, apples, plums, grapes, gooseberries, rhubarb; a team of gardeners produced vegetables and hot-house flowers of every variety. The remnants of this operation still exist on our grounds. We have two large greenhouses and can grow all our own flowers and plants.

The fruit beds have diminished, but we still have apples, plums and raspberries in the summer and fall. And the vegetable garden, under Michael's loving and skilled care, flourishes. Our tables are laden with fresh vegetables all summer and fall, and our freezers are stocked through the winter. It's a regular little mini-farm here; Dennis keeps telling me that all I need now is a pig. One of these days I'm going to surprise him and come home with a pig in the boot.

JANUARY 19: *Newport, County Mayo*

Liam, Christopher and I are at the Curleys' house in County Mayo for the weekend; Bill had to give a speech to the Chamber of Commerce in Mullingar, so he couldn't come with us. David stayed home to keep him company.

Today was the first time I have ever been shooting; Walter Curley gave us a good lesson in safety and then showed each of us how to load and fire the guns. The boys were thrilled and excited; they have been impatient to come for weeks. Michael Chambers, the Curleys' caretaker, and a neighbor, Jim O'Donnell, went along with us. I was a disaster as a shot. In fact, I usually closed my eyes and looked the other way when I pulled a trigger, and I think that if I had actually shot anything I would have started to cry. But I loved the excuse for the long walk out over the bogs and wetlands of western Mayo, where the purple sky reaches down to the edge of the sea and the wayward clouds, scudding overhead, turn sunshine into rain with whimsical rhythm. The only way to see the countryside, to feel the wind and the rain on one's cheeks, to smell the fresh, wet air from the sea and the bogs, is to walk across the land, over fences, through marshes, Wellington boots squelching. Sometimes the land is so springy I can jump up and down on a patch of wet grass and the land under my feet bobs up and down like bedsprings.

This morning, all of us, heavy with coats, hats, gloves, boots and cartridge belts, headed across a sandy inlet where one could reach a small island when the tide was out. It was raining softly but steadily, the kind of Irish rain that doesn't get you wet. We were crouched down in a long, spread-out line with our guns ready, when Michael suddenly yelled: "Geese!" Liam was quick to swing upwards and take aim, and, on his very first shot of the day (of his life!) he brought down a large, plump Canadian goose. Talk about beginner's luck.

From the island we walked back to a sea bog and sloshed our way through its soft, marshy, uneven surface, looking for snipe. When we had no luck there, we crossed over by car to a mountain bog which gave us a wonderful view of the countryside for miles around. The rain had disappeared and the sun warmed us on the hill top. I sloshed happily along between Jim and Michael, their soft, melodious accents and sure footing on the bogs both signs of born Mayo men. Something flew over; grouse? We all had a go at it but missed, and had begun walking back to the cars when suddenly Liam yelled, from several hundred yards away: "Mom! I'm caught in a bog and I'm sinking." His voice had a scared edge to it, and I began to hurry toward him, but Michael stopped me and said: "Walk over slowly and don't look excited, or he will get scared and start tugging at himself, and that will make him go in deeper." So we walked slowly in his direction and poor Liam, mystified by our seeming nonchalance while he sank even deeper, yelled again: *"Mom!"* There was no mistaking the tone of his voice now. He was up to his thighs and his boots had filled with water, but by the time we reached him, he had managed to extricate himself and was pouring the water out of his boots, and laughing at his predicament. All the men said it was a good thing to have happened because he knows now that if he keeps his head, he can cope. It can be dangerous, however, and a stranger should never walk in a bog alone.

Down the road and into a field for plover, where we *think* Christopher shot one. On to another bog for snipe. And finally, before the light of day was gone, we drove to a lake to look for duck. En route, Walter showed us a holy well, which has been there for thousands of years and where people come to pray for cures.

The lake was beautiful and still. White fleecy clouds were mirrored on its quiet surface, and soft, round-topped hills rolled from its edge to the top of the horizon. We spread out in a line again; I stood by a tree at the top of the lake and leaned my gun against a boulder. I became absorbed in the beauty of the lake and its surroundings, marveling as I always do in the Irish countryside at the stillness. No sound at all broke into the hush of the day's end, so I was startled to hear the crack of a rifle break out across the water as Walter brought down two snipe which fell on the other side of the lake. Rusty, his Irish setter, was delighted to have some work to do at last, and plunged into the icy waters to retrieve the birds.

The light was fading and the day's shooting was over. We climbed back into the cars, tired, exhilarated and, rare for an Irish winter's day, sunburned.

JANUARY 23

Now the state of my car is really desperate. I had the entire motor rebuilt, which took three months. The very day I drove the car out of the garage the transmission failed. When I had the car towed back in, I was told that it must have been a "coincidence." Ha.

I told the foreman they must have ruined the transmission rebuilding the engine, and he denied touching it. Never mind, says I, sounding like a proper Dublin matron, "I'll put the entire matter in the hands of my solicitor."

January 28: *Dublin*

I got up and looked at myself in the mirror this morning and groaned. I am getting old, fat, wrinkled, flabby and soggy. It's disgusting and alarming. I picked up the phone and made an appointment to start a crash course at the Rosebay Health Institute at Brown Thomas. I had an hour of exercise, wearing my old high-school red cotton leotard and a pair of Liam's red ski tights, and I felt pretty tacky when a tiny lady with an enormous bottom came in with a silver lamé leotard and tights. They didn't do anything for her bottom, but they certainly dressed up the place. After exercising, I had a marvelous steam bath and a wheat germ facial. I can't see any improvement yet, but at least I've begun a holding operation.

January 29

The big political news of the week is a ruckus caused by the funeral of a famous Kerry athlete named John Joe Sheehy. It seems that there was a Republican guard of honor, dressed in black berets and black sweaters, flanking the hearse during the funeral procession, and that they fired a gun over the casket. (It's against the law in Ireland to be a member of the Irish Republican Army.) A minister of state, Tom McEllistrim, said: "I was there and there was no guard of honor." But the *Independent* printed a picture of the funeral procession and the Republican uniforms were clearly evident. Then RTE refused to show a film they had made of the proceedings until public pressure forced them to do so. The Republican honor guard was clearly evident in the film. And then that was the end of it.

January 30

I gave a speech tonight to the monthly meeting of the Women's Political Association. The other speaker was a sociologist from Trinity and a single mother. She gave a good speech and I followed with a general discourse on the state of women's affairs in America, beginning with the history of the women's movement in the nineteenth century. I stressed the diversity of cultural, religious, and ethnic backgrounds among American women, something Irish women find hard to comprehend. They were a good audience, attentive and interested, and asked good questions when I'd finished.

The association has a reputation in Dublin for attracting some far-out, radical, strident feminists; the women I know in the organization, its founders, are anything but. The single women in the group have responsible jobs and the married women run comfortable homes; some of them work and all of them have a serious, concerned interest in the welfare of women in Ireland. They feel that the political scene here is dominated by men, which it is, and that women should have a louder voice in the political process, either by holding elective offices or working actively for candidates who are interested in women's concerns. They are a nonpartisan group and give campaign support to women candidates of all parties. I have found neither their views nor their life-styles to be in any way radical or far out. If the same group existed in the United States, it would be considered a middle-of-the road, low-key organization.

Last week, one of the founding members of the WPA, a young lawyer named Yvonne Scannell, who lectures on contract and personal property law at Trinity, won a case before the Supreme Court changing the country's tax laws for married working women. The old tax structure had been extremely unjust. As Yvonne said, when she herself decided to get married, she realized that she would lose so much in taxes that it would scarcely pay her to work. Trying to get around the tax law, she attempted to convince the chaplain at Trinity to give her and her bridegroom-to-be a religious ceremony but to skip the legal one so that she would not be married in the eyes of the state. When that proved impossible, she helped found the Married Persons' Tax Reform Association with Mairead Ui Dhuchain, and the two of them spent the next couple of years speaking around the country about the injustice of the law, and collecting funds to help them prepare their case for the High Court. In October 1979, they won their case in the High Court and the state appealed it to the Supreme Court. Last week, Yvonne and her many helpers and supporters were celebrating victory.

Now that they have won this case, the MPTRA will probably go on to fight other tax injustices. In an article in the *Irish Press,* Yvonne said: "Of course, not everything would be challenged on constitutional grounds. Pressure groups are effective, too; I'm in the Women's Political Association, myself."

There are many more battles to be won. A wife, for instance, can't claim certain benefits from her husband's social insurance, so if she stays home to mind the house and the children, he can get free dental care, but she can't.

Another injustice the group intends to challenge is the age limit on entry to the Public Service. If one is twenty-eight or over, one is ineligible; this means that wives who have stayed home to raise small children and want to return to the work force at age thirty-five or forty are automatically ineligible.

President Carter's ban on the United States' participation in the Olympics this year—a protest against Russia's invasion of Afghanistan—has not been met with enthusiasm in Ireland. The press here often refers to Mr. Carter's "cold war tactics," and there is a great fear in Ireland of armed conflict between the US and Russia, which could engage Ireland as a battleground. So it comes as a surprise to me that when a peaceful, nonviolent protest is offered as an alternative to war, the Irish government and Irish citizens are not supportive.

Lord Killanin, the president of the International Olympics Committee, lives in Ireland and his view, which is that the Olympics shall take place no matter what, is the majority viewpoint in this country. Also, the Irish have two world class runners: John Treacy, who is a student at Providence College in Rhode Island, and Eamon Coughlan. Both young men have a chance to take an Olympic gold medal.

The *Southern Star* newspaper in Skibbereen took the *really* long, historic perspective on the issue, gloomily predicting that "history will regard President Carter's boycott of the games as being the most ill-conceived, stupid act of a politician since Napoleon decided to invade Russia."

FEBRUARY 3

I buttered my toast, poured my tea and opened the *Sunday Press* this morning and there was a big picture of our house in the Park and a bold headline: SÉANCES IN THE PHOENIX PARK LEGATION. THE AMBASSADOR WHO TALKED TO GHOSTS!

What??? I dropped the marmalade into the tea and read the subhead: "Washington is told that Balfour, Teddy Roosevelt, and the Mother of FDR have spoken to a medium." I *knew* there would be some funny story in the paper when our electricity went out last week and we greeted our guests by candlelight, but this is really going too far! I read on and sighed in relief. It was a story not about Ambassador Shannon, but about a former United States minister to Ireland, David Gray, who served here during the Second World War. He was disturbed that Ireland would not enter the war as America's ally and tried unsuccessfully, at the cost of much bitterness between the two, to persuade de Valera to withdraw his pledge of neutrality. A historian named T. Ryle Dwyer has written a book about Gray's sojourn in Ireland and has documented the séances he used to have at the residence. Gray, having become interested in spiritualism while he was a student at Harvard University, employed a medium in Ireland named Geraldine Cummins. She was able to summon up messages for him from President Roosevelt's mother and from Arthur Balfour, a spiritualist himself and perhaps easily accessible to Gray since he had lived in the residence when he was chief secretary here from 1886 to 1892.

Apparently Gray would relay the messages he received to President Roosevelt in his official cables.

"What," I asked Bill over our bacon and eggs, "would President Carter do if you sent him messages from the ghosts of history?"

"Pay my passage home, if I were lucky," was his reply.

"Heavy air," along with its twin, "creeping damp," are mortal but unseen enemies that lurk in every Irish household, ready to pounce if the windows aren't open and the temperature hovers just below that legally permitted in Victorian orphanages. To use central heat as a mode of attack is permissible, but generally considered unsportsmanlike.

The Irish say that heavy air makes it hard to get out of bed in the mornings. I obviously became a victim long ago and have never had it properly diagnosed. The temperature in our bedroom this morning was a heavy 56 degrees. Kitty says it makes you sleep like a saint and I know why: getting up is a sure route to martyrdom. I put on a long woolen robe over my nightgown, and an Irish sweater over that and descend for breakfast, looking like a disheveled Mrs. Perry who has just missed the Commodore's expedition. "Tea!" I gasp, and feel the ice floes breaking up as the hot brew goes down.

David says cheerfully, spooning in his cereal: "You should eat porridge. It makes you feel warm." I don't like to admit to them that I am not a porridge person. It's not the taste or texture that puts me off, it's the color. I sit and hug the teapot to my bosom and wonder if I will develop chilblains. I wonder what chilblains *are*. Ah sure, I'm a terminal case of heavy air, and now the creeping damp's got hold of me.

February 7

We went to dinner tonight with Una and David Kennedy. He's the tall, lanky president of Aer Lingus. One of the dinner guests was Brendan O'Regan, the man who masterminded the establishment of Shannon Airport and the Shannon Industrial Park.

I had met Brendan a few times previously, but this evening was the first occasion when we had a long talk. He turns out to be an exceptionally interesting man. He recalled that during World War II, before Shannon Airport was built, flying boats with American soldiers used to land at Foynes, further up the Shannon Estuary. In the postwar era, before the advent of jet travel, commercial planes flying from the United States to Europe had to stop over at Shannon Airport for refueling. Brendan built up the airport by turning it into a free port with a duty-free shop. Although most airports now sell duty-free items, Shannon was the first, in 1946, to promote such an idea.

Brendan also developed the area around the airport as a tax-free zone for small industries (if the products were exported), and a General Electric firm, E.I. Ireland Limited, was one of the first to build a successful plant in the Shannon Industrial Park.

A natural executive and promoter, a man of boundless optimism and energy, Brendan O'Regan is confident that Ireland, both North and South, has the brains, the managerial talent and the ideas to compete successfully in the modern world. Now that he has retired from active business life, he is devoting his energies to promoting Cooperation North, his plan for alleviating the tensions between North and South by encouraging the exchange of business, industry and tourism between the two. He wants to match up comparable groups in each area so that tourist officials, county managers, farmers, youth groups, women's clubs, newspaper reporters—people from every walk of life—can travel, work and live with their opposite numbers and learn to know each other, appreciate each other's similarities, and understand and accept their differences.

He believes that part of what troubles Northern Ireland is simple ignorance of what the South is really like.

He has received support for Cooperation North both in Ireland and in the United States. If any one man can pierce the centuries-old shield of distrust and anger between the two warring factions, Brendan O'Regan has the energy, the skill and the imagination to do it.

FEBRUARY 14

I slept late and had breakfast in my room this morning, sitting at my little table by the big windows looking out over the lawn, enjoying the thin winter sunshine that streamed into the room. The three morning papers didn't have much news, except a report that we may be close to freeing the hostages, and an item saying that the Olympic Committee has voted to go ahead with the Moscow games. The majority of mail to the *Irish Times* still tends to be antiboycott; David Andrews, the former minister of state in the Foreign Office, had a letter in the paper castigating the US for trying to boycott the games and saying that Ireland must go to them. Although the government has made no official statement one way or the other, the minister for sport, Jim Tunney, goes about the country saying that Ireland will go. A sportive eighty-four-year-old lady from Cork wrote to the Irish Olympic Council with a contribution to Ireland's Olympic fund, saying, "I enclose a contribution . . . as a refutation of President Carter's childish and ineffective boycott of the games. . . . good luck to all the sporting boys and girls who don't care two hoots for Jimmy's moronic dictatorship." I'd love to see her debate the issue with Miz Lillian, another octogenarian who would no doubt match tongues with the wag from Cork.

FEBRUARY 16

Bill and I attended the Fianna Fáil Ardfheis at the Royal Dublin Society this afternoon and evening. It's the annual party conference, with loyal party workers coming up to Dublin from all over the country to hear their leaders speak, form party policy, exchange political gossip, and lobby for seats on the party's national committee. This is the first Ardfheis that Charles Haughey has addressed since he was elected taoiseach, and we were eager to hear his message.

We went up to the press room to watch; it was hot, noisy, smoky, filled with working press and hangers-on, just as it would be in America. Haughey's speech had just been released and we read it before we watched him deliver it. I thought it was something of an anticlimax; it was well written but bland and uninformative. His allusions to Northern Ireland drew a standing ovation, but he really didn't say anything new.

We stopped to chat with lots of friends in the press room, including Seamus and Anne Brennan. Seamus is the young, dynamic secretary of the Fianna Fáil party. Politicians say he has a bright future on the political scene in the coming years; I have always been impressed with his straightforward manner, his knowledge of party strategy, and his common sense and good judgment.

FEBRUARY 20

What a day! I had my ambassadors' wives luncheon at the residence today. They all came, including the wives of the top Foreign Affairs officials, and *all* arrived on the stroke of 1 PM. Dennis could scarcely announce them fast enough.

The dining room looked like a spring garden. The daffodils, crocuses and hyacinths, forced for winter blooming, were in pots lining the walls, filling the mantels and side tables. I had six round tables of five each, with blue and pale green tablecloths, and for a centerpiece, tiny reed baskets with baby crocuses and miniature hyacinths, packed in green moss.

It's the sixtieth birthday of Gwen Richie, the wife of the Canadian ambassador, so we surprised her with a cake decorated with a maple leaf, and a rather off-key "Happy Birthday to You"; Anne had also made her latest dessert extravaganza, a French apple tart which she got from the French Cooking Course running now in the London *Observer*. It's rich and gooey, with light, flaky pastry; served with heavy Irish cream, it's a dieter's downfall.

247

I sat with Anne Lenihan, the wife of the new foreign minister, who has just come back from Bahrain, where she and Minister Lenihan accompanied President and Mrs. Hillery on an official visit. We talked about the Ayatollah and the chances for the hostages' release; I'd just read that he had taken on a seventeen-year-old bride. "Maybe that will use up all his time and energy," I said to Anne, "and divert his mind into directions other than political." I have read that men who take on young mistresses have a significantly higher rate of cardiac arrest than other men, so there's that possibility as well.

The afternoon went off without a hitch and voices rose to a cheerful pitch that told me everyone was having a good time. We had coffee in the drawing room, and at three o'clock sharp, my guests departed, the long black line of cars purring back down the drive and out the gate.

I had to dress for the evening and leave by 5 PM to pick up Bill and go to the Setanta Art Gallery on Molesworth Street, where he was opening a very special exhibit. Joseph O'Neill, the young son of one of our cleaning staff, Margaret O'Neill, is having his first show at the Setanta tonight. We are proud of him and very happy with the quality of the work exhibited.

Then on to the official opening of the new Allied Irish Bank headquarters on the Merrion Road, just across from the RDS. There was a cast of thousands, and of course I saw all my luncheon guests again. Niall Crowley, the chairman of Allied Irish, was bringing the taoiseach through the crowd and stopped to say hello to me. The taoiseach said, without preliminaries, "Is your husband here?"

I pointed Bill out across the room and he walked hurriedly over to him. He wanted to tell him that a story which had appeared in the evening papers saying that the government had decided not to support Carter's Olympic boycott was a complete fabrication; totally false and misleading, he said. Bill was relieved, since he had been disturbed by the story. He had drafted a letter to President Carter just that afternoon saying that the Irish would delay their decision until they saw which way Europe was going. When the story appeared in the papers, he delayed sending his letter. Now, with Mr. Haughey's reassurances, he can send it.

FEBRUARY 21

We spent dinner discussing colleges with Liam. He has applications in for five American colleges, and like parents of high school seniors everywhere, we are awaiting the Letter. He has his heart set on Dartmouth. We tell him he should be pleased to be accepted at any of his five choices. We have a couple of months to wait, but already we have begun to greet the mail delivery with a special edge of anticipation. It was an arduous task to apply for college admission from abroad. The SAT exams are given in Ireland and administered here in Dublin by an American teacher. American boys and girls come from all over the country to take the test. Fifteen of them took it with Liam, but since the high schools here have no way of helping to choose a potential college or to advise on the applications, we felt rather at sea. We had met a very nice Dartmouth graduate who is a student at the Royal College of Surgeons. He came to our house for last year's Thanksgiving party and did a very persuasive job of selling Dartmouth to Liam.

After dinner, we broke open a bottle of champagne and shared it with the boys to celebrate my signing a contract with Atheneum to publish *you,* dear journal. I've begun to think of you, not as white typewriter paper that I write on, pages in a loose-leaf notebook, but as a long-suffering, sympathetic and forgiving friend, to whom I pour out each day's news. Now perhaps you will one day be handsomely printed and bound between hard covers, with no typos, no scribbling in your margins, and we'll all be very proud of you.

FEBRUARY 25

We had a reception here for 145 friends to see Rosaleen Linehan give a performance in the ballroom of *Love Is Pleasin', Love Is Teasin,'* a one-woman show on the theme of love and the Irish. She's taking the show to the US in a few weeks, and gave this preview performance for the Ireland American Society. As her husband, Fergus, said in the program notes: "The ancient Irish, who approached the subject [of love] in a more uninhibited fashion than their descendants, had many definitions. They said it was like the toothache and the colic, that it was like a powerful potion that could make you drunk for a year and give you a hangover for another ten. They said, too, that it was like the smallpox—you could have it mildly but you might carry the marks for life—and compared it to wooing an echo, choking on nectar, or a race with lightning and thunder." They were a long way, Fergus went on to say, from the puritanism of the twentieth century, when a "learned professor announced that lovemaking was 'bad for you,' and priests chased lovers out of ditches with their blackthorn sticks."

But the pendulum is swinging back; the population is growing, and bachelors are being routed out of their hiding places and marched to the altar in ever-growing numbers.

Rosaleen, an immensely talented and charming Irish singer, comedienne and actress, sings and reads from Yeats and Moore, O'Casey and O'Faolain, Joyce and Lavin, giving us their versions of love among the Irish. It was a well-conceived, humorous and touching show, carried by Rosaleen's smiling Irish charm. At least one member of the audience was totally overcome by it, and provided us with our first drunk since we've been in business here. But he was a nice drunk, bobbing quietly about the room like a loosened buoy in a storm, not quite sure which way the wind would blow him next. He left the house at one point, weaving out the front door, and returned shortly, presuming he had arrived home. He stared up at the domed window in the foyer in disbelief, looked longingly at the bar, and finally said to Dennis in a puzzled tone: "I'm not home, sure I'm not?" Dennis assured him that he had just come full circle and was still at the residence. He smiled and weaved out into the dark once more.

I stayed up until 4 AM, talking and laughing with my good friends, Kay Costelloe and Adelaide Sharry, Bill's secretary, about the party, and when I fell into bed, I knew the air would be extremely heavy in the morning. And I have a black-tie dinner for twenty-four in honor of the new chief rabbi tomorrow.

I saw in the United States Agricultural Newsletter that in a 1977 international comparison of food, drink and tobacco expenditures published by the United Nations Yearbook of National Accounts Statistics, Ireland ranks highest in the world for its expenditure on alcoholic beverages, based on the percentage of its national disposable per capita income. It spent 12.6 percent of its income per capita on booze. It ranks second in the world in consumption of tobacco, spending 5.1 percent, toppled from first place for this dubious honor by Sri Lanka (formerly Ceylon).

FEBRUARY 26

The new chief rabbi in Dublin, David Rosen, looks like he came right out of Central Casting, with a young wife as beautiful as he is handsome. They have come to Ireland from an assignment in South Africa, but Mrs. Rosen has Irish roots.

Since they are both kosher and vegetarian, our dinner tonight was a challenge to Anne's ingenuity. We decided to fix two menus, one for any of our Jewish guests who wanted to follow the rabbi's dietary practices, and one for the rest of us. We prepared mushroom salad, carrot and raisin salad, cole slaw, an endive and orange mixture, deviled eggs, and meringues with fruit and ice cream for dessert. While the rabbi's food was being passed around the table one way, our more ordinary menu of roast lamb, potatoes and vegetables was going the other. Finally, Minister George Colley, who was sitting on my right, turned to me and whispered: "What's going on? They keep passing me up!" I explained our double menu, but assured him he could be kosher for the evening, too, if he wanted. The salads looked so inviting that I think all of us ended up eating a fair portion of the Rosens' food.

The chief rabbi, who was born and educated in England, is a very perceptive, quick and intelligent man, with dark, lively eyes and a well-trimmed black beard. He already knows much about Ireland's history, literature and social problems, and I'm sure he will be a success with his congregation here. His wife, whom I felt at ease with immediately, is pretty and chic, with a warm smile and quick wit.

Among our guests this evening were the former Lord Mayor of Cork and Mrs. Gerald Goldberg, who had been our hosts when we made our first official visit there. They are both people of remarkable erudition and their knowledge of history, art and literature is impressive. Another guest at the party was Ben Briscoe, a Fianna Fáil TD, who is the son of the famous Lord Mayor of Dublin Robert Briscoe, a legendary figure in recent Irish politics.

FEBRUARY 27

This afternoon I chose the winners of a craft show at the School for Blind Children on Merrion Road. The students had made an extraordinary variety of knitwear, collages, ceramics, woven purses, and pictures. The children, many of whom are albinos, were friendly, energetic and eager to meet me. One tiny girl came up to sit on my lap and ran her small, thin fingers carefully and delicately over my face. "You have mascara on your eyelashes," she pronounced. "I can feel it. And you have on pierced earrings, lipstick and perfume, but you don't have on hair spray. What color are your eyes?"

"Brown," I told her.

"Right," she says, still "looking." "And your nose isn't exactly *big,* but it isn't exactly small, either."

Another little girl told me she loves the United States and listens to all the American television shows. "I can imitate an American accent," she said, but then turned immediately shy.

"Do it," her friends begged her, and assured me that she was wonderful.

"Are you sure you won't mind?" she asked me.

"No," I promised her. "I want to hear you."

"All right. Here goes." And suddenly her whole stance changed, and she turned down the corner of her lower lip, frowned, and said in perfect TV Brooklynese: "Okay, Sam. Just bring dose guys in here and tie 'em up. I'll do da rest." Her pals giggled madly. "Do your southern one," they begged. And she did a southern belle, and then a flat midwestern drawl all with perfect intonations and subtle nuances. She is a born mimic.

I gave out the first, second and third prizes; it was a difficult choice, and I made the decision based upon the teachers' comments that "he or she worked the hardest," or "she needs encouragement." RTE televised the ceremony and I made a short speech, telling the children what an ambassador does, and what I do, and why we had been chosen to come to Ireland.

One of the things the Irish do so well, with such kindliness and understanding, is to care for the handicapped. The nuns who run this school appear both devoted and professional. The teachers, lay women, showed a great enthusiasm for their work, tempered by a kind and compassionate attitude toward the children. The atmosphere here, as in the school for deaf girls which I visited not long ago, was one of cheerful, busy activity, and the children are as saucy, vivacious, and articulate as children anywhere.

I had mentioned to Mr. McNulty, David's piano teacher, who is also blind, that I was coming to the school today, and he told me that he had attended it as a boy and owes the nuns there much of the credit for his early musical training and encouragement. "If it hadn't been for them, I would never have gotten where I am," he said generously. Over the past three years, I have watched him teach David, direct a choir, play the organ in church, and perform his role as husband and father. It has been an enlightening experience for me.

FEBRUARY 28

I drove the boys to school early this morning (Bill is on a trip to Sligo and Leitrim), and came back to work at my desk till 11:30 AM, when I went to Mountjoy Square to visit the St. Ann Flats, a block of apartments for old folks. I am going to make a radio plea for financial donations to the Flats and wanted to see what they were like before I spoke about them on the air.

The inner courtyard of the block is inviting, with roses and flowering borders and a big open grassy area. The flats form an L shape around the courtyard with a community center on one side. The building is three stories high, and each flat has a small balcony.

I visited three of them. The size of the rooms is so much smaller than their American counterparts would be, that I had to adjust my standards mentally before I could accommodate myself to their smallness. The first one I visited was for a single person and had just one room with a tiny kitchen and bath. The tenant was very welcoming and eager to show me her things, but as we were leaving, she suddenly said, with great feeling: "The architect who designed this building should be hung!" There was a moment of stunned silence, while my guide, one of the building's supervisors, looked at her with dismay. But she continued: "There are no cupboards at all." And she was right, there were none. My guide quickly thanked her for letting me see her flat and we left in a hurry. I admired her spunky critique; I don't think that had been on my planned tour.

The next flat we visited was occupied by two sisters. It had a living room, a bedroom with a double bed (which they shared) and a tiny kitchen and bath. They had fixed it up in an attractive and comfortable manner and it looked much more cheerful than the first one. They both said they were very happy there and enjoyed the company of the community center.

We went on to visit some flats that are being let to young, newly married couples. They are charged a sizable rent, which "gets them in the habit of putting aside a certain amount each week"; and when they move out and are able to get a house of their own, they are returned half of that rent plus interest.

The community center is a very attractive room with a fireplace and a small kitchen for fixing snacks. Much to my surprise, the matron said that not very many of the residents use it. "You know how it is," she said. "They like to keep to themselves." I would have thought that loneliness would have been one of their biggest enemies, but the Irish are funny that way. They *do* like to keep to themselves.

FEBRUARY 29

Bill made a major speech tonight in Sligo, setting forth the reasons for President Carter's tough policy toward the Soviet Union following its invasion of Afghanistan. (I read his speech before he left and knew it would elicit a spate of publicity.) He explained that these measures were an alternative to war, not a prelude to war. President Carter's partial embargo on the grain sales, cutbacks on Soviet fishing rights in American waters, reduction in the number of flights into New York by Aeroflot (the Soviet airline), and his ban on the sale of high-technology items are all attempts to make the Soviet leaders think twice before committing another act of aggression. The way to make them more cautious, Carter believes, is to force them to pay some economic and political price for the Afghanistan invasion. The ban on American participation in the Moscow Olympics is part of this effort. Since the Olympics are to be a major propaganda show demonstrating the "success" of the Soviet system, for which the Soviet government has been preparing for years, the cancellation or transfer of the games, or even the reduction in participation by foreign countries, would deprive the Russians of the prestige they value so much and have been seeking.

MARCH 1

Bill's speech in Sligo has drawn a lot of press coverage in the morning papers, as I knew it would, but as yet no editorial comment. When he returned to Dublin this afternoon, he agreed to give a radio interview on

RTE's news program to be broadcast at 1 PM on Sunday. He has been avoiding radio interviews because once they are taped, they can be cut, and the person being interviewed has no control over the shape of the interview as it actually goes out to the public. But he decided to make an exception in this case. Having gone to Sligo to make a speech explaining the president's foreign policy, he felt he should continue his "missionary" work over the radio, and this program commands a large audience.

We had a brush with the Law this evening. A glint-eyed garda on a sharp lookout for lawbreakers thought he had bagged a sure one when he stopped us tonight. We were on our way to Nick and Mary Robinson's for dinner, and Bill decided he would drive us there himself. Our own car is *still* in the garage, having its transmission overhauled (more on that later), so we are driving a small "banger" that the embassy owns.

We had never been to the Robinsons' house before, but we had their address on Wellington Place. In the dark and the rain it was difficult to read numbers, and we paused in front of several houses, pulling in toward the curb and pulling away again. Suddenly, a motorcycle cop appeared at our side, motioning for us to pull over. Bill rolled down the window and said: "Good evening. I'm glad to see you. I'm trying to find a number on Pembroke Place."

"Wellington Place," I whispered.

"Wellington Place," he repeated for the garda. "I'm *always* getting those two mixed up. Ha ha. Ahem."

The garda looked at him in silence for a few seconds and then asked very suspiciously: "Are you all right?"

"All right" is an Irish euphemism for "sober."

"Tell him you're the American ambassador," I whispered.

"I'm, er, the American ambassador," Bill said, looking more than a little uncomfortable.

The garda took this as a whimsical sally and asked: "Is this your car?"

"Yes, it is. Well, actually, it isn't. That is, it belongs to my embassy."

"Do you have the registration papers for it?"

Bill looked as if he had just been asked to recite the alphabet in Sanskrit.

"Registration papers? No, I wouldn't have those. You see, I don't really get involved with that kind of thing. I suppose my administrative officer would have them," he added encouragingly.

"Would you mind to step out?" the garda asked in what could only be interpreted as a Firm Tone.

Bill got out and stood in the rain with the garda in front of the car. His red carnation and his derby looked very ambassadorial, but our garda was unimpressed.

"You're also driving with your bright lights on," he said accusingly.

Bill leaned in the window to turn on the dims, and flipped the switch for the window wipers instead. The cleaning spray shot out over the windscreen as the wipers went into play.

"Whoops," Bill said.

"What's that?" asked the garda, who by this time had his notebook and pen poised.

"I said, 'Whoops,' " Bill replied. "This is the first time I've driven this car and I'm not too sure where everything is."

"Could I see your identification?" asked our friend, who was now writing in his little book. I wondered if he knew how to spell "whoops." Bill fished endlessly through credit cards and calling cards, and finally came up with a piece of identification. The garda looked at it very carefully. Either he had a reading problem or he was memorizing it. The rain was coming down harder. He finally handed it back to Bill and looked at him earnestly.

"Be careful," he said, and sped off into the night.

MARCH 11

"When Irish Eyes Are Smiling" and "The Rose of Tralee" are two of the most popular and oft-sung Irish songs. I went to the Burlington Hotel this evening to help choose the Dublin "Rose," the girl who will compete for the title in Tralee next summer. I was the only woman on a panel with four men. We had nine contestants to chose from, each a pretty and poised girl. We spoke to them individually, questioning them on their schooling, families, jobs, current favorites in music, books, films and theater, boyfriends, aspirations for the future.

Each summer the Roses come to Tralee from all over Europe and America to vie for the title of Rose of Tralee; at the festival they appear before another panel of judges and are interviewed on national television by Gay Byrne. They also must do a "number," whether it's a song, story or joke.

The Rose we chose tonight is not only lovely to look at but intelligent and articulate. Dublin will be proud of its Rose in Tralee next summer.

MARCH 12

I popped into Switzer's Department Store today to buy some trim for a chair I am reupholstering. I was in a hurry because I was meeting Mab Moltke for lunch, but the sales clerk was deep into conversation with a jovial, elderly, red-faced gentleman and his thin, cheerful wife, who were up from the country to buy a little brass ring for her to fasten her neck scarf.

"I have all the time in the world," the man boomed at the clerk. My heart sank. "I'm not one of your pressurized men who don't have time to say a pleasant word to anyone, much less a sales clerk." The clerk didn't flinch, but I did. "Or even to do a day's shopping with the wife, even if it is just for a trivial thing like a scarf ring, which, if it makes her happy . . . well that's just what life is all about, isn't it?" He looked enormously pleased with himself and had the definite air of a man who was only warming up. The wife, smiling and nodding and looking just a *teeny* bit simple, tossed her head in the direction of her husband and said: "Just listen to him." That seemed to end her contribution to the conversation. She had obviously spent a lifetime doing what she urged us to do.

The clerk was in accord with their sentiments and eager to join the conversation. "Most people *are* pressurized," she agreed. (I wondered by this time if we were on to people or steam cookers.) "It's a shame," she went on, "and it certainly doesn't make *my* day any more pleasant, with people coming in the way they do, demanding to be waited on instantly." (I closed my purse and immediately stopped waving my trim in her face.) The man tried to break in, but she was away and running now.

"It could be plain that I'm busy doing something else, but no, they want instant attention and they want it *now*. People don't take the time to be courteous, much less friendly. If only they knew where this world was headed," she added ominously, "they might slow down and make time for the amenities."

The man was clearly irritated that the floor had been snatched from him, and he banged his hand down on the counter for emphasis. And attention. "It's *city life* that does it," he said. "Down in the country we *know* what civilization is. We make time for the amenities." He looked around for confirmation and his eyes rested on me. Clearly I was expected to say something.

"It's not nearly as bad here as it is in New York," I ventured. "Now that place *really* is pressurized."

The thought of New York stunned them into silence. The little wife stopped smiling and the jovial, time-laden husband stared at me aghast, then said, "New York. Well. That's something else again." The two of them paid and left. The clerk turned to me and said: "They come in often and they always have time for a chat. Aren't they sweet?" I didn't dare disagree.

As I left the store, smiling to myself about the conversation, I realized that it is true that during my three years in Ireland I haven't had one single "run in" with a rude or impatient or surly clerk. A few may have been overly nonchalant ("Excuse me, can you tell me where I would find the sheets and towels?" "Haven't a clue"), but everyone I have dealt with has been courteous and willing to take time to make selections. Many of the large stores are understaffed, and a customer has to wait to be served. But when it's your turn, like the lady said, there's time for the amenities.

The women selling fish on Moore Street

I salute all those foot-weary men and women up and down Grafton Street, Dawson Street, Henry and O'Connell streets and all those other places in Dublin where they spend their days serving the public with time for a smile. And I particularly salute all those tough, old, hoarse-voiced gals on Moore Street, cigarettes dangling from their mouths, hawking their fish or fruit on cold rainy sidewalks, flirting with the world and turning their daily routine into a burlesque of themselves, and they their own best audience.

MARCH 13

One of the inspectors from the Department of Education, Sean McGowan, came by the house this morning to pick me up and take me on a tour of several Dublin schools. Our first stop was at the Aughrim Street School, St. Gabriel's, which is in a relatively poor section of town, just behind Dublin's old cattle markets and near the army barracks. Many of the parents of the schoolchildren there have been recently relocated and have severe social and economic problems. By rights the school should be a "difficult" one; but it isn't, thanks mostly to its industrious, skilled and exuberant principal, Grainne O'Sullivan.

I walked in on her cold, which isn't a very courteous thing to do, but I wanted to see the classes unprepared for a visitor. After her initial shock at my arrival, Miss O'Sullivan welcomed me warmly and we set out to see the school. The girls were lovely and friendly but very shy. Some of them spoke so softly I couldn't hear them; others put their hands up in front of their faces if I looked in their direction. The teachers were devoted, and their hard work with the children showed in every aspect of the classroom. The tiny four-year-olds were reading from their texts. The ten-year-olds knew who the first president of the United States was, and the twelve-year-olds could name five American rivers and tell me which one is the biggest. Bright as they are, Miss O'Sullivan told me that most of them will not go on to higher education. They will leave St. Gabriel's at twelve and go to a "tech" or a community school, but not many will go beyond a "group cert," which is the exam for leaving school at fifteen years of age. She said that most of their parents don't look upon education as a stepping-stone to higher wages, a better life or more security. "They will often encourage a child, especially if she is an older child in the family, to quit school at fourteen or fifteen and go out to work to bring wages home."

During the recess, all the teachers joined us for coffee in one of the small classrooms while we continued talking. I wanted to know about the relationship between the Department of Education and the Church.

"The parish, or the diocese, nominally owns the school property," one of the teachers explained. "The parish priest is the 'manager' of the school and he appoints four people to serve on a managerial board. The board also includes the principal, one or two teachers, and one elected parent. The Department of Education provides the money for teachers' salaries, school maintenance and so on."

The girls at St. Gabriel's don't wear uniforms as girls would at a private convent school, but their clothes were neat and serviceable. Some of the classrooms had that strong "wet puppy dog" smell of children who need a bath. The teachers explained that many of the students live in homes without bathing facilities and have to attend public bathhouses. Many times the younger children are taken from school early in the afternoon so that they can get to the baths before the hot water runs out.

I left St. Gabriel's and headed downtown to visit a school in the city center, behind the Gresham Hotel. The Rutland Street School building is as dilapidated as the neighborhood it serves. Most of the population around the school is in the process of being relocated to newer housing developments on the fringes of Dublin. The school population is dwindling as the neighborhood moves out, and part of the building is now used for a government-sponsored hotel training school.

I visited a "special class," where many of the children had been in trouble with the law and been taken to Children's Court. They were dirty, smart, articulate and street-wise; one very small boy told me with obvious pride that his brother had just been "sent up" for five years for arson.

They sang a couple of songs for me with gusto, and their teacher was obviously proud of them. "You can't find better kids," she said. "The school is their only stabilizing atmosphere. Home for most of them is grim; tiny, two-bedroom flats for six, eight, ten or twelve kids." One little girl was the youngest of eighteen!

The older flats in Summerhill, which is the neighborhood adjoining the school district, are being phased out, but some of the flats there are still occupied. They don't have bathrooms, but still the people cling to their old neighborhood and resent being moved. One of the teachers told me about a young mother who was relocated about ten blocks away from Summerhill. She was given a good Council flat with a bathroom. All her relatives from the old neighborhood come to see her and take baths but, in spite of that, she is very unhappy there and says the neighbors know the poor area she came from and are snobbish to her. She misses her old friends and is trying to have herself moved back to her old down-at-the-heels neighborhood. "I grew up there," she said. "It's where me and my family belong."

MARCH 18

We drove down to the National Museum today to see a chalice that has just been dug up by an amateur archaeologist in County Tipperary. He was apparently using a metal detector and found the twelfth-century artifact, along with a paten, wine strainer, and stand for the chalice, which is supposed to be similar in style and design to the famous Ardagh Chalice, one of Ireland's most revered relics. It is black with age and sediment and must be sent off for cleaning before the amateur can tell what it really looks like. It's an important find, and there has been much controversy, Irish-style, over the discovery. The newspapers first said that it was found by an "English amateur archaeologist." Then they said he was Irish but wouldn't reveal his name. Then they said he would be given a monetary reward for finding the objects, and *then* they said he would be fined for using a metal detector and digging on someone else's property without permission. And so on.

MARCH 19

The murder of the archbishop of El Salvador has turned attention to the United States' involvement there. The embassy in Ballsbridge was the site of a twenty-four-hour vigil protesting that involvement. The Irish are particularly intense in their criticism of the United States and its connections with El Salvador because the bishop of Galway, Dr. Eamon Casey, attended the funeral mass in San Salvador for the slain archbishop and witnessed firsthand an outburst of violence directed against the congregation. It was a traumatic experience, and Dr. Casey is so incensed at what he regards as American support of the "wrong side" in that tragic country that he has suggested Ireland break off diplomatic relations with the United States. The minister of foreign affairs, Brian Leinhan, appeared on a television show, "Today Tonight," recently and poured oil on troubled waters. He suggested that breaking off diplomatic relations with the United States would not be a "constructive approach ... especially when dealing with an old and valued friend."

MARCH 20

I went to the American Women's Club the other day to hear Senator Catherine McGuinness speak about women's legal rights in Ireland. She traced the history and origins of various discriminatory laws affecting women throughout the ages in Ireland. Since I had just finished reading an excellent collection of essays called *Women in Irish Society: The Historical Dimension,* I was particularly interested in her remarks on the rights of women before the twelfth century and the Norman invasion of Ireland.

Women's rights in that pre-Norman era were far-ranging. They could divorce and own property, two rights that they were soon to lose. A woman could divorce her husband because he was sexually unsatisfactory: sterile, impotent or a homosexual. She could also collect a fine from her husband for assault and the equivalent of her full bride's price if he beat her. As Donncha Ó'Corrain points out in his essay "Women in Early Irish Society," the German scholar August Knock remarked that the laws governing marriage show a "frankly astonishing concern for the dignity and individual personality of the wife in marriage." This statement certainly could not have been made about the marriage laws affecting Irish women in later centuries.

Although women then held no inherited political powers, they were influential and powerful in their own right. Abbesses of large monasteries, for instance, could wield great power; Irish queens often played a formative role in guiding their husband's destiny. They were sure of their positions, and the ancient Irish or "Brehon" Law protected them and gave them a certain independence of action and thought that the imposition of English law in the early seventeenth century denied them. As Ó'Corrain says: "In its attitude to women and their place in society, as in its attitude to many other matters, modern Ireland enjoys no continuity with its Gaelic past."

Through the seventeenth, eighteenth and nineteenth centuries, the role and status of women in Ireland were as dismal as anywhere else in western Europe. Their property and inheritance rights were governed by English common law, they had no political rights, and they were expected to play only a submissive, domestic role within the context of their family. Not until 1879 were they admitted to University. By then, the wind was blowing in a different direction.

Senator McGuinness said of the suffragette movement in Ireland: "It coincided with the move for Irish independence, and many women fought hand in hand with both movements. It was an exciting and exhilarating time for women in Ireland." (While I was lunching recently at the Royal College of Surgeons, across the street from Stephen's Green, the doorman showed me the bullet holes inside the College that had been made by British soldiers deployed in the Green during the Rising of 1916. The remarkable Irish feminist and patriot Countess Markiewicz occupied the College and with great courage defended it until the Rising failed.) The wave of nationalism and the women's movement absorbed the energies and the passions of women just emerging into an organized political force. Their emergence was not, however, limited to politics; Lady Gregory and Maire Nic Shiubhlaigh were instrumental in the formation of the Irish National Theatre; women in the arts, in teaching and in academic professions were adding new, feminine dimensions to Irish society.

But after the War for Independence was won and both men and women had to get on with the more mundane jobs of making a living and raising their families, Irish women went back to their more traditional roles. It was as if the fire and creativity that revolution had inspired in them had burned itself out in their generation, and they didn't pass on the flame to their daughters. Like the postsuffragette women in America, Irish women in the twenties and thirties were passive, home and family oriented, and almost totally apolitical.

Men in Ireland have, throughout the ages, found women's rights movements hard to accept. Even Yeats, who was in love with Maude Gonne, a leading political activist, once talked about "women climbing on a wagonette to scream."

In her talk to us, Senator McGuinness, who practices law in Dublin, went on to talk about present-day legal rights for women in Ireland.

"Although broken marriages are rife—you have to wait four months to get a place in court to hear a separation trial—you still can't get a legal divorce. The court procedure is simply to settle on children's care, property, and maintenance allowances. Even though the Catholic Church will grant an annulment, which says in effect that the marriage never took place, the couple cannot obtain a legal divorce which would allow them to obtain a legal certificate of civil marriage. In the eyes of the state the second wife, or husband, is illegally married and any children from that relationship are illegitimate. Even though the husband of such a marriage could make a will and leave everything to his second wife and his children by that second marriage, his first, or legal, wife will still inherit one-third of his property, his money or his land."

During the question period I asked Senator McGuinness what "criminal conversations" are. My women friends frequently bring up that phrase, roll their eyes and groan, but I've never known exactly what it meant.

"It's an archaic law still existing in Ireland which says, in effect, that if a married women runs off with another man, her husband can sue that man for taking his 'property.' The same is not true, of course, if a man runs off with another woman."

APRIL 7: *County Kerry*

We left Dublin this morning for a week's Easter trip to Sneem, in County Kerry. A Dublin friend, Dermot Kinlen, has a house there by the sea and has very kindly loaned it to us for the holiday. When I mentioned yesterday to Sybil Connolly that we were headed in that direction, she said we must see Lismore Castle en route. She promised to phone and arrange a visit, and it turned out that the owners, the Duke and Duchess of Devonshire, were in residence. They hospitably invited us and the boys to stop by for lunch.

There is a spectacular view of the castle as one approaches Lismore, in County Waterford—all turrets and towers and a banner waving in the warm spring sun. Although it is a nineteenth-century Gothic reproduction, it looked wonderfully romantic and ancient to us.

The Duke and Duchess met us at the door and welcomed us warmly. I was immediately struck with her beauty, especially her vivid, startlingly blue eyes, set off by her blue Fair Isle sweater. I wasn't surprised when I learned that she is one of the Mitford sisters, and Desmond Guinness's aunt. She has those "Mitford blue" eyes.

The Duke is very tall, gregarious and charming. He made a special effort to make the boys feel at home, and they were enchanted with him. He introduced them to his huge billiard table, and that was the last we saw of them until we went in for our lunch. Our hosts were both dressed informally, she in knee socks, a skirt and sweater, he in slacks with a sweat shirt and a jaunty red kerchief at his neck. We had sherry in front of a fire in the small sitting room, and then went into an excellent lunch. The salmon was caught that morning in the river that runs alongside the castle, and the chocolate meringue cake called out for an encore, which it received from all the Shannons.

The Duke told us that they are trying to decide what to do with the Castle. It isn't your ordinary country home that you can pop in on for a weekend's fishing or rest. The care, upkeep and maintenance all belong to a bygone era, and for one family to live in it for only a few weeks a year and to maintain it is an enormous responsibility.

The gardens are lovely, filled with flowering shrubs and spring bulbs.

The Duke filled my arms with pink and white camellias as we were preparing to leave, and then turned to the boys. "On Easter Monday in England we have a tradition of giving children a treat," he said, grinning, and slipped them each a thick white envelope with an embossed crest on the back. The boys, surprised but accepting, put on their most endearing smiles and made profuse and charming thank-yous. They were delighted to find a generous little monetary treat when they tore open the envelopes.

APRIL 8

We spent the night at a small country inn where we had a very good dinner, a drink by the fire, and an early night . . . or so we thought. At 4 AM I was awakened by roars of laughter and loud voices. I looked at my watch and couldn't believe the time. Were they early risers who were cheerful in the morning? Hadn't they gone to bed? Were they off on an early hunt? I climbed out of bed and felt in the dark for Bill's robe (I never travel with robe and slippers when I'm with Himself; I borrow his, to his patient annoyance). I tied the sash twice around my waist, put on his slippers and flip-flopped down the darkened hall in the direction of the noise. I wasn't averse to joining the party if it seemed worthwhile, but at this stage it was hard to tell whether it was the milkman flirting with the kitchen maid or the dregs of last night's party in the bar. The laughter led me down a flight of stairs and into the kitchen. There, perched on kitchen counters and stools, sat the family, the boys who had served us in the bar and the dining room during dinner, and their mother, telling stories, hooting and hollering and having the time of their lives. When I pushed open the swinging door and stood there, illuminated by the overhead light of the kitchen, a deathly hush settled on everyone. They stared at me as if a long-awaited ghost had finally arrived in their midst.

"Glory be to God," said the mother.

"Hello," I said. "I heard you talking. And laughing."

They stared at me in silence.

"It *is* 4 AM," I said, defensively, obviously needing some excuse for appearing in their kitchen in the wee hours of dawn in a man's paisley bathrobe which hung down to the floor. They stared. I began to wish I had combed my hair and put on lipstick. I glanced down at my feet. One of Bill's house shoes had an enormous hole in the toe and my toe showed through. Everyone in the room seemed to be looking at it, and I tried to shift my toe to another spot.

"Well," I began again, "it *is* late and we couldn't sleep for all the noise. I guess our room is just above the kitchen."

The mother suddenly jumped, as if released from a mysterious trance,

263

and said in a most matter-of-fact voice: "Right you are. Off to bed with you, boys." The boys scattered like lightning. The overhead light went out and I began making my way back up the staircase in the dark, tripping over the long hem of the bathrobe and flipping out of the slippers. When I curled up next to Bill, he muttered: "What was that all about?"

"Nothing. I'll tell you in the morning."

In the morning, I thought I might have dreamed it. But no; at breakfast one of the handsome little boys who had served us at dinner the night before brought orange juice to our table and said in a voice scarcely above a whisper: "Mammy says she hopes you got back to sleep."

"I did," I said.

APRIL 13

On the way back to Dublin after our week's holiday, we had a blowout on the road outside Cork. We didn't have a spare in the car, which isn't an encouraging situation in which to find oneself on a Sunday afternoon on a small road in Ireland. The reason we didn't have a spare is very complicated. Just outside of Lismore, we had a flat. We took the tire into a garage in Youghal (pronounced Y'all) to have it repaired, and when the boy put the "repaired" tire back in the car, it was making a strange hissing noise.

"Isn't that a funny noise for it to be making?" I asked. (Isn't that a dumb question to be asking?) "It sounds like all the air is coming out."

"Ah, no," he reassured me, his forehead crinkled up into a responsible frown. "That's just trapped air. It'll stop in a few minutes."

And it did. When the tire was flat again and we were too far out of Youghal to turn back. We made it to Sneem and tried the local garage. The young man there agreed that it was hard to get a decent day's work done anywhere anymore, and promised to have the tire fixed by the next day. He did, and it lasted an hour this time. In despair we gave up and trusted to our spare, and that's why we found ourselves on the Cork Road with a blowout and no spare on a Sunday afternoon.

Bill and Christopher walked down a small country lane to a pretty farmhouse set in a lovely site overlooking a glittering blue lake. They returned in a few minutes with a handsome young farmer on his tractor and an air pump. He helped us take off the ruined tire, and he blew up the other one. All we could do was hope it would last until we could find an open garage in Cork that sold tires.

While we were changing tires, another car pulled up, filled with a family on a Sunday outing. They asked if they could be of help, then immediately recognized us. Out came the camera and we all posed together by the side of the road, while the young farmer took the pictures.

They said they would follow us into Cork, just to make sure we got there safely without another blowout, and they directed us to a garage that was open and, happily, had a tire to fit our small borrowed station wagon. (Our own car was still in the garage. More on that later.)

APRIL 16: *Dublin*

Daffodils and house guests are arriving, our two sure signs of spring, and both are a welcome sight. The Joneses and the Smiths arrived today. Richard Jones, the novelist, and his wife, Moussia, are over from London, while Eddie and Beth Smith are here from Kansas City. Eddie is a fellow trustee with Bill of their alma mater, Clark University. I also entertained a seventy-four-member teenage band from Rhode Island. They were agog at the house and the gardens and one of them asked: "What exactly do you do here?" When I tried to explain some of the duties of an ambassador serving abroad, he said in stunned amazement: "You mean we taxpayers pay for you and your husband to live in *this* house and give parties?" I admitted that was the case. "I bet you never even eat plain food," he went on. "I bet you guys *live* on eggs Florentine!"

A very happy boy, with a wide smile stretching across his freckled face and his eyes dancing with delight, came racing into my bedroom this afternoon, tripping himself on the three steps that lead up from the hallway, waving an envelope and a piece of paper in his hand.

"Look!" he shouted. "Look at this!" His hand was trembling as he handed me the paper.

"Dear Liam Shannon," it said. "Welcome to the Class of 1984. Congratulations. Dartmouth College."

I couldn't decide whether to laugh or cry, so I just hugged him and said: "Wonderful. Now I can form the Dartmouth PTA." He looked at me in horror for a split second before he burst out laughing. "Knowing you . . ." he said.

APRIL 17

I met the ambassadors' wives for lunch today at the Central Remedial Clinic for physically and mentally handicapped children. Lady Valerie Goulding started the clinic twenty years ago, when she saw what a great need there was in Ireland for schooling and training for the handicapped. Almost single-handedly she begged, fought for, cajoled and wheedled the money for the school. It is now a model for similar establishments all over Europe, and its spacious, sunny rooms are filled with children and young adults doing schoolwork, gymnastics, swimming, physical therapy, craftwork and just having fun. It is not a residential school; the students are brought in each morning by bus and private car.

One of the teachers at the school, Vicki Moltke, is the daughter of my friend Mab, so we made a special visit to her classroom and I was introduced to a small American student there, a tiny girl with cerebral palsy whose family has moved to Ireland.

Valerie wants the ambassadors' wives to be honorary patrons of an "Ambassadorial Ball," to be given as a fund raiser for the Clinic and also to honor Jimmy Saville, an English radio and television personality who has given unstintingly of his time to raise money for many good causes, including the Clinic.

APRIL 18

I was up at dawn, not having slept a wink. My hands were shaking so I could hardly dress, my tea cup rattling in my saucer. Unable to eat a bite. "How can you all just sit there, stuffing it in, chatting away as if it is an ordinary day?" I asked the others. "Don't you think we should be leaving?"

"It's only eight o'clock," Bill said, looking at his watch. "You don't have to be there until nine."

"We don't want to be late. In fact, we want to be *quite* early. We should leave in ten minutes." Everyone just kept on eating.

"You'd think he was making his debut at the Metropolitan," Christopher said.

"It could be the *beginning* of his debut at the Met," I replied. David was singing this morning in his first competitive Feis or festival at the Father Matthew Hall, and although he was coolly professional and wondered what all the fuss was about, I was a wreck.

We had to be at the Hall at nine o'clock. All the children draw lots to see who will play or sing first. David's singing class is first on the program, and David drew the first lot, so he has to open the Feis, poor fellow. He says he's glad, he would rather get it over with. Bill wasn't able to come, so Steffen, the Danish boy who took Siobhán's place when she left, accompanied us. He has helped David practice his solo for weeks, and is almost as nervous as I am.

The stage is huge! And although the hall was half empty, the adjudicator was already in place when we arrived, seated at a table in the center of the main aisle. He's over from England to judge this Feis, and one of the more experienced mothers in the hall whispered to me: "He's one of the tough ones."

All the children in Ireland who study music will be competing in one Feis or another around the country during the spring months. It's a great honor to take a first prize in one of them, especially at the prestigious Feis Ceoil in Dublin.

The adjudicator called the hall to order. David had been taken backstage with the rest of the eight-year-olds, ready to be called in the order of their lots. The accompanist settled herself at the piano and announced that she was ready. Each of the boys in David's group had been asked to sing "Paper Boat." Another more difficult song could be substituted, however, and it was announced that two of the boys had made the substitution. There were fourteen boys in the group.

"Number One, please." The adjudicator spoke in a deep, serious tone.

David walked out alone to the center of the stage. It looked as big as the stage at the Metropolitan. And he looked very small in his brown cord pants, cord vest, white shirt, brown and white houndstooth coat and little striped tie. My heart was thumping so hard I thought I would be asked to leave the hall.

"Good morning," the adjudicator said to David, in a softer, friendly voice. "It's not so easy to have to be the first one. Are you ready to sing?"

David nodded. He had one hand in his jacket pocket and the other one hung by his side, just as Mr. McNulty had told him.

"Fine. We'll begin when you are ready."

David nodded to the accompanist, who played the opening chord. He came in right on time, his tone was sure and clear, but his voice sounded very small. After a few bars he gained confidence and expanded his tone. He seemed calm and relaxed and sure of himself. I began to feel a little light-headed, then realized that I hadn't taken a breath since he began to sing! David had been practicing "Paper Boat" for two months. He sang it just as well as he could, without a mistake or a forgotten word. He finished to a round of applause and turned and walked off the stage.

"That was very nice. Thank you very much," the adjudicator said. "Number Two, please."

We sat through eleven more "Paper Boats" and two substitutions, then waited twenty minutes for the verdict. Each child was given points for his performance, based on the quality of his voice, his diction, his musical interpretation and so on. First, second and third winners were announced, to enthusiastic applause. David came in fifth in his group.

"Well done!" Steffen said, shaking David's hand. David was pleased with himself, as he should have been. I couldn't have stood up there and sung "Paper Boat." I would have taken one look at that adjudicator and fainted dead away.

APRIL 21

I went by myself to the Botanical Gardens today. I've been many times and take visitors in the spring and summer, but I wanted to go alone today, notebook in hand, to do some gardening homework. It's a wonderful place for the serious gardener to study, with "classrooms" of labeled plants, trees, shrubs, creepers, vines, herbs, annuals and perennials; one can go home reeling with enthusiastic, ambitious plans for one's own garden. Also, it's a peaceful, quiet place of beauty, with rustic, winding footpaths, arboretums, ancient and majestic trees, elegant vistas and mossy, sylvan glens. A small green river runs through the Gardens, with footbridges crossing from one side to the other. I've often thought what a wonderful place it would be for a garden party, but then, of course, one couldn't count on the weather.

Today was a perfect spring day, warmer than usual for April, with blue, cloudless skies. After I had spent an hour jotting down names of potential plants and flowers for the residence gardens, I closed my notebook and walked toward the river, marveling as I always do at the green luxuriance of the grass, its delicate softness and its thick, spongy feel. The Gardens were empty, as they usually are early on a weekday morning, so I was startled to see the figure of a very tall man striding purposefully in front of me, down by the river. He didn't have the concentrated, squinty look of a person studying plants or trees. He glanced neither right nor left but walked straight on, shoulders squared under a very handsome, well-cut tweed jacket. His pants were crisp and pressed, his shoes highly polished. I followed along at a discreet distance, wondering who he was, if I perhaps knew him, and what he was doing there in the Gardens at ten o'clock on a Monday morning.

I was taken aback when he suddenly spun around and began walking just as quickly back in my direction. I saw him then in full face. Did I know him? No. And he gave no sign of recognizing me. He was about mid-fifties, very handsome, with the ruddy cheeks of a country person. He passed by me with a perfunctory nod of acknowledgment, but he gave himself away by looking at his watch as he passed. Clearly, he was there to meet someone and that someone was late. Who was that someone?

All thoughts of flowering fruit trees, deciduous hedges, herbaceous borders fled. I was no longer Capability Brown, planning great eighteenth century gardens, I was Miss Marple on the scent of something peculiar. I followed him, making random jottings in my notebook so that he would think I was solely engrossed in the vegetation. He walked very fast and stopped again suddenly. I thought he was going to retrace his steps once more, but instead he sat down on a bench and crossed his legs with the resigned look of a man who knows he must wait.

I bent down to examine the leaves of a small sapling. Neither of us had long to wait. She came suddenly and unexpectedly from a small side path, not, as I had thought she would, from the direction of the main entrance. She came so quickly and quietly I didn't even know she was there until I heard her voice, soft but tense with excitement and slightly breathless. "Hello." My back was to them and I was still bending over my sapling. How long can one look at a leaf? They began walking in my direction; I kept my head down but peered up under the brim of my hat for a second to see that he had his arm around her and she was tall and slim. As they passed, I caught a quick look at her face. She was smiling at him. I became intensely absorbed in a blade of grass as they passed in front of me, but I needn't have worried. They had no eyes for anyone but each other. Miss Marple gave way to Barbara Cartland. What a romantic, secluded place to meet. Do they come here every Monday morning? Whom would they expect to encounter in the Botanical Gardens at this hour? Hardly me, which is just as well, since I know her intimately, and, of course, I know her husband, too.

APRIL 23

We went to the Allied Irish Bank Headquarters again this evening to see one of our favorite writers and a dear friend receive the AIB Writer's Award. Benedict Kiely is one of the kindest, most generous men I have ever met; he and Frances Daly are often at our house and we heard the news of his award with great pleasure. I was a fan of his long before I ever came to Ireland; his novella *Proxopera* is a powerful depiction of the obscene tactics of the IRA.

I often hear Ben reading his short stories on the radio, and his soft, Northern accent brings an additional dimension of life and wit to the characters he writes about. I recognize his voice the second I flick on the radio, and when I hear it I smile to myself, stop whatever I am doing, and settle back for a wonderful, amusing and robust story.

MAY 6

New carpets are being installed all over the house and it's a mess. Dennis is trying to cope with all of that, a dinner party tonight, and a reception for 120 on Friday. Mr. and Mrs. Alfred Knopf, Jr., of Atheneum Publishers (*my* publishing company!) came to dinner tonight, and we had a "literary evening" for them with Mary Lavin and Michael Scott, Seamus and Marie Heaney, John Banville and his wife, Bruce and Mavis Arnold, the Hugh Leonards (another Atheneum writer). Etcetera, etcetera, etcetera, as David would say. And as usual with literary guests, everyone enjoyed each other and themselves enormously and stayed until the wee hours. Seamus spoke to me so eloquently on Northern Ireland and its problems that I made everyone be quiet and listen to him repeat it. He laughed and said: "Every time you get two people together talking about the same subject, you start a seminar."

MAY 7

John Burke, the young farmer who "rescued" us when our tire burst on the road to Cork, came to tea today with his pretty fiancée. We had made him promise to come by and see us, and since he was in Dublin for the Spring Show at the RDS he took us up on the invitation. I also entertained a group of Irish Countrywomen's Association ladies from Galway this afternoon.

MAY 9

The house echoed with soft southern voices as a delegation from Birmingham, Alabama, came through. Their city put on an Irish Festival this spring, and we were returning some of the hospitality shown the Irish participants. We invited all those who had gone from Ireland to Birmingham, including a group of actors from the Projects Art center, a very bohemian, long-haired, grubby, friendly sort of group. I asked a slim, tall, bearded fellow who was wearing a tattered gray fedora if he had ringworm, but he didn't get my joke and left his hat on throughout the reception.

When all the guests were leaving, Brian heard someone clanking; his coat pockets dragged suspiciously downward. When Brian stopped him, it transpired that he had four bottles of whiskey tucked away in his pockets and was hoping to make a clean getaway. He put them down without a murmur, and slipped out, chastened, I hope, by being caught. That's the very first time since we've been here that anybody   at least to our knowledge—has tried to slip off with some booty. I hear that it happens all the time in other embassies around the world. The Irish, among other virtues, practice honesty.

MAY 12

We received a very eloquent and sweet note this week from Jack and Máirín Lynch, sending us condolences for the death of the eight American soldiers who were killed attempting to free the hostages in Iran. We were both very touched by their thoughtfulness; it was particularly meaningful and appreciated since it was the only note of sympathy we received.

MAY 20

My mother and her friend Alice Jobes have been visiting from Texas this week. They both laughed uproariously at a headline in the paper yesterday saying: TEMPERATURE SOARS TO 70 DEGREES. They cut it out to take back home and show their Texas friends when the thermometer in Kerrville hits 110 degrees in the shade!

Today I took them both out to the cliffs of Howth, one of my favorite walking spots along the Dublin coast. I don't find the time anymore, but last year I used to drive out here on a weekday morning with Molly, my Labrador, park the car, and go walking alone along the steep, rock-strewn cliffs that line the shore high above the water. The Howth Lighthouse sits at the end of an arm of land that stretches out to sea, the Head of Howth. From the other side of Dublin, standing by the Joyce Tower at Sandycove, in Dun Laoghaire, you can look over the bay and see the lighthouse blinking and twinkling across the dark expanse of water, guiding the ships that come into Dublin Harbor.

There are a few small cottages hugging the edge of the cliffs, nestled into a lonely and isolated niche with nothing for company but the friendly, blinking, constant signal of the lighthouse. I often stand on top of the cliffs, looking down upon those cottages, and wonder who lives there? I picture myself in one of them, sitting by a warm peat fire, with the waves pounding against the rocky side of the cliff, spraying silver and green jets of seawater high into the air as they crash outside my window. I hear the wind howling off the ocean, slamming into my snug little cottage, making the yellow gorse that grows up to the doorway cling to its sturdy roots for dear life. I am writing novels inside my whitewashed, wind-dashed cottage, listening to the sounds of the gale and watching the waters of the bay recede, exhausted, out again to sea.

My mother is as fanciful a dreamer as I am when it comes to choosing a place to live, and she's even more prone to act upon her fancy than I am. When I was a child, it wasn't an unusual occurrence at our house for my father to come home from the office, looking forward no doubt to a quiet evening at home with his family, only to be met at the door by my mother, her eyes shining with excitement to announce: "Guess what! I sold the house today!" One time she moved us all out to a farm for two years, even though my father had to drive some distance into town to his office, so that my brother and I could have a "farm experience." Another time she took my brother and me all the way out to Arizona to "look at some property," but she came home empty-handed from that prospecting trip.

She was enchanted by the tiny houses when I pointed them out to her from atop the cliff, and saw in them what had attracted me. "Let's find out who owns them," she said with that particular gleam in her eye and authority in her voice that means her prospecting blood is running and she's on the verge of doing something rash, romantic and fun, something that will give my father nightmares. "Maybe they'll throw in the lighthouse."

"No," I said. "I couldn't do it now. I don't have the time to invest in it, much less the money. But maybe, someday."

She looked disappointed. "No time like the present," she offered hopefully. Those five words, attached to "time for a change," are her guiding philosophy. But I led her away from our impractical dream and back up the path toward the car.

MAY 23

The Irish government has voted to support the US Olympic boycott, but the Irish Olympic Committee has said it will send the team anyway. The Vintners' Association has promised that they will work very hard to help raise the money for the team, and Sinn Fein The Workers' Party, has also said they will support the team and contribute to a nationwide money-raising campaign.

MAY 29

We had a small farewell luncheon party today, just the four of us, for Kevin and Kay McGuire, who are being transferred from our embassy here to Gabon, where Kevin will become the deputy chief of mission. We will miss them both very much; Kevin's work as the economic counselor at the embassy has been invaluable to Bill, and Kay has contributed her energy and organizing skills in many areas. She's the one who organized all the classes I have attended on Irish history, poetry, and literature. She has served energetically as president of the American Women's Club, putting on fund raisers, giving teas, and arranging speakers for the meetings. She and Kevin and their two boys have traveled the length and width of Ireland and are leaving with a detailed knowledge of its culture and history. They are a great credit to the embassy, to the foreign service and to their country. They are an example of what makes diplomacy work.

JUNE 2

The leader of an American junior college tour offering course credits for a trip through Ireland got in touch with me to ask if he could bring his students out for a tour of the house. I agreed and gave them my talk on the house and paintings. They were an attentive bunch and made notes furiously on everything I had to tell them. While I was giving them coffee and cakes after my lecture, one of the students, a thin, short girl with a funny topknot on her head, cornered Dennis as he was pouring coffee and whispered to him: "Can you tell me any gossip about the Shannon family that I can put in my notes?" Dennis thought it was amusing, but I was offended by her rudeness.

"What'd you tell her, anyway?" I asked him.

"Oh, just the usual," he replied, and closed the door quickly before the teacup could bounce off his head.

For once I feel as if I may be in over my head, that I am sinking in a sea of invitations, lists, arrangements, plans, parties and guests. That I don't know what I am doing from hour to hour. I've got a reception for three hundred members of the Friendship Force from Worcester, Massachusetts, coming up in two weeks, followed by a Fourth of July reception for everyone in Dublin who can walk or talk; I've got eighty women from the Irish Countrywomen's Association coming to tea this afternoon, and a party for the National Press Club, four sets of house guests arriving over the next four weeks, and a black-tie dinner for twenty-four on July 5th. We're going to have a marquee put up in the Pretty Garden, pray for clear weather, and hope for the best.

In the meantime, I'm trying to make summer plans for all of the boys. Liam is taking his leaving examination this week, even though he already has his plans made for college in the fall. The exams are *very* hard, and the Irish boys and girls at his school are under terrific pressure. My heart goes out to them. David and Christopher are both going to Camp Ireland for two weeks in July. David has sworn that he will not get homesick and phone us in the middle of the night to come and get him. Christopher is taking a sailing course in August. We're losing Steffen in July and all of us will miss him. He's been a wonderful addition to our family and very dear to David. Thank goodness Patricia Roche has entered our lives. She came for a few months earlier this year and cooked for us while we were without an assistant cook. She's going to return to Dublin in the fall and has agreed to live with us and take care of David.

Later

I had my eighty ICA ladies to tea this afternoon. As we were walking through the gardens to show them my vegetables, I asked the president of one of the clubs why more Irish women, farm women especially, don't grow their own vegetables. Her answer was direct and to the point: "They're too damn lazy, that's why!"

"You mean," I asked, "that there's no deep sociological or historical reason?"

She threw back her head and laughed heartily. "Your sociological reason is laziness. Your historical reason is apathy," she replied.

She may be too hard on her fellow countrywomen, but it has always puzzled me how few vegetable gardens one sees in Irish farmyards as one drives around the countryside. Ireland has such a good climate and soil for growing most vegetables that it could be an economical and very satisfying hobby here.

I had to take Christopher out to Dun Laoghaire this morning for a swimming test, which he has to pass in order to be eligible for the sailing course. The children were being tested outdoors, in a pool filled with seawater. It was a beautiful spot, built into the rocks jutting out into Dublin Harbor, but it was *coooolllllllddd*. The children were all moaning and groaning and gritting their teeth as they prepared to jump in and swim their laps. "It's no colder than it would be if you capsized out in the middle of the bay," one of the teachers wisely told them. "So you'd better get used to it now." Christopher gave me a soulful look as he stood on the edge of the pool, begging silently for mercy, and his look turned to pure rage as he made the plunge.

One little girl was standing by the edge of the water, blue with cold, and crying her heart out. "I'm *not* going in," she sobbed. Her father picked her up and threw her in. I was sure she would sink to the bottom, but instead she nimbly grabbed hold of the side of the pool as she went down, and held on for dear life.

"Swim!" her father roared.

"No!" she cried. "I can't. I'm too cold. I want to get out." I was on her side.

"All right," said the frustrated dad. "That's perfectly all right with me. You just won't take your sailing course this summer, that's all. And that's *fine* with me."

"I don't *want* to take my sailing course," she moaned. "I want to go home."

"You *do* want to take your sailing course"—he had shifted gears and was red in the face with fury now—"and you are going to swim."

"I hate sailing." She was sobbing.

"You do not hate sailing. You love sailing. And now I am going to count to five and on the count of five you are going to start swimming. *Do . . . you . . . understand?* One. Two. Three. Four. Five." Nothing happened.

He knelt on the edge of the pool and began pulling her fingers from the side, one by one. I knew that if I gave him just the slightest, the tiniest little shove, just a nudge, really, he would join his daughter in the water for a father-daughter swim-along. I wondered if he'd press charges if I did that.

I knelt down next to him and put my hand in the water. It was icy. "Gee, it's really cold, isn't it?" I said to the little girl. "Should I push your dad in so he can see how cold it is?" She stopped crying and looked almost cheerful.

"You seem to find this very amusing," he said between clenched teeth and walked away. I never did find out what the outcome was, but

if I had been that dad, I would have gotten her a pony and left her on
dry land.

June 17

John Boorman, the film director who made *Deliverance,* is making a
movie here in Ireland about the King Arthur legend. Bill and I drove
out to the National Film Studios at Ardmore today and had lunch with
Seamus Smith, the director of the studio, and Mrs. Boorman. We toured
the sets after lunch; the last time I had been on a movie set was when I
was a movie-mad sixteen-year-old and toured M-G-M in California; Sonny
Tufts pulled my ponytail and I almost fainted. The set for Merlin's cave
was a fantastic creation, where grotesque shapes and vibrant colors
formed a blaze of wild make-believe imagery. One could easily imagine
magical things happening there.

Some of the battle scenes were being filmed on another set in a riding
stable out near the Park. We jumped at the chance to drive out and
watch the filming. The stable was crammed with men roaming around in
beards and armor, plus the film crew, and, in the midst of it all, lying on
the floor looking through a camera lens, was John himself, preparing for
Arthur's death scene.

We were motioned into silence as the action began, but it was immediately stopped and someone said: "Just a little bit more blood, please, on
the forehead, and more sweat on the upper lip." A man came running up
to the dying Arthur with two spray cans in his hands, one marked BLOOD
and the other SWEAT. Arthur, bloodier and sweatier, looked more authen-
tically near death and the action continued.

July 4

We have survived our first Fourth of July party at the residence. Each
of us pitched in and worked on the party all day. I drove downtown to
pick up cheese, pâté and French bread at McCambridge's; Liam spent the
entire day in the kitchen making meatballs; and the other two boys carried plants, chairs, linen, glasses, ashtrays and bottles from the house,
helping Dennis and Brian set up shop in the marquee. I put a dozen
small round tables along the wall of the tent, and I lined the walls and
the interior posts with pots of geranium and ivy from the garden. We
put a bar table at either end of the tent, and had a hot and cold buffet
table.

Earlier in the day, I had done a radio interview on the telephone with
RTE about the Fourth of July, its historical significance and how Ameri-
cans celebrate the holiday at home. "What would you eat on a Fourth of
July picnic in America?" the interviewer asked.

"Fried chicken and cold beer," I replied.

"Will you be serving fried chicken at your party this afternoon at the residence?" he asked.

"No, I'm afraid not," was my reply. And I hadn't been off the phone for ten minutes when it rang again; this time the caller was a representative of Dublin's Kentucky Fried Chicken. He had heard the interview, and said that Kentucky Fried would like to donate several barrels of fried chicken to the party this afternoon.

"Wonderful!" I said. "Bring it along and I know everyone will enjoy it." And they did. One woman came up to me, wiping her fingers and lips, and said: "Oh, it takes you Americans to know how to fry chicken. All we ever get here in Dublin is Kentucky Fried, but you folks really make it wonderfully!" I didn't have the heart to disillusion her.

All through the day little puffs of rain blew in, then the sun would come out. The afternoon cleared, but the wind came up. It would be a rather spectacular celebration if the marquee blew down with five hundred people in it.

Bill and I stood by the wall of the Pretty Garden, where the iron gate leads in from the courtyard, and greeted our guests there. We were protected from the wind by the high brick wall surrounding the garden, and by the walls of the courtyard. The diplomatic corps arrived first and promptly, as they always do. A new Russian ambassador has recently arrived in Ireland, and I met him today for the first time, a big, burly bear of a man, quick to crack a joke or wink at a pretty woman.

Ireland has two women ambassadors now, Johanna Nestor from Austria and Ruth Dobson from Australia. They will soon be joined by a third, when the Chinese embassy opens here. The Nigerians were there in their handsome national costumes, adding so much color to the somber pinstripes of the other ambassadors. When the last of the guests had been greeted and tucked safely into the marquee, we joined the party. The tent was filled to overflowing, which was just as well, since we had to depend on body heat to stay warm. Virtually every invitation had been accepted and the din in the tent grew as the wine flowed.

I love to listen to the radio in Ireland, and Valerie McGovern, of the deep, throaty voice and the smooth, polished delivery, is one of my favorite announcers. I don't know if she was having us on today or was playing it straight, but I tuned in to her "Summer Look Around," a program about out-of-the-way places in Ireland, and heard what can only be described as one of the most obscure interviews imaginable. She was visiting a place called Fahart. (Fahart?) Presumably the gentleman she interviewed knew something about Fahart, but if he did he was keeping it to himself. Perhaps he feared that painting a beguiling picture of the town would bring hordes of tourists upon it, spoiling the quiet tranquillity of the village. Or perhaps Fahart just doesn't have an abundance of tourist attractions.

Valerie opened the interview: "Can you tell us something about Fahart?" Anticipation and expectation hung in her question, and left open a wide range of possibilities. But her interviewee obviously did not want to be caught up short. He gave the question a lot of thought. Finally, in a deep, sonorous voice, he replied: "It's the birthplace of Saint Brigid. And it has some interesting cemeteries."

"I see," says Valerie, her anticipation dropping several decibels and her enthusiasm ever so slightly dimmed. "That's very interesting. I suppose Saint Brigid is buried here, then?"

"No, she's not," came the answer, promptly this time. But then, with an unexpected sigh, he continued: "I think she's buried somewhere around Kildare. Or Meath, perhaps."

Valerie plunged bravely on. "And what else is Fahart noted for?" she asked. (The "else" seemed just a tiny bit extravagant under the circumstances.)

There was another long, long pause, for consideration, reflection. Perhaps for a short nap. Then: "Well, it's noted for the Long Kick."

"The Long Kick," Valerie repeats desperately, enthusiasm edging into gloom. "I suppose that's a football term."

"I wouldn't know," responded the gentleman unhelpfully. "But it's probably something to do with a sport, like, you know."

"Yes," said Valerie. "Now, what would a tourist visiting Fahart be interested in seeing here?"

Another thoughtful pause, followed by a sigh; a yawn perhaps? "Well, there's a Smithwick factory here, like, you know. You could take a tour of it, I guess. Although I don't know that they let tourists visit it. But they might now, you know. I wouldn't care about seeing it myself," he confessed gloomily.

July 6

Every four years, Ireland hosts an exhibition of modern art, called Rosc (which means the "Poetry of Vision"). It's always a controversial exhibit, and filled with paintings and sculpture that make the conservative, traditional art lover cringe in horror. Juxtaposed with the contemporary art, Rosc also offers an exhibition of works from a much earlier period. This year an American collector, Dr. Arthur Sackler, has loaned his collection of Medieval Chinese paintings. He and Mrs. Sackler are staying with us for a few days, and we all trooped down to the National Gallery for the official opening tonight. The place was mobbed; Bill had prepared a very nice speech, welcoming the Sacklers to Ireland, describing the aims of Rosc and officially opening the exhibit. Unfortunately, the microphone in the National Gallery didn't work, so no one except those standing right in front could hear his speech. Brian Lenihan, the foreign minister, was going to introduce Bill, but decided at the last minute that it would be better for Michael Scott, the founder of Rosc, to do it. Michael took over the dead microphone and said: "May I introduce to you the most beloved, respected ambassador the United States has ever sent to Ireland, Mr. William ..." then he turned to Bill and drew a complete blank! He just couldn't remember Shannon! He recovered after some seconds and since the microphone wasn't working anyway, scarcely anyone heard but those of us on the stage. We kidded him unmercifully about it afterwards.

JULY 7

The headlines in all the Irish papers are blazing with stories about Sean Donlon's abrupt dismissal as the Irish ambassador to the United States. An able, well-liked, and hard-hitting opponent of Irish-American support for the IRA, Sean's recall is analyzed in the Irish papers as a placating gesture on the part of the taoiseach, Mr. Haughey, to Mr. Neil Blaney, a Donegal deputy and member of the European Parliament. According to Sean Cronin in the *Irish Times,* Mr. Haughey, who will face a general election in less than eighteen months, must build support where he can find it. Mr. Blaney is not in accord with the Lynch/Donlon line on Northern Ireland, and when he spoke in the United States last year as a guest of the Irish National Caucus, he said that Ireland should take a stronger line in making the United States aware of British involvement. Presumably bringing Sean home and sending someone in his place who will support a policy more in line with Mr. Blaney's will deliver the votes from Donegal.

Although we would personally welcome the Donlons back to Dublin as valued friends whom we have missed during their stay in Washington, I was stunned to think he would be recalled after just twenty-one months, when he has been such a forceful and courageous voice against the use of violence in Northern Ireland and has done so much to educate the American public on the differences between the peaceful, nonviolent organizations that are trying to help Northern Ireland in a positive way and those who support the guns and the gun runners.

Mary McGrory of the Washington *Star,* an accurate reporter of Irish-American affairs in the United States, wrote today that relieving Sean of his post in Washington "promises to be the most unpopular move since British Prime Minister James Callaghan dislodged Sir Peter Ramsbotham in favor of his son-in-law, Peter Jay.

"... Donlon has waded into the thick of Irish-American politics with a vigor and force not seen in a generation of Irish diplomats ... he traveled the country to stem the sentimental tide of money and support pouring into the coffers of the IRA."

JULY 13

We dropped the younger boys off at camp today and returned to an almost empty house. Liam is here working in the gardens for the summer, but our staff have gone on their summer holidays, so we are rattling around this big house by ourselves and loving it. Bill has taken two weeks off; he and I go out into the gardens every day to pick raspberries, and I freeze them. It's marvelous to slouch around in my jeans, to see no one, hear no one, shake hands with no one! I make a concession by answering the telephone in case it's an emergency or the boys calling from camp. We do, however, still read the papers each morning, and they are still full of "the Donlon Affair." His dismissal from Washington has turned into the biggest diplomatic controversy since we've been in Dublin. The government announced a few days ago that he would stay on, after all. Brian Lenihan said in the *Irish Press* that press speculation in recent days that Mr. Donlon was to be moved because of a change in government policy on Northern Ireland was entirely without foundation. The government, he said, had complete confidence in Mr. Donlon as its representative in Washington.

Rumors had floated in the press that he was going to be transferred to the United Nations, that Eamon Kennedy would be sent from London to Washington, that Andrew O'Rourke, the secretary of the Foreign Office, would become Irish ambassador in London, and that Noel Dorr would be made secretary of the department. Now none of this is going to happen. The "Four Horsemen" of American Irish politics, Senators Kennedy and Moynihan, Speaker O'Neill and Governor Carey of New York, were all apparently very displeased with the move to transfer Donlon and made this displeasure known to the Irish government, which had second thoughts. In Northern Ireland, the decision to keep Donlon in Washington was also welcomed by John Hume, the leader of the Social Democratic Labour Party, and by the Alliance Party.

Mr. Hume said: "The removal of Ambassador Donlon would have done serious damage to the hard work of many people for many years in building up the most influential support that this country has ever had in the United States, culminating in the historic declaration on the Democratic platform in the presidential election. Senators Kennedy and Moynihan, Speaker O'Neill and Governor Carey have been solid and true friends of Ireland.

"In order that all shreds of suspicion be removed and this unfortunate affair closed, it is necessary that it be made clear that the activities of Congressman Mario Biaggi and the organizations with which he is associated enjoy no support whatsoever among any substantial section of Irish opinion."

Mario Biaggi, the New York congressman who heads a paper organization called the Ad Hoc Committee on Ireland in the House of Representatives, had been accused by Donlon of "serving the interests of terrorism." Biaggi's reaction to the Irish government's retraction on removing Donlon from the Washington scene was: "If Mr. Donlon's role as a spokesman for the policies of Mr. Haughey has been clarified, then his retention presents no problem."

JULY 19

We went to the Abbey Theatre tonight to see Hugh Leonard's play *A Life,* starring Cyril Cusack. It was an excellent production and the acting superb, as it usually is at the Abbey. The theater was crammed; the play has been a success here, as are all of Hugh Leonard's plays. His ear for language, his acerbic wit and poignant recreation of the past make him one of Ireland's gifted playwrights.

At the intermission, I saw Louis le Brocquy's new portrait of Michael Scott hanging in the second floor lobby of the theater for the first time and admired it.

Bill had to take me out to lunch this week and buy me a hat to pay off a wager. He bet me that Gerald Ford would be Reagan's vice-presidential candidate, and I bet on George Bush. So I get a new hat; thank you, George.

We lunched at the Grey Door and then wandered over to Brown Thomas to look at hats. I found a pretty navy blue straw with a big brim that I can decorate with a bouquet of flowers and wear to the Horse Show. The clerk there showed me two designer hats—beautiful, chic, eighty pounds each! Imagine paying eighty pounds for a hat! Bill would have bought both of them for me if I hadn't stopped him. He has no sense at all.

We stopped on the ground floor of BT to buy freezer containers for the fruit and vegetables that are pouring into the kitchen from the garden. The clerk said: "Sorry, luv, we're out. We'll have some more in six weeks."

"Six weeks! No one will want them in six weeks. By then the harvest will be over. You should have them *now*." She gave me the same kind of look Liam gives me when I say: "You can't cram for an exam all night before you take the test."

I had to calm my nerves by stopping at the Austrian bakery beside the Royal Automobile Club and buying four Danish.

We walked up Dawson Street past the Lord Mayor's mansion and saw two young men washing windows on the fourth floor of a building with no safety straps of any kind. I wanted to yell up to them to be careful, but Bill stopped me. "You'll distract them and they'll fall for sure." I walked on, butterflies in my stomach, certain I would hear a thud on the pavement any second.

One week has passed with no phone calls from David, no parties, dinners, receptions, meetings, speeches, and I haven't shaken one hand. I am totally revived and rested. And getting just a tiny bit bored. I took a long walk by myself today in the Park and sat on a bench and talked to an old man. He told me he was a widower and lived alone. "Are you lonely?" I asked him.

"Sure the peace and quiet of it is worth the loneliness," he replied.

JULY 25

We're home again from our three-day holiday in the west. We spent a night at Creggan's Castle in County Clare, right in the middle of the Burren, on the Corkscrew Hill. It's a lovely country hotel, one of the nicest I've stayed in, with a very good dining room. On Monday evening we drove over to Doolin to see Bill's cousins, Brid and Michael Shannon. Brid has recently opened a small restaurant in Doolin called Killala House, which Michael built, and we were eager to see it and have a meal there. It's small, attractive and charming, with whitewashed walls, slate floor and simple, good food. Brid has just had a new baby, which I bounced on my lap for a while after dinner. Two American ladies came in while we were there, and were ohhhing and ahhhing about the place in the loud, enthusiastic, unself-conscious tones that Americans abroad so often use. One of them said to her friend: "It's so quaint and charming; and look! There's a woman holding a baby on her knee. Now if that isn't Irish for you!" As if the Irish had a franchise for producing babies!

The next day we made the rounds of Bill's County Clare relations: his Aunt Nora, who is going strong at seventy-eight; his bachelor cousin Jimmy, who farms the land Bill's mother was born on; Jimmy's sister Agnes and her handsome family. The wind-swept green hills and gray rocks of west Clare are full of McNamaras and Shannons, and most of them are related in one way or another to Bill. You can spot them a mile away. They all look alike.

We headed for Galway the next day, with a cold, biting wind at our backs. We first went south to Ennistymon, then picked up the coast road through Black Head. The scenery along that stretch of coast is glittering and majestic. The gray, rough stone carpet of the Burren gives way to steep, fearsome cliffs holding back the land from the pounding waves that lash into the west coast of Clare off the Atlantic. The landscape is forbidding, harsh and beautiful, but it is softened by the wild flowers that bloom in and around the crevices of the stones and by the brilliant fuschia that lines the narrow road. We passed beautiful stretches of bare, unpeopled beaches, empty today because of the uninviting icy waters and the chill winds that swept the sand along in gusty puffs.

We returned to the residence to pick up the ringing phone.
"I'm coming home," David announced firmly.
"No. Stay and finish out the week. That was our agreement."
"I'm going to run away then." He hung up.
I held the phone in my hand. Would he? Should I worry? Remembering some of his past adventures, I had decided to phone him back when he rang up again.
"Mom?"
"Yes."
"Remember what I just said about running away?"
"Yes."
"Forget it."

The staff is back from their summer holidays and life begins in earnest once again. How could we be so busy all over again and so *soon?*
The floor man is coming again, to resand and restain the dining room floor, rectifying the sorry job done on it last summer.
The men who are supposed to have fixed the oven doors are here again, working away, but without much luck.
My car is back in the garage again. My solicitor has given them an ultimatum. Their fourth.
A sofa for the ballroom, ordered from Washington via Susan McQueen, is missing, and we have to put a tracer on it.
The children have an appointment with their dentist this week. David's two front teeth are coming in almost on top of each other, and Christopher's canine teeth don't seem to be coming in at all.
An American show jumping team is coming to the Dublin Horse Show for the first time since 1972. We're excited to have them here and will give a reception for them. That means invitations for 240.
My VAT returns from the embassy are months behind schedule. (VAT means Value Added Tax, and on certain items that we purchase in Ireland, most particularly wine and liquor, we are reimbursed for that tax, as diplomats are everywhere in the world. In Ireland, there are certain forms that must be filled out, duplicated, mailed, approved, and returned before, sometimes, a check arrives, reimbursing us.)
And then, a farmyard tragedy occurred last night. My dear old chicks out there in their henhouse, laying away, minding their own business, came face to face with a fox—or perhaps a badger—and their bell tolled. He was a greedy fellow and killed twenty-three of the twenty-four. He bit off their heads, sucked their blood and left their carcasses on the ground. Why was one spared? She, poor traumatized creature, will she ever lay

again? Michael discovered the slaughter early this morning when he opened the gate of their pen to feed them. He was even more upset than I, and both of us were puzzled at the extent of the killing. I would have thought he might have had his fill after a dozen.

I cuddled the lone survivor in my arms. She was shaking with fright; she is used to my picking her up and usually relaxes and lets me hold her, but she is rigid and trembling now.

Yesterday I thought a fox was an interesting, fey, elusive and handsome fellow that adorned our woods. Today I loathe him. Nature has curious ways of setting creature upon creature and involving the emotions of humans.

Michael and I picked up all the limp, dead hens and stacked them in a pile by the dump. We set fire to them and the smell of their burning lingered over the farmyard all day.

JULY 29

Liam Shannon would rather fight than write, but he may have changed his mind after tonight. He's been taking out a girl and decided it would be all for the best if he didn't date her any longer. He had his "farewell" speech prepared and knew exactly what he was going to tell her over the telephone.

He dialed discreetly from the empty pantry. "Hello?" he murmured into the phone. "This is Liam."

The connection was so bad she could hear only waves of distant thunder and the occasional crackle and pop of the giant bowl of Rice Krispies that is hidden in every Irish telephone exchange and activated by the dial tone.

"What?" she shouted.

"Liam. It's Liam *Shannon,*" he shouted back, discretion lost to the faulty line. "I don't think we should see each other again," he tried.

"See each other *when?*" she shouted back.

"Again!" he screamed.

"Again *when?*" she bellowed.

"Oh, God," he muttered and slammed down the receiver. The entire household had hung on his every word.

AUGUST 4

We picked up John Peate, our Dublin friend who spends part of the summer with us out here "on the farm." The household has been looking forward to his return. I've promised to take the boys out to Kilcullen, in County Kildare, the site of my favorite pub in Ireland. Right there in plain sight, smack in the middle of the pub, for all the world to see, is an exhibit the likes of which you won't see anywhere else in the world. You can gaze upon the Withered Arm of Dan Donnelly, preserved for posterity in a bottle. Dan Donnelly, for all those not conversant with the Irish boxing scene, was one of the greatest boxers Ireland ever produced. He was a champion among champions, fearless, strong, skilled, agile. His name became a legend in Kildare and spread through the country. His prowess was due, in large part, to the extraordinary length of his arms. It is said that when Dan Donnelly stood up straight, his fingertips reached below his knees. He'd make a shirtmaker cry. But those long arms knocked out many an opponent who, no matter how strong, just couldn't get past them.

Today, Big Dan has left the world of boxing for the big ring in the sky, but some thoughtful and imaginative fan didn't want the rest of the world to be deprived of the opportunity to see the longest arm ever grown in Kildare. So, although I don't know the details of the actual operation, nor am I certain how the arm came into the possession of the pub, Dan's arm is on display right there in Kilcullen, and anyone passing that way ought not to miss the chance to go in, have a pint, and take a look. It's impressive. It's a unique opportunity. Stand up and see where *your* fingertips come to when you hang your arms at your side.

AUGUST 5

The Dublin Antique Fair began today in the Mansion House. Bill and I went with the intention of buying each other an anniversary present but saw nothing we fell in love with. I thought the prices were high, even though stories in the papers had said it was a depressed year and a buyer's market.

I'm looking for a lorgnette. I saw a beautiful one there last year and coveted it but couldn't make up my mind to buy something so frivolous. Bill went back later to buy it for me, and, of course, it was gone. There aren't any at this year's fair. There was plenty of old silver, which doesn't interest me, and a beautiful collection of Victorian jewelry, which does.

We ran into dozens of friends at the fair, and on the way back to the car, dashing through the rain, ran headlong into Oliver Gogarty, a Dublin barrister and good friend. He is the son of Oliver St. John Gogarty, on whom James Joyce modeled his character Buck Mulligan in *Ulysses*. Oliver had come into town to buy a newspaper, forgetting that it was a bank holiday and all the shops were closed. Knowing he likes Irish silver, I told him about the exhibit at the Mansion House, and we left him headed in that direction.

AUGUST 8

It's put a special edge on the Horse Show this year to hear the American National Anthem being played. Our team has made us very proud right through the week, at every event. We gave a big reception for them out at the residence on Wednesday. They had won first place in the Shell Slalom that day and were pleased and happy about their performance. They are bright, charming young men and women, as delightful to talk with as they are exciting to watch on the jumping course. They were tense about the Nations' Cup, the Aga Khan competition that was held today. Ireland won it three years in a row and by doing so retired the trophy. This year, the Aga Khan has come to Dublin to donate another trophy and to present it himself to the winning team. Germany, Australia, Ireland, France, the United States and England are competing for it.

As always for this event, we sat in the box of the president of the Royal Dublin Society. President Hillery was at the show this year, but Mrs. Hillery did not accompany him, nor did the taoiseach and Mrs. Haughey attend, although in past years Mr. and Mrs. Lynch were regulars on the Aga Khan Day. The Aga himself was there, however, tanned and handsome, with a warm and friendly smile and a gracious, charming manner.

We sat on the front row this year; we're now one of the "old" ambassadorial couples. Ambassador and Mrs. de Vogelare of Belgium and Foreign Minister and Mrs. Lenihan also sat with us. It was clear from the start that the US team was giving a superior performance. They rode with great calm, skill and decision. The only thing I worried about was their time. The two girls, Melanie Smith and Katie Monahan, are the best riders on the team; both blond and pretty, they bring experience and confidence to their performances. The two handsome young men, Armand Leone and Norman dello Joio are also superb, but I think the girls outrode them today.

I grew more and more tense as the scores mounted, as clear rounds followed faults. Ireland's hero, Eddie Macken, and little Paul Darragh were both riding wonderfully, as always. Jeff McVean of Australia, the crowd's favorite because of his peculiar style of splaying his legs straight out to each side as he takes jumps, was also coming up with clear rounds. The German team was having bad luck and mounting up faults with almost every round.

I was knotting my hands together and leaning far out across the railing when Norman dello Joio cantered out into the ring for his second course. A clear round would give the US team a victory. The bell rang. Horse and rider sailed over jump after jump, their control and timing perfect. The water jump, which had already given several horses and riders trouble, presented no obstacle. He took it with room to spare, whirled his horse around to the left and headed for the last three jumps, lined up in a row right in front of our box. The arena was silent; not a breath was drawn as he gathered his horse for the first jump. A low hiss of expelled air echoed over the stands as the crowd breathed again when the horse landed clear with a soft thud on the wet ground. He approached the second jump. The clock was ticking away and he was hard-pressed for time. His horse's hoof hit the top rail of the second jump but it stayed in place. He was over safely. One to go. He had four seconds left. Up and *Over!!* I could feel my whole body lifting up as he drew his horse clearly over the last jump. We won! I burst into shamefully wild applause, jumping up and down and pounding Bill on the shoulders as the announcer's clear, precise voice came out over the loudspeaker: "And a clear round for number seventy-four, Norman dello Joio, riding Allegro. The Americans have taken the Aga Khan Challenge Trophy."

Melanie and Katie told me afterwards that they could see me in the box in my red hat and matching suit, jumping up and down and waving to them. The Foreign Minister and Ann Lenihan congratulated Bill and me, as did all our ambassadorial friends in the box. The Aga Khan came over with a wide grin on his face and shook our hands and complimented the riders on their cool, steady performance.

The American team rode out onto the field once more and lined up in front of the president's box, while "The Star-Spangled Banner" was played and the trophy was presented. The Chef d'Équipe of the American team, Bert de Nemethy, received the trophy on behalf of the team. The victorious foursome then made the ritual circle of the field, passing in front of all the stands and holding the large, gleaming silver cup high for all to see. We descended into the reception room to celebrate, and I asked one of the RDS officials if he could bring our team down just as soon as they dismounted. Within a few minutes, they joined us, looking remarkably clean and relaxed after their grueling afternoon on the muddy course. We hugged and kissed; champagne corks popped and someone, I don't even remember now who, made a short speech of congratulations. The Aga Khan shook their hands and beamed his radiant smile on them, and all the while they enjoyed the fun and excitement of it just as much as we did and showed good-humored zest and pleasure at winning. We finally broke up, they to go on to a Hunt Ball, Bill and I to go home and change for the annual reception at the British Embassy. I told them we would be in our regular box tomorrow to cheer them on for their last day at the show.

AUGUST 10

I am very nostalgic about being at the Horse Show today; perhaps it is the anticlimax after the big win yesterday. Or perhaps it is because I have a feeling that it may be my last Horse Show as hostess in this box. Even though I'm not "horsey," I have loved these six days each summer.

At the end of today's show, the prizes for "highest points in the week" were awarded. Harvey Smith, a magnificent horseman and the veteran member of the British team, won first place, with the two American women, Melanie Smith and Katie Monahan, coming in second and third. Armand Leone took fifth place. When the show is over, all the riders and horses pass slowly in parade around the ring one last time. As they rode directly under our box, each one tipped his hat and smiled up at us, and we heard Katie's soft voice float up from the field: "Hello, Mr. Shannon. Hello, Mrs. Shannon." We were strangely touched by it. And that was the end of the show. The day had turned cool and I felt tired and chilled. We dropped Oliver Gogarty off at his house—he was a guest in our box today—and went straight home.

Talk about bad manners and poor losers! I just couldn't believe my eyes when I read the report about the Aga Khan Cup event in the *Irish Times:* "What irked them [the Irish], however, was the knowledge that the American team were just passing through Dublin on their way to Rotterdam for next week's show jumping festival—a sort of equestrian anti-Olympics designed to make up for the poor show in Moscow."

The Aga Khan didn't fare any better; after having donated the beautiful and valuable trophy and having traveled to Ireland to present it to the winning team, he was described in the same story as the man in the "ill-fitting blue mohair suit." For heaven's sake, Your Highness, will you please visit your tailor before you come to Dublin to present another trophy? We're very particular here about the way our donors dress.

Describing the crowd (quite inaccurately) as losing interest in the show once it became apparent that Ireland wasn't going to win, the writer goes on: "As Ireland's hopes faded, the sky turned grey and the general lack of interest in the outcome was almost palpable."

Well, he got one thing right in the story, "Up in the box, the US Ambassador and Mrs. Shannon were almost overcome with delight." We sure were.

AUGUST 11

I've been thinking lately about the price of beef, and it gives me a headache. And then I think about our grassy, green fields which are empty except for three fat, greedy donkeys. (The embassy did not rent the fields for cattle-grazing this year.) And here I am, the granddaughter of an Irishman who in his youth drove his herds of cattle along the Chisholm Trail, across the Red River and into Kansas City to market. And not a cow on the place here.

"Dennis," I said, "we need some cows around here."

"Don't look at me," Dennis said, alarmed. "All I know about is horses. But I have heard stories about an ambassador here who raised dairy cows once. He had too much milk and went into the business of selling it, and I think that caused some consternation in certain quarters."

"But we'll just raise a few cows for our own use," I said, and went to the phone to consult with Robin Mosse, an aide in the Agriculture Office at the embassy. Robin is a frustrated farmer himself, so he was delighted with the prospect of a trip to the cattle market in Maynooth in quest of some good heifers.

The very name Maynooth conjures up the scholarly academic world of the historic university there, which has trained priests for Ireland and for the rest of the world for two centuries. Today I saw an earthier part of town, the big, noisy, bawling, smelly livestock market, where Irish farmers come to buy and sell their cattle and other livestock.

Robin had arranged for someone more qualified than we to do the bidding for us; as at an auction at Parke Bernet in New York, where fine art and antiques change hands, the subtle signals thrown out by the bidders to the auctioneer can be easily misinterpreted by an amateur. You want to know your cattle and you want to know your bidding, or you may end up with a nasty bull when you thought you were buying a goat for the missus.

Dan Hardy knew what he was doing. In fact, when the time came for him to begin bidding for us, I thought he was scratching the side of his nose, and instead I ended up with my three heifers.

The interior of the market is built like a small amphitheater, the rows of benches banked sharply upward from the floor to the ceiling. The auctioneer stands behind a plate glass window and calls out the bids through a microphone. The owner of the particular lot of cattle being bid up stands below the auctioneer, out of sight of the bidders, where he can signal to the auctioneer whether or not he wants to accept the bid. If he feels the price is too low, or that he will do better later on, he gives a signal to withdraw his cattle.

Prospective buyers can wander out among the stalls and look over the day's market. We had decided to buy three heifers; we will graze them for six months to a year and, one by one, fill our freezer with them. With Robin's practiced eye, we soon picked out two beautiful red and white curly-haired cows, a Shorthorn-Hereford mix, and a doleful-looking, sad-eyed black and white Friesian. We settled on what would be our top bid, and we all went inside to await the start of the bidding. The cows are led into the center of the ring, and the bids start immediately and move fast.

I had said to Bill before we went: "You are *not* wearing your carnation and pin-striped suit to the Maynooth Cattle Market," so he had on his Irish cap and an old trench coat. But even so we didn't exactly fade into the background when we arrived. For one thing, I was the *only* woman in the market and even though Bill had on his cap, he wasn't pulling on a pipe, and he can't look out of the sides of his eyes the way a real Irish farmer can. He also has all of his own teeth and almost none of his hair, while the opposite tends to be true of Irish farmers.

So there was just a little bit of a stir when we settled ourselves on one of the benches, and we got a few of those sidelong glances, but, as always, the Irish were too nice and too courteous to do anything so rude as to stare at a stranger. Still, I wish I could have heard the stories at the tea table this evening:

"There he was, up from Dublin in that big black car he goes about in, poking in among the muck, looking over the cattle as if he could tell one from the other, and he brought herself along, too. Thanks be to God, they had another lad with them who looked as if he knew what he was about. Tell me this, what are they going to do with three heifers up in the Park?"

Robin arranged for someone to drive the cows up to the Park that afternoon, and as we were leaving the market, I stopped at the entrance to put some money in the box an elderly nun was holding.

"Thank you, dear." She smiled. "Up for a visit?"

"No," says I. "Up to buy."

I left her with a startled look on her gentle face.

This evening we took a walk down to the pastures to have a close look at our herd. They were "settled in" and chewing contentedly on the lush

Making friends with one of the cows

green grass that was thick around them. The donkeys seemed absolutely thrilled to have company on their home turf, and Vincent, the male, was prancing about, running in circles around the cows, waving his tail in the air and flattening his ears, looking at them with his mean eye as if to say: "Despite the vagaries of nature, I just might be of some possible use to you, in a male sort of way. Why be satisfied with a bull when you could try me?" Brogeen, used to his wiles by now (mother of many), was content to stand guard over her youngest daughter and watch the heifers calmly, giving Vincent the bored look from time to time of an experienced veteran who had been through it all one time too many.

Bill asked me what I was going to name them, and after some thought we decided on a Shakespearean theme. Portia, Juliet and Ophelia.

"How do you like that, girls?" I asked them, scratching their soft, fat sides. They just stared up at me for a moment, pausing in their slow, thoughtful chewing long enough to wave a fly from their backsides with their tails, then placidly returned to the grass.

AUGUST 16

The embassy Marines organized the annual picnic at the residence this year, and did a marvelous job, grilling hamburgers and hot dogs on the patio, playing games with the younger children and, as always, starring in the softball game. I was catcher this year; bend, stoop, catch, throw. Oh, my aching back. It's our fourth annual picnic and we haven't been rained out once. One might even be extravagantly generous and say today was "summery."

Bill's two nephews from Worcester, Massachusetts, and their wives are staying with us, and my cousin Julia from Iowa is here. I hadn't seen her for years and years, and we're having a great time catching up on each other's news and children. Tad Szulc, who used to work with Bill on the *New York Times,* and his wife, Marianne, are visiting Ireland with their friends the Edelsons from Washington, so we had everyone out tonight after dinner to meet some Irish friends, and we sat around and exchanged stories till 1 AM. The talk turned at one point to hunting and shooting, two of Ireland's favorite sports, and Mary White, one of our Irish guests, told about visiting friends in America. Their host was an avid sportsman who loved shooting: duck, pheasant, snipe, you name it, if it flew, he was out there aiming. He had a brand-new wife, some years younger than himself, who didn't know a muzzle from a trigger, but she doted on her new husband and his hobbies. They served the Whites a pheasant for dinner and Mary, a marvelous cook and collector of recipes, complimented her hostess on the bird. "It's delicious," she said. "How long did you hang it?"

"Oh no," said the bride, looking with wifely pride at her husband, "he didn't hang it. He shot it."

I've decided to give Liam a surprise birthday-graduation-bon voyage party; if I suggest such an idea to him, he will veto it, but I discussed it today with Mick Murphy, his pal, and Mick thinks it's a grand idea. I mentioned it to Paul Noctor, Gerry's son (who is now all recovered from his car accident), and he thinks it will be "great crack." So Mick is helping me draw up a guest list and is trying to round up all the boys and girls from Liam's class who spread out around the country after they finished school. We'll have the party in the ballroom. Paul is going to make dancing and listening tapes for me. We'll serve them supper.

I was thinking the other day about the price of pork. And about the little pen that is just off to the side of our "dumping grounds," which would be perfect for a pig or two.

"Dennis," I said, "we need a pig."

"That's what I've been saying for two years," Dennis replied.

"Well, the time has come." I went to the phone and dialed my friend Marie Louise Harhoff, the wife of the Danish ambassador. If there is a pig available in Dublin, Marie Louise will know where it is. She could find you a three-legged elephant if you gave her twenty-four hours to work on it.

She picked up the phone, and when I told her what I wanted, she replied: "My neighbors, the Bradys, have pigs. I'll see if they have any for sale."

They did, and this morning we went out to Bray in a convoy; the Grahams (Bill's nephews), David, John Peate and I in two cars, Michael and Jimmy following up in their car with a wagon attached to it. Michael was just as enthusiastic about the idea as I was. "Sure, they're fine little creatures and no trouble at all," he said. "If you get one, you might as well get two. They'll keep each other company."

We stopped by the Danish embassy en route to pick up the Harhoffs' housekeeper, who was going to direct us to the Bradys'. So we were quite an assemblage when we drove up the narrow, winding, rocky lane to the farm and descended on the Brady family. The pigs were kept in a little enclosure up in a field, and we trooped up, bringing the car with the wagon to the side of the pigs' pen. Michael, Mrs. Brady and I climbed into the enclosure (I was only there for moral support, not having the slightest idea in the world how one caught a pig or what to do with it afterwards. It seemed to be more of a job than catching turkeys).

Daffodil, posing for the camera

"Don't come in here," Michael said, as I climbed over the fence with him.

"Moral support, Michael," I said. But he looked worried. The pigs took one look at us and set up a cacophony of squealing; we might as well have been the big bad wolf descending on their house. They knew an enemy when they saw one. And run! Those fat little bodies could skitter away from our outstretched hands just as fast as we could corner one. It was definitely harder than catching turkeys and was going to take more skill.

The Bradys' German shepherd, who decided to join the fray, jumped into the pen, barking wildly and chasing the pigs, and adding greatly to the general noise and confusion. My sunglasses fell off and then I slipped on some wet cabbage leaves we had taken out to entice the pigs, and I landed in the muck, just missing a piglet by inches. It backed off into a corner and watched me with its little piggy eyes, screaming hysterically. I got up and brushed off the mud and headed after it. Michael finally caught one. "Hold it by its ears and hind legs," Mrs. Brady shouted. It was squealing so loudly, and the dog barking so wildly, that I couldn't hear what Michael said, but I *thought* it was: "Open the gate," which I did, and instantly all the little pigs saw their chance and headed for the open spaces. Michael had to drop the pig and slam the gate shut before all the pigs disappeared into the hills of Wicklow forever. He wiped his muddy, perspiring face and dove in again, grabbing another one. The rest of our group had congregated on the fence railing by this time, shouting encouragement, clapping and hollering when one of us came close to a catch, like an audience at a bizarre pig rodeo.

We finally caught them, two fat, noisy, squirming muddy little bodies, and got them into the wagon, their flat snouts pressing up against the slits in the side, highly incensed at being removed from their happy home. I scratched their big, pointed, hairy ears and named them Tulip and Daffodil. "What good bacon you'll be," I said, feeling just like the big bad wolf.

I've been reading (and loving) *The World According to Garp,* which a friend gave me recently, and it's been sitting on my bedside table for weeks. Tonight, David came running into my room, leaped through the air, bounced on the bed, flung his arms around me and said, with his head buried in my shoulder: "Hi! I'm Garp, and you're *my* World!"

God bless all eight-year-olds.

AUGUST 19

Had two guests for lunch today—Liz Sharlitt, an old friend from Washington, and a friend-of-a-friend, an Irish-born woman who lives in the States now. She said something very interesting on a subject none of my Irish friends in Dublin would broach: "It must be rather hard being the American ambassador here in Ireland now, when so many people would assume that relations between the Irish and America were so calm and peaceful and unstrained, whereas in reality there is an awful lot of anti-American feeling in Ireland, particularly among the young and the 'pseudo-intellectuals.' "

She's the only person (except for my phone caller just after our arrival here) who has said that to me during my stay in Ireland.

I said: "Well, my personal relations with the Irish have all been warm, friendly, and hospitable, with no exceptions. I occasionally get angry with press reaction here, but that's true of anyone who serves in public life. But what do you base your opinion on?"

"Oh, I have to take a lot of flak when I come home to Ireland to visit. People aren't polite to me the way they are to you," she said, laughing. "I think it's partly a residue of the Vietnam years, partly envy of a rich, powerful country, partly the 'in' thing to believe, and partly a rather vague, anti-Western, anticapitalistic political philosophy. And of course, it's partly fear, too, fear of a US-Soviet clash, with Ireland right in the middle!"

The contemporary half of the Rosc exhibit has opened in Dublin, at Earlsfort Terrace, the old UCD campus, and Bill and I went there this morning to meet Cecil King, the painter who is one of the driving forces behind Rosc, and tour the exhibit under his expert guidance. It's very avant-garde; contemporary artists from Spain, Germany, France and the United States are on exhibit, as well as Irish painters, but it's not as far out as I had expected after reading the criticisms of it in the papers. There are one or two paintings that you might call physically graphic— one of a man having a *very* large erection (you wouldn't have to look at its title to know it was a self-portrait), and another very lovely painting of four women in the nude, sitting, or rather squatting down, with their legs open and, as the nuns would say (telling us to sit with our ankles crossed), "everything they own on display for the world to see." The faces of the nude women are very tender and beautiful, and their pose seems relaxed and natural instead of vulgar. I liked it. A woman has written a letter to the *Irish Times* saying: "On behalf of all decent Irish-women, I protest . . ." Well, I'm not Irish, but I'm decent, and I thought it was a fine picture.

We missed seeing the exhibit of the nude young man who rolls himself in a box of flour; he performs once each morning and afternoon, and we had to leave before he came. I was disappointed to miss it, because I was eager to see what possible effect he could achieve. One tends to scoff, but not having seen it, I'll reserve judgment.

Cecil was a wonderful and knowing guide. He talked about many of the paintings, explaining to us what the artist was trying to do, pointing out details on each canvas that escaped our untrained eye. We came away far more impressed than we had expected to be and, we hope, with some greater understanding of abstract art. To find beauty where one hasn't seen it before is an accomplishment worthy of the effort, expense and energy needed to hang the Rosc exhibit. And also, bringing Rosc to Ireland every few years gives young Irish artists, who might not have had the opportunity to travel, a chance to see what their contemporaries in Europe and America are doing. This is particularly important, I think, for Ireland, which remained inward-looking for so many decades in the early part of the century.

AUGUST 21

We went racing today, not to the track but under a brilliant blue sky, skimming along Dublin Bay. Our enthusiastic sailing friends, Tricia and Graham Crisp, had asked us to go out one day with them, particularly on a Thursday or Saturday when the members of the Royal St. George

Yacht Club race their boats in the bay from Dalkey Island toward Howth and back again. We met the Crisps at the Club in the late afternoon to change and to join Pat and Brenda Brannigan on their boat for the race. It was a perfect day for sailing (and, just for the record, this is what the "well-dressed" sailor wears on a late August afternoon in Dublin: woolen undershirt, cotton shirt, sweater, another, heavier sweater, woolen tights, jeans, and oilskins). The wind was up, turning the glittering bay into choppy, white-capped foam. From out on the water, the face of Dublin looked very European, with the tall, narrow pastel houses and the little peaked roofs of the shops in Dun Laoghaire forming a colorful, sharp outline against the sky.

Not being sailors, Bill and I simply sat still and tried to keep out of the way and not get hit by the swinging boom. This was the last race of the season; it was such a beautiful, clear afternoon that most of the members of the club were out, and the bay was soon filled with the white and occasional red or blue sails of the Royal George. For us, it was a new look at Dublin, a wonderfully exhilarating, fresh, exciting adventure. I would have been quite content if our skippers, Pat and Brenda Brannigan, had simply announced that we were headed out to open sea and we had sailed off to a distant port, leaving all our responsibilities behind. I can understand a sailor's love of the sea; the beauty of movement as the sails pick up the wind and send the boat sweeping through blue water, the sense of freedom from a land-bound life, the sense of adventure one has being dependent on wind and wave.

My daydream of distant ports ended as we dutifully turned around when the race was over and came back to the harbor. A little put-put met us at the boat and took us in to shore, where we dressed for the dinner party the Crisps were giving for us at the Club.

Not long ago, the members of the Royal St. George Yacht Club defeated a resolution to allow women to become full members. Their ladies are "associate" members with no voting rights in the club, the same status the Golfing Union of Ireland, which controls all the golf clubs in the country, grants to women. Even more inexplicable is the ban on women members in the University Club (something akin to the situation in the Cosmos Club in Washington), despite the fact that three out of the six University seats in the Irish Senate are held by women.

The ban on women members of the University Club was brought to my attention not long ago by a funny story my good friend Dr. Mary McEntagart, a Dublin surgeon, told me. She had been asked to give a paper at a symposium at Trinity College. One of the members of the committee organizing the symposium asked Mary to join him for a drink in the University bar before the proceedings began. When he brought her in, a member of the club ensconced in the bar huffily demanded of the manager that her presence "be withdrawn."

"Ladies aren't admitted to the bar, madam," the embarrassed bartender had to tell Mary.

"But," argued her host of the evening, "Dr. McEntagart is a featured speaker."

"Sorry, sir. No ladies, I'm afraid. It's the rules, you know."

So the featured speaker could instruct a packed auditorium on the intricacies of vascular surgery, but she couldn't get a drink in the bar. And so it goes.

Tricia Crisp and some of her friends at the Royal St. George have for some time been trying to pressure the male members of the club to admit women as full members, but so far they have been unsuccessful, and the recent vote taken in the club was a disappointing setback.

As I sat there this evening, having a wonderful time, enjoying the company and the very good dinner, I couldn't help thinking all through the evening that were I a single woman, a widow or a divorcee, and were I an avid sailor like Tricia, perfectly as capable of handling a boat as her husband, and had I wanted to join the club, to enjoy the privilege of sailing in Dublin, I would be excluded.

AUGUST 27

Ireland has changed its social and cultural patterns so drastically in the last three decades that the story we heard tonight, a story of religious bigotry in rural Ireland twenty years ago, is hard to believe. We went to dinner with Judge and Mrs. Donal Barrington at their house in Dun Laoghaire. We enjoyed the evening especially; their guests were lively and witty and the talk around the dinner table didn't end until 1 AM, and only then because we reluctantly got up and left so the rest of the guests could do likewise!

Anyway, Donal told us a fascinating story of a famous boycott which took place down in County Wexford about twenty years ago. A Protestant woman had married a Catholic in England and had come back to County Wexford to live. They had several children and, although she had signed the "pledge" to bring up the children as Catholics (required then of all "mixed" marriages if the Catholic partner wanted to be married by a priest), she eventually took her children and moved up to Northern Ireland, where she raised them as Protestants.

The local parish priest in Wexford announced this disgrace from the pulpit and urged the local community to boycott all the Protestant shops and businesses in the small town to "punish" them.

News of the episode quickly spread all over Ireland and became a cause célèbre. During the height of the controversy, Donal Barrington, then a young barrister, was asked to speak at a large Catholic conference being held in Dublin. He decided to attack the boycott in Wexford, a brave and courageous thing to do then, I would think, given the climate of the day and the fact that *he* might be boycotted himself. He made a ringing denunciation of the whole disgraceful episode, and to his astonishment, he received a standing ovation from his audience.

Happily, those days are over for Ireland, and whatever a priest or lay person, Catholic or Protestant, may think in his darkest heart, he won't be making denunciations in public. (In Northern Ireland, it's another story.)

I can remember as a small girl being chased home from my Catholic school one day by a band of "non-Catholics," as we smugly called them, being ridiculed and teased and called a "Cat-licker"; Ireland doesn't have a monopoly on religious prejudice.

AUGUST 30

Liam is eighteen years old today, a man now by legal right, who can fight, vote, drink and one hopes, have the good sense to do all those things responsibly.

We had his surprise dinner-dance last night. It was a marvelous affair and I *think* he was surprised, although I'll never know for sure. All the guests but three could come, along with Brian and Paul, Jimmy and Mary, from our own household.

To my astonished delight, they were all dressed to the teeth! Mick and I had discussed what they should wear, and I didn't want to set down any rules. "Let them do what they want," I told him, thinking that fifty pairs of blue jeans or cords would arrive at the residence gates. But they came instead bedecked in shirts and ties, pretty dresses, fancy pants, and they all looked marvelous.

I had told Liam earlier in the week that I was having a big reception on Monday and that was why the ballroom was "set up." He didn't blink an eye about that, since it happens about three times a month. Anne and I cooked turkeys and hams, made cold salads and apple tarts. I ordered a big, decorated cake from a supermarket in Blanchardstown, near the Park, and when I went to pick it up yesterday morning, emblazoned with "Happy Birthday and Bon Voyage, Liam" across its top, the young clerk behind the counter, whom I had never seen before, said: "Would that be for Liam Shannon, who's having the big party up in the Park tonight?" That's Dublin for you.

We took Liam over to Kay Costelloe's at seven in the evening so she could give him his birthday present and tell him good-by. We headed back to the Park about 7:40.

"Come into the ballroom and see the new chairs that arrived today," I urged Liam.

"Can I see them after dinner? I'm starved." And he headed toward the dining room.

"*No!* Come and see them now." He gave me a fishy look but walked

297

with me to the ballroom, and I opened the big double doors. There they all were, sitting quietly in the dim twilight with the curtains drawn. I flipped on the lights and they all sang "Happy Birthday!" Liam looked surprised but not stunned. When they finished singing, he quipped, "Actually, my birthday is tomorrow. Could you all go away and come back then?" They laughed, and the party began.

We brought in the food right off; I decided if they were going to have beer and wine they should have it on a full stomach, but I needn't have had any fear of that. They ate as if there were no tomorrow. Bill and I served them, carrying platter after platter of food from the kitchen into the ballroom, scooping up salad, dishing out ham, sending around rolls and butter. Seconds? Yes, please. Thirds? If you insist. Apple tart? Yes! Cake? Of course. The food all disappeared as if some giant digestive machine had descended upon us and slurped it up in one big gulp. In fact, it did, and it's called a teenager.

We left them then with music that was shaking the old house to its rafters. Bill and I settled down in the library to wait it out . . . or to be on hand if we might be "needed." We weren't. They were a great bunch and they had a good time; they talked and danced and listened to music. There was one blissful respite when the tapes were turned off and one of the guests, a talented pianist and composer from their class, played some of his songs on the piano.

When they began leaving about 3 AM, Bill and I stood by the door with Liam to tell them good-by, and as we stood and watched him shaking hands I remembered his first birthday party when he was two. He stood then by the door and told all his guests good-by and tried to give them back the presents they had brought. It's a hard farewell for him tonight; although he'll be home at Christmas, his life now changes course, and the memories he shares with these, his pals through high school, will dim and blur and finally become a part of "those years in Ireland." Well, they were happy years for Liam, and King's Hospital is a wonderful place in which to grow. We shall always be grateful to Dr. Magahy for taking Liam in and for turning him back to us, three years later, such a fine boy. And grateful for all the friendships he has made here.

AUGUST 31

"She was lovely and fair as the rose of the summer.
Yet 'twas not her beauty alone that won me.
Oh, no! 'Twas the truth in her eye ever dawning
That made me love Mary, the Rose of Tralee."

Gerry and I sang it all the way to Kerry today as he and Bill and I— along with a majority of the under-thirty population of Ireland and parts of America and Europe—descended upon this pretty little town this afternoon. Ordinarily a quiet and peaceful place in the north of County Kerry, for four days each year in late August, Tralee takes on the slightly delirious air of Munich during Oktoberfest; a certain inebriated gaiety permeates the town, enlivened by the anticipation Atlantic City must feel while waiting for its new Miss America. Tralee is going to crown its 1980 Rose this week.

"The pale moon was rising above the green mountain,
The sun was declining beneath the blue sea,"

as we checked into the Ballyseedy Castle Hotel, just outside Tralee, changed our clothes in a hurry, dashed down a cup of tea, and headed into town where we met the festival committee at the Mt. Brandon Hotel. The road was clogged with people, all in a good-natured, festive mood, and we could scarcely navigate our big car through the jammed, narrow streets. Pedestrians patted the back and sides of our car, and children knocked on the windows to wave. One man came over and motioned for Gerry to put the window down.

"I've a bet with the two women in that shop," he said, pointing across the street, "that this is the American ambassador."

"You've won," Gerry said, rolling the window back up.

We had dinner and spent the evening with the festival organizers and Gay Byrne, who comes down to Tralee each year to preside as master of ceremonies. An army band led the Roses in a parade through town, then we all assembled in the Dome, a huge tent set up in a civic parking lot in the center of town, for a late supper and dancing. Bill has his eye on Miss Cork. Gay B. thinks Miss San Francisco has great potential. "Remember," I said to them, "it's 'the truth in her eye' you're looking for." When the dancing began, Bill had a turn on the floor with each of the American Roses; Miss Pennsylvania kissed him, which cheered him enormously, then she asked him for a job at the embassy! Another American Rose told him she was over in Ireland studying . . . he thought she said, over the din of music . . . "Greyhound Law."

"Isn't that rather a narrow field to bring back to America?" Bill asked her.

"Oh, no, it's a fascinating historical and sociological study of Ireland," she responded, and Bill felt he didn't have anything more to contribute to the subject. When he got back to the table, he said to our group, "Isn't it extraordinary that an American girl would want to come to Ireland to study Greyhound Law?"

The minister for justice, Gerry Collins, was sitting at our table, and he said: "I think she must have said 'Brehon Law.'"

The night wore on. I danced with all their escorts as Bill waltzed Rose after Rose around the floor. One of my partners told me he had been an escort for ten years but hadn't nabbed a Rose yet. Next Wednesday night, in a gala ceremony here in the Dome, the 1980 Rose of Tralee will be chosen. Unfortunately, Bill and I have to go back to Dublin tomorrow, which is probably a good thing. I think the pace down here in Tralee might kill me.

SEPTEMBER 1

Summer is officially over at our house. Blue blazers came out of mothballs, ties were tied, and Christopher and David hit the road at 8:15 this morning to start school. C. is in eighth grade, taking Latin, French, Spanish, Commerce, Math, History, Georgraphy, Science, English and Religion. If he were Irish, he would be studying Irish as well.

SEPTEMBER 3

Today I opened an Antique Lace Exhibit at Sachs Hotel for Deirdre Ryan, a friend who has a lace shop in Dublin and has gathered her own private collection of old lace for the past twelve years. She has hung the lace against a dark red brocade wall in a private dining room at Sachs, and it looks stunning. I felt as if I had entered a delicate Victorian boudoir when I arrived at the exhibit.

While I was reading up on lace this morning in the Irish Heritage Series, I discovered that one of the women responsible for reviving the lace industry in Ireland in the 1880s was Florence de Vere O'Brien, the very same Florence who lived in this house when her father was chief secretary. She later married in Ireland and moved to Limerick, where the making of lace on a commercial basis had been established around 1829 by an Englishman named Charles Walker. He had brought over girls from England to teach the women in Limerick how to make the lace, and the industry prospered. At one time more than fifteen hundred people were employed in their homes making lace; but without artistic guidance, the quality diminished, and by the 1880s lace making had begun to decline as a flourishing industry. The nuns from the local Convent of the Good Shepherd came to the rescue and kept the skill alive, and about this time Florence O'Brien arrived on the scene. She became interested in the art and put her enormous energies and organizing abilities to work establishing a school of lace making, creating new designs herself, sponsoring public lectures on the subject and finally making the name "Limerick lace" synonymous with some of the finest lace produced during that era.

Lace making, both commercially and as a personal hobby, gradually declined again in Ireland, but now there is a growing revival of interest in this unique, elegant, gossamer craft. Women's organizations teach lace making; the nuns in convents around Ireland still make lace, and some of the couturiers, particularly Sybil Connolly and Mary O'Donnell, are using it on their clothes. Just as needlepoint, crewel work, weaving, quilting and other handcrafts have seen a revival in America in the past few decades, Irish lace may once again make a comeback. Nothing—no fabric, no style—flatters a woman as much as a delicate piece of fine lace framing her face, touching her throat, falling gracefully over her wrist.

We watched the end of the Rose of Tralee Festival on television tonight. Bill cheered on his Cork Rose, and I cheered my Dublin Rose, but in the end the Galway Rose won; she was "lovely and fair" and a social worker besides.

The hoopla is over for another year, and the girls will fade back into their ordinary, everyday worlds. I wonder if the ten-years-an-escort plucked a Rose this year?

September 5

Liam left for Dartmouth today. Bill went with him, to see him "settled in" and then to return to Boston, where he will make a speech as part of the city's Jubilee 350 celebration. He's going to talk at the JFK Library on the role of American Irish mayors of Boston.

The two younger boys had to leave for school before Liam got up, but I took them in to say good-by to him. David just stared solemnly and wouldn't say a word. Liam is his hero, going off now to fight the battles of adulthood.

I took pictures of his leave-taking, and instead of succumbing to the tears that were waiting to fall, we all laughed as the black car rolled slowly around the curve in the driveway and down the lane toward the gates. "Don't forget to brush your teeth!" I cried, as Liam stuck his head out to wave a last good-by. "And remember. I'm coming to Dartmouth next year to organize the PTA. Pave the way!"

And he was gone.

Maeve hugged me, she in tears and I dry-eyed, and we turned back to the house to get to our day's work. I had a luncheon date with Mavis Arnold today and was glad to have to get out of the house. I'm resisting a lonely trip to Liam's room, orderly and clean now, the way I've been nagging him to keep it for years. Orderly, neat, clean. And empty.

I picked up Mab on the way to Mavis's. She had the "sisterhood" there, plus a friend whom I hadn't met before, a beautiful, vivacious lady who obviously didn't know she was in a hornets' nest of liberated women! As we were sitting down to lunch, Hilary Pratt asked her if she would like to come to the Women's Political Association fund raiser we are having at the residence soon.

Liam, with his father, leaving for Dartmouth

"Oh, I don't know," she said. "That sounds like something those women's lib types would put on, and I have no time for anything like that."

Well, you could have heard a pin drop, and we, women's libbers to our cores, all looked out of the corners of our eyes at our hostess for instructions on how to proceed. Hilary Pratt took over, calmly and persuasively leading the heretic out of the Fog of Unreason and into the Sunlight of True Faith. I think she had won a convert by the time lunch was over.

September 7: *Clonbulloge, County Offaly*

I often receive requests to open festivals and exhibits around the country and regretfully have to turn many of them down for sheer lack of time.

I had a phone call from the chairperson of a festival in Clonbulloge, who asked me to open their annual (I thought she said; our connection was not the best) "thrashing" festival.

"*Thrashing* festival?" I shouted into the phone. (The Rice Krispies were at it again.)

"Yes!" she yelled back. "It's our seventh annual festival; we try to reenact some of the farming practices of long ago that are no longer practiced in Ireland in order to preserve our traditions and heritage."

My mind immediately pictured a kind of reenactment of an ancient rite of autumn, when old grudges and family feuds that had simmered through the summer were settled in a harvest combat; I imagined broad-shouldered, hot-blooded farmers' sons engaging in a sort of communal Irish karate match on the village green, their grunts and snarls echoing across the town, each kick, each blow wiping out the anger over a stolen lamb, a poisoned well, a daughter's roll in the haystack.

"Oh, I'd love to come," I said, trying to sound as much like Margaret Mead as possible.

"I'll write you the details," my caller promised, and rang off. When her letter came, all my anthropological appetites were squelched. I was being invited to open the Seventh Annual Clonbulloge *Threshing* Festival. Oh well. I've never seen one of those either. I accepted.

The road leading out of Dublin toward Clonbulloge was clogged with traffic when we set off this morning. Cars were pouring into Dublin for the All-Ireland Hurling match, and the petrol truck drivers' strike is still on, so there are long lines in front of every filling station, adding to the general traffic chaos. "Maybe we should turn back home and not try to go," Christopher suggested hopefully. His enthusiasm for threshing festivals did not match mine, but Robin Mosse, my "agricultural adviser," David S. and I outvoted Christopher, and we went on, arriving in good time. Mrs. Allen, the chairperson of the festival, met us, or rather flagged us down, in the center of the main street (we're not hard to identify in our big black car) and led us out to a farmhouse luncheon party, where we were joined by Monica Carr, the radio personality, who was there to judge the babies in the baby contest.

After lunch, it was time to open the festival. The organizers had erected a small platform in the center of the village green and had dragooned the parish priest into introducing me. The streets were thronged with townspeople and neighboring farmers, all patiently waiting for the "opening ceremonies," and to see what I looked like. Old ladies came up to me and murmured softly, as if I weren't present: "Oh, just look at her! Isn't she lovely?" a comment guaranteed to make one *feel* lovely.

"Good afternoon," the priest began over a loud-speaking system. "I'm sure all of you here have seen this lady on the 'Late, Late Show.'" Nods of recognition rolled around the crowd. "She was Gay Byrne's Finest Hour," he continued, to my delight and embarrassment. The crowd tittered. He showered me with undeserved compliments, making me sound like a cross between Joan of Arc and Eleanor Roosevelt.

Then it was my turn. I've noticed that foreigners in any country like to think they know the local slang and often misuse it, to the bewilderment of the natives. I think I fell into that pitfall this afternoon when I began by telling the townspeople of Clonbulloge that I was a "jackeen" (a city person) by necessity but a "culchee" (a country bumpkin) at heart. The response to that statement could be generously described as "a courteous chuckle." I went on to describe my heifers, pigs and hens up in the Park. That was met by puzzled silence. Christopher said later: "They wanted to hear what it's like in an embassy and you start telling them about chickens and pigs. They must have thought you were nuts!" He's probably right. Anyway, I soon had them warmed up, and finally ended the speech by walking to the center of the main road and cutting the white ribbon that stretched across it, announcing: *"The Seventh Annual Clonbulloge Threshing Festival is now open!"* The local band played a very resolute version of "The Stars and Stripes," and the parade began, consisting of an Irish Countrywomen's Association float, the threshing machine, a beautiful vintage Rolls-Royce, three tractors, a Model-A car and—the star turn—a big, black shiny, hissing steam engine.

"Come on." Monica Carr took my arm as the parade ended and we headed toward the festival grounds. "Now that you're here, you've got to see how a threshing machine works."

The grounds were teeming: babies beribboned for their contest, dogs washed and brushed for a dog show; rides and vending machines, stock car racing, an army tank exhibit, griddle-bread making on an open fire, buttermilk churning (which I tried to do for the benefit of the television camera and discovered it's more of a skill than meets the eye).

And then there was the ancient threshing machine, hooked up to the steam engine, which was huffing and puffing gallantly, shooting clouds of steam out of its chimney while the thresher shook and rumbled and groaned and vibrated, spraying whiffs of straw and grain into the air as its mechanism began separating the straw from the grain. I thought it might be dangerous to stand too close to it, and I was eyeing its rumblings and shivers with feigned enthusiasm when I heard a voice at my side saying: "Don't you want to climb up on top of it and see how it works."

I stared incredulously into a pair of round blue eyes twinkling under a cloth cap, and looked around at a circle of old farmers who had gathered round the machine, puffing on their pipes and looking at me out of the sides of their eyes. Some culchee I was!

I gathered my full skirt around my knees and began ascending the shaky ladder, hoping and praying that I had on a good pair of knickers, since they would soon be visible to all the world. Happily, the TV cameras had disappeared.

One rung of the ladder was broken and my high heels nearly slipped off, but I made it to the top, where a strong pair of hands pulled me upright. My head bobbed in rhythm to the vibrations of the thresher. A man below was handing up bundles of "corn" (in Ireland, grain is called corn) to a co-worker standing on top of the thresher with a pitchfork. A woman cut the string, then handed the grain to a man who put it into a hole, where it went down through a mechanism which separated the grain from the straw. The grain goes down into a large funnel and comes out the side of the thresher into big canvas bags. All the time, the thresher is shaking and rocking like a rural rock band, and anyone standing on top could easily fall off or stumble into the hole that the grain is going through. I was clinging tenaciously to the arm of my guide, my enthusiasm for farm life ebbing by the second. "It seems like a very dangerous operation," I whispered to him as I swayed to and fro. He replied, providing no reassurance: "It is that. There's many a bad accident and death that took place during threshing time."

Nowadays, of course, the kind of threshing machine I saw at the festival is just a relic of the past, a nostalgic reminder of the "old days," which weren't always so good.

After I gingerly climbed back down the ladder from the thresher, stepping onto solid ground to a round of applause from the clutch of farmers, Monica persuaded me to help her judge the baby contest, a thankless task since all you end up with is three winning parents who are reaffirmed in their knowledge that their babies are the prettiest in the world, and fifty other moms and dads who are convinced you're either totally blind, hopelessly prejudiced, or an aunt of the winner.

I made my choices on the basis of (1) a mother who told me she and her husband had been trying to have a baby for fourteen years, and (2) the infant of the only father who entered the show and sat in line with all the young mothers. I thought perseverance and courage should both be rewarded.

I declined to judge the dog show and finally, as the sun was beginning to go down over the festival grounds, I found David in the stock car pit (after a long search), said farewell to Clonbulloge, and we returned to Dublin. The late afternoon had turned warm and sunny as it so often does in Ireland. Galway had beaten Limerick in the Hurling Final and all the Galway cars, their red and white banners and flags streaming out behind them, were heading west toward home.

It was a memorable day; I loved it, and when I hear people describe in glowing terms the loveliness of Wicklow, the majesty of Kerry or the lonely beauty of Connemara, I shall speak up for the warm heart of Clonbulloge.

SEPTEMBER 11

I stopped in town today and bought a package of yellow ribbon. When I drove in through the residence gates, I parked the car and took out my yellow ribbon and tied a bow on the branches of each of the chestnut trees lining the drive up to the house, and finally one around the trunk of the big sycamore out in front. We too, in Dublin, are waiting.

We were scheduled to go to the All-Ireland Gaelic Football match today, but when I got up and opened the shutters I thought we had sunk into some sort of subterrestrial swamp. It was dark and windy, with the rain sweeping in across the Park and hitting our windowpanes with angry gusto. A vengeful day. I thought surely the game would be called off, but when I mentioned that to Dennis and Brian at breakfast, they hooted. Nothing short of a national emergency calls off an All-Ireland game.

We drove through thick fog to mass at "Mary's Chest," our little chapel attached to St. Mary's Hospital in the Park. It's now an orthopedic clinic, but it used to be a hospital for chest diseases in the melancholy days when tuberculosis was rampant in Ireland, and is known fondly to those in the neighborhood as Mary's Chest.

The electricity in the chapel was out as a result of the storm, but the darkness lent a peaceful and contemplative atmosphere to the service and the priest couldn't see in the dark to read his sermon, which I still consider, as a carryover from childhood, a blessing.

Back to the residence for lunch with our Worcester house guests, Milton and Alice Higgins, and then on to the game.

The field at Croke Park was a beautiful sight; the grass so green and well tended, and the Kerry and Roscommon flags waving in the stands bobbing like colorful clouds among the somber browns and grays of an Irish crowd.

The VIP stand was full. The foreign minister was behind us, the minister of health to my left, with a priest friend between us. The minister for justice and his wife were in the front row alongside the taoiseach and his wife. The minister of education, seated in front of me, leaned back to whisper: "There's not a McNelly on the team!" (McNelly is my maiden name.) The tanaiste and his wife took their seats, then the band marched out onto the field, the flags of Roscommon and Kerry mingling with the Irish tricolor. When the president of Ireland arrived, the band struck up the National Anthem. The two teams came streaming out of their dressing rooms to the hysterical joy and roars of the crowd. They lined up in two rows behind the band and marched the full oval of the field. The sky, though still heavy and sullen, had ceased and desisted from its morning onslaught.

The band marched off the field and the game began. Roscommon got off to an aggressive start with a first-minute goal, bringing the Roscommon supporters to their feet with ecstatic roars of encouragement. But it was clear even to me, a novice, that the game belonged to Kerry. They ran faster, caught the ball more times, kicked farther and played a strong offensive game.

Gaelic football is a good spectator sport. It's fast and the rules are easy to understand. The priest sitting next to me said: "I'd explain the rules to you, but you don't really need to understand them, because no one goes by them anyway!" The players (fifteen to a side) can kick the ball, catch it, run as much as four steps with it (then they have to bounce, dribble or pass it); they can kick the ball or carry it into a goal. In other words, anything goes. Each half is a frantic, fast, nonstop 35 minutes. You have to be very fit for Gaelic football, and the boys on the field today looked like prime specimens.

Kerry pulled ahead and stayed there, playing a very good game. Roscommon was on the defensive most of the way, and when it was over, the men of Kerry, mud splattering their green and gold shirts and pants, lined up to come forward to the VIP stand and receive their enormous silver cup. Their captain, Ger Power, his handsome, mud-streaked face beaming, brown hair curling over his collar, accepted for the team, thanked his fellow players and then held the cup aloft for the crowd to see and cheer.

We all crowded into a little office below the stands after the game and were served tea or Irish whiskey. Someone came up to Bill and had a long whisper in his ear; when we were leaving, I asked him what it was all about.

"Just a rumor about someone who wants to be the next US ambassador to Ireland," Bill said.

Already? They could at least wait till the election is over.

I'm enjoying the last volume of Anne Morrow Lindbergh's *Diary* very much. I so totally empathize with her conflict between time to write and time to spend on one's family, home, husband, outside responsibilities. As she says, it is not so much the hour or the three hours of the day you need—you can find that—it's the stretch of peace, of quiet, of nothing to think about, no child's problem, no clock to watch, no dinner to plan, no drain to unstop, no house guest to listen for; time to empty one's mind, to plan and think and create, rather than just to grab the free hour, sit down and begin writing in frantic rushes.

It's no wonder so few famous women writers have had children. It's very hard to empty one's mind of them. Bringing up children and running a large household is such a minute-by-minute operation. Most men can plan and schedule their days so as to make optimum use of their time. A homemaker must catch it on the fly. I have a friend who rents a room in a neighbor's house and goes there each day to do her writing. I wonder if President and Mrs. Hillery have a spare room to rent?

SEPTEMBER 25

I had the men out today from James Adam and Son to do a complete inventory of the furniture, silver, chandeliers, and rugs in the residence. We have never been inventoried, except for the standard embassy list, which doesn't take antique value into consideration. In among the standard "Grand Rapids" pieces from the State Department are some very fine pieces of furniture.

When that was finished, I dashed down to Bill's office to meet the new Chinese ambassador, Madam Gong. The Chinese have just opened their embassy here, buying up three houses on Ailesbury Road, to the consternation of a few of their neighbors, the astonishment of others and the amusement of some. Given the price of real estate in that fashionable neighborhood, the Chinese do not seem to be "wanting."

Madam Gong paid her official call on Bill this morning, and he invited me to come in at the end of it to meet her. She is a charming woman, dressed today in a pale gray silk suit with a mandarin collar, and plain black leather pumps. She has a simple, short hairdo, and wears no make-up but has wonderfully young-looking skin for a sixty-seven-year-old woman (mother of two). I was sitting at dinner the other night with the man who is going to be the doctor for the Chinese here, and I made him promise me to "find out her secret." I know that all the members of their staff in Dublin are very fitness-conscious and can be seen early each morning walking very briskly in a little line up Ailesbury Road toward the sea at Sandymount, and back again.

Madam Gong was accompanied to Bill's office today by a young man on her staff with a pleasant, warm smile who took notes of everything Bill said; I tried once to peer into his notebook, and I thought at first that he was taking shorthand, but then of course I realized that it was Chinese! (Or was it Chinese shorthand?)

Madam Gong has been widowed for a long time and has two daughters whom, she said, she misses very much; and "no grandchildren yet, unfortunately." She went to graduate school at Columbia University in New York and her English is excellent. She said she was delighted to come to Ireland, that everyone here seems so friendly and helpful. Several people on her staff, particularly the domestic help, do not speak English, so life has been difficult for them. But they are studying the language and I'm sure they will master it soon, and probably Irish as well. After the experience one of them had yesterday, I'd give them six months to become fluent. One of the staff phoned his doctor late in the evening to explain that he had a "nosebleed." At least, that's what the doctor thought he said. Listening to very broken English over an Irish telephone can be tricky.

"Have you had it long?" he asked.

"All day."

"Good heavens! Is it a heavy flow?"

"Yes."

"Come right over," the doctor told him. "I'll take a look at it."

Although the bleeding had stopped when the patient arrived, the doctor thought to be on the safe side he would pack his nose with wads of cotton wool. The poor little fellow just lay there patiently, getting first one nostril filled up and then the other.

"There!" exclaimed the doctor, satisfied with his job. "That should hold it for the evening. Come back and see me tomorrow if it starts up again.

"Doctor," the patient began timidly, with the impeccable courtesy of the Chinese, "you think this will cure me?"

"Oh, I should think so," the doctor said confidently. "You don't seem to have any other symptoms. Blood pressure is normal."

"I see," the patient said, obviously confused by Western medical practice. "This is the way to treat my problem?"

"It is," the doctor replied, getting just a tiny bit impatient with the questioning. "Of course, if it should continue, we could do something more drastic and cauterize your nose."

The patient's eyes opened wide at this prospect, and he dug into his pocket for a tiny medical dictionary.

"Perhaps," he began again, "you did not understand me perfectly on the telephone. Forgive me please, but I think you are treating the wrong end. This is my problem." And he held open the dictionary, pointing to the word: "Diarrhea."

"God help us," the doctor muttered, unstuffing his nose.

On to a luncheon party where I met Moira Wood, a Dublin doctor who works at one of the "well-women clinics" here, where women can go for contraceptive advice or fittings, vaginal smears, breast examinations and so on. We talked about the new Contraceptive Act which is to go into effect in Ireland on November 1, and which is, in the words of Senator Gemma Hussey, "a ridiculous piece of nonsense." Dr. Patrick Leahy, who works with many of Dublin's poor in the Ballyfermot area, said: "As a doctor I am going to challenge the Act by ignoring it."

The Act ("An Irish Solution to an Irish Problem") stipulates that contraceptives, even condoms, can be dispensed only by doctors on a prescription and only to marrried people. Doctors, naturally, don't want to become the keepers of the nation's morals. There is supposed to be a very steep fine for giving out contraceptives at a family planning clinic, plus several weeks in jail. I can't imagine that the penalty will be enforced.

"Ah well," said one of the guests at the luncheon party, "if they can't get condoms they'll just use Saran Wrap."

We moved from contraception to battered wives. The new Legal Aid Centres for battered wives were officially opened this week. Customers arrived at a "staggering rate." Some of their complaints: raped in front of their children; burned and scalded by their husbands; beaten by husbands and boyfriends when they "confessed" they were pregnant.

Mrs. Maeve O'Brien-Kelly, chairperson of the Limerick branch of the Association for Deserted and Alone Parents, said in an interview the other day: "The family, that sacred institution glorified in our constitution and in sentimental song, is for many women a place of torture."

After we had been in Ireland a few months, David tagged on "and bless the drunk" to his list of those to remember in his prayers each night. Residents of Ballina seem to be following his example. I read in the *Irish Press* the other day that "publicans in Ballina are to observe a two-minute silence on their premises so that customers can recite a prayer for parishioners with drink problems."

OCTOBER 4

The American presidential campaign, as seen from here, looks worse and worse for President Carter. Many of our American friends who have visited us over the past several months, Democrats and Republicans alike, say that they are disillusioned with Carter's administration, that he won't be able to pull the election off. The press in Ireland is certainly not enamored of either candidate. An editorial in the *Irish Press* last summer said: "Mr. Carter still has his fans, but even they must acknowledge that his presidency has been undistinguished, unmemorable even ... it is a cruel reflection on the political system of the world's greatest democracy that, in the end, the choice to fill the most important and powerful office in the free world should lie between an honest amateur and an old-age pensioner."

I think that Carter's Arab-Israeli peace negotiations, the Panama Canal Treaty, his willingness to do unpopular things such as send arms to Turkey, his conservation and energy measures *were* "memorable," but certainly his campaign hopes look dim.

And so my thoughts are beginning to turn homeward. Thoughts of home are already mingled with moments of nostalgia. I watch the flowers that I planted in the courtyard withering and dying this autumn with a special sadness, knowing that I probably won't see them bloom again next summer; I watch Brogeen's belly swell once more, realizing that I won't be here to see a new donkey in the meadow. And I wonder: Should I make curtains for the upstairs bathroom or just leave it now? On the other hand, I scour the Quays in earnest, looking for bits and pieces of brass, porcelain or glass that I can afford to take home with me. I plan an "Irish room," filled with my Irish paintings, glass, pottery and woolens. And *you*, dear journal, loom in front of me looking more and more like a book, and I find myself devoting more and more attention to you.

Going home seems something of an anticlimax. Is it the letdown of returning to normal, everyday life? Or is it Creeping Middle Age?

It's a disquieting, unsettled time. I'll be glad when the election is over and we can start making some decisions.

OCTOBER 10

The Women's Political Association came out to the residence this evening for a fund-raising reception. They are getting into high gear for their annual Seminar in November and are bringing Betty Friedan to Ireland to be the featured speaker. One of the "sisters," Audrey Conlon, attended the Conference on Women in Copenhagen last summer and met Ms. Friedan there. Audrey told her about the WPA and nabbed her to come to Ireland. All of us are eager to meet and hear this famous, controversial "mother" of women's liberation.

And speaking of motherhood, Robin Mosse thinks two of our three heifers are in the family way. It's an unexpected development, but not so unusual, Robin assured me. "The low fence, the odd bull; you know how it is."

We called in Mr. Barrett, our veterinarian, to come and have a look at the cows. He arrived today and I, mother of three, and gentlewoman farmerette, disgraced myself in front of him. He arrived in his van, the back of which looks like a cross between a West Virginia front porch, a 1920s drugstore and a jumble sale. Mr. B. is a vet in the style of James Herriot; he goes about his business with zest, humor and an obvious love affair with all four-footed creatures.

We had lined up the heifers in the stable for Mr. B.'s visit, and the three of them stood there quietly, their great wet mouths still working over their last bites of grass, their eyes rolling from one to the other of us, knowing something was afoot. Did I detect a little glint of regret in Portia's eye, a sense of guilt in Juliet's hanging head? Have these fat, gallumphing creatures who came to me under the guise of three virgins been, in fact, indulging in midnight orgies with the "odd bull"? Is my little beef operation going to turn into a dairy farm?

"Well," says Mr. B., scratching Juliet on the rump. "So they think you are in calf, you naughty girl. Now you just relax and we'll see." He pulled on a plastic glove that stretched all the way to his armpit and said to Michael and me: "If you can just hold her still as best you can, I'll stick my fingers up her nose."

Up her nose?

Michael took her around the neck and held on tight while I scratched her ears and murmured encouraging words as I watched, fascinated, while Mr. B. put his two fingers up her nose.

"Well, you learn something new everyday," I said. "I never knew you felt up a cow's nose to tell if it was pregnant." The vet stared at me with a look of stupefaction for a split second, then roared with laughter. "No, luv," he said, "I'm not testing her up her *nose*. I'm just getting ready to put this iron clip through her nostrils. That will keep her quiet while I slip my hand up her behind, and *then* I can tell if she's in calf." I blushed in mortification as Mr. Barrett winked at Michael and Jimmy. "That's one for the book," he said. I'll never live it down.

The wind banged the stable door back and forth, and the dim overhead light swayed on its cord. "Not the best of consulting rooms," I apologized to the vet, as we stood crowded against each other in the tiny stable.

"Oh, I've seen much worse than this," he answered cheerfully. Juliet finally decided to give in to the whole embarrassing operation; she heaved mightily, sighed and leaned her enormous body against me, pinning me to the stable wall, and Mr. Barrett inserted his fingers into her, then his hand, then his forearm ... was he going to climb in? I didn't dare ask any more questions. He stopped just short of his armpit, and felt and prodded and nodded to himself while we all waited expectantly. "She's pregnant, all right."

We repeated the process with Portia. She was far less relaxed than Juliet, and she snorted and kicked and heaved and moaned, but finally Mr. Barrett got his arm up her and made the same pronouncement. Only Ophelia, it turned out, had minded her manners and been a good girl. Once the pregnancy tests were completed, we held onto the girls once again while the vet gave them each a brucellosis test on the underside of their tail. They've had the test once, but after I read about a speech that Professor J. D. Collins gave last summer on the health hazards of farming, I decided we can't be too careful.

"You've got three grand, fine, muddy heifers," Mr. Barrett told us, as he put away his gear—"muddy" meaning good and fat—"and you'll have five before long." He waved us all a cheerful good-by as he rattled off down the back lane in his little van. Michael seemed a bit subdued. Three heifers to graze for beef are one thing. Two cows in calf are another! I don't believe I'll mention to him *quite* yet about the peacocks I've ordered!

OCTOBER 24

Mrs. Nesterenko, the wife of the new Russian ambassador, came to call on me this morning. She's an ample lady, with a high, upswept hairdo, handsome blue eyes, heavily penciled eyebrows and a nice suit—a blazer and plaid skirt. Her coral-colored blouse had a pearl star pin in its tie. She's vivacious and outgoing, and told me she used to be a singer, a mezzo-soprano. She has a grown son and daughter, and is keeping her year-old grandson here in Dublin so that her daughter can finish her graduate studies in Russia. That surprised me, because I had always heard that Russia has very fine day-care centers for working or studying mothers.

She asked after my children, and I told her that Liam was away in America, attending university.

"Is that expensive?" she asked.

"Yes." I smiled. "Very!"

"Oh, well, in Russia our universities are free and we pay the students a stipend."

"Now you tell me!" I said. "We could have sent Liam to the University of Vladivostok!" She laughed uproariously.

She wanted to see the house and I took her on the tour, ending up in the ballroom, where she sat down and played our Steinway grand. "Marvelous!" she said. "Your house is like a palace."

I told her we would have a musical evening soon and would invite her to come and sing, a prospect that pleased her enormously.

"We must do that!" she said. "I think it's too bad that our countries are on bad terms now and we can't have so many cultural exchanges."

"You be our cultural exchange," I said, and we both laughed.

OCTOBER 29

The Turks are leaving, and they gave a farewell reception, which I attended by myself tonight. Bill is away in Cork. The Turkish embassy is in an apartment building, and as I walked into the lobby, I ran into the Nesterenkos.

"Where is your husband tonight?" Ambassador Nesterenko boomed at me.

"He's gone to Cork," I explained, as we stood waiting for the elevator.

"No," the ambassador said. "He did not go to Cork. *You* ate him!" He loved his joke and shook all over, but just at that moment, the Chinese ambassador, Madam Gong, arrived in the now-crowded lobby and shook my hand warmly. Then she gave Nesterenko a frosty little nod and he wiped his smile off his face and gave her his "I am Russian you are Chinese" official greeting, which is about as warm and friendly as a loan shark trying to collect a bad debt. At that moment, the elevator door slid open and the four of us, Ambassador and Mrs. Nesterenko, Madam Gong and I stepped in. I was in the middle, a certain symbolism not lost on any of us. The door slid shut and nothing happened. I pressed the button again and we waited. I looked at the ambassador, he looked at me. I looked at Madam Gong, and she stared straight ahead. I pressed the "Alarm" button but it didn't ring. "Maybe you could sing," I suggested to Madam N., who had been looking glum but perked up visibly at my suggestion. Suddenly the door mysteriously swung open and we all filed out. We were still in the lobby.

"I will walk," Madam Gong announced, and I followed her up the six flights. I was panting when we reached the top, but Madam Gong wasn't even winded. The Nesterenkos were still two flights below.

313

NOVEMBER 4: *Election Day*

I slept late this morning, knowing that we would have a late night. The embassy is having a big Election Night blast. We invited Maureen Potter and Godfrey James, the current stars of the Irish production of *Annie,* to lunch today at the residence. We enjoyed them and it kept our minds off the election. Bill said this morning that he "smells failure."

I couldn't concentrate on any work at my desk this afternoon, so I put on records, lit the fire, and sewed patches on the boys' jeans. We went down to the embassy about 10:30 PM and it was jammed and overflowing. Bill made a short welcoming speech to the crowd, avoided an interview with an eager journalist, and went up to his office to listen to the returns. By midnight the heavy Reagan turnout was clear. (Ireland is five hours ahead of the United States.) We left at 12:30 and came home again, to sit by the fire in the library and talk until 2:30 AM. Somehow I don't feel as sad as I thought I might. Certainly I would have liked Carter to have been reelected, and I would have preferred to leave Ireland with him still in office, but I feel ready to go home and now we have the decision made for us. We talked of Bill's options at home, of where we would like to live, of what we want to do. He is saddened and dismayed at the election results.

We finally banked the fire, turned out the lights and locked up.

NOVEMBER 5

The phone started ringing early this morning, friends commiserating on the outcome of the election, saying how much they will miss us, and so on. I keep telling them that I haven't packed my bags quite yet. Someone phoned to say she had heard *for sure* that Gregory Peck was going to be appointed the new ambassador to Ireland!

Bill went off to morning mass. He had gone on Monday and Tuesday, to pray for one of his sisters who is having minor surgery this week. He said he thought he'd better go today, too, in case someone saw him there Monday and Tuesday and thought he had been praying for a favorable outcome to the election. Oh, the trials of public life, they follow you right up to the Communion rail!

NOVEMBER 13

We gave a "literary" dinner tonight for Bill and Joan Roth, our American friends who live part of each year in Cashel, a two-hour drive from Dublin. After dinner, Bill tried to get everyone at the table to speak, but it began to turn into a eulogy for us, so he stopped them and we got on to other subjects. Charles Acton, the talented music critic of the Irish *Times,* spoke passionately about the need for a large concert hall in Dublin. I remembered what a member of the Juilliard Quartet had said to me years and years ago at a wedding reception we were attending in New York, when the Kennedy Center was being built in Washington: "No one will ever go to it," he said, "because Washington isn't a theater- or concert-going town." It wasn't, because they had never had any place to go. Now, of course, you have to book tickets weeks in advance for concerts or plays at the Kennedy Center, and it has transformed the cultural life of Washington. Dublin will be the same, if they ever get a concert hall worthy of their own musical and artistic talents.*

Late in the evening, we started talking about H-block and the hunger strikers. The prisoners at Long Kesh Prison, in Northern Ireland, who are "on the blanket" (since they refuse to wear prison clothes as part of their campaign to be recognized as political prisoners, not criminals, they wear a blanket instead), have been on a hunger strike for nearly three weeks. Seamus Heaney, a poet and a Northerner himself, spoke eloquently this evening about the strike: about the prisoners' feelings of bitterness and isolation that have created the mentality needed to carry out a hunger strike; about the history of hunger strikes as a political tactic in Ireland; and about the violence and bloodshed that are likely to follow the first death of a striker. Seamus was very moving in a quiet way, articulating the tragedy of the strikers, their families and all of Northern Ireland.

Garret FitzGerald, the Leader of the Opposition, said that Britain must not even *pretend* it would change its stand on the strike. He said that Ireland has always refused to yield to hunger strikers in its own prisons and that the prisoners at Long Kesh know that, so they don't try it with the Irish government. He recalled that when Eamon de Valera was taoiseach, he let two IRA hunger strikers die in 1940, and a third in 1946. They had been interned in World War II so they wouldn't cause trouble between Ireland and Britain. In the months leading up to the war, there had been 250 IRA bombing incidents in Britain, including a devastating explosion in Coventry that killed six people and injured dozens.

December 2

This was Betty Friedan Week for us in Dublin. She left her mark on Irish women and on the WPA, and she even changed Bill's views of liberated women! Her schedule in Dublin made a presidential campaigner look like a laggard. TV appearances, radio shows, her speech at the Sem-

---

* In September 1981, the new concert hall in Earlsfort Terrace opened, and all the reports about it have been highly favorable.

inar, dinners, receptions, and some shopping and sightseeing took up every hour of her waking day. We gave a dinner party for her at the residence on Friday, and she was a great hit with all our guests, liberated or not. Even the most chauvinistic of our guests—and there were a few—forgave her feminist views because she turned out to be such a good storyteller. In Ireland, that gift makes up for most political, philosophical or social aberrations.

She had been booked to do a television show called "Countryside" on Friday afternoon, but at the last minute one of the staff members connected with the program phoned apologetically to say that the producers of the show were "fed up" with women's shows and canceled her appearance.

"I could lie to you," the caller said, "and say we couldn't get a camera crew, but that's not the truth."

Her speech at the Seminar began at 3 PM on Saturday. The ballroom of the hotel held twelve hundred people and every seat was taken. We rigged up the loud-speaking system so that latecomers sitting in the lobby off the main ballroom could hear the speech. Men are invited to the Seminar, and about two hundred of them, including the American ambassador, came this year. I introduced Betty, and she stood up and began a one hour and forty-five minute performance that was probably the most effective speech I've ever heard.

She spoke without notes or prepared text and never faltered or hesitated to find a word or enlarge on an idea. She drew laughs from the audience at tense moments and she made them weep. She outraged them and then beguiled them with a quick turn of phrase. She amused and moved them; she held them in the palm of her hand. It was a tour de force and when it was over and the audience was giving her a standing ovation, I slipped a note to Mavis Arnold, the president of the WPA, who was sitting on the platform with me: "I think that was the most captivating speech I ever heard."

We dispensed with the question-and-answer period; it seemed superfluous after the speech. When she had finished signing autographs in the crowd, I took her arm and said: "Come on, I'll take you home now. You deserve a rest after that performance." She turned on me, outraged, and shouted: "*You* promised to take me to a pub after the speech. I've been in Ireland for three days and haven't seen the inside of a pub."

"Aren't you exhausted after all of this?" I asked her, incredulous that anyone would have an ounce of energy left after that performance.

"No," she laughed, obviously riding high on the crest of the successful afternoon. "Let's go." So we rounded up a half dozen "sisters," and with Bill as the only man in tow, we introduced Betty to the charms of a "real" Irish pub. We took her to Madigan's, which is Ben Kiely's neighborhood "local."

Betty wanted to see the Joyce Tower in Sandycove, so we went out there early Sunday morning. We discovered a champagne reception going on, sponsored by Margaret Mason, the agriculture attaché of the American embassy. She had organized a Food and Wine Week in Dublin to encourage the sale of more American food products here, and the reception was the end of the week's festivities. We joined them, and I gave Betty my quick tour of the Tower. It's beginning to sound like a 78 rpm record turned down to 33, but she went through the Tower with all the enthusiasm of a lover of Irish literature. (She had been delighted to read in the paper the other day that she was "a Yeatsian incarnation with her mass of flowing gray hair ... who wove her own magnetic magic.") At the Tower we met David Green, the director of Celtic studies at the Institute of Advanced Studies. He's a big man with a flowing beard and a booming laugh, and we all left the Tower together with Mavis Arnold to lunch at Nieve's in Dalkey. David, a newcomer to American feminism but curious to learn, punctured the Sunday propriety of the restaurant by booming at Betty: "Where does your movement stand on the question of lesbianism, abortion and issues like that?" Betty answered in clear, ringing tones. Necks stiffened and a certain disapproving quiet settled over the other diners. But David's infectious, ringing laugh echoed through the room and knives and forks clattered once more.

Betty left Dublin that evening, heading for Paris and London and more speeches, and I went home to bed. It takes a *lot* of energy to be a feminist on the road.

DECEMBER 9

I was dressing for dinner tonight, putting on nail polish and listening to the evening farm news ("Black Leg Can Strike Without Warning!!! Vaccinate *NOW!*" Must check with Michael about that. I remembered yesterday to buy the World's Only Eight-in-One Wormer), when the intercom on my night table jangled suddenly and it was Mick, one of the guards at our front gate.

"Mrs." he said in his rich Dublin accent, "there's a lad here with a pig in his front seat, and he's wondering would it be all right if he left him here for the night."

"Run through that again, Mick," I said, turning the radio down.

He repeated himself.

"Is he all right?" I asked.

"Oh, he's sober all right, Mrs. He's with the Department of Agriculture." That, in Mick's eyes, was obviously the Seal of Sobriety.

"But what's he doing at our gate with a pig in his front seat? That *is* what you said, isn't it?"

"Don't know, Mrs."

"I'll come down." I gathered up my long black-lace skirt, kicked off my sandals and slipped on my boots, and ran down the front drive to the gate. There, just as Mick had said, was a very small van parked inside the gate with a young man standing beside it, and a *very* large pig sitting in the driver's seat. I thought for one mad second that I had stumbled onto some Beatrix Potter movie set and that any minute the pig would get out of the van, shake my hand and invite me home for tea and crumpets.

The young man was shy. "What seems to be the problem?" I asked, trying to be serious in a situation that cried out for the Mad Hatter's touch.

"Well," he began, "it's like this. I was driving this boar down to a farm, like, and I was cutting through the Park, when all of a sudden this big fellow broke through the partition I have in the back of the van, you know, like he just pushed his way into the front seat. I couldn't keep on driving with him giving me the nudge all the time, like leaning on me, you know, and finally he just seemed to want to take over the driving entirely and I saw your gate here and thought I should stop, like. As soon as I got out, this big fellow just moved over to the driver's seat, like that's where he wanted to be all along, and now there's no way to move him."

We peered into the cab of the van and there he sat, a very large boar, quite calm, and making contented little grunting noises to himself. He seemed to be looking intently at some middle-distance spot up the road, and ignored us completely.

"But what should we do?" I asked the driver, wanting to be hospitable but not quite knowing how to handle the needs of a large boar with driving ambitions.

"I was wondering if maybe, like, I could leave him here for the night?" the man suggested. "In the morning I could bring some more lads around to help me get him back in the van. I heard somewhere that you keep pigs, like."

"I don't really keep pigs," I explained. "I just have two of them and they're really sort of like pets." It was his turn to look incredulous.

But we called in the help of Michael and Jimmy, and they managed somehow to get the boar out of the van and into the pen, where he spent the night, graciously received by his two fat hosts.

I thought about telling the story at dinner, but then I thought there's only so far one can stretch one's audience's imagination. And then too I thought: Did it really happen?*

There was a letter in the *Irish Times* not long ago, written by a "guest

---

* A few days later, I received a very nice note from the Department of Agriculture, thanking me for my help in the matter of the pig in the van. I hadn't dreamed it after all.

in Ireland," expressing amazement at the "inexhaustible depths of Irish patience."

"Surely," the writer went on, "there must be a line between patience and indignation, between docility and righteous wrath." I've thought of that so often while living here. The Irish have no sense of outrage; they are put to terrible inconveniences and even hardships by illegal strikes and poor public service, often caused by just a few men, and they seem willing to take it. So many friends tell me frustrating stories of incompetent laborers, untrustworthy companies, of work promised and left undone, but they just accept it as a fact of life. The Irish triumvirate of answers to any problem is: "I'll phone you." "I'll write you." "A letter is in the mail."

I kept a list of a few of the strikes during 1979/1980: A city-wide bus strike hit Dublin, nearly causing the city to shut down. A nationwide postal strike brought untold financial hardship to businesses around the country. The dustbinmen struck; they said their waterproof coats made them sweat. The farmers threatened. Taxis went out for a day, the buses had a slowdown, the switchboard operators at the Department of Foreign Affairs went out, envelope makers struck; electricity in parts of Dublin was cut off; the deep-sea section of the Dublin Port, the psychiatric nurses, the buses again, buses in Cork, the Alcan plant in Limerick, the cement plant in Drogheda, Aer Lingus, the switchboard operators at the Electricity Supply Board, petrol truck drivers and sugar beet factory workers were all into the striking game during the year. Almost all of these strikes were in the public sector. Are the Irish trying to say that Socialism doesn't work?

The strike against Aer Lingus, the post office shutdown, and the petrol truck drivers caused serious upheavals in the nation's economy, and hardships to almost every citizen of this country. If I were Irish, I'd *protest*. I'd strike!!

CHRISTMAS SEASON

The hunger strike at Long Kesh Prison was called off. One of the seven was very near death and had already lost his sight. The prisoners said they had "won," that England had given them the concessions they wanted, but the British said they had given nothing, that the prisoners only reinterpreted the concessions they had been offered much earlier to make the strike look like a victory. Everyone was relieved, as Christmas approaches, that the strike was called off. The strikers received very little support here in Ireland. The march for the strike in Dublin was a fiasco; University College Dublin voted not to support it, as did Coleraine University in Northern Ireland. However, the papers are full of stories saying that the prisoners in H-block are "out of control" and that there will be more strikes after Christmas.

I was just reading a report on health statistics for EEC countries, stating that Ireland has by far the highest number of beds in psychiatric hospitals and that alcoholism accounts for the highest number of male admissions, while manic depressive psychosis is the more prevalent illness for women. The Irish spend one pound in every eight for alcohol, according to economist Dr. Brendan Walsh. Since many Irish households spend nothing at all on drink, that pushes the figure up much higher.

A friend was telling me the other day about her husband, who is drunk every weekend and on each holiday. "At least he pulls himself together to get to work during the week, but every night during Christmas he's been drunk. I'm lucky, though. He's a cheerful drunk and comes home at night singing, hooting and hollering and trying to get me out of bed to dance with him. I just trip him up on the sofa where he falls and sleeps it off. But you take my son-in-law, now he's a rotten drunk. He comes home from the pub, wakes up the children, scares them out of their wits, teases my daughter until she's frantic, and talks to himself all night. When he's sober the next morning and confronted with all these things he says: 'It's not true. You're making it all up.' "

Ten percent of work absenteeism in Ireland, at a cost of thirty million pounds per year, is due to alcoholism, according to official figures. Others put it as high as 30 to 50 percent.

NEW YEAR'S EVE 1980–1981

It hasn't been a good year, economically, for Ireland. After three years of rising prosperity, strikes and inflation have begun to take their toll. That thirty-four-day Aer Lingus strike last summer cost the country 21,000 visitors and £2.4 million in revenue. The cost of living rose by 18 percent during the year. Even though the taoiseach, Mr. Haughey, warned the country in his State of the Nation address on television in January that Ireland was on a disaster course if industrial strife continued, the strikes have persisted throughout the year.

One of the saddest incidents of 1980 was the death, by her own hand, of Mrs. Anne Maguire, the mother of three children who were killed in the strife in Northern Ireland and whose deaths led to the formation of the Peace Movement. Mairead Corrigan (the sister of Anne Maguire) and Betty Williams, the two women who founded the movement and who later won the Nobel Peace Prize for their efforts in Northern Ireland, have split up. Many people feel that the movement, which started with such high hopes and generosity of spirit, has lot its potency and is incapable of further leadership.

But there were bright spots during the year as well; that previously all-male bastion, the Irish Army, has taken in its first female cadets!

1981

January 13: *Belfast*

I made a quick run up to Belfast on the train to visit some Ireland's Children projects. Happily, the Dublin-Belfast train was neither blown up nor threatened to be blown up, so my trip was safe and uneventful. I made my first stop with Sister Bernadette in Moyard, Belfast, to see the home for battered wives she has established, then on to Ballymurphy to see Sisters Magdalene and Ita, whose work is similar to that of Sister Bernadette and whose needs are identical. The areas these nuns service (all are social workers) are extremely depressed economically, with an unemployment rate of nearly 60 percent.

A quick stop at the City Hall, where I paid a courtesy call on the Lord Mayor, drank a cup of tea and posed for pictures, while the Lord Mayor, a most genial host, and I—both of us being enthusiastic mini-farmers—discussed the price of heifers.

My last stop of the day was in the Ardoyne, where I had an "Ulster fry" with Bridie Maguire. An Ulster fry, beloved in Northern Ireland, consists of fried sausage, bacon, eggs, tomatoes, potatoes and bread. It was delicious but one fry would feed me for a week. Bridie and I then spent the rest of the evening at the new Youth Center. I didn't really think, two years ago when I was last in Belfast, that I would ever see the Center built and in use during my time in Ireland, but there it stands, having risen out of the rubble, the dirt, the broken glass and shattered dreams of the Ardoyne, a tragic, desolate, battered neighborhood which has been nearly destroyed by the vicious sectarian fighting of the past decade. Fortunately, there are people like Bridie and her husband in the neighborhood; people who wouldn't bow under the weight of the fear, the heartbreak, the madness going on around them. Their primary concern was for the children, their own and the neighborhood's—to get them off the streets and make them a less vulnerable prey to subtle political pressures, to get them out of the drinking clubs, to get them involved in sports and a community life, to make them proud of their neighborhood and responsible for something that is uniquely "theirs."

Bridie cajoled, begged, harassed, and prodded the funds for her Center from every pocketbook she could think of. And when she got a little money in the bank, the construction began. The kids in the Ardoyne gathered around to watch the foundation dug, the bricks laid, the basketball hoops go up, the pool rooms and games rooms come to life, the Ping-Pong tables arrive, the snack bar stocked, the electricity turned on. Finally, Bridie announced that the Center was ready. The night before the opening ceremonies, she and her husband made a last-minute inspection. As they switched on the lights in the shining new gymnasium, they discovered to their horror that the gleaming varnish of the basketball court, just applied that day, had turned into a sticky glue. Somehow the wrong formula had been used and it was ruined—a total mess. There was no way the Center could be opened in the morning. "Their wee feet would stick to the floor," Bridie said, telling me the story.

But the kids had been promised the opening and had waited a long time, and Bridie's devotion to the boys and girls of Ardoyne is astonishing. She and her husband found a store open where they could buy varnish remover and the proper varnish. All through the night, on their hands and knees, they removed the sticky mess, they sanded, stained and varnished. At dawn, the floor was complete. They turned up the heat to dry the finish, and by the appointed hour it was ready.

I had been looking at Bridie's hands all evening; they were red and raw-looking, with half-healed sores over some of her fingers. I took one of her hands in mine. "Is that the varnish?" I asked her.

"No, luv." She laughed her cheerful, husky laugh. "That was the remover and the wee sandpaper."

When I had finished my fry, Bridie and I walked up the hill to the Center. It had snowed earlier that day, then the snow had turned to rain and the sidewalks had become an icy, slippery obstacle course. We clung to each other, fighting the wind, slipping on the ice, picking our way around the rubble and debris in the unlit streets, until we saw the lights of the Center ahead.

Dozens of boys and girls were waiting outside in the bitter cold for the building to open at 7:30 PM. They streamed in as Bridie unlocked the doors, and soon the whole place was rocking with noise and laughter; the thump of balls, the screech of tennis shoes on wood, referees' whistles, the light click of Ping-Pong balls, giggles and squeals from little girls as little boys chased them from room to room. There was a quiet refuge where teenage girls sat learning needlework, and a dim and subdued room, off limits to the younger children, where a group of boys held a

324

serious pool game. In the midst of it all, Bridie: keeping the peace, answering questions, sellling a soft drink, sending troublemakers home, and beaming at her kids, safe, off the streets, having fun, just where she had always dreamed of them.

I spent the night in Belfast with the Michauds, the new American consul and his wife, and I fell madly in love with a new puppy they had, a tiny Tibetan terrier. I've never seen one before; it looked like a miniature sheep dog. Mrs. Michaud gave me the name of a breeder in Dublin.

We sat up and talked about Belfast. Although the political situation there seems less tense and raw than it did on my last visit, the economic situation is desperate.

The social workers in Moynard and Ballymurphy told me that the social service cutbacks have created a sense of financial urgency in a situation that was always hovering on the edge of despair. Prolonged unemployment, a shocking housing situation and the psychological scars of the Troubles have taken their toll: a sharp increase in vandalism, increased drunkenness, more broken marriages, a huge increase in battered wives.

As my train sped back to Dublin this afternoon through the bleak January landscape, I could only sit and stare out the window and wonder, again, where will it all end?

JANUARY 15

All the ambassadors and spouses drove up the lovely, tree-lined drive to Áras an Uachtaráin, the president's house, for the annual New Year's greeting this morning. The nuncio read his greeting on behalf of all of us, and then the president responded, in Irish and in English. It's a very short ceremony, and after it was over we filed into another room to line up for our official photograph. They had put our names on the floor so we would know where to stand, and all those short-sighted ambassadors were practically crawling around on hands and knees, looking for their names! We were placed in the second row, right behind President and Mrs. Hillery. I had worn a big hat for the occasion and I'm afraid it rather stood out. Way out. The poor Japanese ambassador was placed right behind me, and as I'm very tall and he's very small, my hat just about finished him off.

When I returned to the residence this afternoon, Maeve had a message for me: there *is* a breeder of Tibetan terriers in Dublin.

JANUARY 19

We have been glued to the radio all day. The earliest word was that the Iranians have signed the papers necessary to transfer their money out

The official New Year's photo—we've moved up to the second row

of American banks, and a team of Algerian doctors has flown to Iran to examine the hostages. Two Algerian planes have landed in Tehran to take the hostages to Algeria, then on to Germany, where they will apparently spend a few days before they leave for America. Is it really about to be over for them?

It seems so close to the end. The planes are on the tarmac, the hostages have been brought to the airport, but they still haven't left. How can they stand it? Every second now, after their long internment, must seem an eternity.

JANUARY 20: *Inauguration Day*

It's still touch and go about the hostages. Just when they were ready to leave yesterday, there was another holdup. But apparently minutes after Reagan was sworn in, they were airborne and on their way home, via Algeria and Germany. I feel so deeply sorry for President Carter—ex-President Carter—that he didn't get the thrill, and have the honor of announcing their release, but Bill thinks that this final two-day delay was almost certainly a deliberate act of revenge by the Ayatollah Khomeini against Carter.

We watched the inauguration ceremonies on television and had a few friends in for dinner in the evening. We invited our guests out into the foyer where the ambassadorial and the American flags stand, and where we keep a picture of President Carter on display. Bill made a little speech about the hostage release and then about President Carter's administration, pointing out his achievements, and then we toasted the release of the hostages, President Carter and our new president, Ronald Reagan. Before we left the foyer, I took down the picture of President Carter and handed it to Bill. And that, for us, was the end of the Carter administration and the beginning of the end of our Irish sojourn.

JANUARY 23

Michael O'Donohoe's daughter Deirdre was married today, and a more beautiful bride couldn't be found in the length and breadth of Ireland. John Fearon, you are a lucky man!

As we were sitting at the table with Mr. and Mrs. O'Donohoe and the bridal party, Bill was called away to the telephone. When he returned, he whispered to me that he had just learned that the hostages are coming through Shannon Airport on Sunday on their way home from Germany. I was so excited I wanted to jump up and grab the microphone in the middle of the bridal toasts and announce it to the world, but of course we have to keep it quiet as they want no publicity.

The party continued through the afternoon, with dancing, singing, recitations, poetry readings, and all the things that make Irish weddings the best in the world. I *finally* learned how to do the Siege of Ennis; panting, perspiring and breathless, I got through it from start to finish this time.

A very funny thing happened during the party; Maeve and I laughed about it afterwards, but it reflects the tension that permeates one's subconscious these days. One of the groom's uncles had gotten up to recite that moving speech of Robert Emmet, the Irish patriot, "Let No Man Write My Epitaph." He delivered it with elegance, force and grace, and the crowd in the ballroom were moved to silence by his oration.

Maeve had gone out a few minutes before he started the speech and as she returned she was surprised to find that the room had fallen into a hush. When she heard the booming words from the patriotic, stirring speech, her heart started racing. Oh, dear God, were her first thoughts, the IRA has taken over the wedding party and they'll kidnap the ambassador. A second later, as more words from the speech came pouring out, she peeked through the doors, realized what was going on, and laughed at her own fears.

We have a new puppy at our house tonight. We named her Fling after searching in vain through the encyclopedia for appropriate Tibetan names. Bill thought "Fling" sounded faintly Oriental and it describes the way she throws herself around.

JANUARY 25: *Shannon Airport*

We were up at six this morning, pulling sleepy boys out of bed, eating a hurried breakfast in order to be on the road by seven. It was a glorious morning, cold, clear and still. Although we left in darkness, within a half hour the sun had come up. Not a car was on the road, and the villages as we passed through them were still, empty and sleeping.

Midway down to Shannon, just as we passed the sign marked KILLA-LOE, we stopped the car, had cold drinks and fruit, and got out of the car to exercise and take the kinks out. After a few jumping jacks, deep-knee bends, and a jog down the road and back, we got back to the big black car, revived, and set off again.

We pulled into Shannon Airport at 10:10 AM and went straight to the VIP room, which was laid out with coffee and cookies. All air traffic in and out of Shannon had been diverted, and the airport seemed strangely quiet and empty with no one in the usually crowded Duty-Free Shop. The taoiseach, Mr. Haughey, and some government ministers and members of his staff were due to arrive in a private plane at 11 AM. The press, about forty strong, were lined up behind a barricade on the tarmac. Many of them had flown over from England this morning, and their tiny chartered planes were lined up near the runway. They were not allowed inside the airport to interview or photograph the hostages—the "returnees," as we call them now.

Bill and I went out to chat with the press while we awaited the taoiseach's plane. Upon his arrival, we went back into the lounge to wait. One of the airport staff came in and whispered to Bill that the hostages were not going to get off the plane while it refueled at Shannon. Bill got on the telephone and called directly to the plane, telling them that the airport had been emptied, there would be no press allowed in, and that the prime minister was there to greet them. When they heard that, good diplomats that they are, they decided they would get off; very soon after that, their plane was announced. We left the VIP lounge and walked down to the door leading out to the tarmac. I stood between Bill and the taoiseach and the two boys stood behind us. I have seldom taken our boys to official functions, but this is one episode in American history I didn't want them to miss. I also wanted to be able to share it with them.

There was no band or fanfare. We simply waited quietly, Irish government officials and several members of our embassy staff mingled with airport officials. Someone pointed skyward and we all looked up, and there was the plane, big and silver, winging its way down for a landing, with "The United States of America" printed on its side. I felt tears spring into my eyes as it eased down into a smooth landing and cruised to a stop. The taoiseach, Bill and I walked out to the ladder, which unfolded almost as soon as the plane touched down. The door of the aircraft opened and I looked up to see a slight, neatly dressed man standing at the door. We ran up the steps and the man grabbed me immediately and gave me a huge bear hug and a kiss.

"Hi!" he said. "I'm Bruce Laingen and I'm kissing all the girls today." He was the chargé d'affaires who had been at the Iranian Foreign Office on the day of the takeover and had remained there throughout the or-

Leaving the plane with the hostages at Shannon airport

deal; a "hostage," free and smiling and well. I clung to him to make his physical presence real.

The control officer from the State Department took us down the aisle of the plane, introducing us as we went. I stood in the aisle, my eyes sweeping over the faces of the occupants and I felt a sense of unreality. *Here they are!* I had a wild impulse to grab each one of them and hug and squeeze them. They were all smiling and they seemed to be looking at us very intently, far more so than with the normal curiosity of strangers. It was almost a hungry look. Do they know, I wondered, how we have prayed for them, cherished them, kept them in our thoughts each day, hung our yellow ribbons for them?

Mr. Haughey told them there was Irish coffee waiting for them in the lounge, and they all let out a whoop and a cheer. We left the plane, the taoiseach first, with Kathryn Koob and Elizabeth Ann Swift, the women returnees, on each arm, then Mr. Laingen holding onto my arm, and Bill with us, followed by the rest of the returnees, the crew, doctors and State Department staff. The crowd of bystanders, many of them Americans, who had gathered behind the barricades by the entrance to the airport, clapped and cheered as we came down off the plane. One of them held up a big sign that read: "We didn't forget." The airport was festooned with yellow ribbons; each of us wore one on our lapel and Joyce Bournes, the wife of our military attaché, gave one to the taoiseach. As we walked into the building, the loudspeaker was playing "Tie a Yellow Ribbon 'Round the Old Oak Tree."

We assembled in the lounge, where the Irish coffee was waiting, and Mr. Haughey made a very warm and touching welcome-home speech to them, then produced a letter Bruce Laingen had drafted and which he had been able to smuggle out of the Iranian Foreign Office for delivery to the Irish embassy last St. Patrick's Day. Bill spoke after the taoiseach, and Bruce Laingen responded on behalf of the returnees. I whispered to him that one of their group, Mike Kennedy, had a cousin-in-law who lived in Dublin (my friend Mab Moltke), so he spoke a few words of thanks "on behalf of the Irish in the group."

Everyone lined up and shook hands with the taoiseach, with Bill and me, and I had a chance to give out a lot of hugs. The two women seemed in marvelous shape, cool and calm, with witty stories of their experience. One of them commented on how good the Irish coffee tasted; while they were in captivity, she said, the guards continually harped on the evils of alcohol. He went on and on, until finally all she could think about was how much she wanted a drink! She told me she had been bound hand and foot to a straight chair for the first three weeks of her detention and could sleep only on a hard floor with no mattress.

"It was so boring," she went on, "and we longed for things to read. The only magazines lying around were 'How to Install the Bell Telephone System' and a handbook on racing cars. Neither was exactly mesmerizing." Finally they were given books from the library of the American School in Tehran.

On St. Patrick's Day, someone cut out a green paper shamrock and pasted it on the wall of the one toilet everyone used. It was their only means of communication; soon, everyone was writing messages to each other on the shamrock.

I thought the returnees looked physically tired and depleted. To a man, they had dark circles under their eyes, and they all seemed thin. Most, however, were in good spirits, elated in fact, with the "high" that I'm sure accompanied them for the first weeks of their freedom. Two or three of the men seemed somewhat dazed and depressed, as if they were heavily tranquilized, and one poor boy's hands shook so badly he could hardly hold his coffee.

The Duty-Free Shop was opened up exclusively for them and they were eager to take advantage of it. I saw them trying on Irish sweaters and woolen caps. They were each given a bottle of Irish Mist and a beautiful Waterford "Christmas Bell" as gifts from the Irish government.

The hour and a half was up very quickly. The taoiseach took both women by their arms again, and on the way back to the plane he walked them over to the waiting press. Mr. Laingen gave a short interview to the group of journalists and then, with many more hugs and farewells, they climbed aboard and left us for the last, happy lap of their long, long journey. They will be home again, in the arms of their loved ones, in just six more hours.

We had lunch with the taoiseach, Minister and Mrs. Gerry Collins and some of the staff. It was a subdued lunch, an anticlimax after the drama of the previous hour. We left immediately after and headed back to Dublin. I was exhausted, exhilarated, high, and happy. It has been one of the most momentous days we've had in Ireland.

JANUARY 28

After all the excitement of the hostages' homecoming, I'm ready for a little peace and quiet, a tranquil respite. So what do I get? I get this morning's *Irish Times* handed to me at the front door by Gerry, as Bill and the boys dash out to the waiting car. I pour my tea, open the paper, scan the front page, and my eye is caught by a headline across the bottom of the page: WARM IRISH BUT DULL COUNTRY. Idly, I began reading the story, and when I got through the first two paragraphs I simply had to stop, put my head in my hands and groan, before forcing myself to keep on reading:

"A diplomat at the American embassy in Dublin, who is shortly to be reassigned to Japan, has described Ireland as 'an isolated, provincial country,' and said he will not be sorry to leave.

"Mr. Robin Berrington, cultural affairs and press officer at the embassy, in a copy of a letter apparently intended for American colleagues and included accidentally in a publicity handout about President Reagan, said Ireland has been a 'disappointing assignment.'" The letter goes on: "Ireland has food and climate well matched for each other: dull. The one bright spot is the people, but after two and a half years they remain enigmatic and unpredictable despite their easy approachability and charm ... the high cost of goods, their unavailability, the dreary urbanscapes, the constant strikes and the long, dark and damp winters combine to gnaw away at one's enthusiasm for being here ...' He went on to describe Ireland as pretty small potatoes compared to other countries in Europe."

Not satisfied to bemoan Ireland, Mr. Berrington took a swipe at Britain as well. Having taken a trip to England at Christmas, he gained, he said, a " 'greater appreciation of the similarities and differences between the inscrutable Irish and the insufferable English. Whatever reservations I may have about Ireland, at least the Irish are warm, lively human beings.'"

How did the paper get that letter? Apparently Robin always kept piles of surplus handouts in his office. As he was preparing a mailing list for the new brochure on President Reagan, copies of his Christmas newsletter intended only for his personal friends at home and around the world got mixed up in the pile of brochures and were sent out in the general mailing.

Since the *Irish Times* received it accidentally, should the editors have published it? I think that was fair. It would have been heroic self-denial to do otherwise, although Bill told me this evening that it had also gone out by mistake to an Irish magazine where the man who received it mailed it back to Berrington without using it—a gentlemanly gesture, but not a journalistic one.

I wonder what the reaction will be to this? I am sure it will be heard far and wide, whatever it is.

JANUARY 29

No one is talking about anything else, naturally. Last night's *Evening Press* carried a big banner headline on the front page: US ENVOY NOT SORRY TO BE LEAVING "DULL, PROVINCIAL IRELAND." Lots of our friends who saw the headline on the street thought it was referring to Bill!

Bill is being pushed by incessant press demands to make a statement about Berrington's letter. He prepared the following statement today and distributed it to the papers:

"I love everything about Ireland, especially including its weather, but I cannot guarantee the opinions and emotions of all my colleagues. The Irish are famous for their sense of humor and I think I shall have to rely on it in this instance."

Robin has been recalled to Washington by his agency, the International Communications Agency (previously the US Information Agency). He has been given twenty-four hours notice to "vacate his post." Luckily, he is a bachelor and doesn't have family arrangements to make.

FEBRUARY 5

The Berrington Affair is still making news every day, on radio, TV, in the papers. There was a very nice editorial in the *International Herald Tribune,* via the *Washington Post,* praising Bill for his reaction to the affair. Berrington also received some praise in the *Irish Times* for his "outbreak of candor that must do much to restore one's faith in the humanity of diplomats."

Bill put up with a lot of teasing for his remarks about "loving the Irish weather," but in fact, it's the truth. Having grown up in Worcester, Massachusetts, where winter blizzards sweep across the city with chilling regularity from December through March and the snowbanks mount higher than the tops of cars; and then having spent most of his adult life in Washington, D.C., where the summer temperatures soar to 90 and 100 degrees and where the humidity lines closets with mold, he finds the cool, mild, even temperatures of Ireland, just as Goldilocks found Baby Bear's soup, not too hot, and not too cold . . . just right.

Dr. Noel Browne, an independent member of the Dáil, a political maverick, physician, psychiatrist, left-wing Socialist and outspoken critic of the United States, came to lunch today. I found him to be a most sympathetic, sensitive observer of the social scene in Ireland. As minister of health in 1948, he was given a large budget in an emergency move to wipe out tuberculosis, which had long been a plague in the country. He succeeded in the war against TB. The only reminders of it today are the large, fortresslike gray stone hospitals that stand forlornly across the Irish countryside, empty now, desolate and ghostly reminders of grimmer, darker days.

Dr. Browne tried to follow up his success in the war on TB by initiating his now famous and failed "Mother and Child" scheme, which would guarantee free health care to women from the onset of pregnancy through birth, and aftercare for their babies. A powerful alliance of the Church, the medical profession and government bureaucrats fought vehemently against the scheme—bizarre as that seems now—because, they argued, the family is a sacred unit and morally responsible for the health of its own members. In the end, the scheme was defeated.

Dr. Browne spoke passionately and with clarity about the social tensions among the underclasses in Ireland that so often result in alcoholism: overcrowded housing, families too large to be maintained responsi-

333

bly, anxiety over unwanted pregnancies, worry about job security, lack of education and training for a good job. Violent crime in the poor and underprivileged neighborhoods of Dublin, almost unknown a few decades ago, now exacerbates the tensions of living in overcrowded, undermaintained tenements. All the urban problems that America has been unable to resolve Ireland is now bleakly and unhappily encountering.

Underneath Dr. Browne's cool, detached manner, one could sense a compassionate involvement and a sympathetic attitude toward the poor and the troubled. Although we would disagree about American foreign policy, I was grateful that he would come to our home and talk to us about his perceptions of Ireland. And thanks be to God, he didn't even mention Robin Berrington!

FEBRUARY 6

Out to the John Dillons' for dinner tonight, where one of the guests, political commentator Brian Farrell, said he thought there would be an election in Ireland sometime this summer, perhaps as late as September. Bill's face lit up. He's like an old fire horse, ready to go to the scene of the action everytime he smells the smoke of an election in the making. Having covered every American presidential campaign since Eisenhower first ran in 1952, he is eager to witness an Irish election in process before we leave.

Lots of rumors floating around about our successor. Still no official word, however. We are hoping we can stay on until June, when the boys finish their school year, but we'll have to play it by ear and see what transpires. I'm asked a dozen times a week: "When are you leaving?" I just smile and say I don't know, but I'm beginning to feel like the guest who stayed too long to dinner.

FEBRUARY 14

One of the saddest nights in Ireland's modern history: forty-nine Dublin teenagers were burned to death in a disco fire in Artane, North Dublin, just after midnight. One hundred and forty more are injured, many of them critically. Bodies are lined up at the city morgue and queues of frantic, grieving parents and relatives wait to go in and identify them. Many are unrecognizable. May God have mercy on all those who suffer tonight in Dublin.

At about 1:30 AM, in the disco-dance hall, someone spotted smoke drifting into the main ballroom. Within minutes, the building was in flames; the synthetic fibers in the chair seats exuded a poisonous smoke. The ceiling, also of a synthetic fiber, "melted," and fell in. The electricity went off, and the boys and girls stampeded for exits in total darkness.

Some ran into bathrooms to try to climb out windows, only to discover that the windows had been boarded up to keep gate crashers out.

One of our guards, Ian Higginbottom, had a son at the dance. He said he felt his eyes burning and decided to go into the cloakroom to get cigarettes and escort his date to the bathroom. He smelled smoke, grabbed his date and dashed out. They were two of the lucky ones.

Bill wrote letters of condolence to the taoiseach and to the Lord Mayor, Fergus O'Brien, and we drove downtown and delivered them by hand this afternoon. The city is silent and cloaked in mourning.

FEBRUARY 26

We had our annual ambassadors' wives outing today, given by the foreign minister's wife. We met at Iveagh House and climbed aboard buses to drive down to Barrettstown House, the "hideaway" in the country for the Irish government. It's a handsome old house, about an hour outside Dublin, which once belonged to Elizabeth Arden. She restored it and decorated it (lots of foundation cream shades and lots of pink), and then died before she really had a chance to use it. She willed it to the Irish government.

After a hearty lunch, we sat by a roaring fire, gossiping and admiring the lovely woods and landscapes outside the tall Georgian windows. As I sat there, I began thinking of all the terrific adjustments I'll have to make—we'll all have to make—when we get home. Bill said he will miss his car and Gerry the most. I'll miss not having to clean up after a party or empty the dishwasher. David said gloomily: "I'll have to learn to wash the car." But there are things I look forward to, and long for: To be in my own home again, to wander down into the kitchen at midnight barefoot in my nightgown to make a cup of tea or raid the refrigerator, to have neighbors and friends drop in during the middle of the day for a chat and coffee over the kitchen table, to belong to civic organizations, to be able to speak out for or against political issues, to be nearer Liam.

MARCH 10

Bill has arranged with the State Department for his resignation to take effect in June.

The American Women's Club paid a beautiful tribute to me today. I was moved to tears by the kindness and the generosity of spirit that prompted it, and thrilled by their sensitive planning of an event that was just perfect for me.

We gathered in Jury's Hotel at 10 AM. They had invited all the other ambassadorial wives, the female ambassadors, and our own embassy wives and members of the club. After a coffee hour, we were entertained by two women musicians, a singer and a harpist, who played and sang all the Irish songs I love the best. And then Mary Lavin read a story of hers that I particularly like. Louise Lewis, the pretty, petite president of the club, made a gracious speech about my work in Ireland over the past four years. I wonder if they really know how touched I was by it all? I had to stand up at the end of the performance and find words to thank them, but I'm afraid they were only a hollow echo of what I really felt. As I stood speaking to them, I saw that Bill had slipped into the back of the room, an invited male in this all-women world, and he looked like a cat who had found the cream. I could almost hear him purring.

MARCH 13

I never forgot my intention, made four years ago when I first went down to the State Department to look at pictures of the residence, to find a suitable name for our house here. Last month, I initiated a contest at the embassy and asked all the employees and their spouses to submit names. They came pouring in: Lincoln House, Kennedy House, Roosevelt House, Tall Trees, The Park House, "Shannondoah!" Deerfield, Hoover House, Phoenix House.

I submitted the nominations on a ballot last week and members of the residence and embassy staffs voted. Dennis got busy with cardboard and his paints and has created a perfect replica of the residence. We took it down to the embassy this afternoon and had a proper christening party. I made a little speech about the history of the house (they surely know it as well as I do by now!) and then, in the best Academy Award manner, Bill handed me an envelope with the winning name. I opened it and announced: "It's Deerfield." An apt choice for a house set in fields alive with deer and also a name rich in American historical connotation.

Ted Brennan, one of the embassy employees, handed me an open bottle of champagne and I poured it over the model of the house, officially christening it and, I hope, naming it for posterity.

Good-by, residence. Hello, Deerfield.

MARCH 22

I had planned to have a quiet weekend packing books and being home with the children. Then Bill phoned this morning from Boston with some exciting news.

"You always said you'd like to live in Boston," he began, and he didn't need to say another word. I *knew* he had accepted a position at Boston University. His relationship with President John Silber and the university dates back to 1976, when he made the commencement address there and received (along with Julia Child) an honorary degree. I *have* always loved

Boston, on quick and infrequent visits; I find it a city full of bustling charm, with an elegant, old-world ambience.

We began discussing housing, schools, his job, neighborhoods; finally I said: "We can't settle any of this on a transatlantic phone call. I'll see if I can get on the Aer Lingus New York flight tomorrow, and I'll meet you in Boston in time for dinner."

MARCH 27: *Boston*

It's been a busy four days. But everything is settled. We've got a house to live in, the boys are enrolled in schools in Brookline, I've rented a house in Cambridge for the summer while the Brookline house is being renovated, and tomorrow night we're flying back to Dublin. Everything has gone so smoothly that I think we are going to love being in Boston. I visited the high school and the elementary school where the boys will be and was very much impressed with them. And we'll be close to Liam at Dartmouth. I liked the friendly taxi drivers, the exuberance of the Quincy Market, the wonderful slide show of Boston we saw at the Visitors' center; I liked having lunch one day at the Ritz and the next at Jimmy's on the waterfront where our good friend Joseph Gannon took us. I like the neighborhood look of Brookline, the tree-lined streets, the quiet old handsome houses with clutches of kids on the street corners. And I like the challenge of decorating a house from top to bottom, from *scratch*.

Bill is enthusiastic and happy at the prospect of going back to his first love, university teaching. When he left graduate school at Harvard, his first job was editing the Theodore Roosevelt papers at MIT. He was way-laid on his way up the academic ladder by a detour to Washington to write a book, and that led to a newspaper job. He never returned to academia, but his stints as a fellow in Morse College at Yale, and his visiting lectures at Princeton always confirmed his love of university life. So, as he began a diplomatic career at fifty, he is beginning again four years later.

MARCH 30

Home again and flooding the boys with news about their new home, new schools, neighborhood. They are wildly curious and enthusiastic; I think going home is a reality to them now. They, like I, will have to do a little heart-mending at not returning to Gramercy Street, but a new adventure is good medicine. I've tried to remember every detail for them, and I took pictures of the house and their schools.

Walter Curley, Bill's predecessor, was in Dublin today and came out to the house this evening. While we were having coffee after dinner, Brian came in to tell us that he had heard on the news that President Reagan has been shot.

We raced upstairs to see what kind of news we could get on television. First the reports said he had not been hit, then later, more accurate stories began coming in. There was still no assessment of the president's condition at midnight, so Bill and I went down to the embassy to see if anything was coming in on the wire. Bill prepared a statement for the newspapers and radio, but RTE News is on strike and no one from the press phoned to ask for a statement, so about 3 AM we went home to bed, relieved and grateful to hear that the president's wounds were not life-threatening and sickened to hear about the near fatal head wounds of his affable press officer, James Brady.

April 10

I can't keep track of the days and nights, much less find time to write my journal. The packers have been here to assess our move. Christopher is in France for a month on a student exchange program. I had my itinerant girls from Galway in for a last, farewell tea party. They were delightful as always and quite a changed group from the shy youngsters who appeared here three years ago.

Went to dinner at the Chinese embassy on Monday. The only other guests were their own embassy personnel and some of ours. We sat at a plain, round table in a rather spartan, undecorated dining room in Ambassador Gong's house on Ailesbury Road. The many-coursed dinner was good, especially the octopus, which was sort of crunchy and went pop! in your mouth when you bit down on it; and the Peking duck was delicious. The conversation at dinner was all serious and substantial; no funny anecdotes or raucous laughter at this dinner table! Ambassador Gong is thoughtful and intense, and determined to learn all she can about Ireland, from politics to farming methods to economic structure.

After dinner, we were shown three movies that supported the Chinese claim to superiority in cuisine, porcelain and . . . of all things . . . monastic life! As soon as the lights came on again we stood up and made our farewells.

Gerry told us on the way home that because the renovations to the kitchen in the house where we had dinner had not been finished on schedule, all the food this evening had been cooked at another of their houses down the road and rushed up in the backseat of a car.

April 27

Days and nights are crammed to their fullest now with good-by parties, farewell interviews, packing, planning our own farewell receptions at

Deerfield. Our close friends in the diplomatic circle here, Ambassador and Mrs. Zepos of Greece, are also leaving Dublin this summer, and there are rounds of farewells for them, too. Greta Zepos, Marie Louise Harhoff of Denmark and I have formed a close and warm friendship in our four years together. We share a deep attachment to Ireland and hate the thought of separating. When and where will we all meet again?

Niall and Una Crowley gave a warm and lively farewell luncheon for us today at the new Allied Irish Bank Center on Merrion Road, and we all laughingly recalled the day four years ago when I innocently came to lunch at AIB with Bill, making history by being the first female guest in the Board Room!

I'm giving three farewell interviews to the press this week, and we're giving our annual St. Michael's College library fund-raising "do" at Deerfield on Friday, with 150 guests. The library shelves at the school are filled with books now, thanks to the hard work and perseverance of the committee.

Two house guests arrive on Saturday, Libby Donahue from Washington and Marion Schlesinger from Cambridge, and we're off to Waterford on Monday for a Chamber of Commerce luncheon and a tour of the Waterford Glass factory, something that has been on our list of "musts" ever since we got to Ireland and somehow has been put on the back burner until now. I also want to bring home a Waterford stove, the little cast-iron stove made in Waterford that can burn peat or wood and is a mighty source of heat, to warm our frigid Boston winters.

MAY 4

Five weeks left. I feel like an astronaut on countdown.

Bobby Sands, the angry and charismatic young hunger striker, died today in Long Kesh Prison, the first of the H-block hunger strikers to succumb. It is such a tragic waste of human talent and misplaced idealism. And more are bound to follow.

I'm packing books with Dennis and Brian each day. We made a round of the house this week, collecting all our own possessions and lining them up for the packers on long tables set up in the ballroom. I'm amazed—I'm flabbergasted!—at the things we have acquired in four years here: glassware from Pearce and Ledbetter; Waterford crystal, Irish ironstone, copper and brass from the Quays in Dublin; pottery from Nicholas Mosse down in Kilkenny; gorgeous Irish woolens from Avoca and the Weaver's Shed; prints of Dublin (one a gift from the St. Michael's Library Association, one from the "sisters" of the WPA); contemporary Irish paintings and drawings. The house looks absolutely barren. The paintings on loan to us from the Art in the Embassy program have been taken down, packed and shipped back to their donors. The bare walls, with outlines of the frames on them, stare back at us in silent reproach for leaving.

A marvelous dinner party with a small and intimate gathering of some of our closest friends at Joe and Imelda Malone's; each guest sparkled and each story was better than the last. Laughter floated through the Malones' dining room until two in the morning.

A repeat performance with another group of friends the next night in the beautifully restored Georgian town house of the John Lowes on Baggot Street. It has the only "penthouse" I've seen in Ireland, where one can stand and look out across the rooftops of downtown Dublin.

A farewell luncheon given to us by the Ireland-America Society, where Beta Whelan, this year's president, dissolved our table into helpless laughter telling us about her first week as a qualified podiatrist down in her native Listowel, in County Kerry. She proudly hung out her shingle on her front door: "Beta Whelan, Podiatrist." Shortly afterwards, on a warm summer's evening, as she and her parents were sitting in their living room with windows open onto the street to catch the evening air, two locals passed the house and stopped under the newly hung sign. After puzzling over it for a few seconds, one asked the other:

"Podiatrist. Now Tom, what do you think that would be?"

"Ah sure," said Tom, wise to the ways of the world, "it's some new kind of Protestant."

I giggle at everything I hear these days. Maybe it's the frenetic pace. Maybe the laughter softens the lump that always seems to be in my throat.

MAY 11

The movers descended on us today with mounds of cardboard cartons, mountains of brown wrapping paper and enough masking tape to reach from Dublin to Boston.

I solved the question of our official gift at the diplomatic farewell. I put the equivalent of the cost of a silver tray toward the purchase of a Sheraton sideboard, a beautiful inlaid mahogany piece that will grace our dining room in Boston and remind us always of our friends in the diplomatic corps here. It arrived at Deerfield today to be wrapped and packed with the rest of our belongings.

I asked Bill if he had started packing the files and books and papers in his office. "Packing?" he asked incredulously. "How can I pack when I have so much work still to do? And anyway, I've got lots of time."

I refused to make further comment, although I've noticed that Adelaide Sharry, his devoted and superefficient secretary, has a wild and rather frantic look on her face lately.

My cousin Martin Coyne arrived today from Washington. I've been trying to lure him to Ireland for four years, but he's of the "better late than never" school. He's going to walk around the Ring of Kerry with a backpack, the best way of all to see and feel its beauty.

In the middle of pouring tea for fifteen women this afternoon, I stopped in midstream and to their astonishment exclaimed: "The donkeys!" We have all forgotten to make arrangements for the donkeys (the pigs and heifers have long since graced our dining room table!). The Italian ambassador's wife wants one, so that will take care of the baby. Brian de Breffney had mentioned needing a donkey on his estate in the country. I wonder if he wants two (going on three)? I must phone him. I went back to pouring tea.

Dinner at David and Una Kennedy's; everyone shocked and subdued by the news of the attempted assassination of the pope.

MAY 14

We took Marty Coyne with us last night for a small farewell dinner with Gay and Kathleen Byrne out in Howth. The other two couples— Eamon and Grainne Andrews and Ted and Kay Bonner—were both from the world of show business. On our way home in the car, as we followed the dark shoreline, Marty asked in amazement: "Is every dinner party in Ireland like that? No wonder you've had such a good time. You wouldn't get that talk and those stories in Washington." Sure, you wouldn't.

At a farewell party at Mab Moltke's this evening, she presented us with a huge cake decorated with a big blue eye lined with false eyelashes and tears outlined in icing dropping from it.

MAY 16

The US Chamber of Commerce in Ireland gave us a splendid, black-tie farewell dinner tonight in the Burlington Hotel, with a wonderfully gracious and generous toast to Bill and all the work he has done for business in Ireland since becoming ambassador. He was very touched and proud.

MAY 23

And it goes on and on; we've become whirling dervishes, pushed along by the momentum of emotion, excitement, activity; no time left now for contemplation, no time for a peaceful, quiet moment to savor our waning days. And it's just as well. As Bill said to me the other night: "All the activity surrounding a death—the wake, the funeral, the influx of relatives and friends—keeps the mourning at bay. We don't have time to think about how much we regret leaving Ireland. We're too busy saying good-by!"

Vincent Jennings, the editor of the *Sunday Press,* and his wife, Mary, gave us a warm and intimate farewell dinner tonight, and we held our own two very large farewell receptions at Deerfield this week. I couldn't fit everybody into one occasion, so I simply divided up the guest list alphabetically and had the A through M's on Tuesday and the N through Z's on Thursday. Dennis, Maeve and the staff are almost on their hands and knees with exhaustion, but they keep going. Anne must have made her thousandth meatball this week, and Kitty hung up her five thousandth coat.

My car left Dublin this week, shipped to Boston to await our arrival. I never told the outcome of the trials and tribulations of my poor auld engine. I left off the story just as my transmission gave out, a half-block away from the garage, and the mechanic assured me that it was only "coincidental" to the work done on the engine. At that point, I no longer trusted to my own sane judgment; the possibility of murder, arson or bodily harm all passed before my eyes in vivid Technicolor. That's when I put matters into the hands of a solicitor. He and I and the garage eventually reached a compromise: a new transmission system installed, with my paying for parts and the garage footing the labor charges. I thought that was fair and everything would end happily. And it would have, except that the new transmission didn't work. It would give out on me on colorful, fun-filled occasions such as traveling the North Circular Road during rush hour, or leaving an ambassadorial luncheon in the middle of a long line of limousines, or pulling out of my driveway, late for an engagement in town. With infinite patience, the garage would send a tow truck, take it away, return it a day later with an inexplicable diagnosis, and a few days later it would stall again. I had to give up; I was bruised, bleeding and wounded. I was losing my perspective. I was defeated.

I took it to a specialist in transmissions. "Doctor," I said, "my general practitioner has failed miserably; he's obviously a quack. Can you fix this transmission or is it terminal?" A very nice, red-headed young man, the kind of person who immediately instills confidence in his patients, heard my long—and I do mean *long!*—story, and said he would see what he could do. A few days later, he called me in; he had in his hands something black and steel and sort of wedged along the sides. He caressed it tenderly. He began his explanation, pointing periodically to a big gash in the steel part he held, which apparently was crucial to his explanation. The long and short of it was that he could prove, without a shadow of a doubt, that the original garage had seriously damaged the transmission while repairing the engine and that this damage had not been repaired by putting in the "new transmission." I imparted this new piece of evidence to the garage via my long-suffering solicitor. When my red-haired specialist repaired the transmission, his substantial bill was forwarded to the garage. It was paid promptly and in full. Perseverance *is* a virtue.

342

The Irish elections have been announced and the campaigns are off to a colorful start. We have many friends running in all three parties. We are especially interested in Seamus Brennan of Fianna Fáil, who is trying to get into the Dáil in South Dublin, and in Gemma Hussey, who is running for Fine Gael down in Wicklow. Bill is eager to go out on the campaign trail with candidates from each party and compare their speeches, their styles and their methods of campaigning with an American presidential campaign. Garret FitzGerald told him he was welcome to come on his own campaign any time.

Bill phoned Brian Lenihan, the foreign minister, this morning, to clear his trip with Garret before he set out. He explained that, if Brian gave his approval, he wanted to follow the campaign firsthand with each of the candidates.

Brian said sure, as long as he was going with all the candidates. "Come and campaign with me in Castleknock on Saturday, will you?" he asked Bill, and they made a date.

MAY 29

How many ways are there to say good-by? And is one easier than another? I told the "sisters" good-by at a luncheon Carol Bradley gave in Killiney. We talked about the campaign; Gemma was there, taking time off from her frantically busy schedule and filling us in on the details.* And then I turned the talk for one last time to women in Ireland, the gains they have made over the past decade, and their aspirations for the future.

"What do women want now?" I asked the group.

The answers were as varied as the women: "A greater role in decision making (only nine percent of the members of State Boards in Ireland are women), a greater quality of opportunity, more retraining. Telephones."

They stood around Carol's doorway waving good-by as Gerry eased the big car out through the narrow gates, and I turned around to wave to them: a small but determined band, eager, optimistic and energetically gaining footholds for women in Ireland.

We said good-by to Ben Kiely and Frances Daly on Leeson Street at 2 AM this morning, after a feast they had hosted for us at Snaffles, laced with many stories as frothy as the cream in the Irish coffees.

---

* Senator Hussey was defeated in her bid for the Dáil in the summer of 1981, but ran again in the general elections of February 1982 and won a seat. (She was appointed Minister for Education in December 1982.) Seamus Brennan won and held a seat.

JUNE 2

It was our turn this afternoon to stand up front in the drawing room of the nunciature, towering over the nuncio while we made our diplomatic farewells. I thanked them all for our sideboard and passed around a pen and ink drawing that Dennis had made of it. Bill's farewell speech was beautiful, elegant and sensitive, as always. Champagne was poured, the glasses lifted, and we were toasted with all the formal, traditional wishes of good luck in our future endeavors; four years less seven weeks from our first farewell reception at the nuncio's to say good-by to the French.

JUNE 3

The minister for foreign affairs, Brian Lenihan, and his wife, Anne, gave us a lovely farewell luncheon in Iveagh House today. I told him I had been startled to read in the papers that BRIAN LENIHAN ORDERS EN-QUIRY INTO AMBASSADOR'S CAMPAIGNING, but he just laughed and said: "Don't believe everything you read in the papers." He gave Bill a warm and friendly farewell toast, and we bade a sad farewell to all our friends in the Department of Foreign Affairs, making them promise to come and visit us soon in Boston.

JUNE 5

This was the boys' last day of school. I went in the car with Gerry to pick them up at noon and had to blink back tears as I watched for the last time all those small, gray-clad figures shoot out of school.

It's a lovely, warm day, just right for the beginning of the school holidays. I went inside to say good-by to Father McHugh, the head of the Junior School, to Father Flood, the headmaster, and to Sister Carmel, David's sweet and wise teacher. Christopher and a school friend, Davitt Sheean, headed downtown to a movie to celebrate the end of school. David sat quietly in the car and looked out the window all the way home. At one point, he took off his little blue and white striped tie, handed it to me, and said: "I won't be needing this again," and returned to his reverie at the window.

I returned to Ballsbridge at 4 PM for Bill's farewell at the embassy. We all gathered in the Rotunda, American and Irish staff and many of their spouses. The deputy chief of mission, Charles Rushing, made the farewell speech, and presented Bill with an antique silver picture frame with a group picture of the staff. He was followed by Colonel Bournes, who has been the military attaché these last three years. He made a charming little speech "on behalf of the Army," and presented Bill with an army plaque engraved to both of us. He ended on a light and whimsical note, saying that he often said to his wife, Joyce: "Gee, I'd like to be like Ambassador Shannon. I'd like to be able to give those wonderful speeches he makes, to always look so well turned out and beautifully tailored, to have his command of language and history . . ." He went on to list a few more of Bill's sterling qualities, and then, patting his own thick head of hair and with a wicked gleam in his eye, he finished: "But I think I'll keep my own hairdo!" We all roared.

When it was Bill's turn to speak, he surprised and delighted the entire embassy staff by making not a serious or sentimental talk but instead a joking one in which he took each employee by name and poked fun at his or her idiosyncrasies, such as Colonel Bournes's passion for collecting and repairing antique clocks. So we ended on a happy, laughing note. Champagne was poured, we visited briefly with everyone, and at 5 PM, we walked out the door for the last time, hand in hand as we had come in for the first embassy party to welcome us four years ago. As we walked down the broad front steps, the Marine on duty saluted Bill for the last time.

I knew that the leavetaking from the embassy would be hard for Bill, much harder than for me, of course. Deerfield has been my life, while the round tower on the wide corner in Ballsbridge has been his ongoing love affair for the past four years. He has given his ambassadorship all his best energies, brought to it his knowledge and sensitivity about Irish affairs, worked both the "day and night shifts" ceaselessly, and traveled to every county in the country. Being an ambassador is a heady experience, all the more so in a country one loves and knows so well.

I wanted our last farewell party to be something special for him, something I knew he would enjoy, somewhere he would relax and have fun. So we headed out through the soft, warm late afternoon toward Blessington, in County Wicklow, where Bill performed his last official function, opening the Performance Art exhibit that Karl and Doreen Mullen staged in the beautiful gardens of Tulfarris, their home and art gallery.

Nigel Rolf's "living art" performance, which I had missed at the Rosc exhibit, was part of this evening's show. He was rained out of the garden and had to stage his performance in one of the stables. Under dim lights, with a spot shining on him, he lay in a trough of colored flour, with a thin mesh screen covering his naked body. As eerie, hypnotic music came out over a tape recorder, he lay silently in the flour, moving his arms and legs slowly back and forth the way children make "angels" in the snow, leaving behind the design of his limbs on the flour. It sounds weird. It *was* weird. And I have to admit that I had come to scoff. But it was in some mysterious, sensual way, beautiful as well as weird.

What a change, I thought, as I left the stable to make way for the crowds of people trying to get in to see the next performance, from the romantic, sentimental visions of those who left Ireland's shores long ago. And it's a good change, an opening of doors that lets in a freshness of spirit, an acceptance of things that are new, a tolerance of things that are strange, visions for tomorrow instead of dreams of yesterday.

We had the gay evening we have come to expect at the Mullens': Doreen sang Bill all his favorite songs, and we had a marvelous meal in the Loft, their daughter's restaurant in the courtyard. Four good friends, Margaret and Desmond Downes, and Dorothy and Robin Walker, joined us, and we sang and danced and finally hugged good night and good-by in the rain in the wee hours. The wet, glistening streets of Blessington were still and empty as we sped through the night on our way back to Dublin.

June 6

My last day at Deerfield. I got up early this morning, despite our late night, and walked over to open the big white wooden shutters that cover our huge windows. Some of the children, my own and Deerfield's own, were already out on the back lawn, kicking a soccer ball around. I have a million last-minute things to do, packing still to attend to, phone calls to

A final photo with the Residence staff

346

make, thank-you notes I am determined not to leave behind, and from five to seven tonight Bill and I are giving our final farewell party for our staff and their families at Deerfield.

Later

It was a subdued party, compared to all the noisy fun we have had together at our Christmas parties. Dennis made a farewell speech on behalf of the staff. Kathleen, whose love for animals exceeds even mine, held Fling on her lap throughout the party, sad tears in her eyes as she stroked our small pet. We tried to make a few jokes, but they fell flat. It's a terrific upheaval for the staff to have to say good-by to us and face a new family, a new ambassador, a new way of doing things. We have been their family for the past four years, a good block of time. They have watched our boys grow and have supported all my projects with enthusiasm and energy. We've grown accustomed to each other's ways, each other's faces.

It's midnight now. Despite my good intention of finishing everything and getting to bed early, I haven't made it yet. My traveling dress is laid out for tomorrow. (The same dress I left Washington in four years ago . . . and the same red hat! They brought me luck.) The boys' bags are shut and already down in the front hall. Fling is shampooed and ready for her long journey tomorrow. Molly is going to follow later when we are settled in our new house in Brookline. I've come down to the library to pack my typewriter.

It's raining, coming down heavily now, and it's cool and windy, much like the day we arrived here. I've left the drapes open, and I just saw one of the guards pass by outside my window. Usually the night watchmen make their rounds of the house discreetly, never looking in the windows, but tonight I saw him stop under the arc of light from the security lamps on the roof, and seeing me at the window, he raised his cap and gave me a big salute. I threw him a kiss.

I took a last, lone walk in the garden this evening, just at twilight. The new perennial border that Michael and I planned through the winter is half up, looking lovely and promising to be the jewel of the garden by mid-July. The roses, early this year, are blooming, and the rhododendrons along the back wall of the Pretty Garden have, like me, packed it in. Unlike me, they'll be back next year, the lucky divils.

We've picked out a spot on the back lawn to plant a tree tomorrow. I chose a copper beech, and I hope that it will live and thrive and grow and watch over this house and these gardens. I hope a small boy will make a tree house in its limbs before it grows too big to climb. And I hope it will add strength and loveliness to its old and towering neighbors.

The rain is coming down harder. Tomorrow night I'll be sitting under a big Texas moon with a hot June wind blowing across my face. It's a reality that's hard to grasp.

JUNE 7

Michael and Jimmy met us out on the back lawn early this morning with the tree. Michael had dug a deep hole and we lifted it carefully into place, then each of us, Christopher and David as well, took the spade and put earth back over its roots. Christopher put in a shovelful for Liam.

The cars were waiting in front of the house, their trunks filled with our bags. I knew a big crowd was going to be at the airport, and Michael had given me an armful of carnations to give to our friends as a final farewell gesture.

We hugged both men good-by as we stood by our tree, then hurried around to the front of the house, where all the staff and children were gathered. There wasn't a dry eye in sight and every cheek I put next to mine was damp. We piled into the two waiting cars. Patricia, Brian and Paul jumped into Patricia's car to follow, and we slowly pulled out from the portico, drove past the outspread arms of the sycamore tree, down the drive, and past the empty fields lined with the small, sturdy chestnut trees Michael and I had planted two years before, keeping the old ones company.

The flags were flying at the entrance, and Ian Higginbottom was there to pull open the heavy iron gates. Each of us jumped out to give him our last, fond farewell, then the cars moved through the gates and out into the Park. I turned around in time to see Ian pulling the gates shut behind us, and my last glimpse was of the new wooden plaque that had been installed on the high, white gatepost:

DEERFIELD

HOME OF THE AMERICAN AMBASSADOR

Index

Elizabeth Shannon grew up in small towns in Illinois and later in Texas, where she graduated from Our Lady of the Lake College in San Antonio. After college she satisfied romantic yearnings, nourished by the novels of Fitzgerald and Hemingway, by traveling for two years in Europe. Upon her return, she became a reporter trainee for the *Washington Star,* and soon afterwards met and married William Shannon, then a columnist for another newspaper. Although they spent three years in New York and one in London, the Shannons called Washington home until Mr. Shannon's appointment to the ambassadorship by President Carter. They now live in Boston, where Mr. Shannon teaches at Boston University and Mrs. Shannon is embarked upon the writing of a novel.